AF576539

Sacred Landscapes

The Threshold Between Worlds

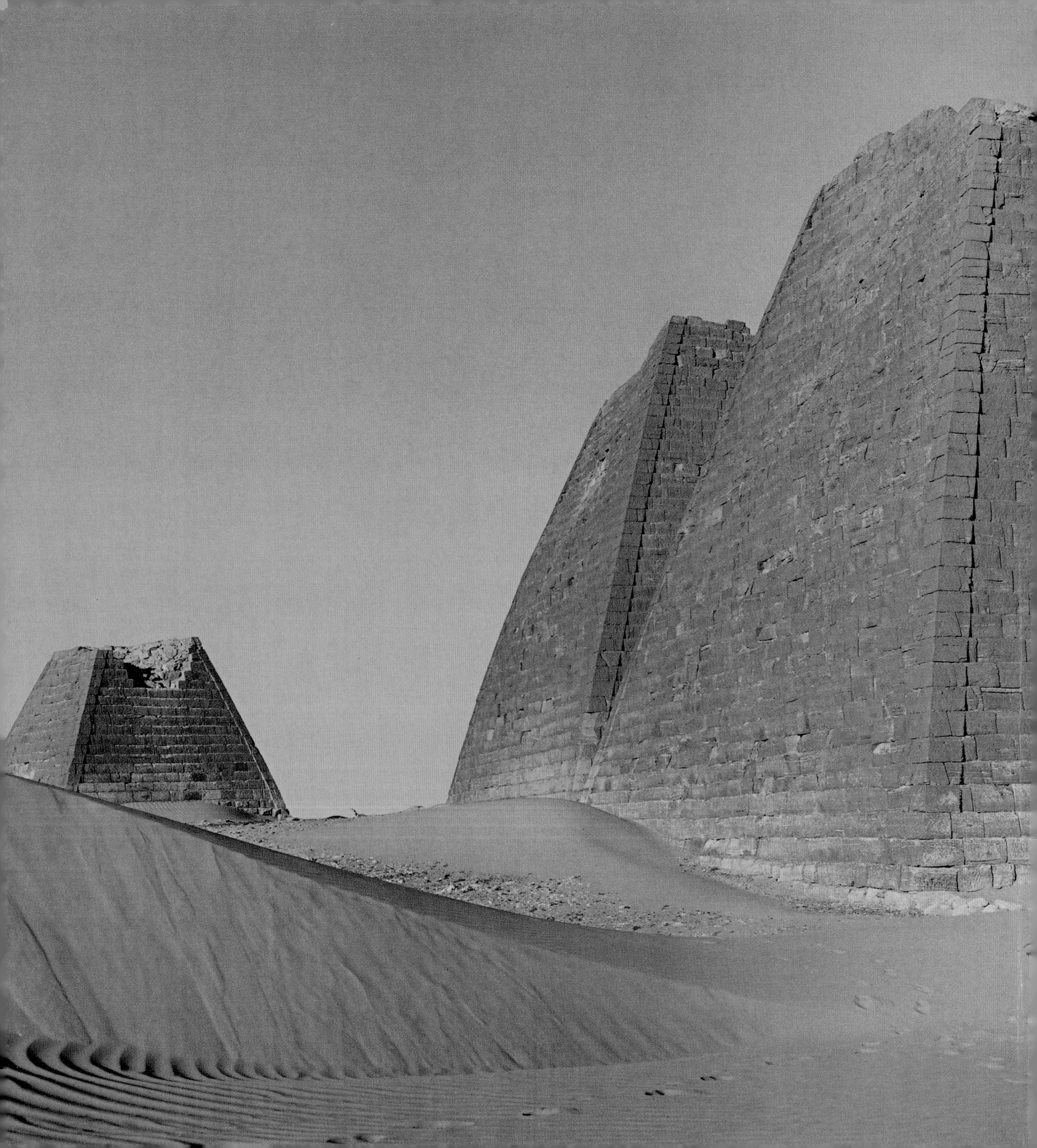

SACRED LANDSCAPES

The Threshold Between Worlds

A. T. MANN

Photographs by LYNN DAVIS

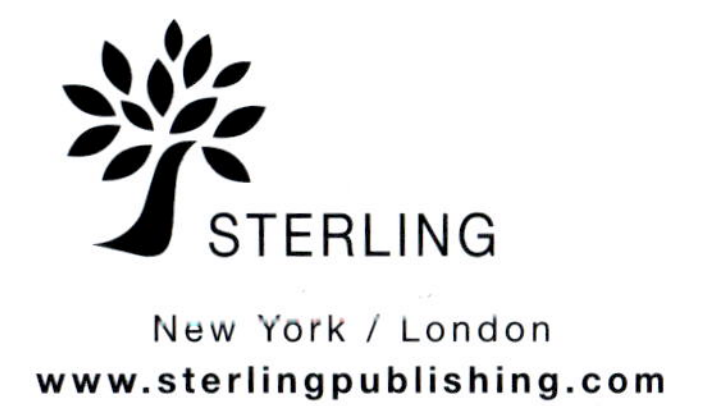

New York / London
www.sterlingpublishing.com

PAGE ii: Pyramids at Meroë, Sudan, 1998

PAGE vi: Monastery, Petra, Jordan, 1995

PAGE viii: Tomb of Zechariah, Kidron Valley, Israel, 1994

Library of Congress Cataloging-in-Publication Data

Mann, A. T., 1943-
Sacred landscapes : the threshold between worlds / by A. T. Mann ; photographs by Lynn Davis.
p. cm.
Includes bibliographical references and index.
ISBN 978-1-4027-6520-9 (hc-trade cloth)
1. Sacred space. 2. Sacred space--Pictorial works. I. Davis, Lynn, 1944- II. Title.
BL580.M36 2010
203'.5--dc22
2010003449

10 9 8 7 6 5 4 3 2 1

Published by Sterling Publishing Co., Inc.
387 Park Avenue South, New York, NY 10016

Distributed in Canada by Sterling Publishing
c/o Canadian Manda Group, 165 Dufferin Street
Toronto, Ontario, Canada M6K 3H6
Distributed in the United Kingdom by GMC Distribution Services
Castle Place, 166 High Street, Lewes, East Sussex, England BN7 1XU
Distributed in Australia by Capricorn Link (Australia) Pty. Ltd.
P.O. Box 704, Windsor, NSW 2756, Australia

Book design and layout by Christine Heun
Printed in China

Sterling ISBN 978-1-4027-6520-9

"Difficult are the gods for men to see."

—Hymn to Demeter[1]

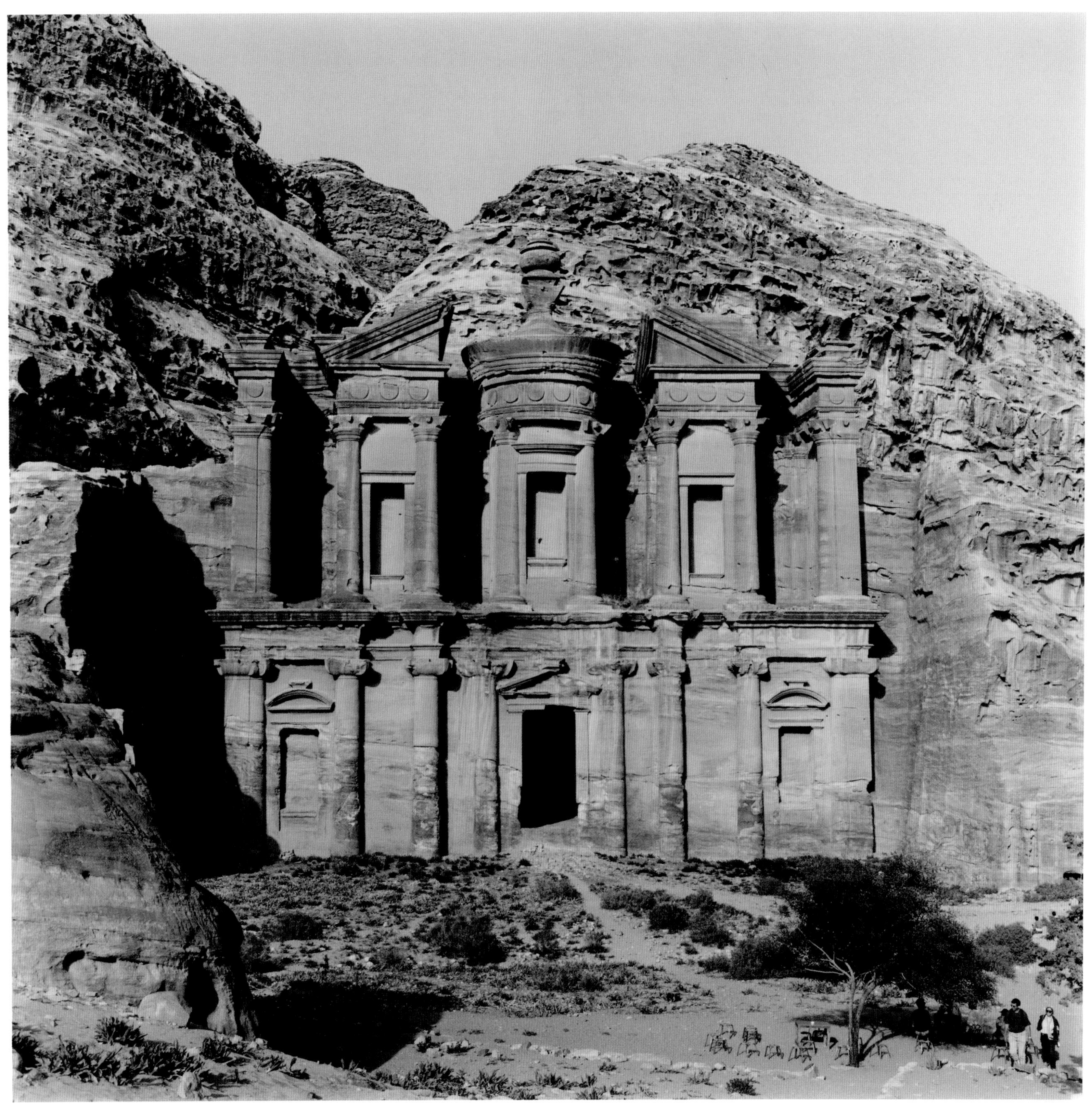

Contents

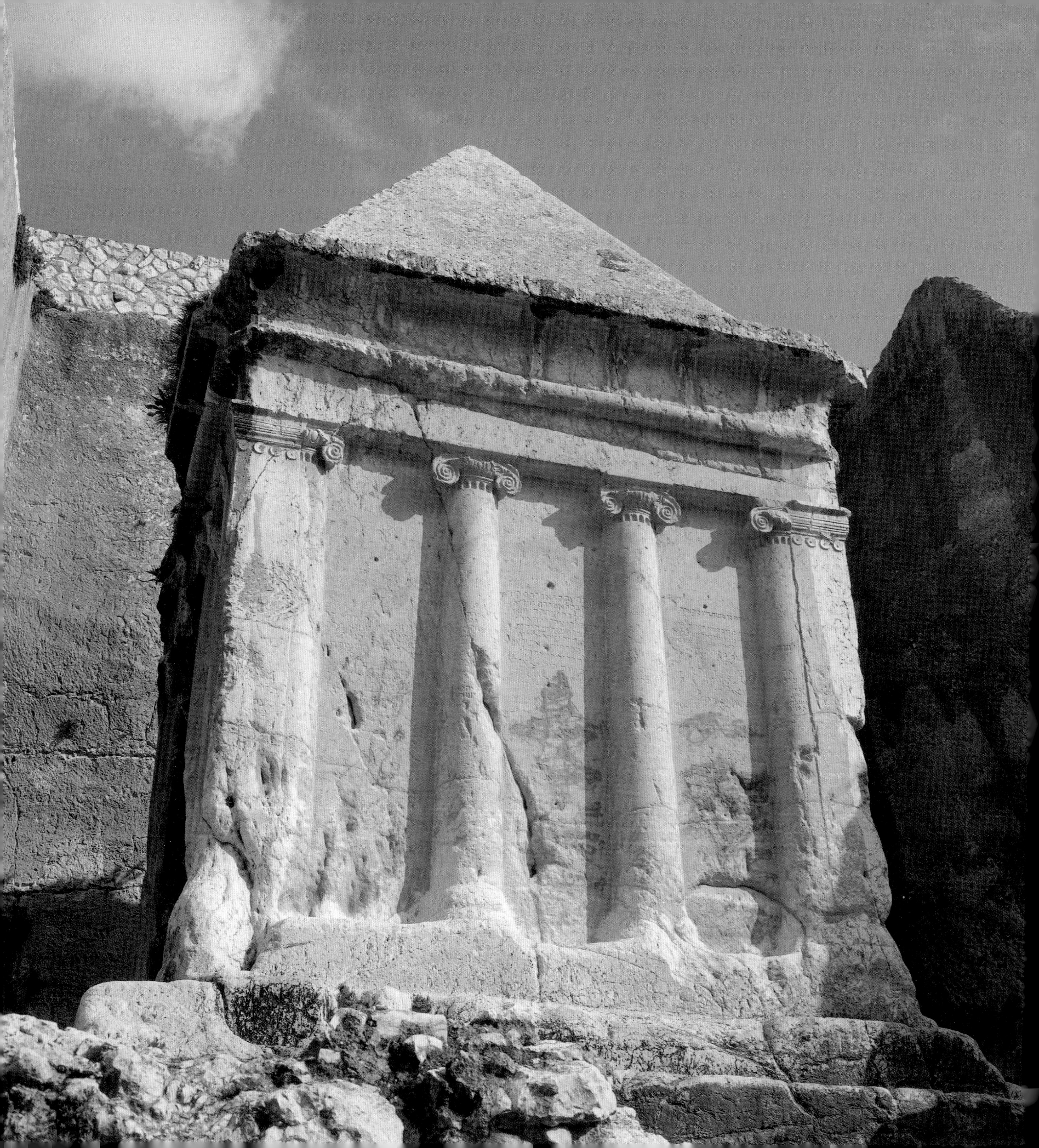

SACRED LANDSCAPES

The Threshold Between Worlds

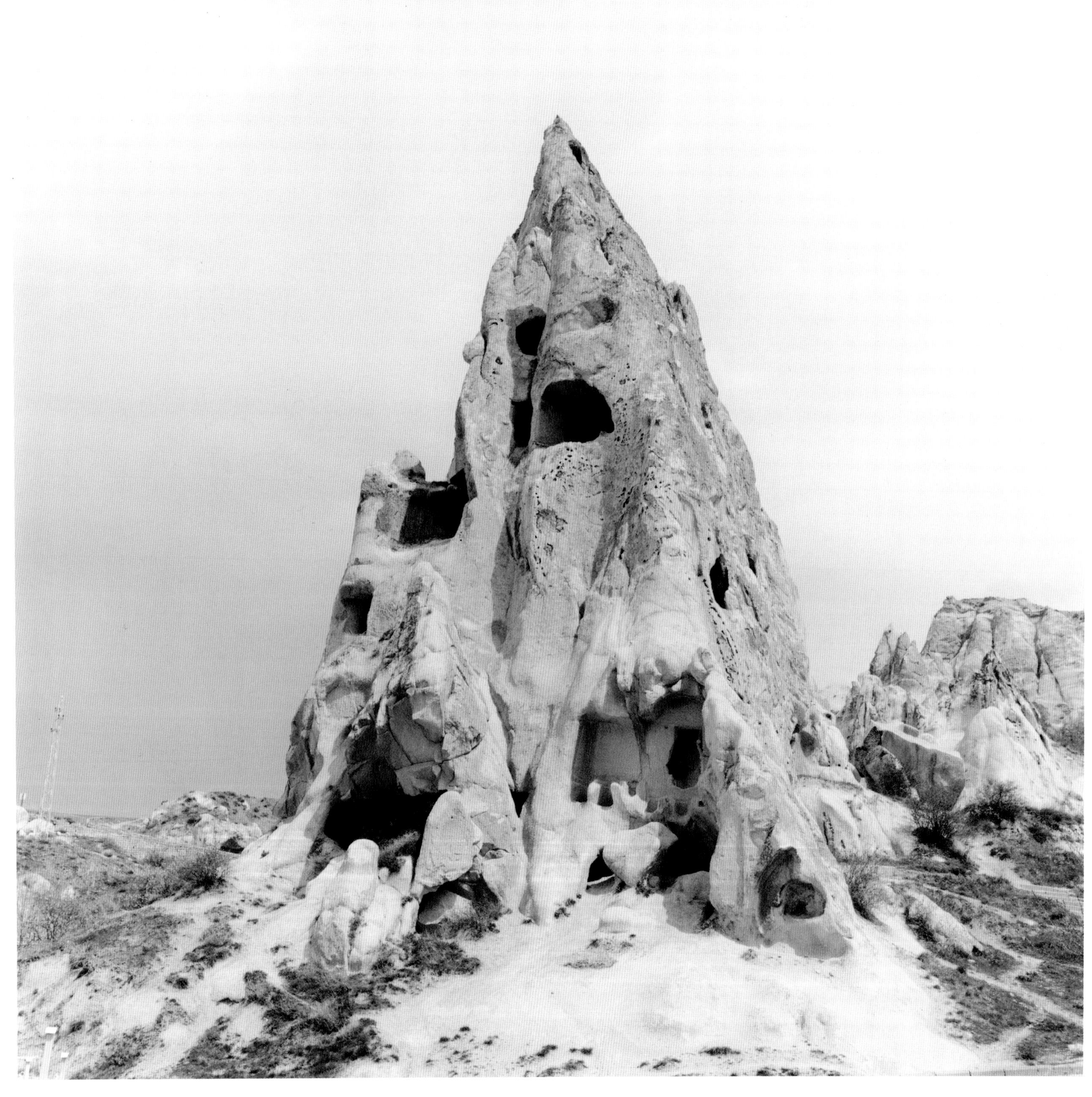

Introduction

After living for half a year in a primitive seaside village near the Sahara in southern Morocco, in 1970 I hitchhiked from Munich to India with a friend, a journey that was like traveling back in time. We wound our way through Austria, Yugoslavia, and back into early European history. Bulgaria looked like the shabby, post-Depression 1930s with its gray and rusty old cars. At the Bulgarian/Turkish border we got a ride with a Viennese college professor who drove a VW bus to Kabul every summer, buying carpets along the way. He spoke fluent Turkish and Farsi and took us with him on condition that we go on his zigzag route via rug-making cities and nomadic tribal settlements across Turkey, Iran, and Afghanistan. His offer was like a dream come true. As we drove, the centuries peeled away with each passing day. We meandered eastward through 1430s Istanbul, along the Turkish Black Sea coast, and then climbed south into the volcanic Taurus mountain range of Eastern Anatolia, haggling along the way in the carpet markets of mountain villages as the back of the van filled up with gorgeous-colored rugs. We emerged many days later near the legendary Mount Ararat, where, legend has it, Noah's Ark landed after the Great Flood. There were no cities for miles on this windswept, largely barren high plain, and it looked like a primal scene from thousands of years ago.

A misunderstanding about our visas at the Turkish-Iranian border forced Wilfred to leave us overnight while he drove on to Tabriz, the famous carpet town in western Iran thought to be the site of the biblical Garden of Eden. Due to the threatening actions of the Turkish border guards and the lack of any acceptable shelter at the border, a group of us retreated into the nearby foothills and spent a glorious full moon night on a hillside overlooking the desolate plain from which Ararat emerges 17,000 feet into the cool, clear air. I reveled at its immensity and sheer beauty, struck by the fact that it probably looked the same to the mythic Noah (apart from the absence of floodwaters). To the others it may have been nothing more

OPPOSITE: Göreme caves, Cappadocia, Turkey, 1995

than a beautiful mountain, but for me it was like a journey far beyond biblical times to a time of origins, and this alternate level of awareness became a primary characteristic of my journey to the East. Ararat provoked an epiphany, an inner understanding that for the first time in my life linked my inner and outer worlds. Ararat was not only present in a physical way, but it also became a symbol of much, much more.

In our lifetime—if we are fortunate—we visit certain places, whether near home or far away, that evoke the sacred in us. They differ from our usual world in magical and powerful ways, resonating with our deeper self, challenging us by their mere presence, and creating such awe in us that we come away feeling ourselves part of a wondrous natural world. There are many sacred landscapes in the world, but *our* experience of them is out of this world. Although such places exist in time, our experience of them is *outside* time. All sacred landscapes were created in the distant past, before modern humans graced the earth; when we gaze at these sublime terrains, it is as if we are transported to a timeless realm or we are revisiting the cusp of creation itself.

According to American scholar and mythologist Joseph Campbell, the power of mythology lies in its ability to awaken the psyche to the wonder of the universe. Most myths began as oral traditions that transmitted the wisdom of earlier ages. Because they were not rigorous written doctrines, myths were almost infinitely flexible, morphing from time to time and from place to place.

In my journeys, I have discovered that virtually all sacred landscapes contain "inner" histories that existed long before their "outer" histories came into being. Often these myths hold a deep and powerful ethos, as well as clues to the profound energies that sacred places transmit to us when we open ourselves up to their language. Since oral traditions have all but vanished in our modern era, we are left with complex, varied, and often contradictory versions of nearly every myth. It is in the nature of myth to be open-ended rather than literal, and, as a result, many of the myths that I have chosen to associate with sacred landscapes express a certain romance and mystery. While they may seem enigmatic to the logical mind, the myths recounted in this volume penetrate deeply into our collective psyche, awakening us to the vital messages of the sacred, natural world.

OPPOSITE: Volcanic tuff, White Valley, Cappadocia, Turkey, 1995

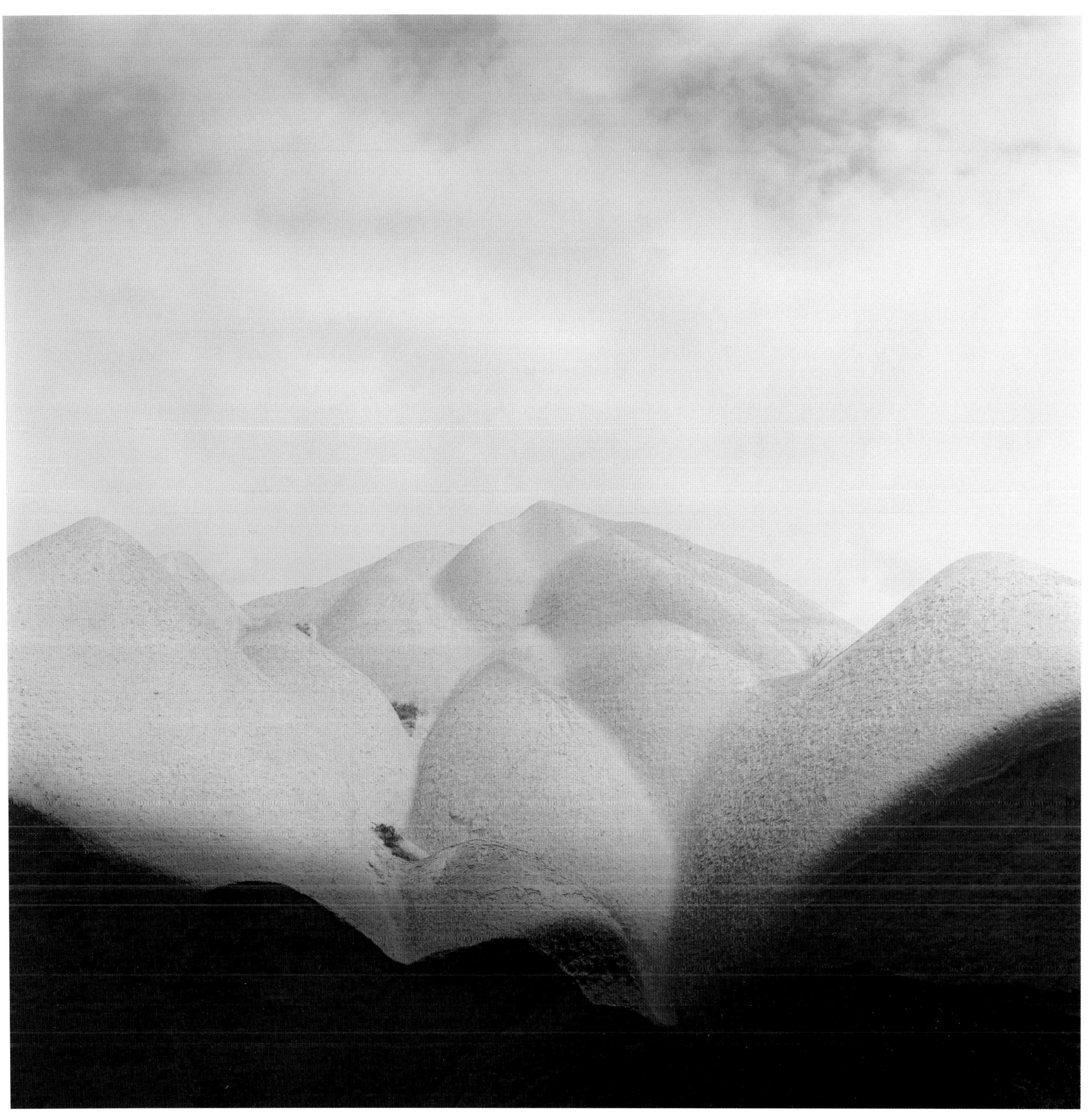

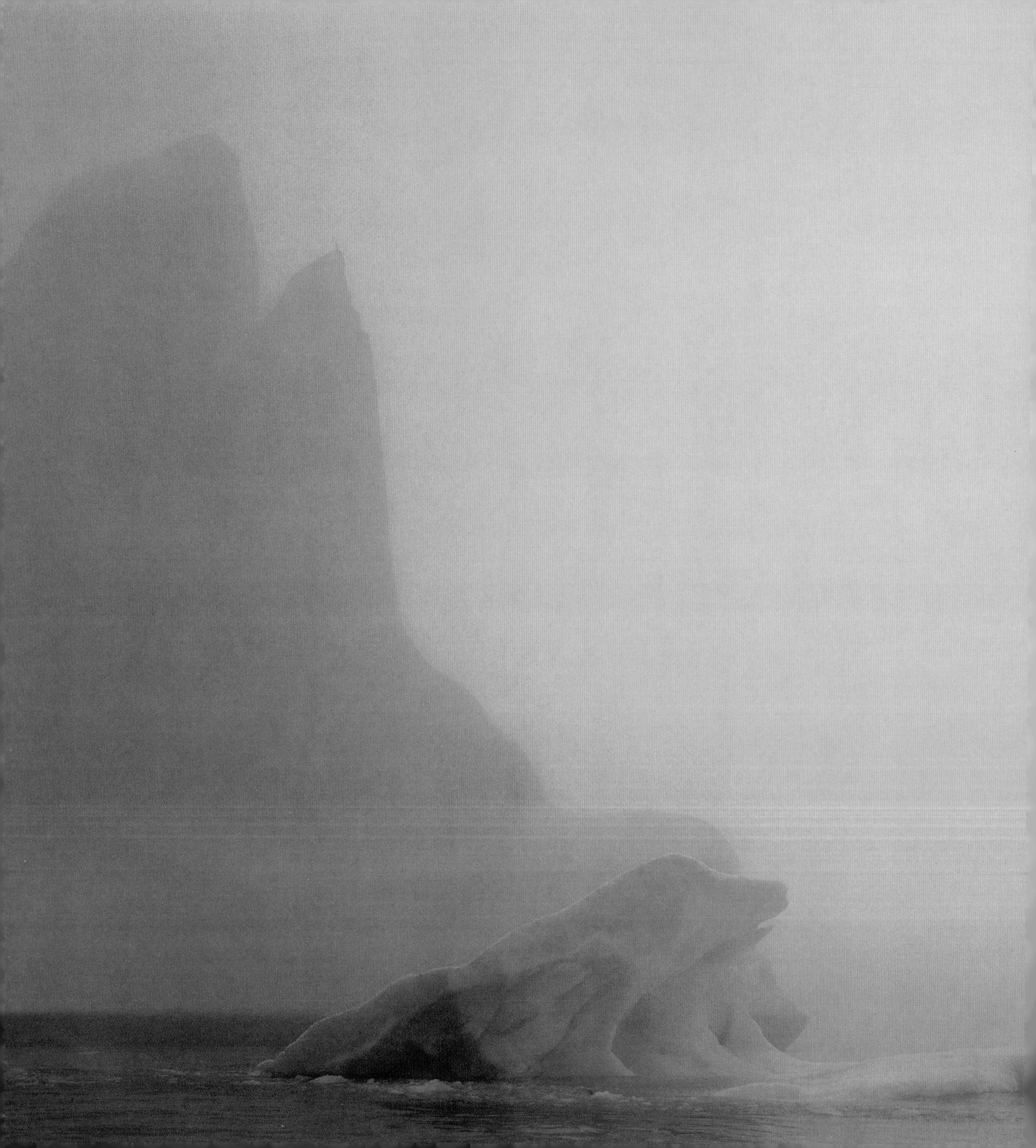

CHAPTER 1

The Threshold Between Worlds

The linear mind is what creates the boundary line between us and the world. Location of consciousness in the brain closes the door to nature. But the door is unlocked.

—Stephen Harrod Buhner, *The Secret Teachings of Plants* (2004)[1]

What exactly is the *sacred?* The sacred is an ethereal quality that has roots in the life of the soul and spirit rather than in any formal religious practice or system. Spiritual qualities are dynamic aspects of the human psyche that are independent of form but that find expression through the world of form.[2] Sacred landscape triggers a spiritual recognition in us when we experience it. Australian Aborigines describe the earth's power as the "dreaming" of a place, because anything that occurs in a particular location leaves "seeds, myths or images, unseen vibrations that provoked the place into being in the first place."[3] Everything in our world is alive with sacred symbolism, imbued with spirit, and pregnant with possibility. Aboriginal art is like a map of this interaction between the spiritual and the physical place. If we are awake, present, open, and engaged, we can pick up these energies and the information they offer. In Vajrayana Buddhism, the sacred isn't beyond thought or supernatural in some vague way, but "rather it has to do with things being so true, so real, and so direct."[4] The great Tibetan Buddhist master Chögyam Trungpa knew that the sacred is a matter of truth and that "the magic is simplicity."[5]

The sacred is also a component of spirituality—that transcendent quality so integral to all people in our present world (whatever their beliefs), many of whom are scientists or even self-described atheists. Spirituality, being both intensely personal and universal, is inclusive of but not necessarily limited to religious beliefs.

OPPOSITE: Iceberg, Disko Bay, Greenland, 1988

A new organization of architects called the Forum for Architecture, Culture and Spirituality uses the following definition: "The spiritual refers to a heightened or alternative state of mind in which one is overcome by, or perceives the presence, insight, or action of forces beyond self-limited consciousness. Spiritual experiences are realized individually and although possible to articulate, they cannot be completely conveyed due to the limited nature of our symbolic language. More specifically, spirituality addresses the human need for transcendence."[6]

Essential to experience of the sacred is a break in our normal perception of the world. Moments of transcendence impel us to abandon ordinary, everyday "profane" time, which is linear and composed of the hours, days, and years of our life. As Mircea Eliade remarks, "by its very nature sacred time is reversible in the sense that, properly speaking, it is a primordial mythical time made present."[7] Because sacred landscapes are typically created by the play of nature over millions of years, they evoke the pure, original state of earth and sky. Such places are wild and chaotic, revealing their history to us in profound ways that we may not understand on a conscious level. Experiencing sacred landscapes is like being present at archetypal realities that occurred at the beginning of time and that continue to repeat *ad infinitum,* if only in the collective imagination and our psyche.

The threshold between worlds is where we offer sacrifices to divinities at rites of passage such as birth, death, and on initiation to adulthood. This threshold is a boundary, like consciousness, protecting us from the wildness of nature while allowing us a glimpse of the higher, spiritual realms. Whether it is a church or temple, a mountain or grove of trees, a pyramid, in the jungle or on an expanse of northern ice, once we cross the symbolic gateway into such sacred territory and allow ourselves to open up to pure spirit, we experience a profound difference. Many of these transitions are also watched over by protective deities that take the form of lions, dragons, Buddhas, and demons, to name a few, as well as symbols or signs that speak their potency as places where the gods descend to Earth, the goddesses emerge, and we ascend to heaven. We don't have to accept or believe any religious or spiritual doctrine in order to feel the power of these landscapes, however, because they precede all modern man-made structures and, by evoking some ancient occurrence recorded in our collective psyche, strike us at our true core.

In physics there is a process called *resonance,* which is a mechanism by which a pair of atoms, objects, wave forms, or beings that move in a similar fashion and at a common frequency instantly communicate information over large distances. This information flows both ways and happens at speeds faster than light travels. We recognize it as the natural but unexpected phenomenon of "being on the same wavelength" as someone else, as when we sense the presence of someone we perceive as familiar across a room full of strangers. In music, resonance is when a sympathetic vibration intensifies

OPPOSITE: Imam Mosque ceiling, Isfahan, Iran, 2001

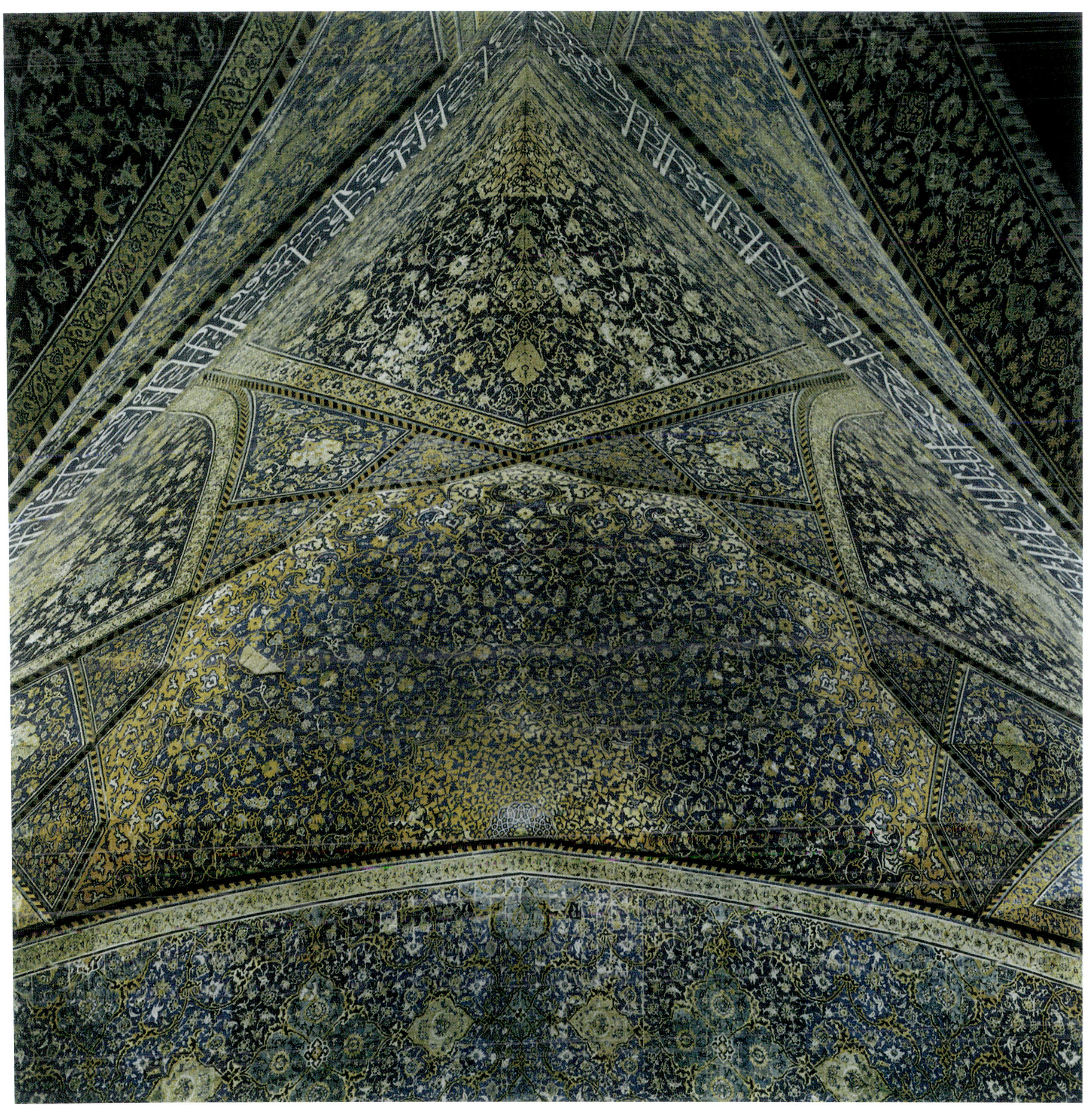

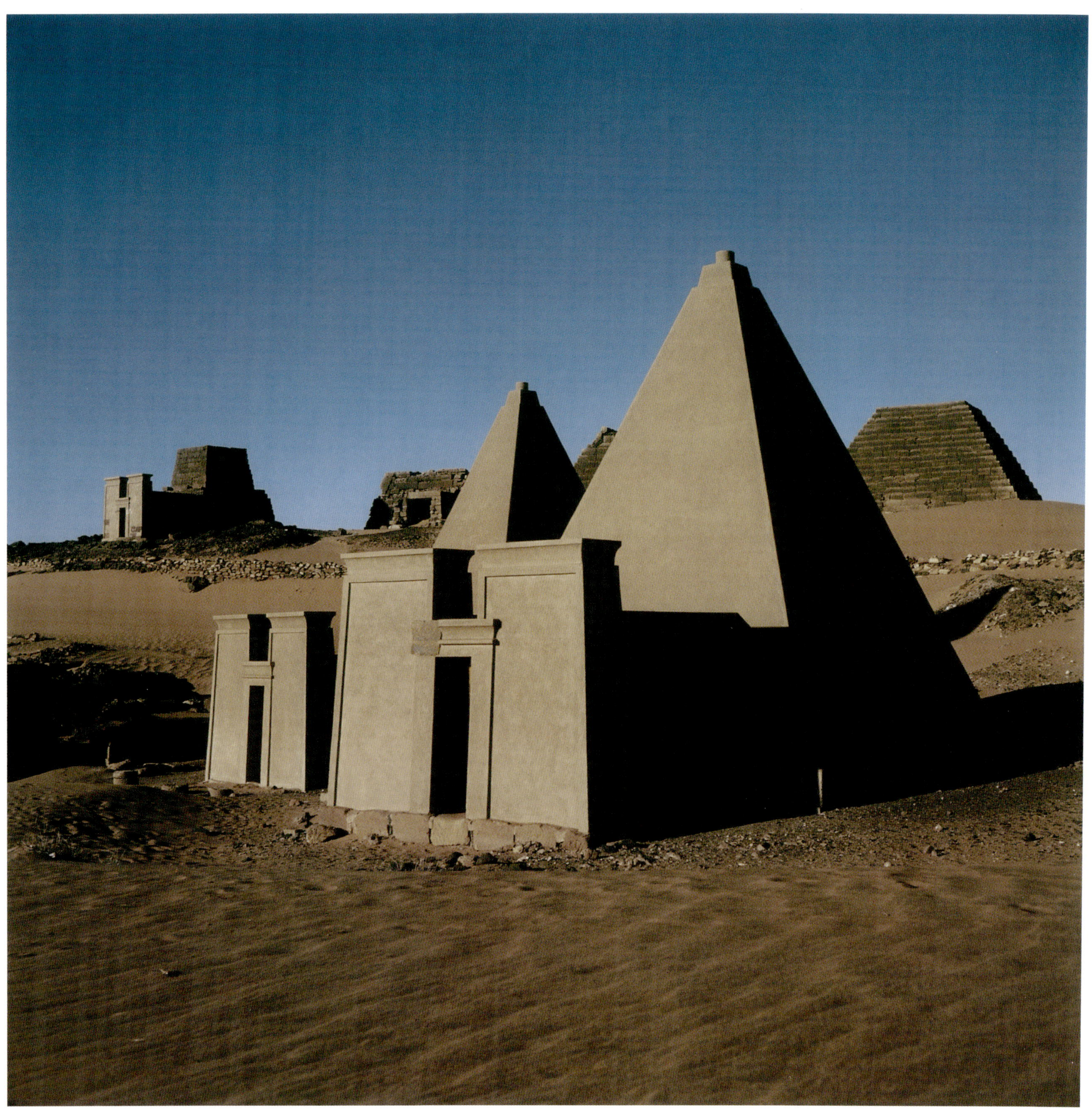

or prolongs an initial sound; some Eastern musical instruments have strings inside the body of the instrument that vibrate with the instrument's outer strings, creating deep resonance. Resonance enriches the significance of things and evokes spontaneous, deep, emotional experiences. Sacred landscapes also act in this way. When we come to such a place we resonate with its energy field, the density of its physical presence, the play of light and shadow, the look of certain angles or curves, or even the depth of experience that the landscape has carried for millions of years. When monuments or sacred buildings are constructed in these places, they act as a kind of focus for these resonant dynamics, and thus the building or object becomes a sounding board for the deep feelings evoked by the landscape, centering feelings and bringing them into more tangible form. In this sense, the resonance of a sacred place is a transition point between heaven and earth, above and below, without and within. We pass between worlds much more easily in such places because the environment contains a sacred presence, and if we are willing to "go there," we can enter the spirit of these landscapes and receive their profound messages.[8]

OPPOSITE: Burial pyramids at Meroë, Sudan, 1998

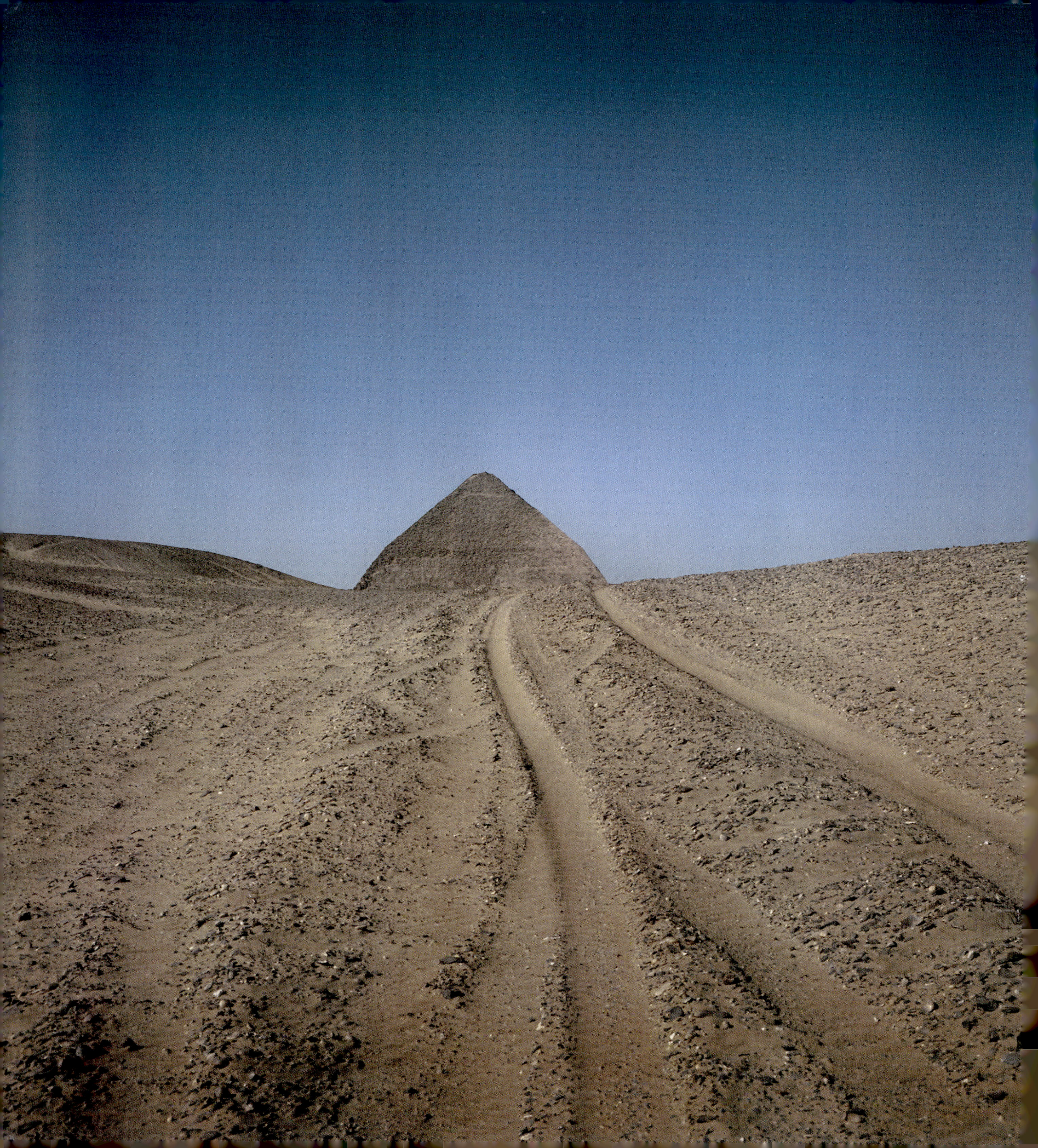

CHAPTER 2

In Search of the Sacred

We have lost the response of the heart to what is presented to the senses.

—Stephen H. Buhner, *The Secret Teachings of Plants,* (2004)[1]

When we experience a sacred landscape, we resonate inwardly with its power, whether or not it conforms to our education or outer knowledge of the world. This may be why so many tourists travel to the ends of the earth to visit such places, even though they may not be aware of what they are experiencing. Indeed, what we experience in sacred landscapes may be in direct contradiction to our formal religious, scientific, or philosophical beliefs. This is because the sacred is a ritual process, a journey we begin at these evocative places, and once we taste it, we remain on the quest for the rest of our lives.

The myriad definitions of the sacred encompass ancient as well as modern sites, ranging from pure, vast landscapes to specific locations. Most often, they date from before human history, although many sites have since attracted religious markers, buildings, or settlements. Sacred landscapes are accomplishments of nature and places of power with the ineffable capacity to confer this potency on those who behold them. They recharge our spiritual batteries and purify the soul.

Essential to sacred landscapes are the myths, stories, and beliefs that early people associated with them. Sometimes they involve places that we cannot find in our modern world, such as the central Asian kingdom of Shambhala, the British Camelot, the Australian Aboriginal Dreamtime, the Three Underworlds of the Navajo, and the mythic island kingdom of Atlantis. Whether or not they ever existed in the material world, sacred sites and their accompanying myths fire our imagination and continue to exist in our mind as we search for traces of them in our journeys across the globe.

OPPOSITE: Bent Pyramid, Dashur, Egypt, 1997

Sacred Origins

To ancient nomadic humanity, the vault of the heavens was the home of their divinities, and this vast dome above, with its infinite stars, seemed to center around and move with them on their travels. They observed stellar movements and created mythologies to worship them. The first temples, including Stonehenge and the other stone and forest circles across Europe and the Americas, were in the open, framing the heavens. When humanity developed agriculture, settled in one place, and created cities and temples, pyramids became sacred mountains; their vaults and domes were re-creations of the sky. These early monuments were also observatories, sacred sanctuaries, and occult centers. They were where humanity met the divine and where observations necessary to the development of astrology, navigation, and calendar-making took place.

To the earliest cultures, the entire earth was sacred. Supernal deities (the highest of the deities) created Mother Earth and Father Sky, rivers and oceans, mountains and valleys, woods and trees and other growing things, and the abundance of animals. Indeed, these deities *were* the land and its creatures—the creators and the created, the embodying spirit on earth and in life. All domains and species were part of the divine, and all were sacred.

Early religious rituals celebrated the creation of the world from primal chaos. Participants relived the mystery of this great birth, stepping out of ordinary time to achieve transcendence, healing, a new beginning, or contact with their ancestors and with primeval gods and goddesses. The same process appeared in holy texts, where mysteries of sacred origin were revealed to prophets at particular sacred settings. Mecca, Mount Sinai, Delphi, Bodhgaya, Jerusalem—these holy places continue to function as symbolic gateways, as portals to our origins. Thus, religious revelations and myths transmit the power of our common origins to subsequent generations.

The traditional Abrahamic religions historically subjugated feminine Earth Mother worship by means of rules and regulations that enforced separation of their followers from the spirits and symbols of the natural world. The "pagan" reverence of the earth and its plants and creatures was seen as a subversive force to be rooted out and eliminated, and this viewpoint persists among large numbers of the current world population. The fact that the world population seems to have striated into those for whom science and atheism are supreme and those with blind belief in religion as a worldview makes the whole situation infinitely worse, because often neither science nor fundamentalism respects the sacred places of earlier times. For example, the expression "tree hugger" has a negative connotation for a large percentage of our population, who consider ecology to be antithetical to commerce and "the American way of life."

OPPOSITE: Great Pyramid of Giza (Dynasty IV), Egypt, 1989

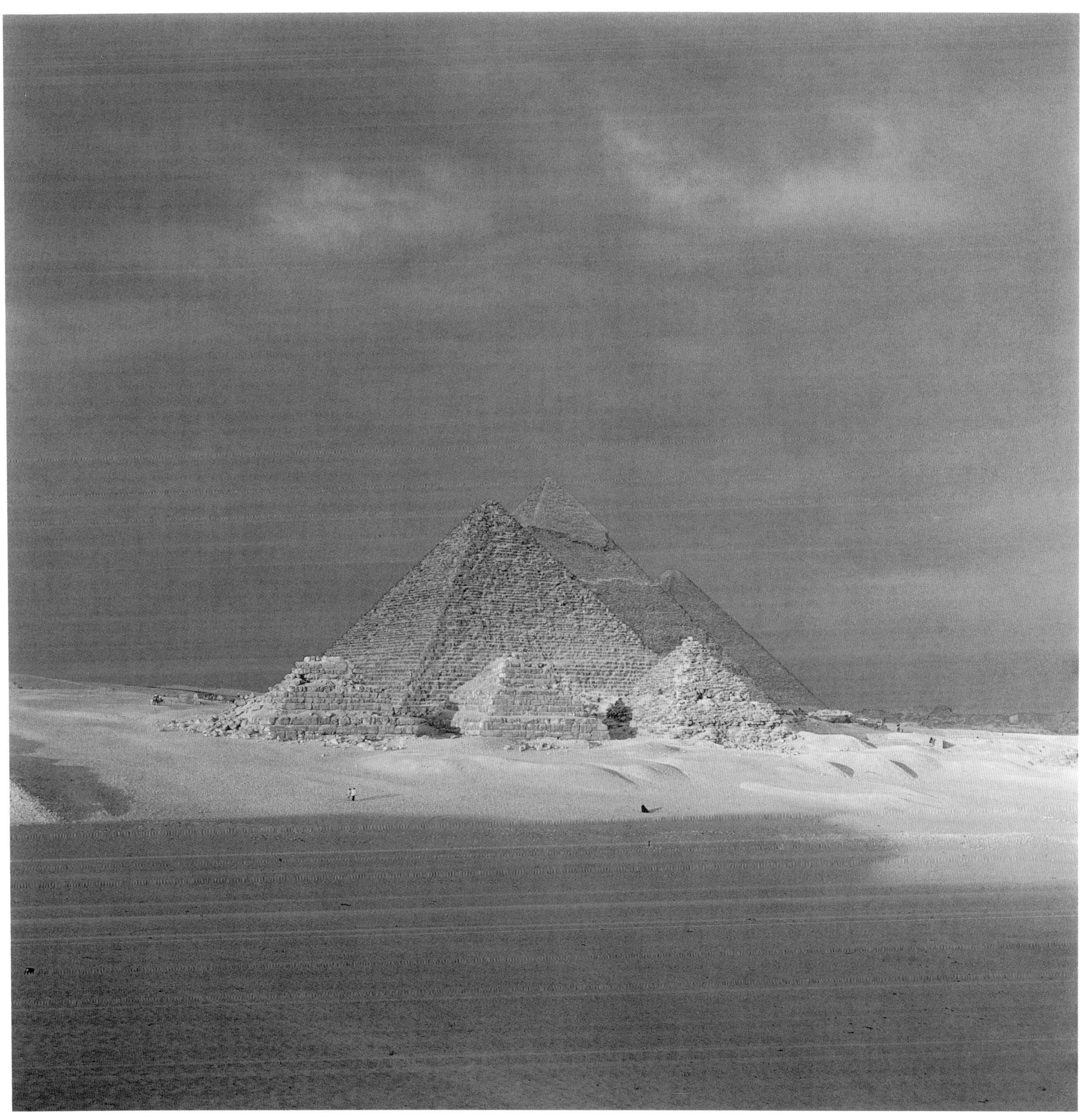

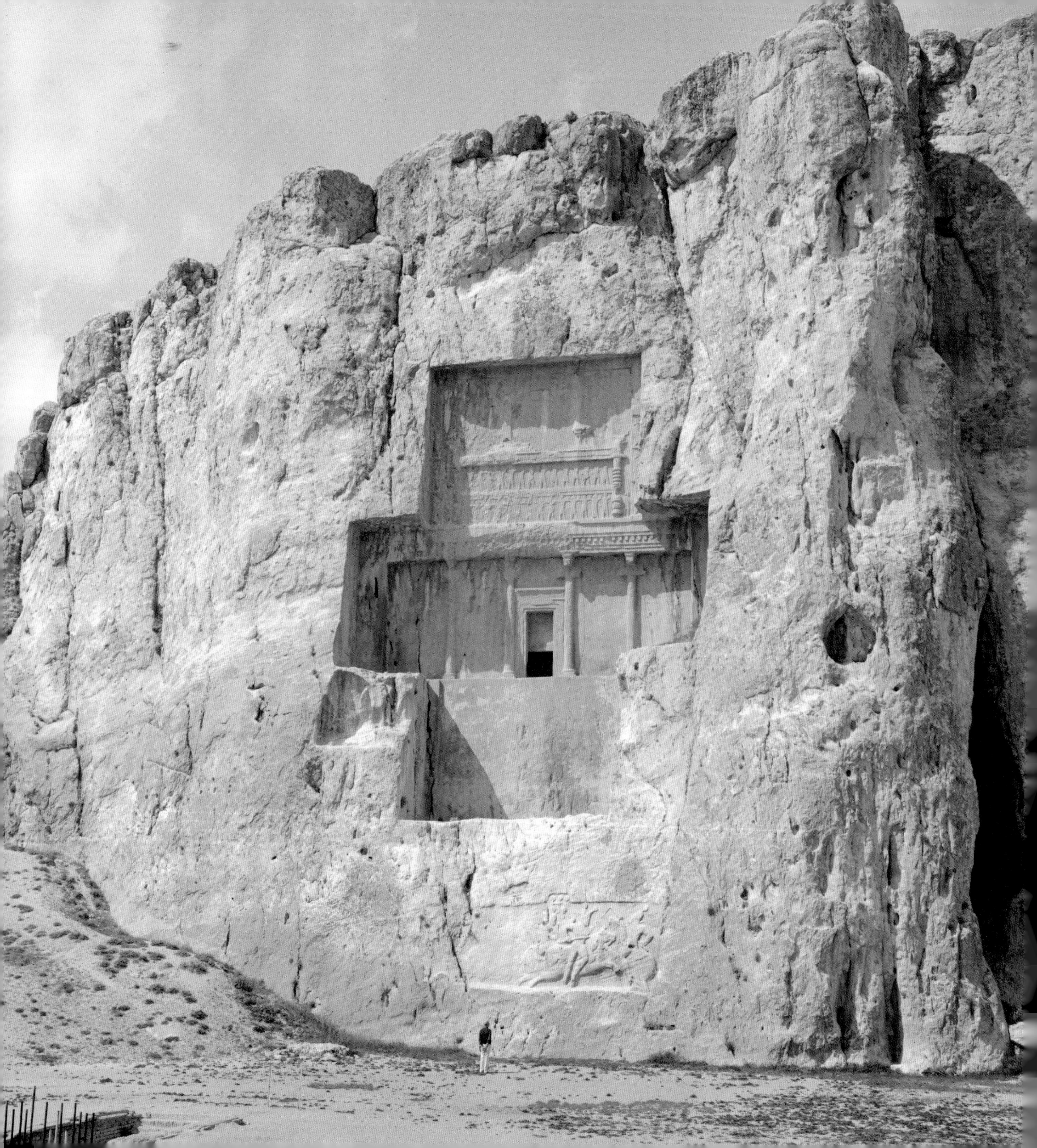

The irony is that many other religions, Eastern and Western, have always built on top of the ruins of earlier sacred places and incorporated their remains, symbolism, and rituals into their own religious observances. Thus, we find groves of trees sacred to the early Middle Eastern fertility goddesses like Ishtar and Isis incorporated into temples, churches, or mosques as columns decorated with floral imagery and carved with vertical flutes like stems and spiraling vines. One of the objectives of this book is to show that the earliest places of nature worship were prototypes and even site-specific locations of later pyramids, temples, mosques, stupas, churches, and holy cities. And although the natural world has become for many people nothing more than an adjunct to the man-made world—existing as merely an abstraction—the original symbols of the sacred continue to exert power over us, albeit unconsciously, rather than with our full comprehension and intentionality.

The Evolution of Sacred Symbolism

It is in the nature of religions to edit out the uncomfortable history of their early matriarchal stages and concepts in favor of the divine revelations of patriarchs such as Moses, Jesus, and Muhammad. The Hebrew Bible is a mythic history of the early Jewish tribes, who continually struggled against earlier Middle Eastern "pagan" nature cults that worshipped graven images, such as winged deities, animals, and plants. The ancient Hebrew culture emerged from one that was historically nomadic; the people were herders and farmers, and it was natural in times of stress for them to revert to their polytheistic earth-worship. The later patriarchies simply neutralized this tendency by incorporating early ritual places and objects as symbols, sacred implements, and influences. Sacred mountains, where revelations and communication with God occur, became symbols, such as the triangular roof of Solomon's Temple, which signified ascent. Likewise, the Tree of Knowledge in the Garden of Eden became a menorah, an ancient Jewish symbol related to trees and tree goddesses. In both cases, the form of the object reminds the worshipper of origins, of beginnings, and of divine revelations achieved through direct contact with God.

Few people are aware of (or understand) the process that, over millennia, has transformed ancient sacred sites into formal, "religious" structures imbued with the symbolism and consciousness of the original sites. Many of us have lost the capacity to understand the "symbol" so integral to understanding the sacred. Like a corporate logo, a sign has a specific meaning that does not vary, while a symbol expresses an inner truth that carries multiple meanings whose accessibility is a function of on our level of understanding. The psychologist Carl Jung defined a symbol as an "expression of the inner unconscious drama of the psyche which becomes accessible to man's consciousness by way of projection—that is, mirrored in the events of nature."[2]

OPPOSITE: Cave tombs of the Achaemenid kings, Naqsh-e Rostam, Iran, 2001

Sacred landscapes are symbolic in that the elements that make them powerful—mountains and rivers, sky and stars, oceans and lakes, majestic trees and jungles, deserts and plateaus—function on many levels simultaneously. They are real and tangible, and they also carry deep symbolism. For example, although we tend to think of the cross as a Christian symbol, it appears in virtually all early cultures—thousands of years before Christianity—as a symbol of the cardinal directions of the compass, or the meeting between heaven and earth, or within a circle as the original symbol of the earth. Ancient symbolism is thus inseparable from our experience of sacred places, and we resonate with these underlying symbols wherever we encounter them. Sacred landscape is beautiful and powerful in its own right, but it also carries a numinous, light-bringing quality that we can't help but notice and respect, whatever our religious beliefs.

Sacred symbols are what Jung called archetypes: universal images that have existed since the earliest time and that are gradually modified, codified, and integrated into the collective psyche through myths, fairy tales or stories.[3] While we may not consciously know what they mean, their meanings exist in our unconscious and can arise to speak to us through dreams, mystical experiences, or visions. We hold on to certain ideas and concepts from the outside world, but when we are in the presence of archetypal symbols, these symbols become alive and bring order to our inner chaos, just as creation myths make the world out of initial chaos. This process—where order arises from apparently random movements and patterns in the physical world—is even reflected in contemporary Chaos Theory.

In his book *The Re-Enchantment of Everyday Life*, Thomas Moore talks about new definitions of the increasingly common word "ecology" that give it more potent moral and ethical overtones. Ecology describes an attitude of someone "who has an ethical concern for all living creatures and for the earth as a living system."[4] This is in direct opposition to the prevailing Western capitalist view, influenced by science, where the earth is considered an inert body available for exploitation. When we understand the earth as an organism in its own right, we rediscover ancient concepts such as "cosmos" and "world soul" from a time when the gods and goddesses were still valued and known by direct experience. I am not suggesting we revert to ancient practices, but it is important to understand that they constitute valid underpinnings that have an ever-increasing relevance today. The ancients recognized and worshipped the forces of nature, attributing divine powers to them. To emphasize how essential it is for us to restore the life we have taken away, Moore repeatedly reminds us that the earth is an organism. Thus, the word "ecology" takes on a new meaning that implies a shift toward feeling, heart, and mystery. More importantly, this modified concept indicates that the only way to truly save our planet is to rediscover the divinity inherent in the earth, apart from or in addition to our religious and scientific conceptions of it.

OPPOSITE: Victoria Falls, Zimbabwe, 1998

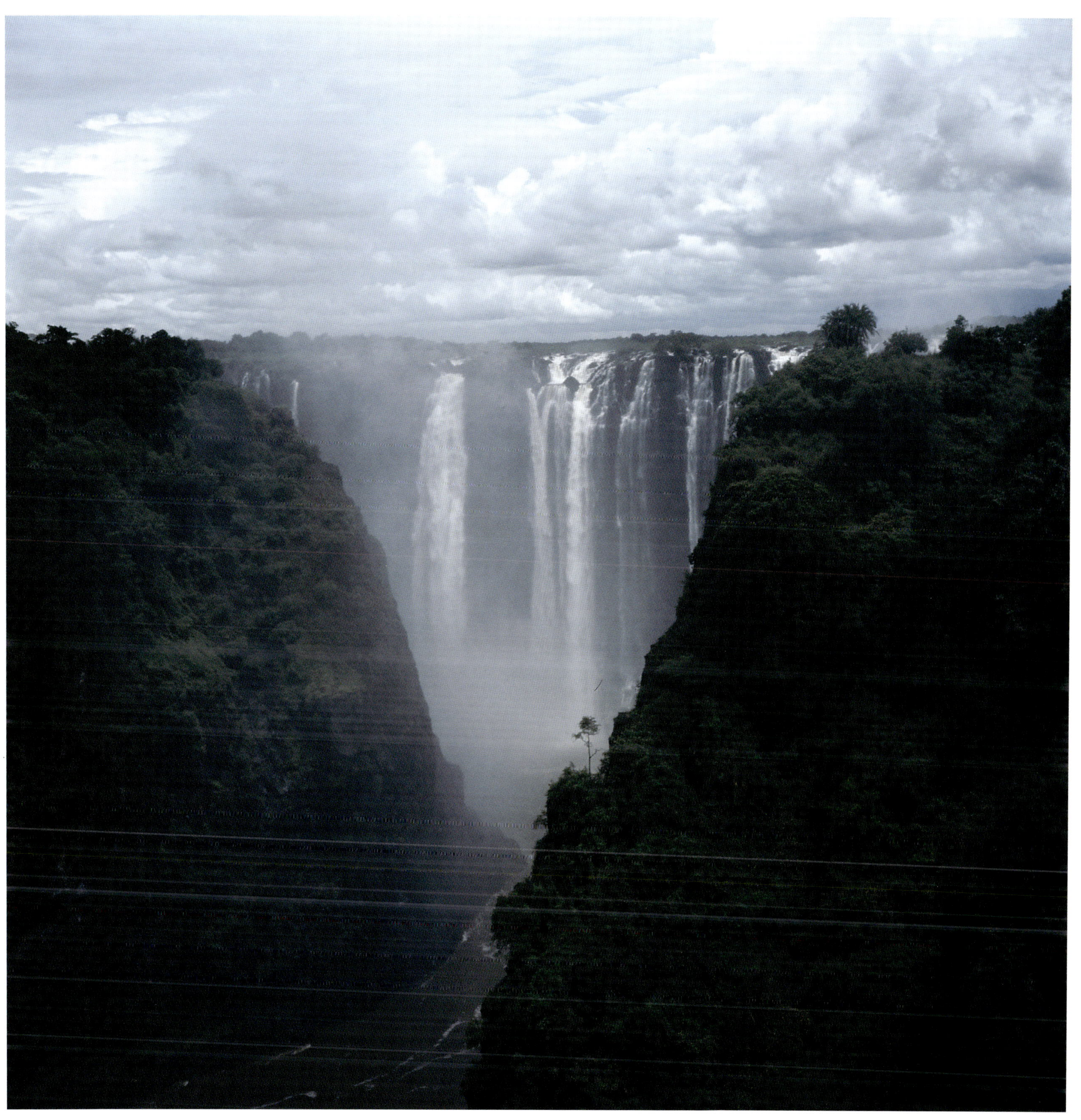

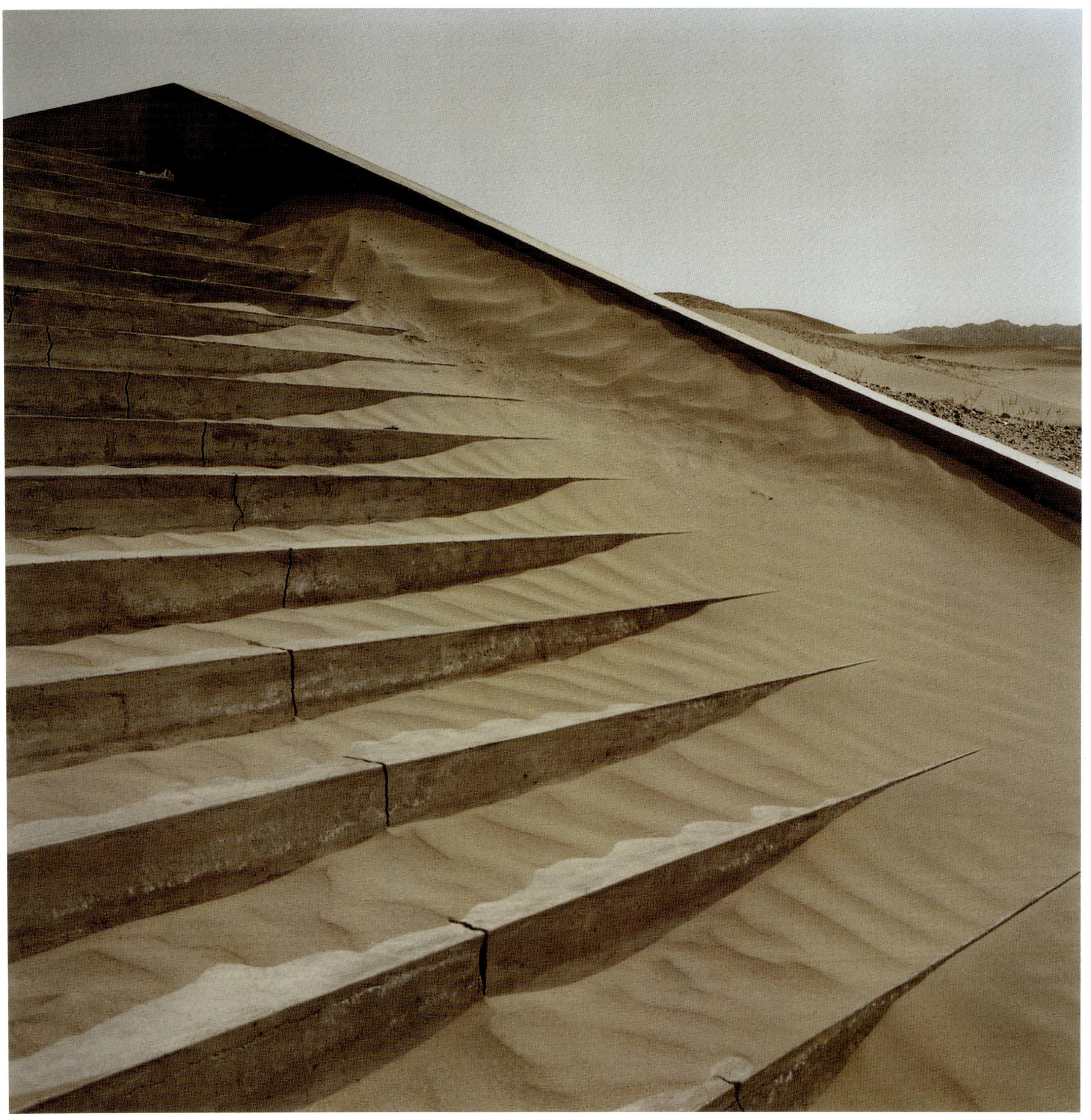

Restoring the Sacred

The earth is the vehicle by which the gods and goddesses seek the utmost respect of humanity, and if they are unsatisfied, they express their shadow sides, causing chaos and disorder. A way that we invite such chaos is to define the precinct or land around a church or temple, synagogue or mosque as "sacred," inferring that the rest of the land isn't. Thus, we fail to recognize the sacred quality of the entire natural world, demeaning all of nature by assigning it a subsidiary role as a mute backdrop to our more important lives. This is a grave mistake. Unfortunately, humanity continues to debase the memory of the spirits by desacralizing the earth, using it as raw material for our vision of dominance through materialism and further desecrating it, to the extent that we are making our only home nearly inhospitable to all living species.

In order to restore the natural world to its proper place, we must encourage the view that all nature is sacred. In this book you will see that although chapters describe certain archetypal manifestations of the sacred landscape, such as mountains, boundaries, gateways, and caves, many of the most powerful sites contain more than one, if not many or even all, of these characteristics. Pyramids, for example, mark important points in the landscape, are oriented toward the cardinal compass directions, evoke sacred mountains in their shape, have inner passageways like caves, and are protected by guardians or with enclosures. In this case, the sacred monument simultaneously functions on many different levels of perception while evoking earlier stages in the development of the sacred.

Our modern scientific and academic establishments tend to consider religion a dangerous force that only prevails when reason fails.[5] At the other end, religious fundamentalists promote creationism and reject scientific theories like evolution.

I think it essential that the sacred be presented as a precursor to formal religion and science. We should not allow later dogma or pronouncements to redefine or negate the sacredness of these landscapes. It is important for us to find a way to express our embrace of a spiritual and ecologically balanced "past-modern" world.

Although pyramids, stupas, sanctuaries, churches, temples, and mosques were built in sacred landscapes, it is the landscape itself that evokes the sacred. Formal religions recognized and attempted to capture the sacred quality that the landscape possessed and willfully disposed of it. Let us therefore rediscover our ancient roots in these sacred landscapes and bring their wisdom into a world that sorely needs it.

OPPOSITE: Cemetery steps in the Taklimakan Desert, Dunhuang, China, 2001

PAGE 20: Bagan, Burma (Myanmar), 1993

PAGE 21: Funerary tower, Ray, Iran, 2001

PAGE 22: Machu Picchu, Peru, 2000

PAGE 23: Window openings, Machu Picchu, Peru, 2000

PAGE 24: Imam Mosque ceiling, Isfahan, Iran, 2001

PAGE 25: Shwedagon Pagoda, Yangon, Burma (Myanmar), 1993

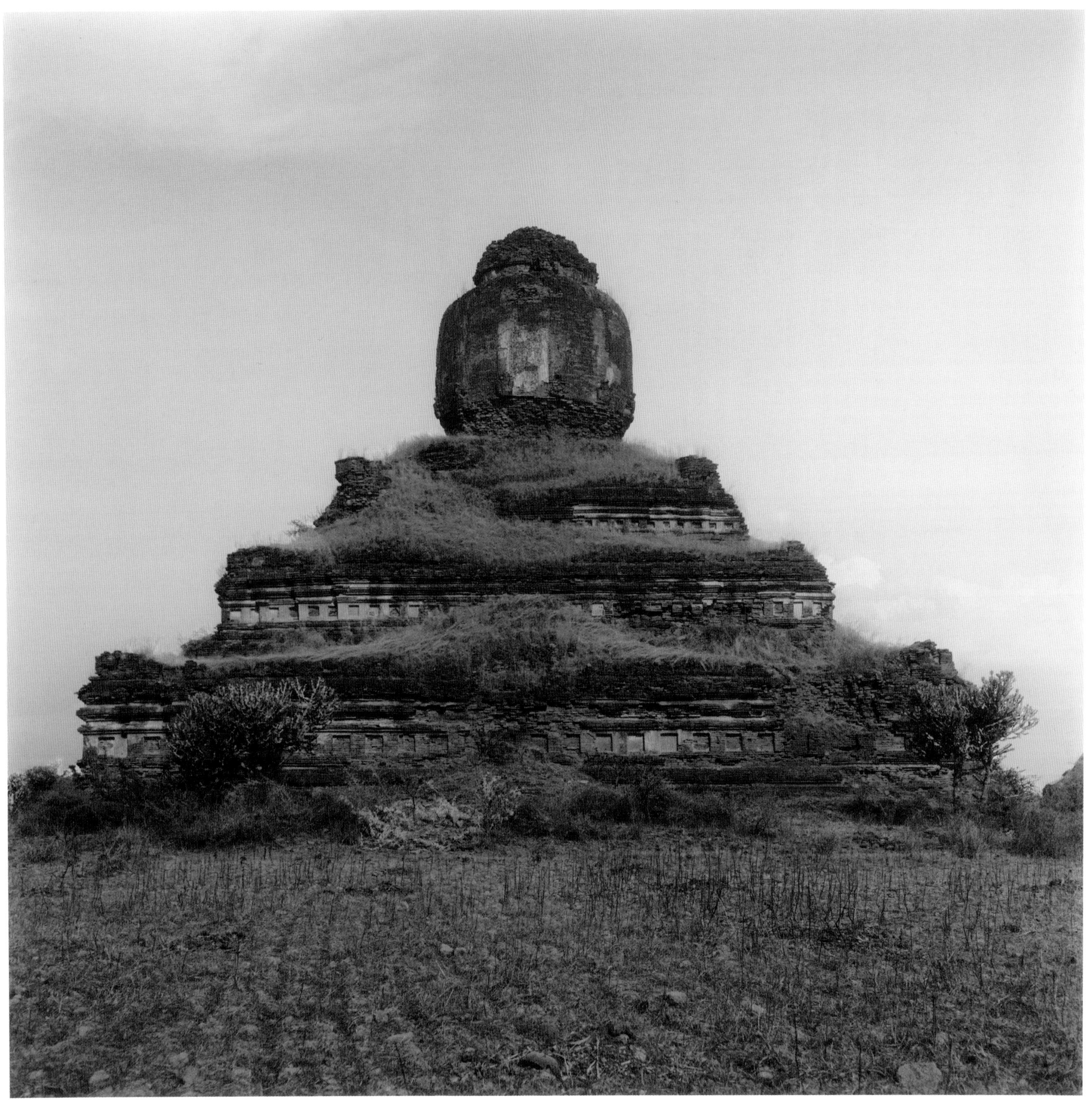

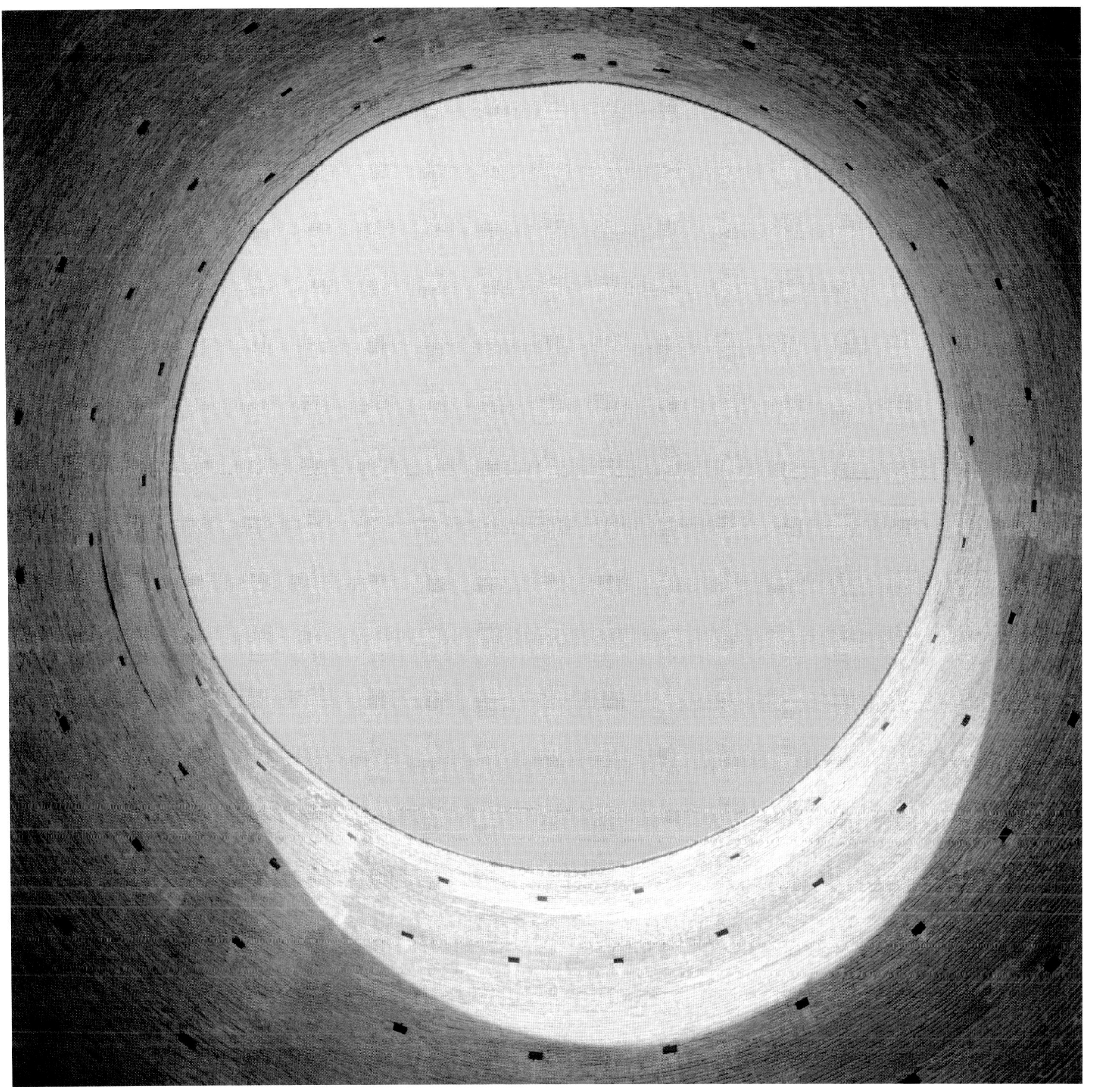

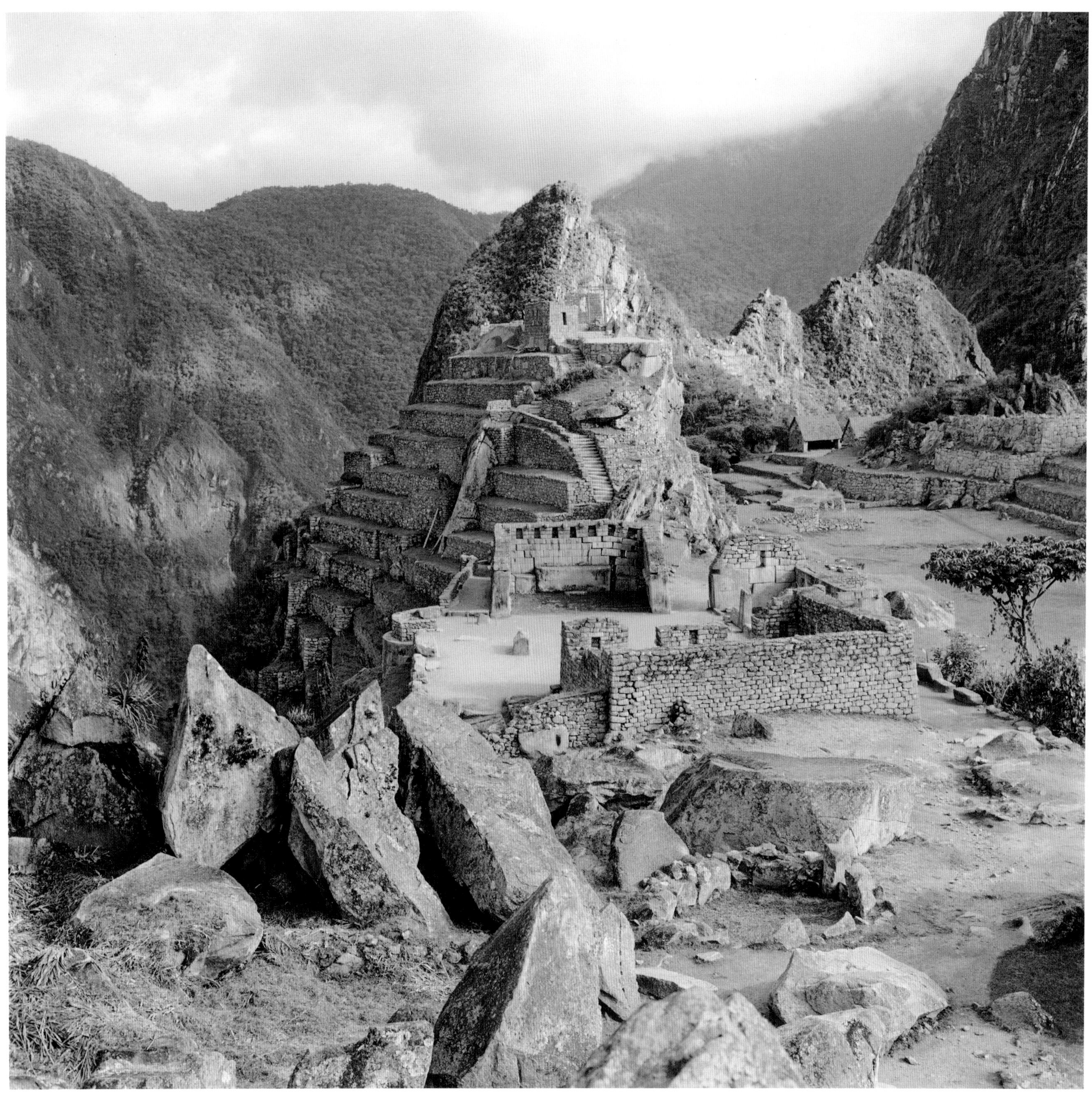

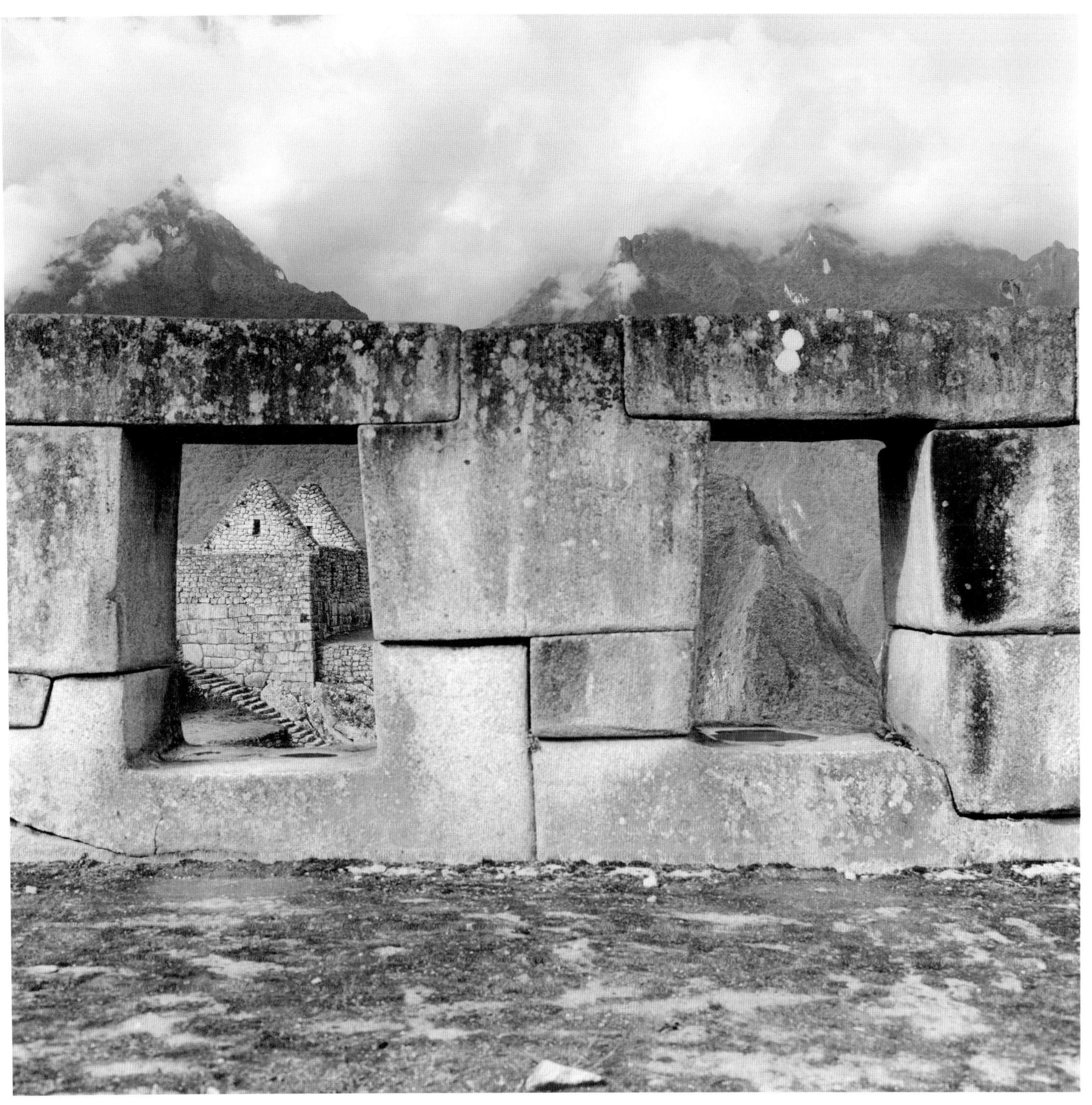

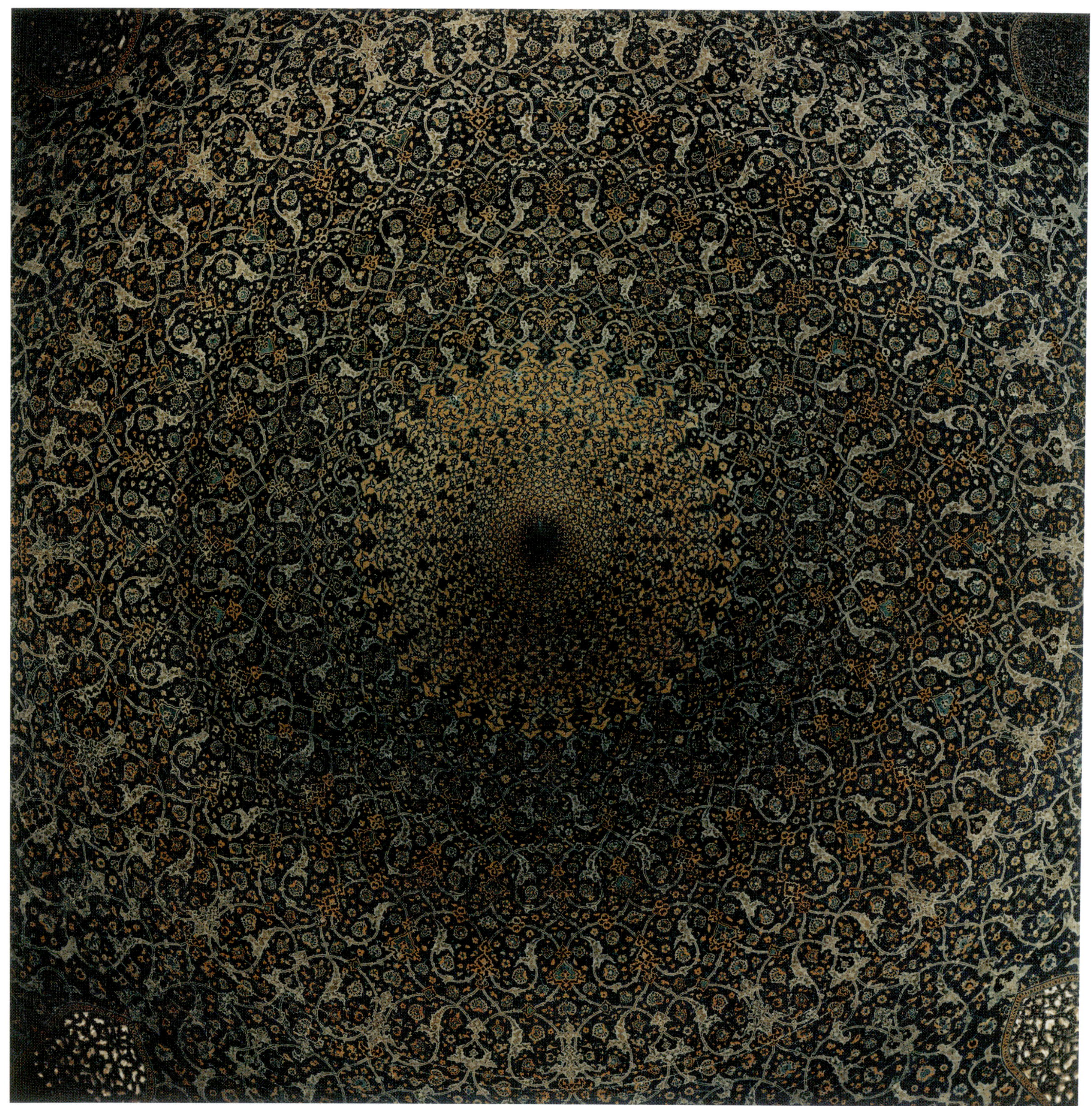

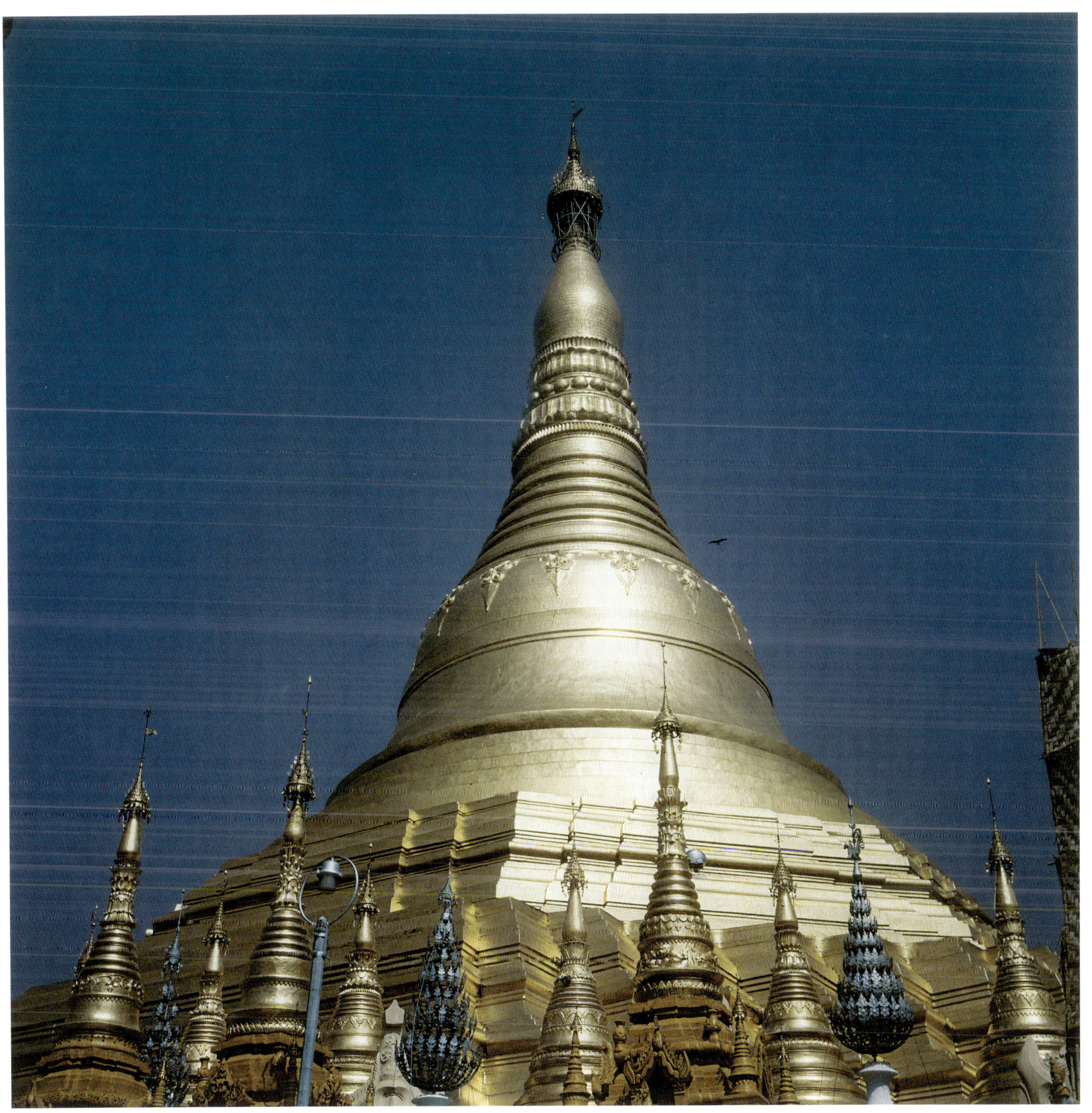

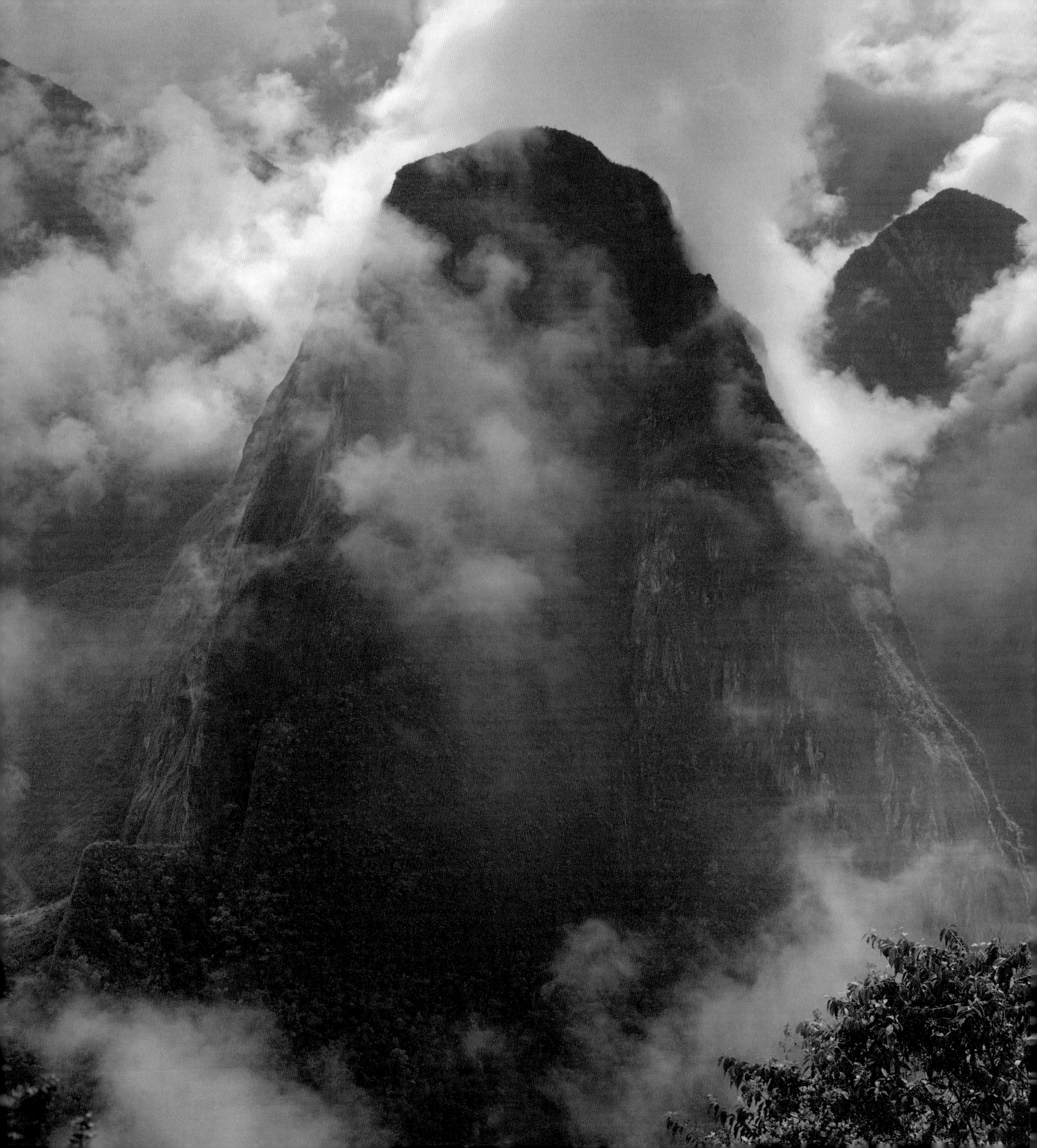

CHAPTER 3

Ascending the Sacred Mountain

Who can understand the secret transmission of the wordless dharma from Mt. Rei?
The mountain where Buddha's first disciple died knows a dawn wind.

~Ikkyu Sojun (1456)[1]

Heaven and earth meet atop the highest mountains, which housed the divinities and supported the heavenly vaults. The only way humans could come into contact with these godly powers was by dangerous quests, although rainbows, earthquakes, and lightning allowed humans to watch this mysterious realm symbolically interact with their mundane lives. Mountains evoke a need to climb them, surmount them, and feel their power and sacredness. They provoke rituals and journeys that are both physical and also spiritual. Their impact is visual, visceral, intensely physical, and tangible—and even more so when they are high enough to penetrate the clouds, are explosively volcanic, or are covered with ice and glaciers.

Jung says that "the mountain stands for the goal of the pilgrimage and ascent; hence it often has the psychological meaning of the self."[2] The mythical world mountains, like Ararat, Sinai, Fuji, Olympus, and Kailash, are places of origin because the gods and goddesses that abide there created the world. Our ancestors celebrated creation as a continuous process, revered the creators, and made continual sacrifices to maintain equilibrium. They were aware that change was inherent in reality. The mountains marked sacred places on earth that protected humanity from the abyss of the underworld and acted as pathways to the profound world of spirit. It is not surprising that later cultures designated mounds, natural hills, and high plateaus as sacred and later created domes and stupas to represent them.

In the creation myths of early cultures, the earth's revolving axis is the navel of the world (*axis mundi*) because the stars and planets in the night sky appear to revolve around the North Pole Star. For nomadic people, the Pole Star remains in the same place in the sky and yet moves with them wherever they wander. This "divine tent pole" links above and below and is the path by which gods

OPPOSITE: Huayna Picchu, opposite Machu Picchu, Peru, 2000

descend to earth, and by which humans ascend to the realm of deities.[3] Mountains are thus revered because they appear to provide access to the axis of the world above. In addition to marking the domain of the sacred, they represent a powerful permanence in a highly impermanent world full of daily threats. Characteristics of sacred mountains appear in myths from all over the world—as twins, containing mysterious caves, surrounded by rivers or a body of water, and, in the case of fiery, volcanic mountains, providing access to the core of the world or the hellfires of the underworld. Above all, however, mountains are places of revelation. The sacred mountain is where Moses was given the tablets of the law and where Zen, Hindu, and Buddhist sages meditate. Likewise, many European cultures make references to the "magic mountain."

The mountains are prophets.

—Honorius of Autun[4]

Machu Picchu: The Eighth Wonder

The twin peaks of Machu Picchu and Huayna Picchu above the winding Urubamba River in Peru are among the most spectacular paired sacred mountains. Although previous explorers had mentioned the site, it was brought to the world's attention in 1911 by American explorer and Yale lecturer Hiram Bingham. He described "great snow peaks looming above the clouds more than two miles overhead, gigantic precipices of many-colored granite rising sheer for thousands of feet above the foaming, glistening, roaring rapids."[5] Although he believed Machu Picchu to be the missing last stronghold of the Inca, abandoned after the empire's eradication by the Spanish in the sixteenth century, it was certainly the most sacred city of the Inca.

Both the capital city Cuzco and Machu Picchu have sun temples with proven astronomical significance; the Inca believed they were descended from the sun. The Inca honored their sun god, Inti, in festivals at the equinoxes and solstices, typically celebrated at the Intihuatana ("Hitching Post of the Sun"), a ritual center in major Incan cities. The importance of this foot-high stone sculpture echoes that of the Greek *omphalos*, or "navel," of the world, which allowed direct communication with the gods, although the Intihuatana is a sophisticated sundial used to determine the yearly Inca calendar. The Inca also used these stone observatories for sun and moon cult rituals,[6] possibly even recording celestial movements with calculation devices made of knotted rope, known as *quipus*, and some scientists even think that the series of stone pillars marking earth lines radiating from Cuzco is a kind of "architectural *quipu*."[7]

As we will see, many cultures worshipped sacred places, where they could see, feel, and measure the movements of the sun and moon, which they regarded as original creator gods and goddesses. These deities were later co-opted and disguised by many of the monotheistic religions.

Machu Picchu is an archetypal sacred mountain; it has stepped layers that are symbolic of spiritual levels, and the natural granite of the mountaintop is utilized in the highest sacred plaza and temple. Bingham named the trapezoidal openings he found there the "Temple of the Three Windows" because they echoed the three ceremonial caves of the primary Inca creation myth, the central window representing the cave from which the Inca people emerged at the beginning of time. Many small temples in Machu Picchu echo the shapes of the surrounding sacred mountains, as do the pitched roofs of many houses in this astounding city. The Inca accepted that Mother Earth and her chosen women held great power, and it was manifested in the sacred places (*huacas*), such as caves, springs, lakes, and mountains, and her priestesses were central to life in Machu Picchu.

Mythic Mount Meru

To Hindus and Buddhists, the mythic Mount Meru—rising vertically amid seven other mountain ranges—is the center of the world. Four heavenly kings reside halfway up the sides, each guarding one of four cardinal directions. Perched atop the summit is Sudarshana, the ultimate realm of the highest gods—the equivalent of Mount Olympus for the Greeks and Valhalla for the Vikings.[8] Spreading out below Mount Meru are the four continents, which constitute the material world of lesser beings. Yogis and yoginis from many religions experience this sacred heaven realm in rituals and trance, aspiring to enter such a realm when they die.[9] Although there is no physical Mount Meru, mandalas, sacred paintings, and diagrams show it simultaneously as a symbol of the cosmos, a map of a celestial kingdom, and a meditation device for achieving enlightenment. The mountain is as alive as if it were a tangible place on Earth. For this reason, ancient Hindu burial mounds for deceased leaders morph into mountainlike reliquaries, or stupas.

Hermits upon Mount Meru or Everest,
Caverned in night under the drifted snow,
Or where that snow and winter's dreadful blast
Beat down upon their naked bodies, know
That day brings round the night, that before dawn
His glory and his monuments are gone.

—William Butler Yeats, *Meru* (1935)

The sacred mountain is a central component of Tibetan Buddhist mandalas—especially as Tibet is the "Land of the Snows" amid the Himalayas and is associated with great awe and mystery. Images of the Buddha giving the Lotus Sutra from Vulture Peak and of Padmasambhava meditating in a mountain cave are central to Tibetan Buddhism and often represented in sculpture, mandalas, and paintings. Another integral concept is the "Pure Land," a divine heavenly realm from which the Buddha emerges

PAGE 30: Machu Picchu, Peru, 2000

PAGE 31: Huayna Picchu, opposite Machu Picchu, Peru, 2000

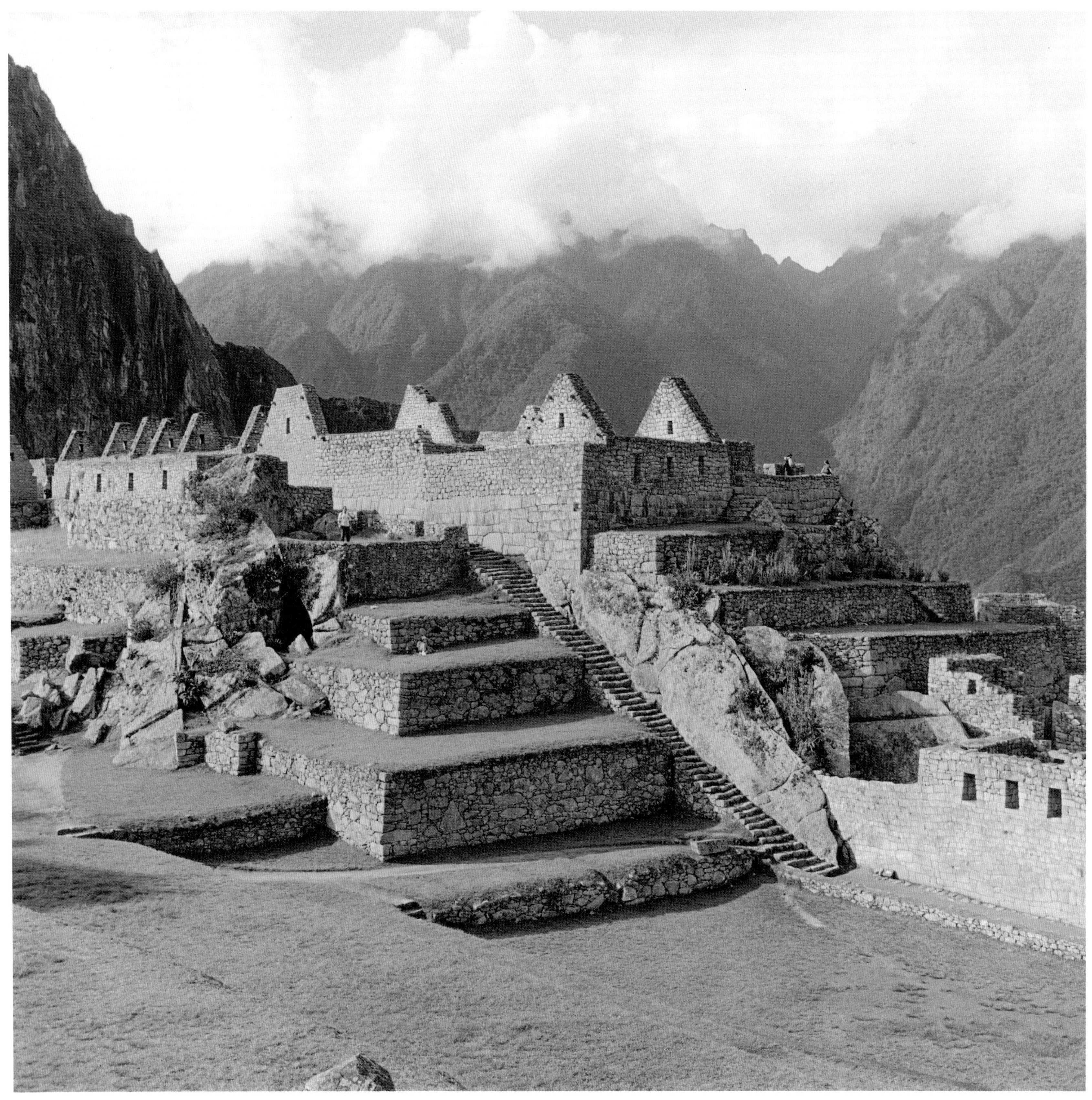

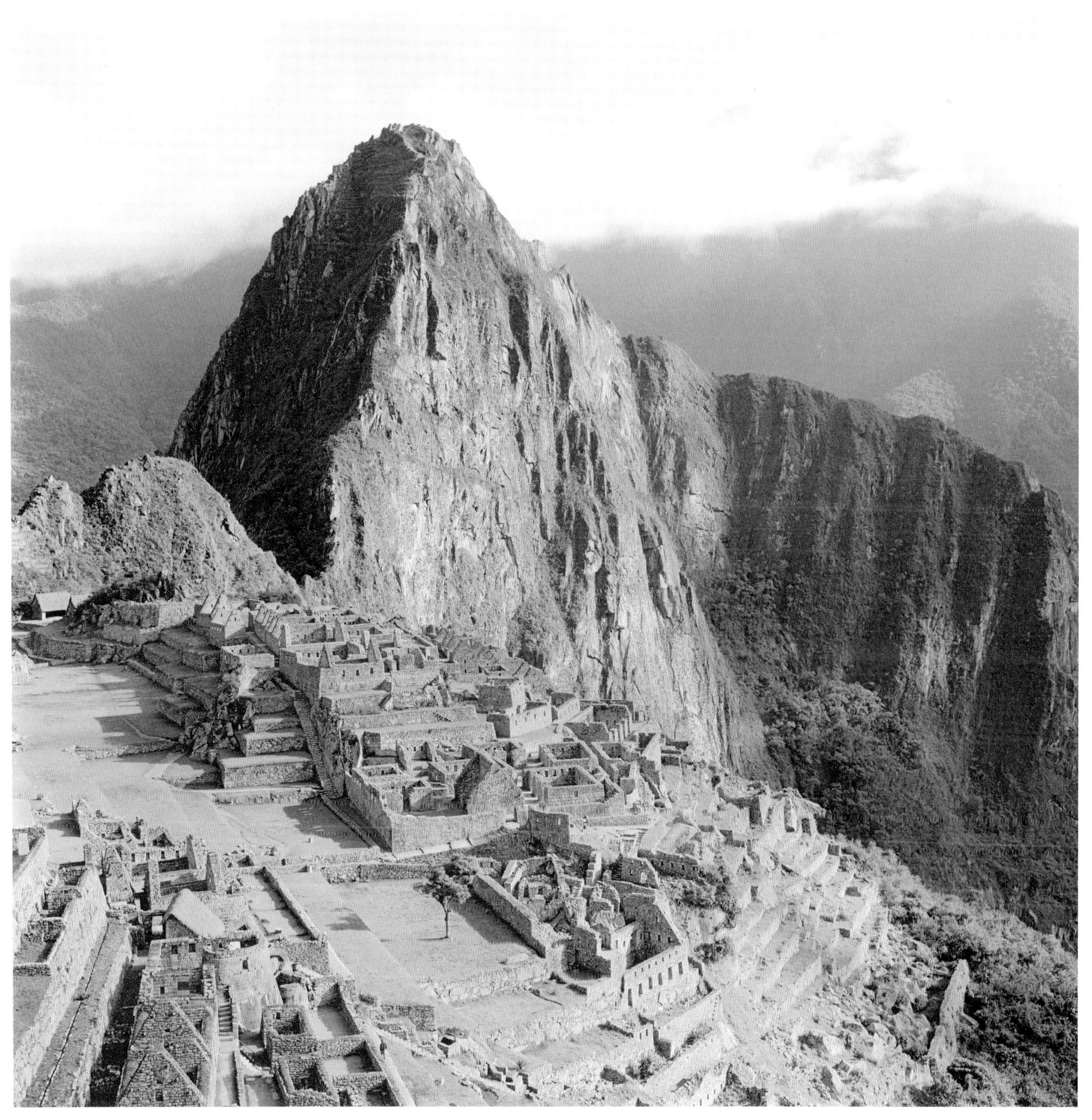

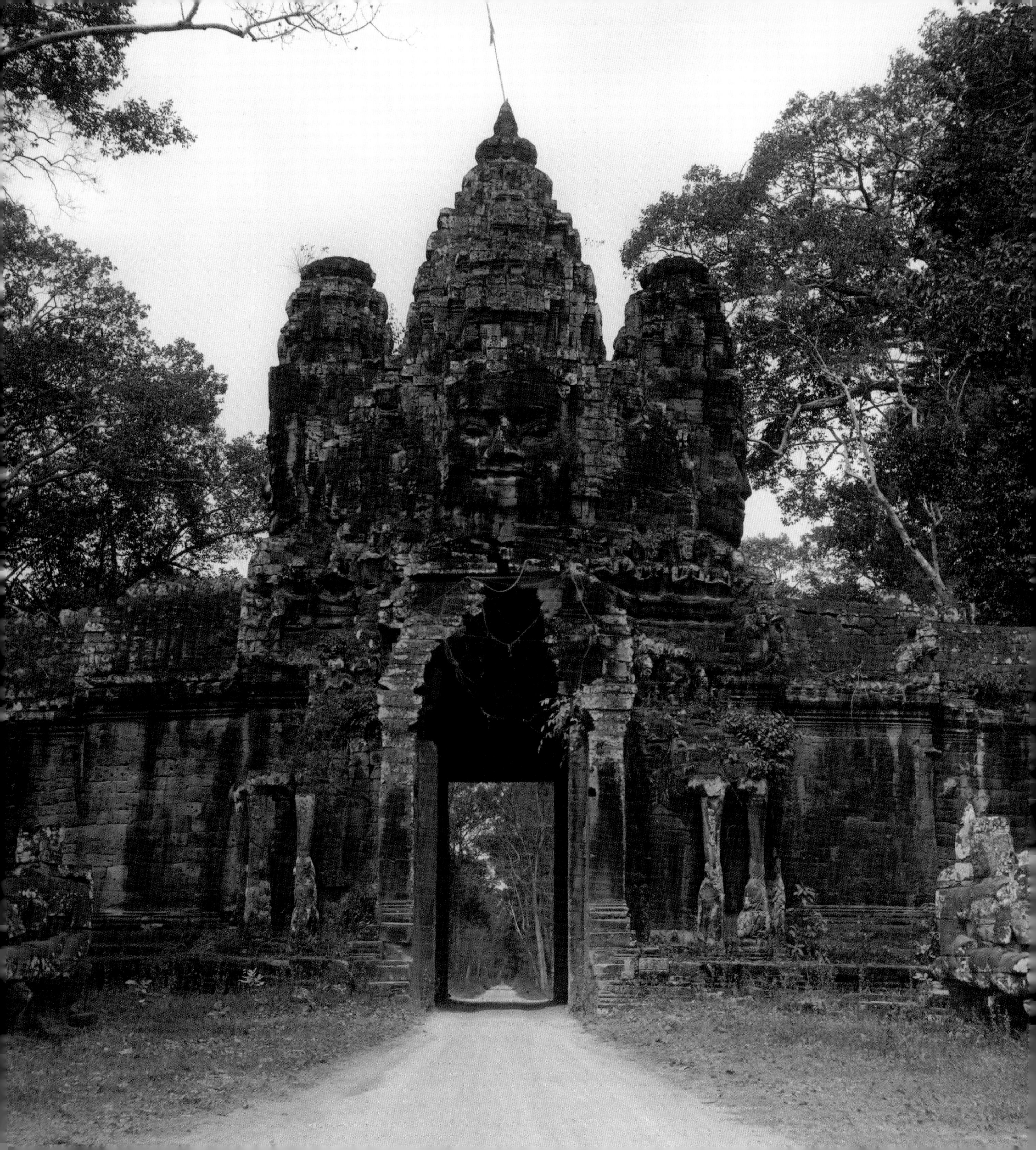

to bestow his teachings. The Pure Land is as much the wish to attain a perfect mind as it is a physical domain of the senses, although over many lifetimes and eons of purification it is possible to attain supreme wisdom and compassion.[10]

In the monumental Hindu and Buddhist city of Angkor Thom is a well-preserved temple whose railings depict a famous Hindu creation myth, the Churning of the Sea of Milk, where the snake goddess wraps around Mount Meru. The myth is powerful in many cultures and has *asuras* (demons) pulling one end of the snake in one direction and *devas* (gods) pulling in the opposite direction, thereby churning the primordial chaos out of which life emerged.[11] The earth's axis creates a cylindrical wobble in its long-term movement, which resembles a churn, and the milk that is churned might refer to the spiraling motion of the Milky Way galaxy itself.

The entire structure of Angkor Thom symbolically supports the Churning of the Sea of Milk myth, and vice versa. Aligned with the four compass-point entrances at the very center of the complex, the Bayon temple embodies mythic Mount Meru. Also, in accordance with the myth, bridges that lead into the complex are lined by gigantic *naga* snakes that are pulled in opposite directions by *asuras* and *devas*. According to Hindu mythology, the *naga* serpents are like a rainbow, linking the world of humanity with the domain of the gods. Entering such a city over bridges lined with *nagas* would "be the equivalent of crossing into Heaven."[12] Angkor Thom is both a gateway between worlds—above and below, human and celestial—and the largest man-made model of the cosmos. With its mandala form of a huge rectangle with smaller, incised rectangles within, and oriented in the cardinal directions with Mount Meru at its center, this extraordinary city of temples is, indeed, a replica of the cosmos in stone.

The flow of the Milky Way headed down to where a corrugation lifted earth to sky. It was the Himalaya. Thus, flowing down from the mountain-tops, the Milky Way became Ganga, Siva's lover and daughter of the king-mountain Himavat.

—Roberto Calasso, *Ka* (2003)[13]

As we will see later, in Hindu mythology the Milky Way comes down to intersect Earth in the Himalayan mountains, creating the origin of the Ganges. Just as Earth's axis can be identified by the North Pole Star, it is also identified by the highest mountains on all continents. The entire universe of stars seems to revolve around these massive, sacred peaks.

OPPOSITE: The gates of Angkor Thom, Angkor, Cambodia, 1993

PAGE 34: Giant Wild Goose Pagoda (Tang Dynasty), Xi'an, China, 2001

PAGE 35: Sacred Way of Xiaoling, Eastern Qing Tombs, outside Beijing, China, 2001

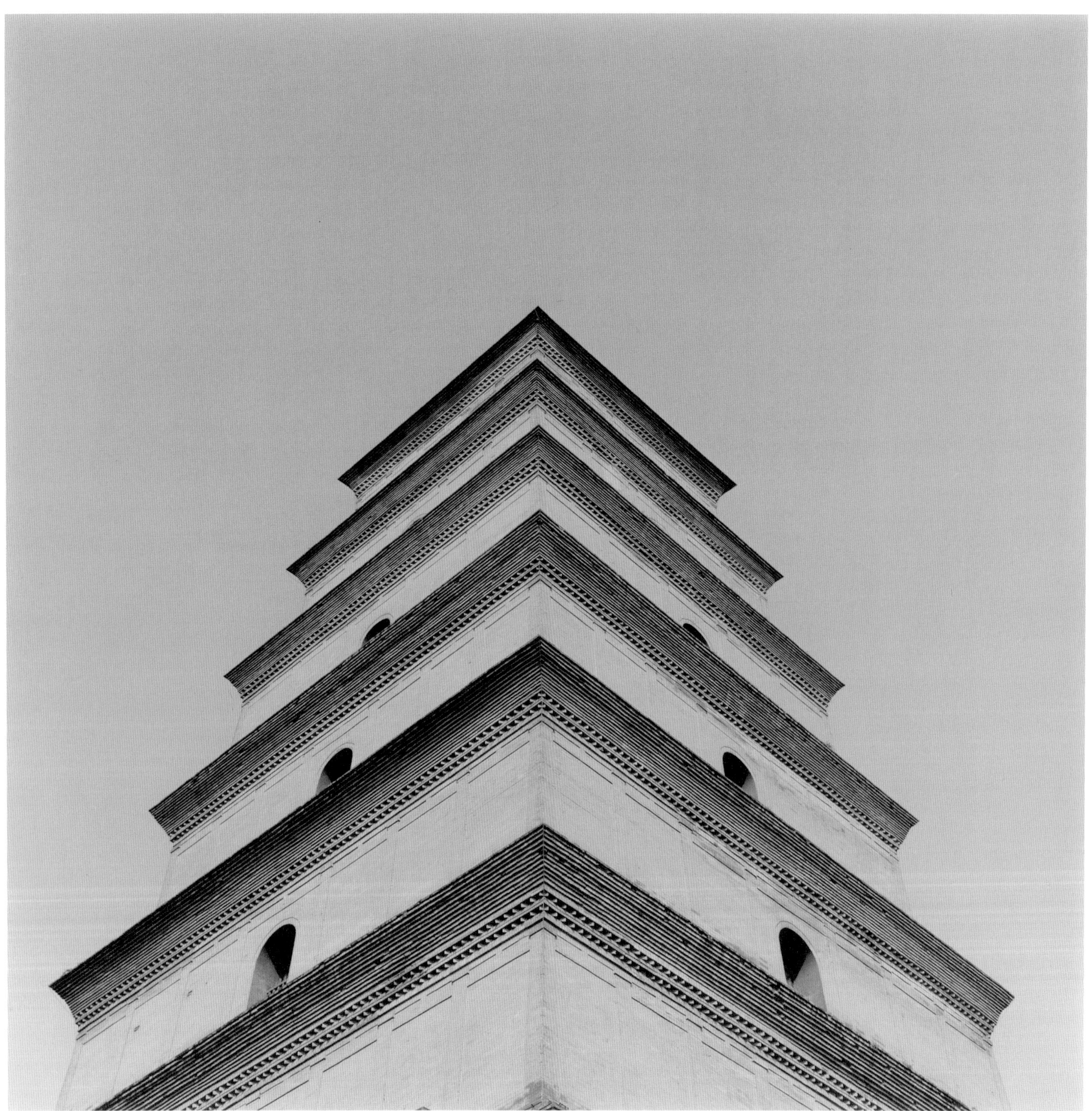

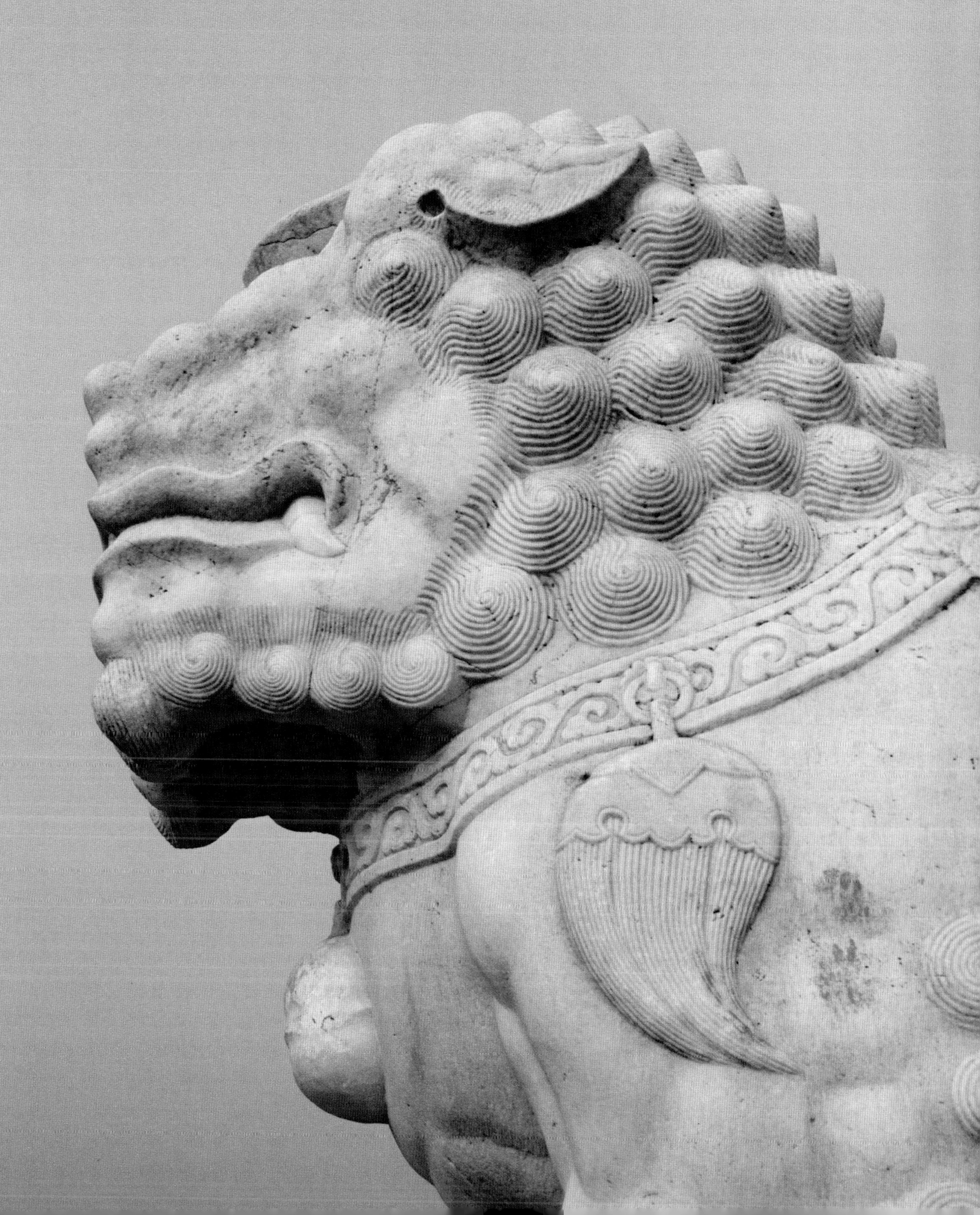

Chinese Sacred Dragon Mountains

Chinese philosophy and medicine are based on the interplay of yin (passive, female) and yang (active, male) energies, These energies originate in the original creation myth that describes the creator god Pangu separating heaven and earth. The dark yin and bright yang energies are forever intertwined, as everything in the world contains them both in varying proportions. These cosmic currents are collectively called *ch'i*. The same term describes life energy in the body, where the earth currents or energies are the acupuncture meridians of the Great Mother,[14] who in turn creates the polarities.

Chinese Taoist philosophy directly emanates from the play of these polarities and finds expression in the Five Great Mountains, supposedly created from the limbs and head of Pangu. However, unlike Meru, these sacred mountains exist in the natural Chinese landscape, not just in temples and sculpture. They also correspond to the four cardinal directions—east being prominent as the head of Pangu—and include a central mountain, following the tradition of Chinese geomancy. The most important is Tai Shan (Peaceful Mountain) in the east, where the sun rises to create the day. To the south lies Heng Shan (Balancing Mountain); to the west is Hua Shan (Splendid Mountain); to the north is Bei Shan (Permanent Mountain); and in the center stands Song Shan (Lofty Mountain).

Chinese Buddhists believe that the four sacred mountains—also present in the landscape—symbolize the four most important Buddhist bodhisattvas (mythic beings whose role is to guide humanity to enlightenment), as well as the cardinal directions. In the north is Wutai Shan (Five Terrace Plateau Mountain, sacred to Manjushri bodhisattva of wisdom), to the east is Putuo Shan (Potala Mountain, sacred to Kuanyin bodhisattva of compassion), to the south is Jiuhua Shan (Nine-Glories Mountain, sacred to Kshitigarbha bodhisattva of salvation), and to the west is Emei Shan (Delicate-Eyebrow Mountain, sacred to Samantabadra bodhisattva of universal virtue).

Feng shui is a form of Chinese geomancy (geographical divination) that analyzes the location, form, and orientation of a building or monument relative to the topography of the surrounding landscape. Buildings that utilize the natural elements of the land and tap into its energy are auspicious places to live, work, or bury the dead; places that are antagonistic to these energies are unlucky.

The link with the environment has magical qualities, and the Chinese believe that the placement of a building in the landscape is of critical importance, because the landscape carries a multitude of qualities that must be counterbalanced. The best possible result occurs when a man-made object enhances and supports the environment from which it, in turn, receives energy. Everything in the physical world interacts energetically, and when sensitivity and knowledge are used together to create an environment, the blend is harmonious and supportive to both the natural and the man-made

OPPOSITE: Great Wall of China at Badaling, China, 2001

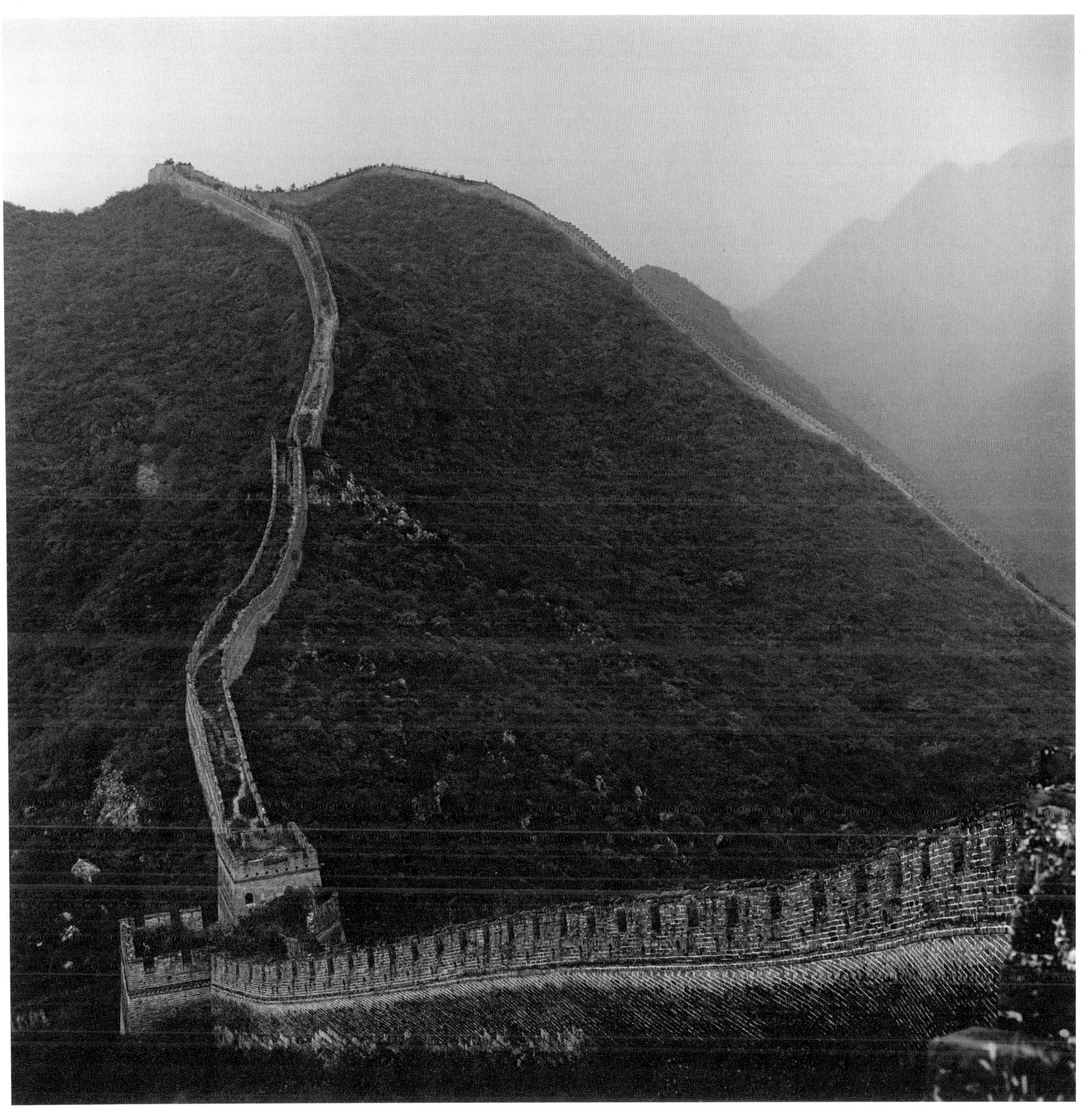

structures. In this sense, feng shui is a legacy that anticipates and brings forth the Green Revolution we so desperately require today.

Mountains meander across the spectacular landscape of China, inspiring early geomancers to liken them to the spines of dragons, because dragons carried immense power and influence for good or evil. They were also seen to govern the health and wealth of the inhabitants. If the inhabitants respected the dragons in the landscape, they remained happy and would prosper, but if the dragons were aroused by ignorance or disrespect, they would cause illness and a loss of wealth—if not outright destruction.

Natural shapes in the landscape are seen to evoke the animal qualities that they correspond to; a particular pinnacle could be a tiger's ear, exhibiting a sense of danger and a difficult boundary, while a quiet mountain might be a protective watchdog that remains very still and vigilant. The direction and siting of buildings in the landscape either utilize or antagonize these forces. For this reason, it is important for everyone to learn to be sensitive to and respectful of the earth energies within which we all live. The shape of a mountain determines the quality of its energy in very precise ways. In the *I Ching*, the trigram *Ken* means "Keeping Still, Mountain," and signifies the northeast, where things begin and end. The five types of mountain profiles correspond to the five elements of Chinese philosophy.[15] Fire mountains are triangular with sharp, pointed tops and carry passionate and spiritual energies. Wood mountains are straight hills with rounded tops and transmit nurturing and protective energies. Metal mountains are soft and gently rounded, carrying the qualities of morality and precision. Earth mountains are plateaus with flat tops and are characterized by their enduring and unchanging qualities. Water mountains are irregularly shaped, often displaying waves or steps and resonating with the flowing and changeable nature of the element. The qualities associated with certain mountain shapes are important, as they determine certain dynamics of an area of the landscape. They also transmit the qualities of energy, health, and wealth to people living near them.

Mythical qualities are also associated with mountains. In Chinese mythology, four celestial animals have counterparts in landscape shapes and materials, and when they are all present, a residence carries great good fortune. The ideal combination is to have both the high hills of the dragon energy to the left and the east, lower and more undulating white tiger hills to the right and west, a range of higher and steady black turtle mountains behind and to the north, as well as flowing water and small hills symbolic of the crimson phoenix to the south. With this combination, inhabitants' lives are balanced, healthy, and auspicious.[16]

Considered interdependent in Chinese philosophy (and in feng shui, especially), the two primary natural forms that we must respect and integrate are water and mountains.[17] Mountains are the source of water and the intersection between heaven and earth. As such, they dispense energy to the surrounding

OPPOSITE: Step Pyramid, Saqqara, Egypt, 1997

PAGES 40–41: Pyramid of the Sun, Teotihuacán, Mexico, 1991

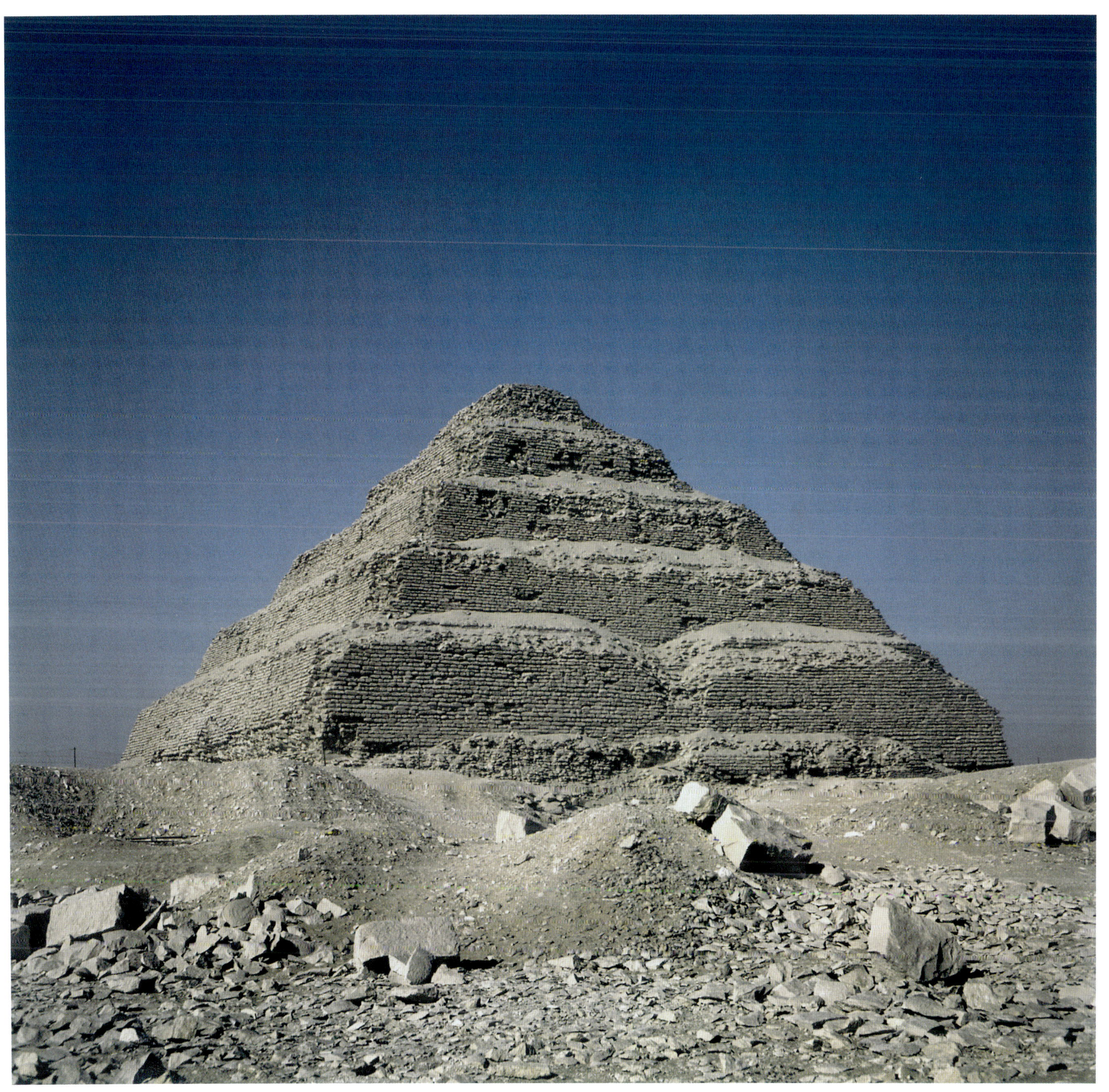

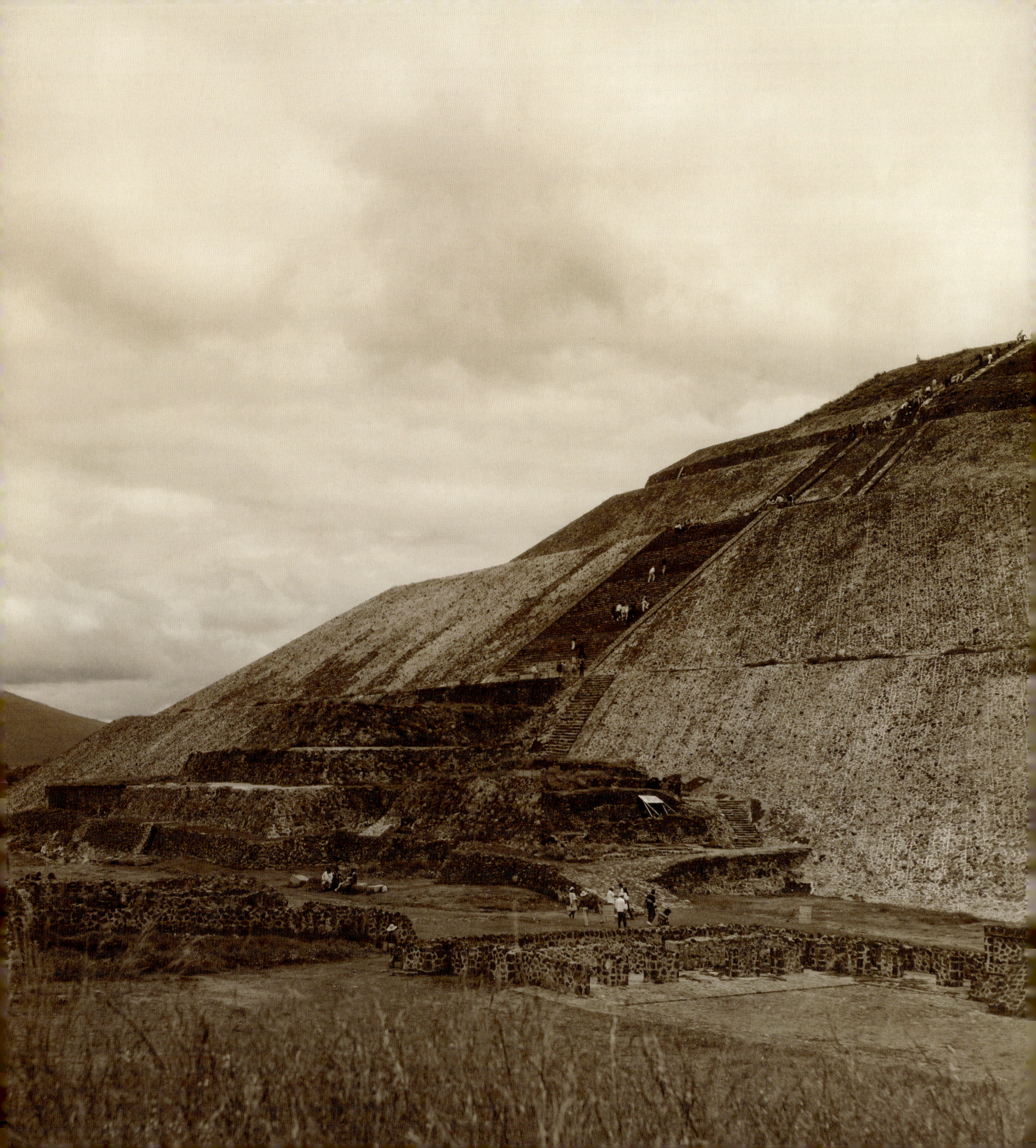

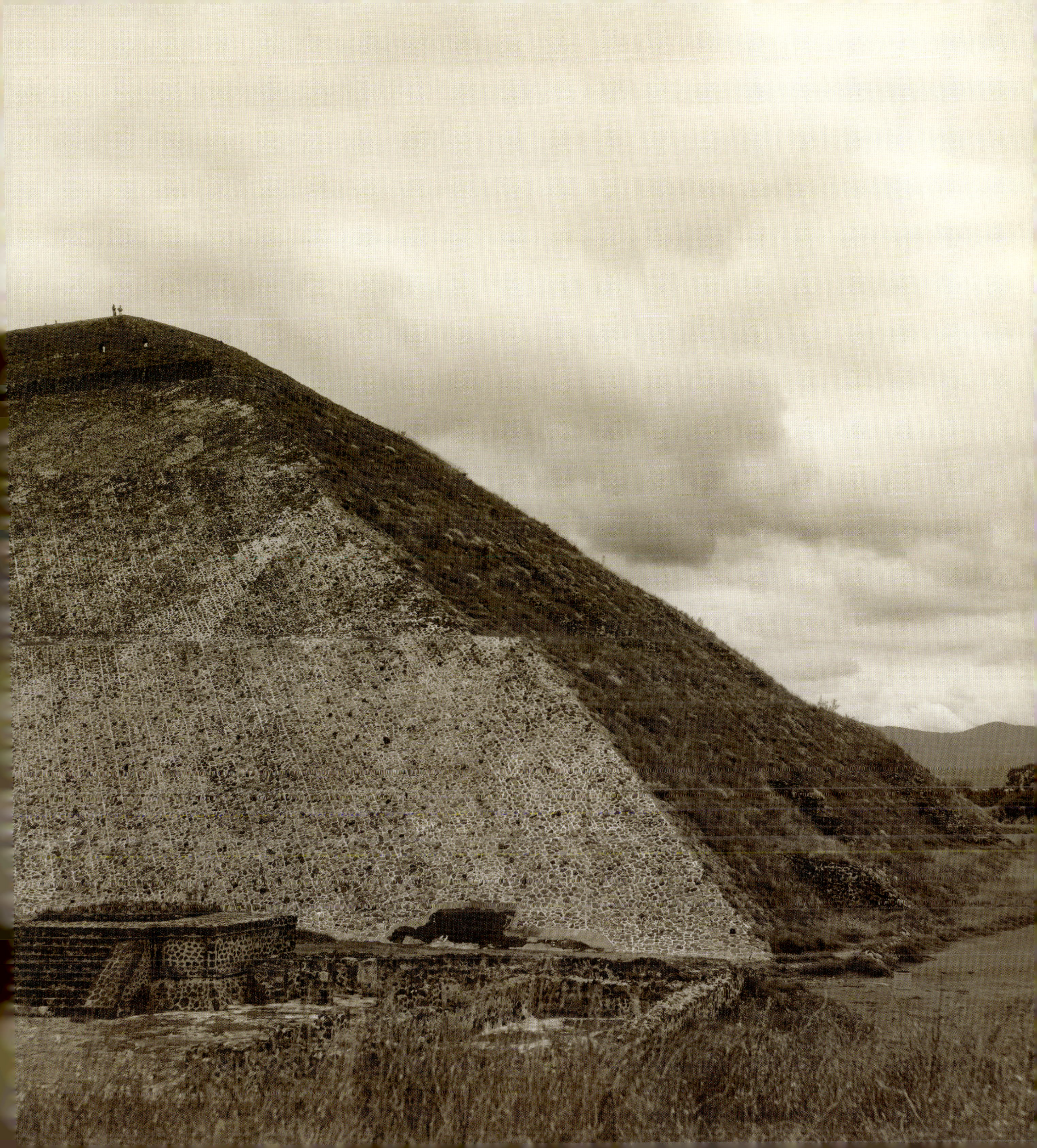

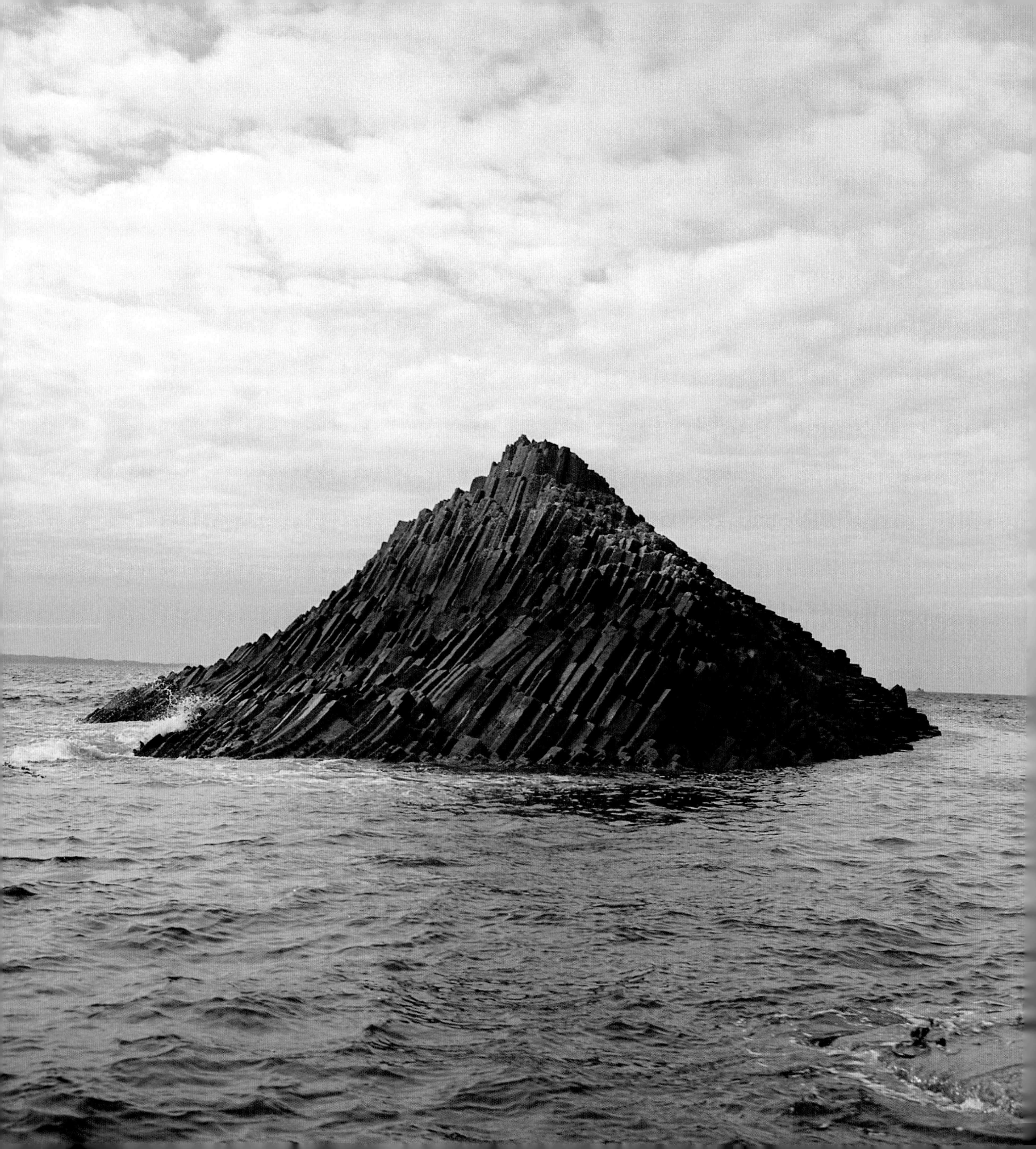

Spring-water in the green creek is clear
Moonlight on Cold Mountain is white
Silent knowledge—the spirit is enlightened of itself
Contemplate the void: this world exceeds stillness.

—Fabled poet Han-shan (c. ninth century)[19]

land or carry it in a latent state—*i.e.,* resources beneath the soil—as it flows from mountaintops in underground streams that feed rivers and create electromagnetic fields detectable across the landscape above.[18] Aside from being the essence of life, water is a critical item on a building's list, so the flow, location, depth, purity, and strength of water are all essential in evaluating the correct location for an edifice. In the Tao (the Way), the primary principle of Chinese philosophy representing the counterbalance between light and dark, male and female, that animates all life on earth, water carries the yang, or active principle, and mountains contain the yin, or passive principle.[20] The intrinsic harmony of water and mountains is considered essential to the proper siting of buildings—powerful dragons guarding the land need plenty of clear water to drink. The flow and clarity of the water determine the potency of the landscape and show the positive qualities of the ch'i that the water carries through the land, just as the purity and flow of blood indicate the degree of health a human body has. However, if water flows too straight or excessively, it can be dangerous, susceptible to flooding, and therefore can be an influence to subdue or avoid. In Chinese philosophy, it is the balance and the dynamics between elements that shape our lives and our destiny.

Zen Buddhism in the Mountains

An essential aspect of Japanese Zen Buddhist philosophy is the symbolism of mountains, epitomized by Mount Fuji. Even the expression identifying Japan as the "Land of the Rising Sun" always shows that sun rising over the cleft of Fuji. The often-described theme of Zen Buddhist monks withdrawing from the world to meditate in isolated caves or monasteries abounds in Zen poetry, literature, and sacred texts. Fuji was probably a live volcano in the twelfth century, and the poet Saigyō describes how the wisp of smoke emitted by Fuji was like thoughts taken to the above, away from the earthly domain.[21] The power and symbolism of such mountains have been incorporated into Japanese architecture, including even in the most modest of meditation rooms. Daisetz Suzuki, author of *Zen and Japanese Culture*, recalls a poem by a fifteenth-century general, describing his residence:

> My hut is on the beach
> Lined with pine trees,
> And the high peak of Fuji
> Looms up above the caves.[22]

OPPOSITE: Fingal's Cave, Scotland, 2006

Volcanic Feelings

Like Mount Fuji, many sacred mountains all over the world are considered active volcanoes. Potentially destructive, fiery mountains of past and present include Vesuvius in Italy, Mount Batur and Mount Agung in Bali, Mount Merapi and Krakatoa in Java, Mount Etna in Sicily, Mount Ararat in Turkey, Mauna Kea in Hawaii, and Mount Shasta in California, among hundreds in the United States and countless others around the world. Volcanoes are so powerful, often dramatically beautiful, and always dangerous that they conjure images of the underworld, with demonic forces roiling below the surface of the earth. The symbolism of the volcano extends far beyond destructive or evil connotations, however, ranging from sexual metaphors to the raw and uncontrolled life force. The volcano is also seen as divine intervention, a world navel, and a place for birthing life and humanity. The amazing stones on Easter Island tell similar stories, and the great burial place of the island is situated in a volcanic crater, which is also a navel of the island and, by extension, of the whole world. In the Rapa Nui way of thinking, such a navel links people with the Mother and ancestors, and the surrounding towering statues perform the dual function of protecting the navel and signaling to the original settlements on the island that were made within the volcanic crater.[23]

The islands that make up Indonesia were created by a string of volcanoes, the most famous of which is Krakatoa, between Java and Sumatra, and it exploded in 1883. That eruption was particularly violent, but the volcano has erupted on many previous occasions, even as early as a few hundred years CE, as noted in accounts in Japan, Australia, and other Far Eastern countries. The nineteenth-century Krakatoa eruption was heard thousands of miles away, and the temperature of the earth cooled by more than a degree for a year afterward. On the nearby islands of Bali and Java, many active volcanoes are considered sacred and have been worshipped by Hindus, Buddhists, and their animist ancestors from the South Seas.[24] The volcanic Mount Batur on Bali erupted more than twenty times in the last two centuries, and the black basalt thrown up around its base is still being used to build temples around the island.[25]

In the eastern end of Java is an amazing ring of volcanoes, one of which is still active. The inactive Mount Merbabu and the active Mount Merapi are two of the four volcanoes encircling the ancient Buddhist monument known as Borobudur. Borobudur was completed by King Sanmaratungga in the ninth century and belongs to the Buddhist Mahayana tradition. The islands had been Hindu for many centuries, but due to a mysterious and still unknown cause, no Buddhist or Hindu monuments were built after 928 CE.[26] The eruptions of "fire mountain" Merapi around 1000 CE showered the monument with ash, until it came to resemble a mountain in its own right, covered with trees and vegetation. Nearly a millennium passed before the English governor of the area, Sir Thomas Stanford Raffles, heard

OPPOSITE: Volcano, Hawaii, United States, 2005

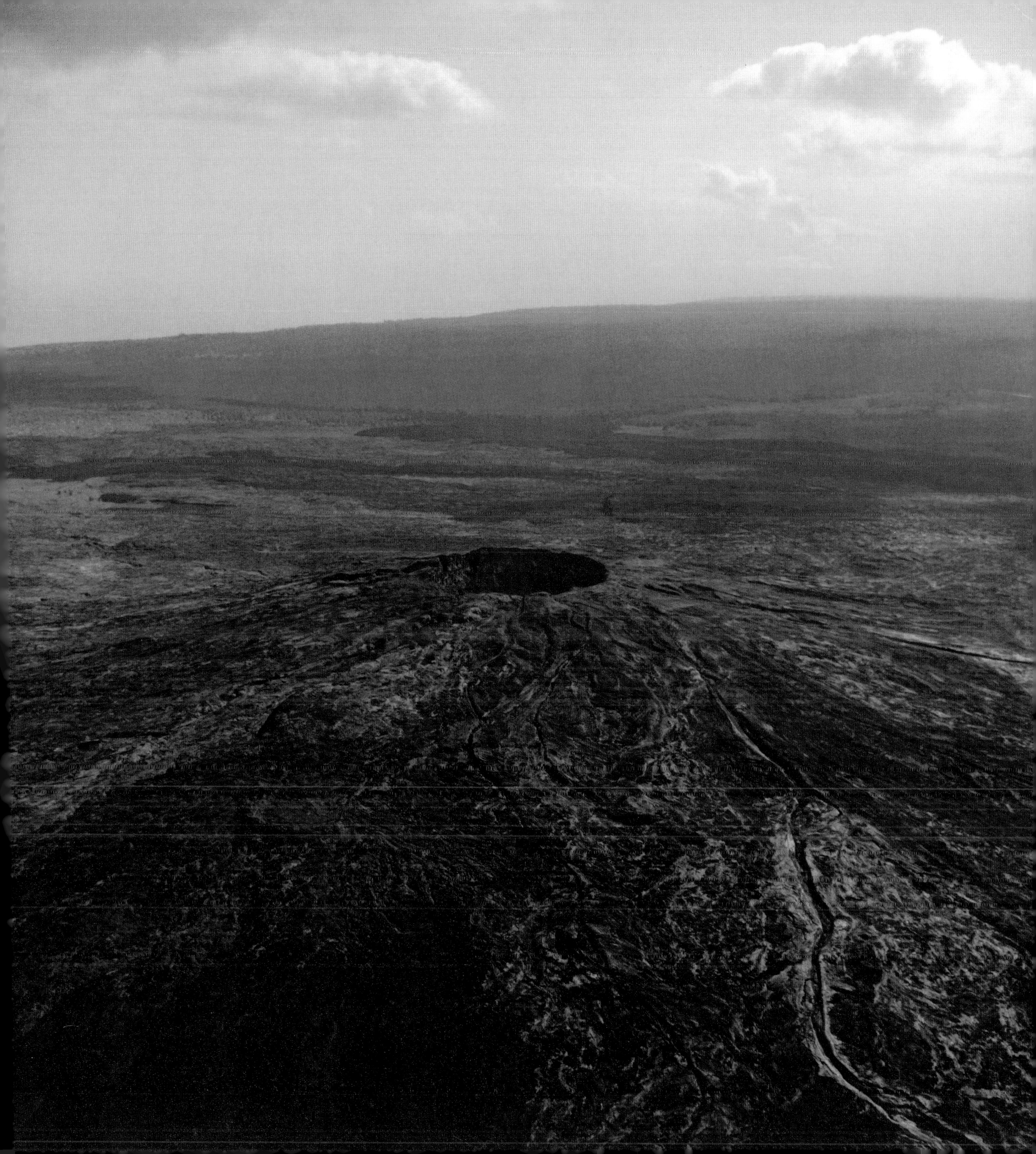

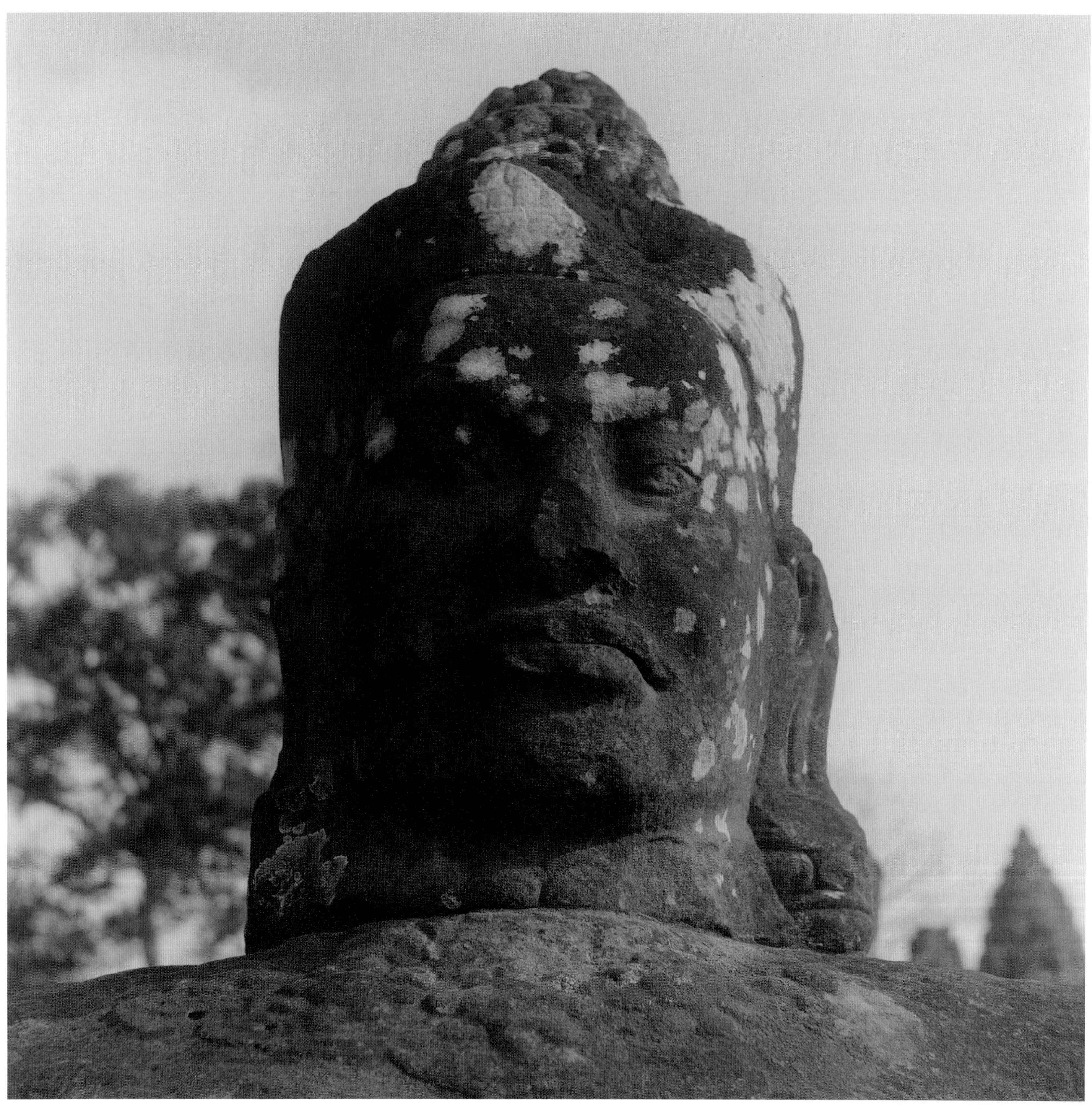

about a mountain that had stone heads sticking out of the soil. In 1814, he found the temple in ruins and had the site excavated. The work was completed only in the last century, and now hundreds of Buddha heads keep vigil in the cardinal directions.[27]

Two sets of twin volcanoes—Merapi and Merbabu to the northeast, Sumbing and Sindoro to the northwest—stand sentinel across the plains within which Borobudur sits. A ridge in the landscape adjacent to Borobudur resembles Gunadharma, its legendary architect, who is believed to keep watch over his creation through the ages. Ascending Borobudur's staircase to the first level, one encounters four series of reliefs—two on each side—exhibiting an account of the Buddha from his birth 2,500 years ago as Siddhartha Gautama, an Indian prince, to his renunciation and spiritual journey toward enlightenment. At the present time, one can ascend to the top of Borobudur and see the volcanic smoke drift westward from the summit of Merapi.

Hopi and Navajo Sacred Mountains

The books of Frank Waters[28] explore Hopi and Navajo mythologies, which involve sacred mountains, and include fascinating comparisons between the Navajo Native American creation myths and Tibetan Buddhism.

According to the Navajo, in the time before creation, people lived in worlds below the ground. When they emerged to the new world, on the surface stood a great rock—the core of the universe, which penetrated through all the known worlds.[29] Rooted in time and space, it was oriented to the four cardinal directions and it glowed with primal colors: white in the east, blue in the south, yellow-red in the west, and black in the north. The people planted the Holy Mountains at the base of the natal rock, which was called the Mountain Surrounded by Mountains or the Encircled Mountain. From this sowing sprung the plants, seasons, sun, moon, stars, and winds. Today, when the Navajo represent this cosmology in their mandala-like sand paintings, it "is the symbol of the great axial rock, the Encircled Mountains; a four-petaled flower, like a four-leafed clover, like a lotus."[30] Waters also states that four sacred mountains still form the boundary of the Navajo homeland: Mount Blanca or the Sacred Mountain of the East in Colorado, San Francisco Peaks in Arizona to the west, Mount Taylor in the San Mateo range to the south, and Mount Hesperus in the La Plata range to the north. The encircled mountain is usually identified as Huerfano Peak near Chaco Canyon, and, similar to the Hindu and Tibetan Buddhist conception of Mount Meru, is a physical counterpart of the mythical core of the cosmos.

OPPOSITE: The Guardians, Angkor Thom, Angkor, Cambodia, 1993

Waters links the core beliefs of Tibetan Buddhism with Navajo, Pueblo, Hopi, Zuni, and Quiche Mayan cosmoses and worlds, noting that each of these universes is four-cornered and four-pointed. All seven concentric circles of mountains in the Buddhist cosmology have their own seas, and each is a separate universe. The Buddhists also understand the sacred mountain as a pyramid of four sides with the same colors as the Navaho great rock and the unusual quality of projecting upward into the sky and also downward into the cosmic core of the underworlds.

In 1979, the Dalai Lama met with three Hopi elders in the American west. Delegation head Grandfather David first said, "Welcome home." Noticing the similarity of David's turquoise beads to Tibetan beads, the Dalai Lama laughed and replied, "And where did you get your turquoise?"[31] Since that meeting, Tibetan lamas have had dialogues with Native Americans, and many lamas have settled in New Mexico. There even seems to be a physical resemblance between Tibetans and Native Americans, which lends credence to the idea that both groups share common Asian ancestors who, thousands of years ago, crossed the Bering Strait to Alaska.

Mountain Wisdom and Dreamtime

The great Swiss psychologist Carl Gustav Jung (1875–1961) lived and practiced near the mountains in Zurich. He was the son of a clergyman, and one of his first formative experiences described in his autobiography *Memories, Dreams, Reflections* (1963) came while on a rare journey in the Alps with his father. After boarding a steamship, the fourteen-year-old Jung and his father arrived in Vitznau. Above the village towered a high mountain, the Rigi, and a slanted cogwheel railway ran up to it.

> My father pressed a ticket in my hand and said, "You can ride up to the peak alone. I'll stay here; it's too expensive for the two of us. Be careful not to fall down anywhere." With a tremendous puffing, the locomotive shook and rattled me up to the dizzy heights where ever-new abysses and panoramas opened out before my gaze. "Yes," I thought, "this is it, my world, the real world, the secret, where there are no teachers, no schools, no unanswerable questions, where one can be without having to ask anything. This was the best and most precious gift my father had ever given me."[32]

Jung regarded mountains and trees as symbols of the personality, of the self, and of Christ. Many years later, when Jung was visiting the Pueblo Indians in the southwestern United States, an old chief asked him. "Do you not think that all life comes from the mountain?" Jung responded that the mountain contains ". . . every sort of knowledge that is found in the world. There does not exist knowledge or

OPPOSITE: Monument Valley Navajo Tribal Park, on the border of Utah and Arizona, United States, 1991

PAGE 50: Dugout Ranch, Canyonlands National Park, Utah, United States, 1999

PAGE 51: Mount Wilson, near Telluride, Colorado, United States, 1998

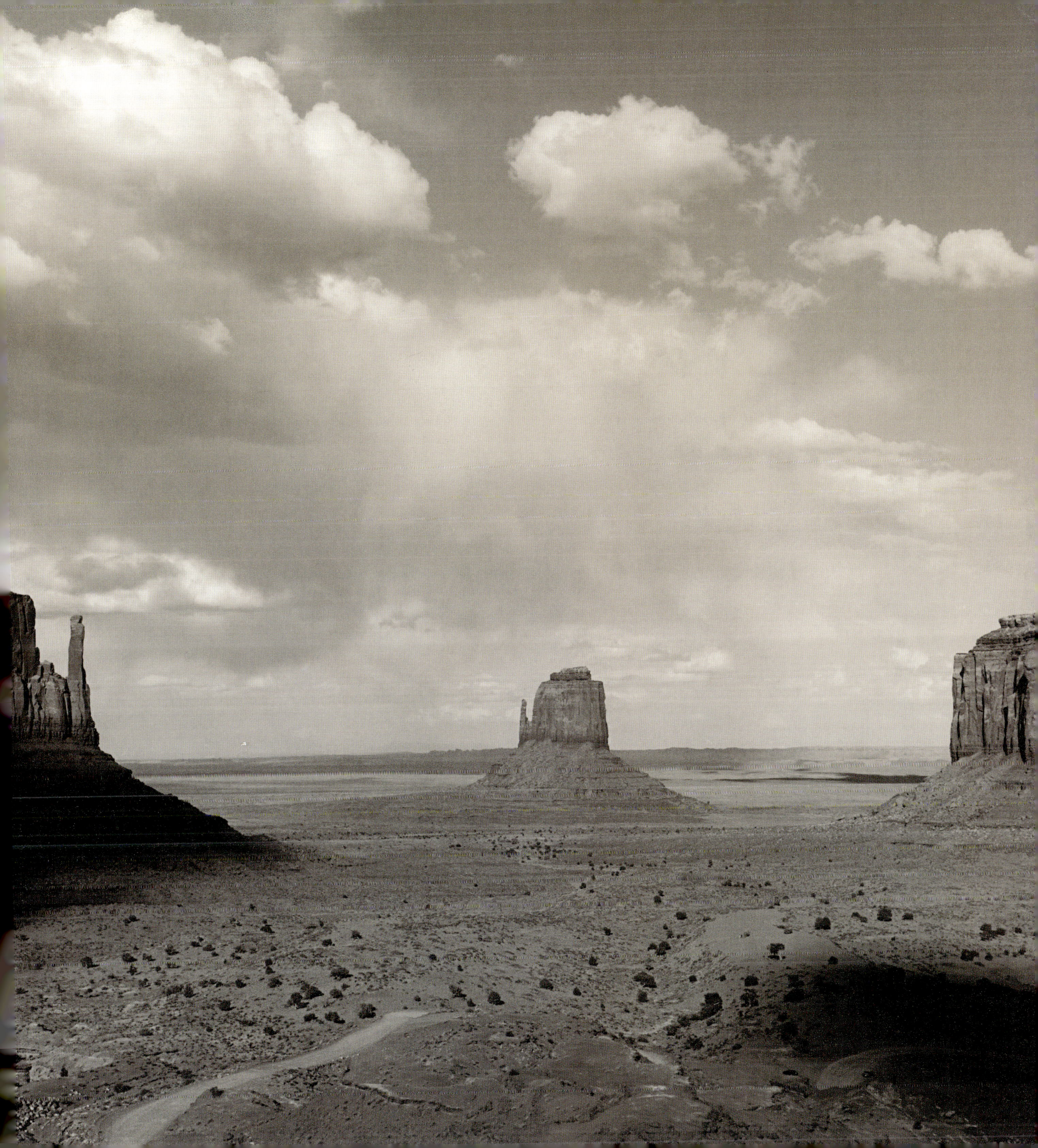

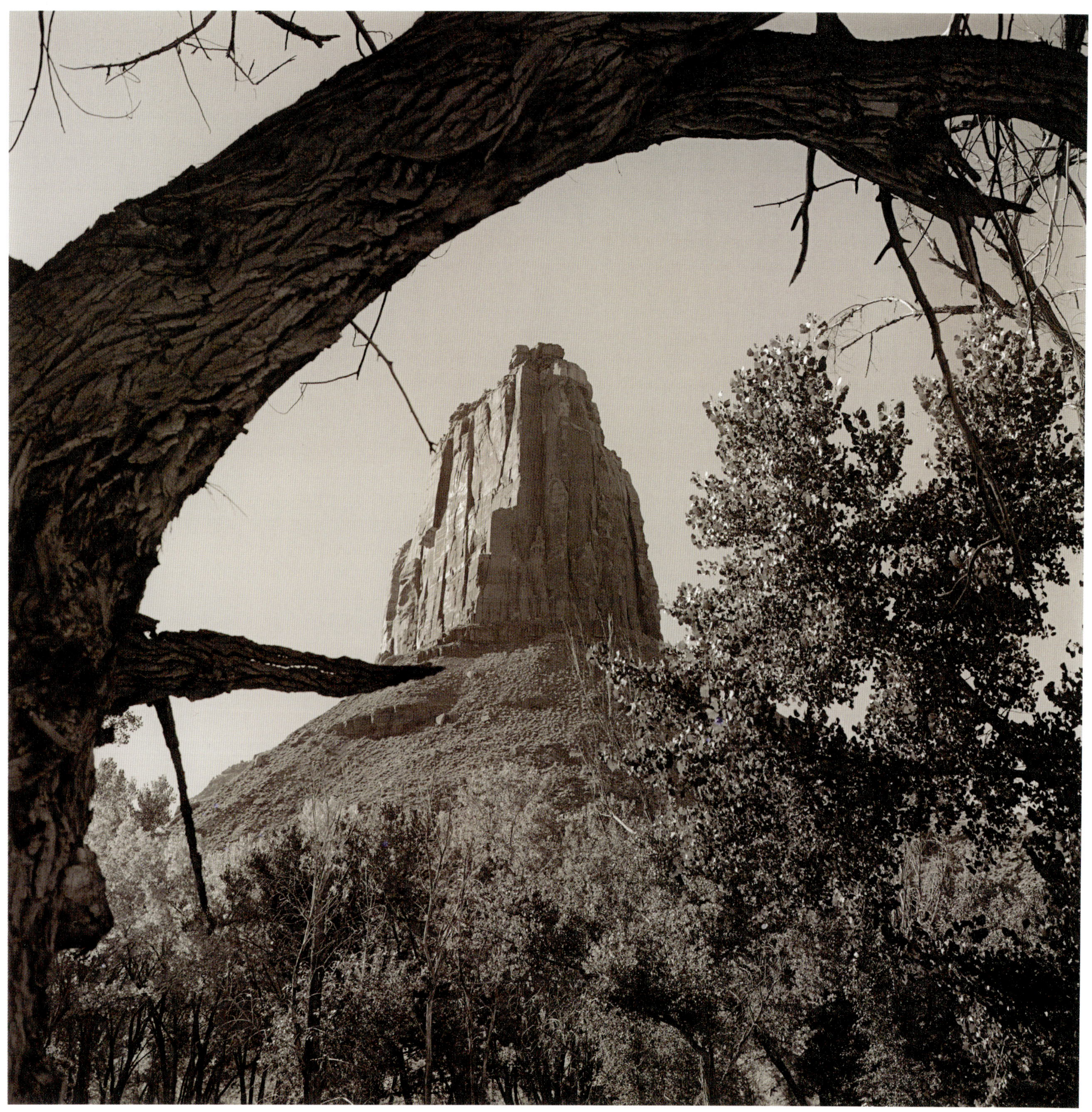

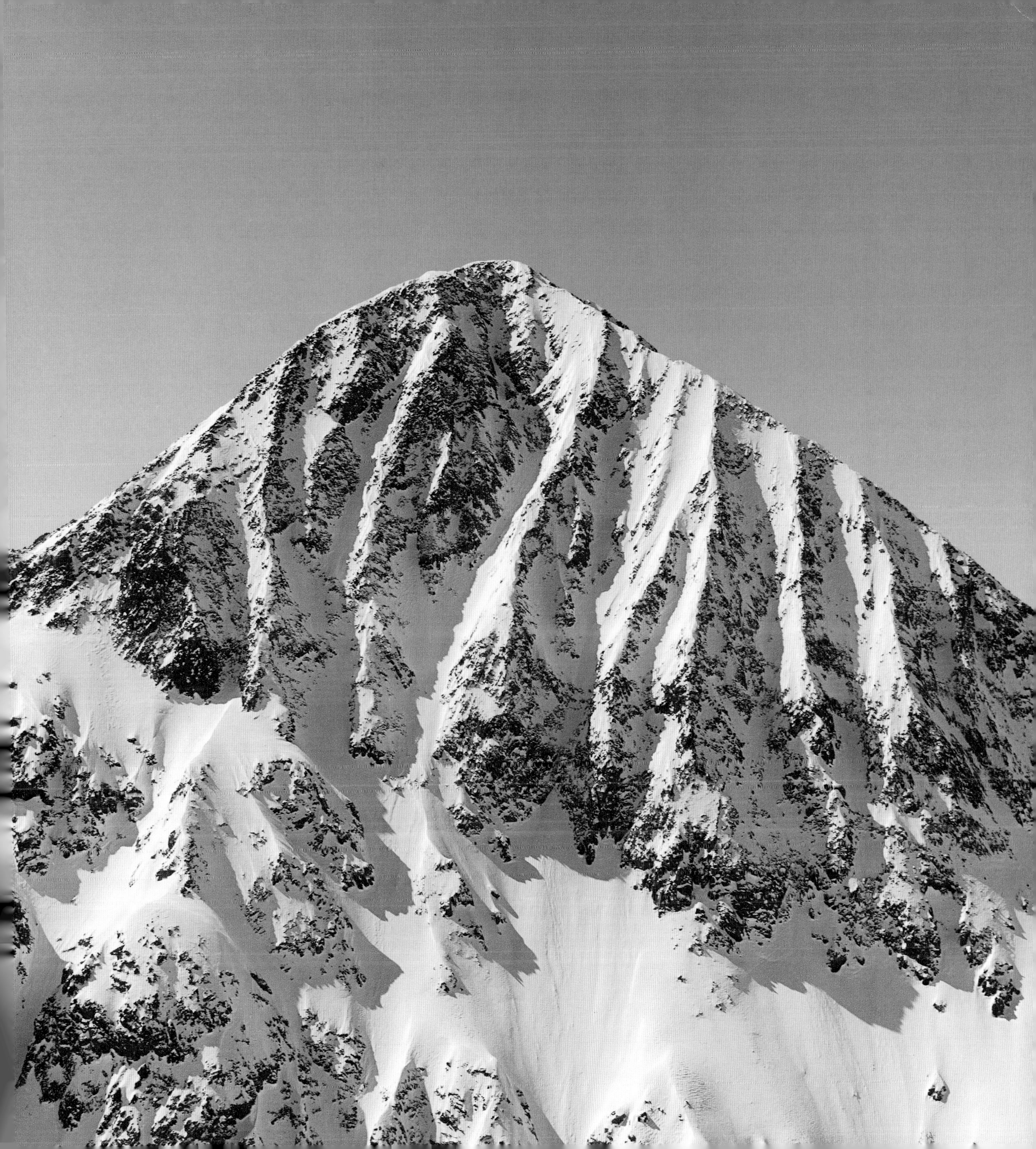

understanding or dream or thought or sagacity or opinion or delineation or wisdom or philosophy or government or peace or courage outside of the mountain."[33]

The 1929 Nobel Prize–winning author Thomas Mann (1875–1955) located his novel *The Magic Mountain* (1924), a meditation on the impact of the mountains on the soul and psyche, at a sanatorium above Davos, the highest town in the Alps. The magic mountain ("Zauberberg") is a myth and a symbol that transmits multiple meanings. To Germans, the quintessential Zauberberg is the Brocken, up whose dangerous paths Goethe's Mephistopheles leads the delinquent Faust, to join in the lawless and phantasmagoric delights of the Witches' Sabbath, or *Walpurgisnacht*:

> But bear in mind the mountain's mad with spells tonight
> And should a will-o'-the-wisp decide your way to light,
> Beware—its lead may prove deceptive.[34]

There is a European tradition of powerful magic mountains. The Greeks, for example, were keenly aware of the horrors of existence, and in their mythology they placed the higher realm of the Olympians before them as an ideal. Several millennia later, German philosopher Friedrich Nietzsche explicitly

> *Early successes, Creation's pampered favorites,*
> *mountain-ranges, peaks growing red in the dawn of all*
> *beginning—*
> *pollen of the flowering godhead, joints of pure light,*
> *corridors, stairways, thrones, space formed from essence,*
> *shields made of ecstasy, storms of emotion whirled into rapture, and*
> *suddenly alone:*
> *mirrors, which scoop up the beauty that has streamed from their face*
> *and gather it back, into themselves, entire.*
>
> —Rainer Maria Rilke, *Duino Elegies* (1912)[35]

referred to Mount Olympus with the word "Zauberberg" in his *The Birth of Tragedy* (1872), and his preoccupation with these powerful, enlightening monoliths became all the more clear in his incomplete great work, *Thus Spoke Zarathustra (1909).* In this book, he presented the concept of the Superman, whose function is to discover the meaning of life by raising himself above "the all-too-human." Zarathustra withdraws to the solitude of the mountains but feels the call to give humanity the benefit of his understanding through a process of repeated ascents and subsequent realizations. To him, the mountains are a metaphor for the spiritual quest:

> When Zarathustra was thirty years old he left his home and the lake of his home and went into the mountains. Here he enjoyed his spirit and his solitude, and for ten years did not tire of it. But at last a change came over his heart, and one morning he rose with the dawn, stepped before the sun, and spoke to it thus: "You great star, what would your happiness be had you not those for whom you shine? Behold, I am weary of my wisdom, like a bee that has gathered too much honey; I need hands outstretched to receive it. I would give away and distribute it, until the wise among men find joy once again in their folly and the poor in their riches. For that I must descend to the depths, as you do in the evening, when you go behind the sea and still bring light to the underworld, you over-rich star. Behold, this cup wants to become empty again, and Zarathustra wants to become a man again." Thus Zarathustra began to go under. And Zarathustra descended alone from the mountains.[36]

In her wonderful study, *The Grail Legend* (1970), Jung's wife, Emma, notes that there is a parallel between descriptions of the Holy Grail and those of the sacred text of India, the Vedas, where the "sun and moon are spoken of as miraculous vessels on the inaccessible mountains of Heaven. There they may be approached only by gods, demi-gods and the blessed dead."[37] She also discusses a legend about Alexander the Great, who discovered a mountain with 2,500 sapphire steps leading to the House of the Sun on the summit. There, Alexander meets an old white-haired man within the golden temple, who asks if he wants to see the lush and beautiful holy trees of the sun and moon in his future. Nearby, a phoenix sits in the branches of a barren tree, forecasting Alexander's early and fated death.[38]

With its mountain symbolism of four sides and orientation to the cardinal directions—also present in the many pyramids in Central and South America—the Great Pyramid of Egypt may be the original manifestation of the sacred mountain as an architectural monument. Indeed, peering from a distance through the desert early morning mists, the three ancient pyramids together look remarkably like a mountain chain. Newgrange, Ireland's great and vast Neolithic cairn located in the Boyne Valley and dated circa 3700 BCE, likewise represents a sacred mountain and has a very long chamber that penetrates to its core, through which the rising sun shines during the annual winter solstice. This remarkable structure also combines the symbolism of the lunar maternal mound, which almost looks like a breast in the landscape, with a womb that the sun penetrates into yearly to ensure the fertility of the crops and the culture.

PAGE 54: The Parthenon, Athens, Greece, 2008

PAGE 55: Red Pyramid, Dashur, Egypt, 1997

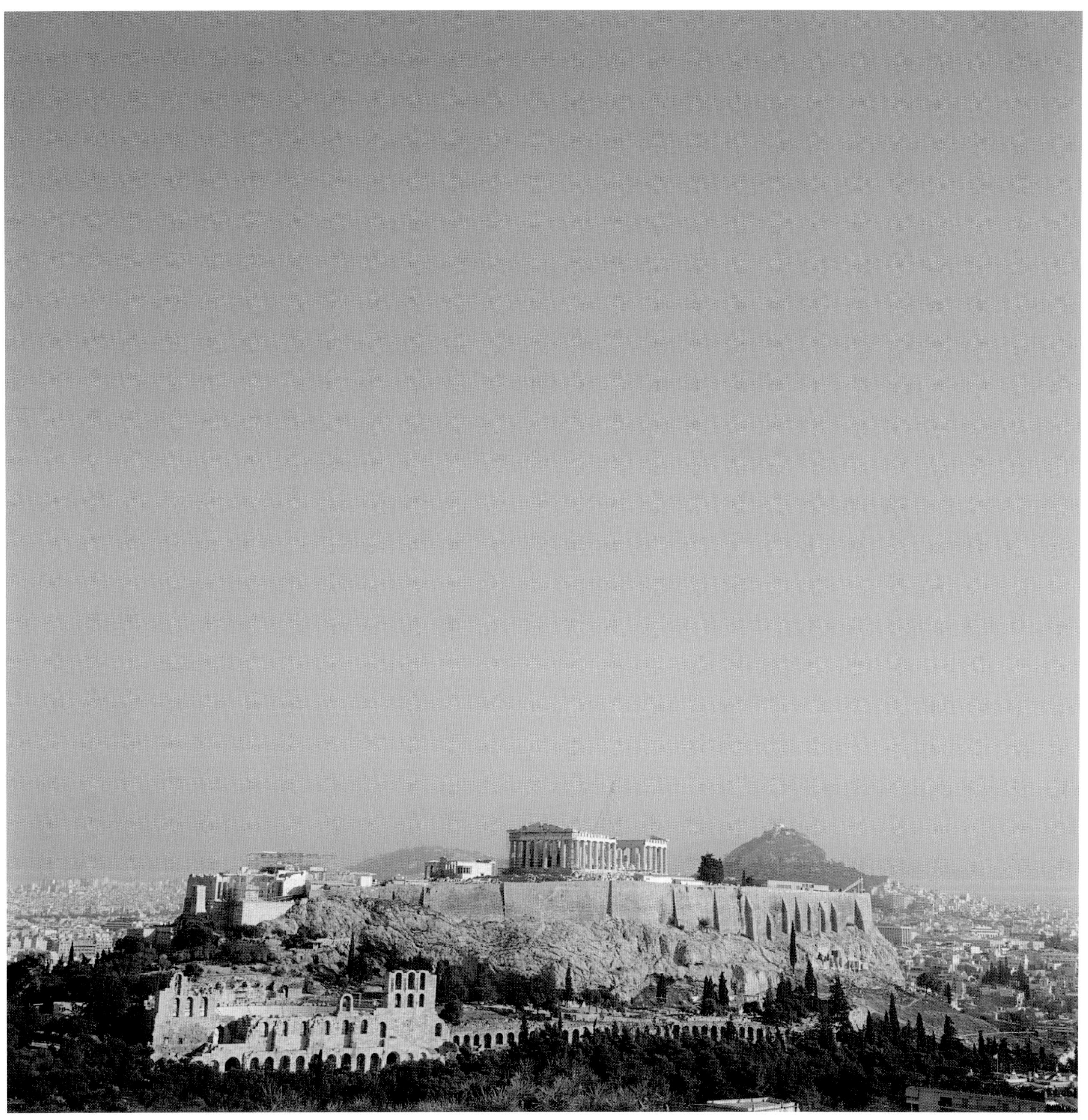

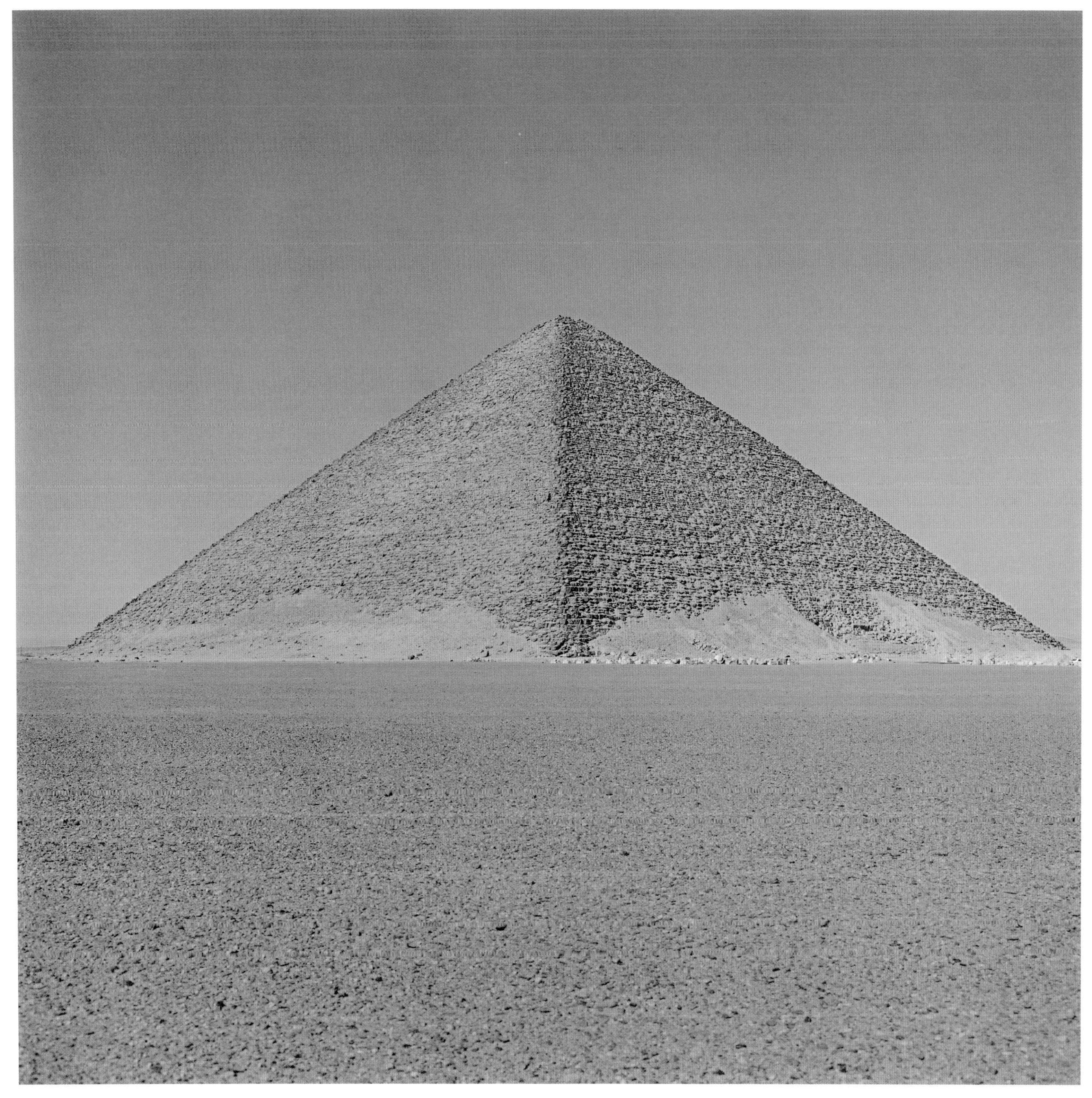

The sacred mountain of the Australian Aborigines is Uluru, or Ayers Rock, a sandstone rock formation in the center of the continent. It is an *inselberg* (island mountain), the eroded remains of an early mountain range and, as such, a potent symbol of the distant past. The Anangu Aborigines are the traditional owners of the mountain and say that the world was once a featureless place until the creator beings—termed Sky Heroes—took the form of people, plants, and animals and traveled over the land. According to the legend, the land is still inhabited by the spirits of dozens of these ancestral creators, generating a kind of "echo" in the material world, known as the Dreaming.[39] In this mythical landscape, the vibrational shape of everything in nature is transmitted through potent "seeds" that carry their creative origin.[40] Events in early history were dreamed by the Aboriginal ancestors as a mythic creative act, and the rituals of the Aborigines are intended to remember the first dreams and bring them into the life of the people.

All nature is so alive with the Dreaming, even conception is considered to be a woman dreaming a child into her womb, which can be caused by a totemic being becoming identified with the child. The child's spirit appears to the father as a voice from nature or a disappearing image in the water or a sound on the wind, and if he is able to catch its equivalent totem animal and bring it home, the family will consume it and take its spirit into their bodies. In some cases a woman is allegedly fertilized through contact with the spirits of a sacred place, such as the many "fertility caves" of Uluru, which are only accessible to women. These caves contain phallic rocks that the women rub their bodies against to intensify their magnetism and fertility. The ancestral beings present at the spot when a woman experiences her first morning sickness become the adopted totems of the child.[41] In this way, the power of sacred sites becomes incarnate in the Aboriginal people, generation after generation.

The mountain is a symbol of our highest aspirations, and the beauty we find in these massive monoliths not only energizes us but embodies our striving for what lies above.

OPPOSITE: Ayers Rock, Uluru National Park, Australia, 1991

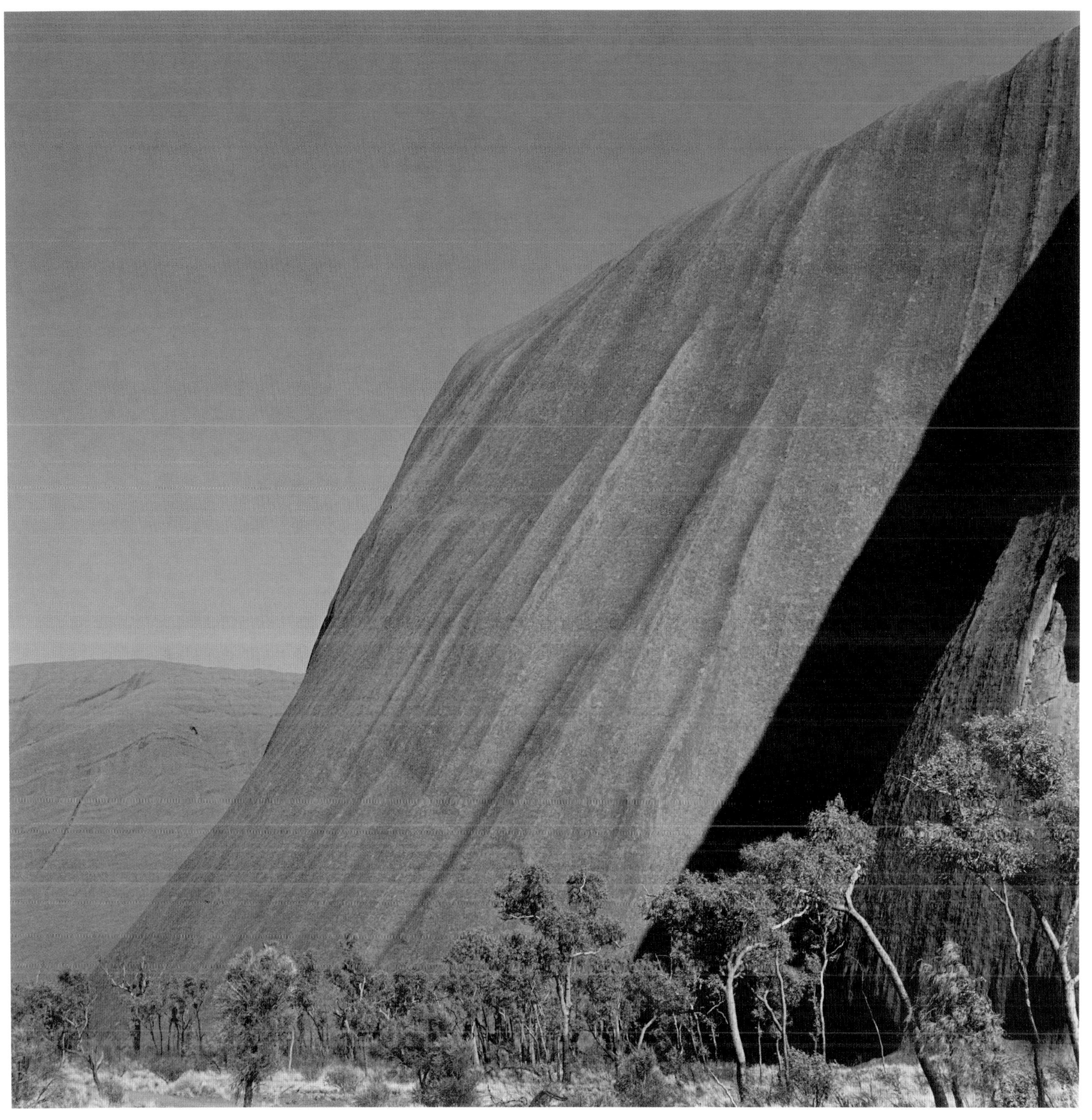

An iceberg is one of God's own buildings, preaching its lessons of humility to the miniature structures of man. Its material, one colossal Pentelicus; its mass, the representative of power in repose; its distribution, simulating every architectural type. . . . But this thing of refraction is supernatural throughout. The wildest frolic of an opium-eater's revery is nothing to the phantasmagoria of the sky to-night. Karnaks of ice, turned upside down, were resting upon the rainbow-colored pedestals; great needles, obelisks of pure whiteness, shot up above their false horizons, and, after an hour-glass-like contraction at their point of union with their duplicated images, lost themselves in the blue of the upper sky.

—Elisha Kent Kane, *The U.S. Grinnell Expedition in Search of Sir John Franklin: A Personal Narrative* (1854)[42]

OPPOSITE: Iceberg, Disko Bay, Greenland, 1988

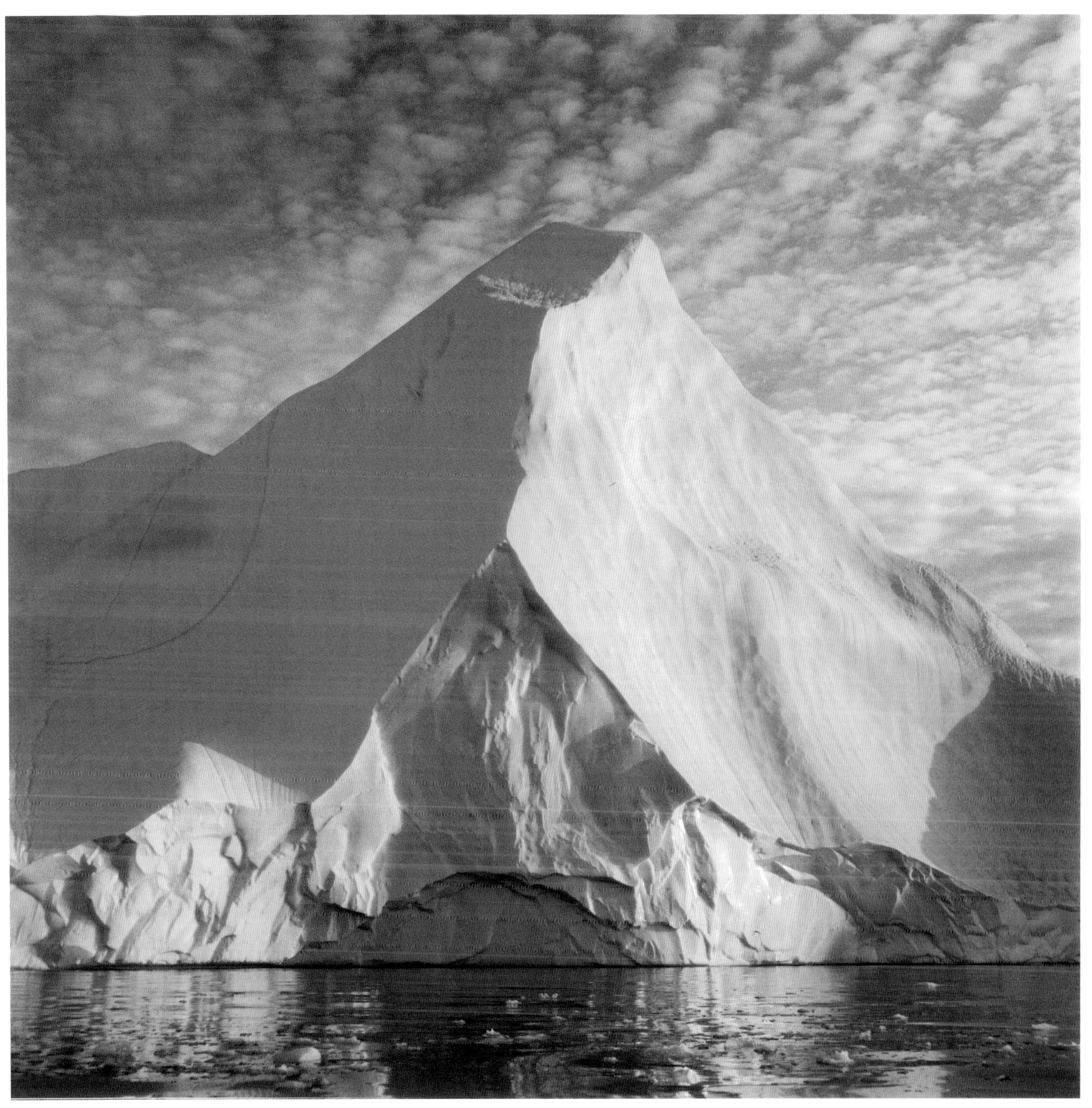

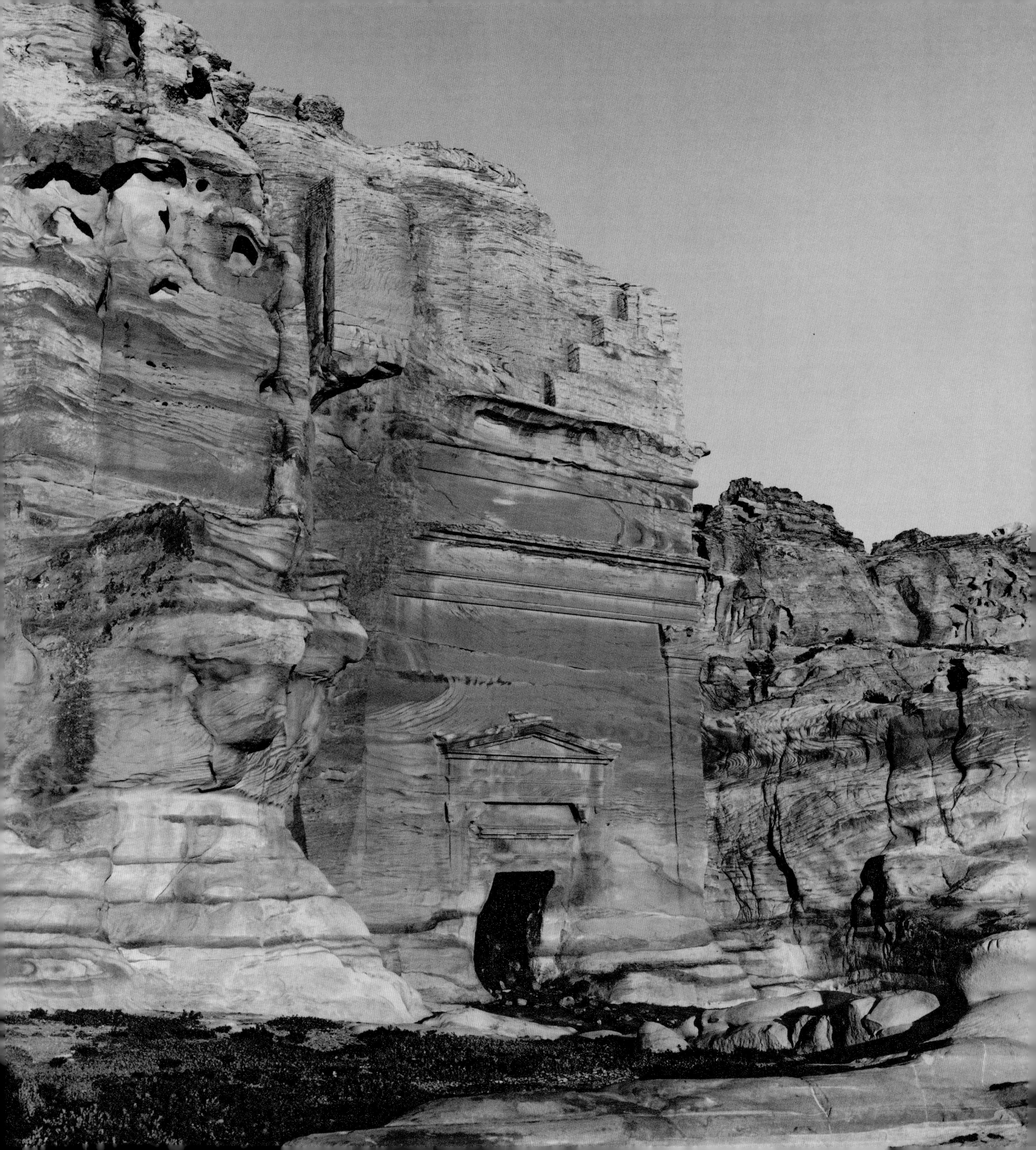

CHAPTER 4

Sacred Cave Mysteries

The cave, as literal fact, evoked, in the way of a sign stimulus,
the latent energies of that other cave, the un-fathomed human heart, and
what poured forth was the first creation of a temple in the history of the world.

—Joseph Campbell, *The Masks of God* (1959)[1]

Before humans built shelters, the earliest sacred places were caves. It was natural for our nomadic ancestors to discover these hollows in the landscape, to take shelter in them, and upon finding the bones of bears and other animals, to consider these animals totemic and magical. Caves became the home of ritual cults and often stored imagery in the form of wall paintings that carried the early generative history of a people or tribe. Some renowned examples include the Upper Paleolithic caves of Lascaux, in France, and Altamira, in Spain, both of which contain paintings of totem animals and the hunt; the oracular cave at Delphi, in Greece, where the priestesses of Apollo sat to receive divine prophecy; the cave in which Zeus was allegedly born, on Crete; and also the many Himalayan caves where hermits obtained profound wisdom.

Most of the sacred caves around the world are appropriately located in sacred mountains, and there is a naturally strong relationship between the two. Mountains are masculine and phallic, ascending up to the sky, while caves burrow into the earth, have huge underground pockets full of strange liquids, and are the natural domain of the Earth Mother goddesses and the underworld. If the landscape above ground is the land of the living, it is only natural to locate the land of the dead below ground, only accessible through such caves. A common idea in Eastern religions is that the feminine force that gives birth is, simultaneously, the force that reigns over the dead, as life leads inexorably to death. This is a central tenet of both Hinduism and Buddhism, embodied by the terrifying black goddess Kali in Hindu mythology and by the many-armed demonesses in Tibetan Buddhism. The gateways that lead up from

OPPOSITE: Tomb, Petra, Jordan, 1995

one level to another at Borobudur in Java are mounted by arching Kala figures that appear to guard the cavelike steps.

Joseph Campbell writes, "The cave has always been the scene of the initiation, where the birth of the light takes place. Here as well is found the whole idea of the cave of the heart, the dark chamber of the heart, where the light of the divine first appears. This image is also associated with the emergence of light in the beginning, out of the abyss of the early chaos, so that one senses the deep resonations of this theme."[2] This thinking ties the cave with the archetypal feminine and birth, seen in many early cultures as the birth of the Sun from its mother, Earth. A hidden element of the sacred landscape, the cave is also a powerful initiation space. First used in its natural state, the cave then morphed into an architectural form present in some of the most magnificent historical monuments, including the King's Chamber of the Great Pyramid at Giza, the corridors inside Mayan pyramids throughout Mexico and Guatemala, the stone chamber at Newgrange in Ireland, temples carved in stone at Ajanta and Ellora in India, the church and caves at Petra in Jordan, and even some of the darkened naves of early Romanesque churches. Even though distant and removed from actual caves, as Homer describes in *The Odyssey*,[3] these cavelike spaces evoke the passage between worlds via darkness:

> Perpetual waters through the grotto glide,
> A lofty gate unfolds on either side;
> That to the north is pervious to mankind:
> The sacred south t'immortals is consign'd.

The Neoplatonist philosopher Porphyry (233–305 CE) wrote a commentary about Homer's description of the Cave of the Nymphs, near Ithaca, which possessed unusual and magical powers. According to Porphyry, the cave is an image of the cosmos, where through one door mortals descend on their path to generation, while through the other door immortals ascend the path of liberation toward the realm of the gods. Because in ancient times caves were almost impossible to light with torches, they remained an "invisible realm," where secret initiations took place. The resident nymphs, who carry the potency of this realm, guard over the cave—a place of gestation and birth, as well as passage to the beyond. The ancient Greeks understood that the inscrutable, womblike interior of the cave flows without visible form, and that its darkness represented all the matter he world contains, an astonishing precedent to the very recent discovery in physics that the universe is teeming with pulsating, invisible dark matter.[4]

To the Maya, the geography of the entire world was sacred, but this sacredness was particularly concentrated in places such as mountains and caves—channels through which one could pass to the

OPPOSITE: Buddha, Yungang Grottoes, Datong, China, 2001

PAGE 64: Great Pyramid of Giza (Dynasty IV), Egypt, 1989

PAGE 65: Petra, Jordan, 1995

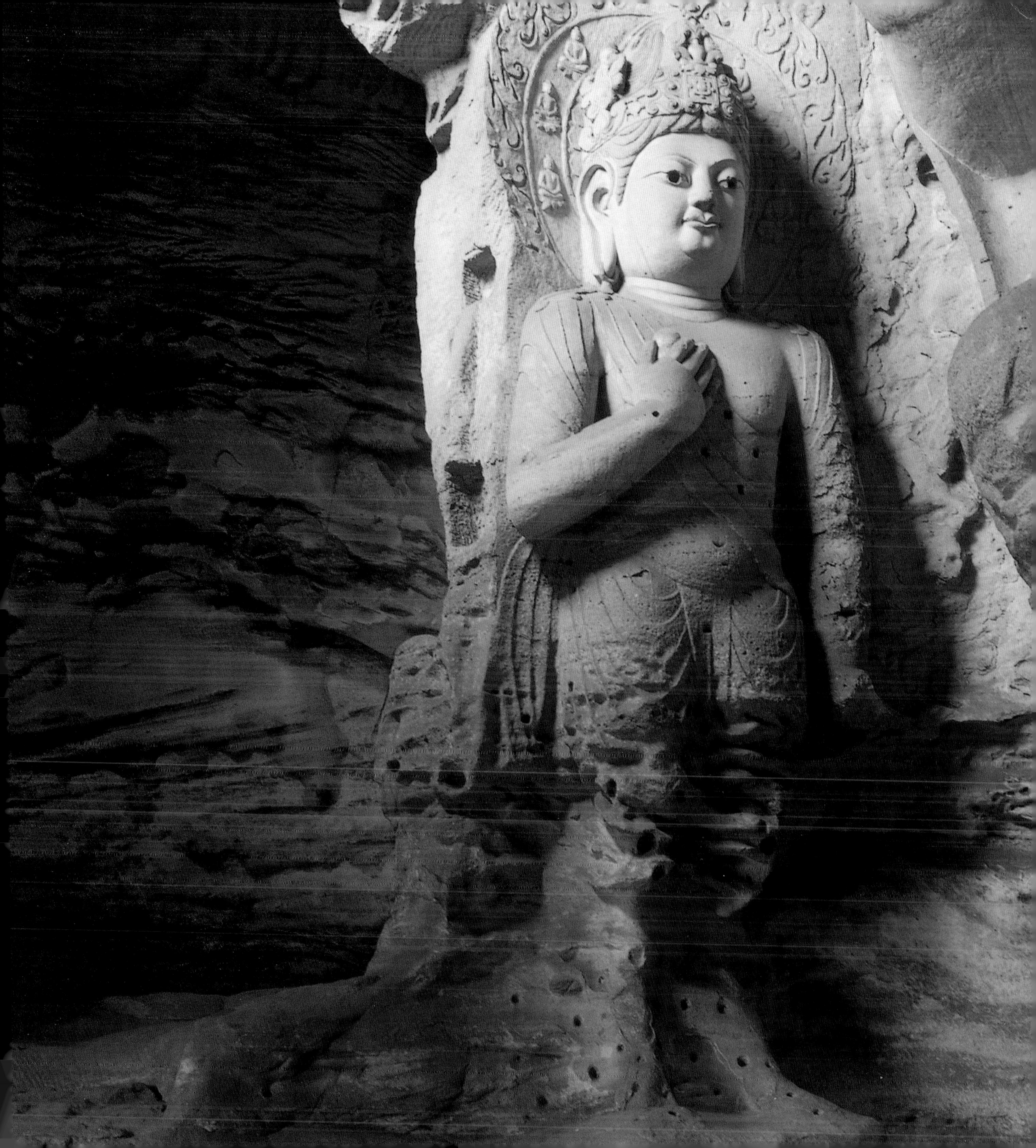

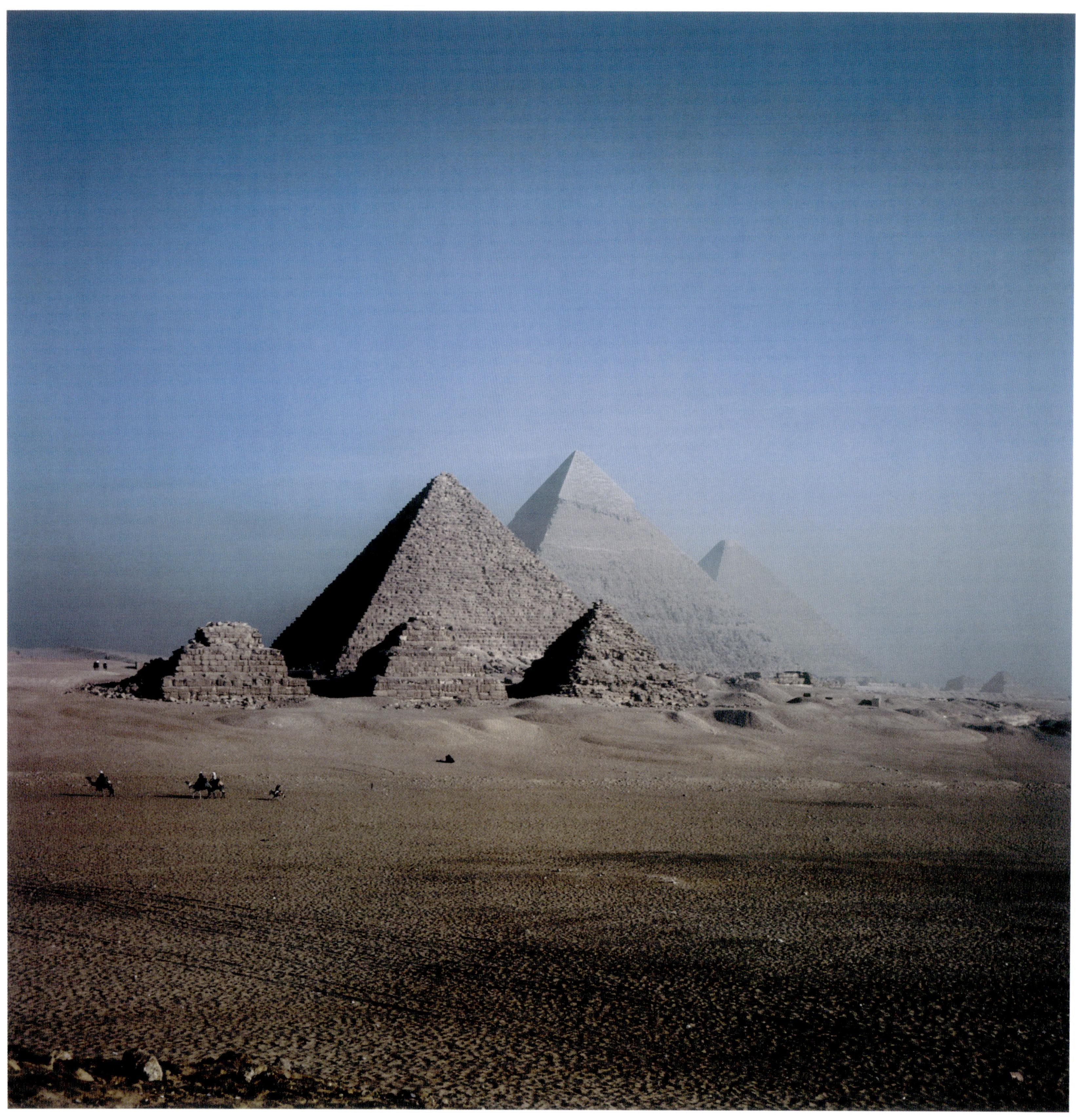

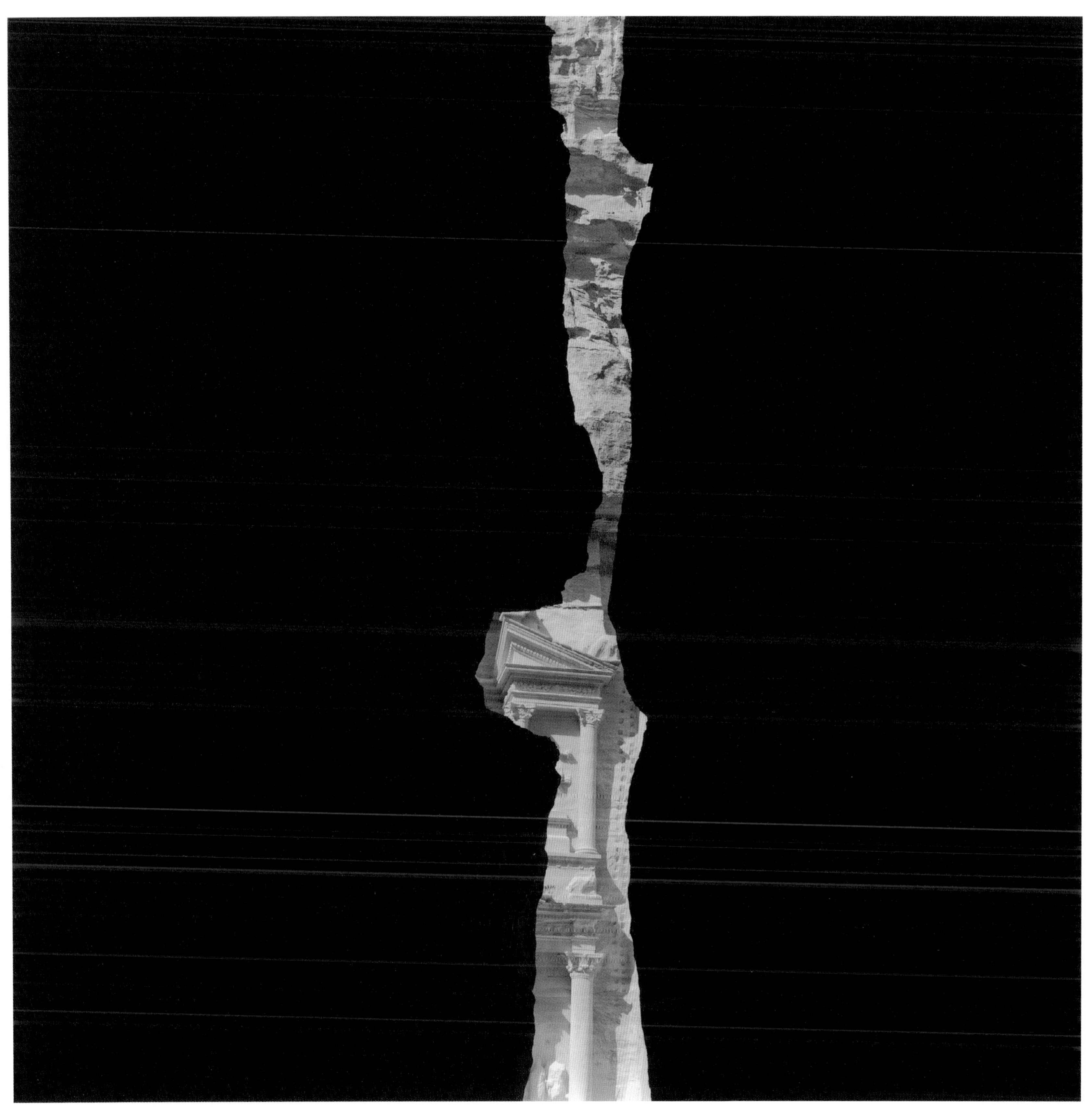

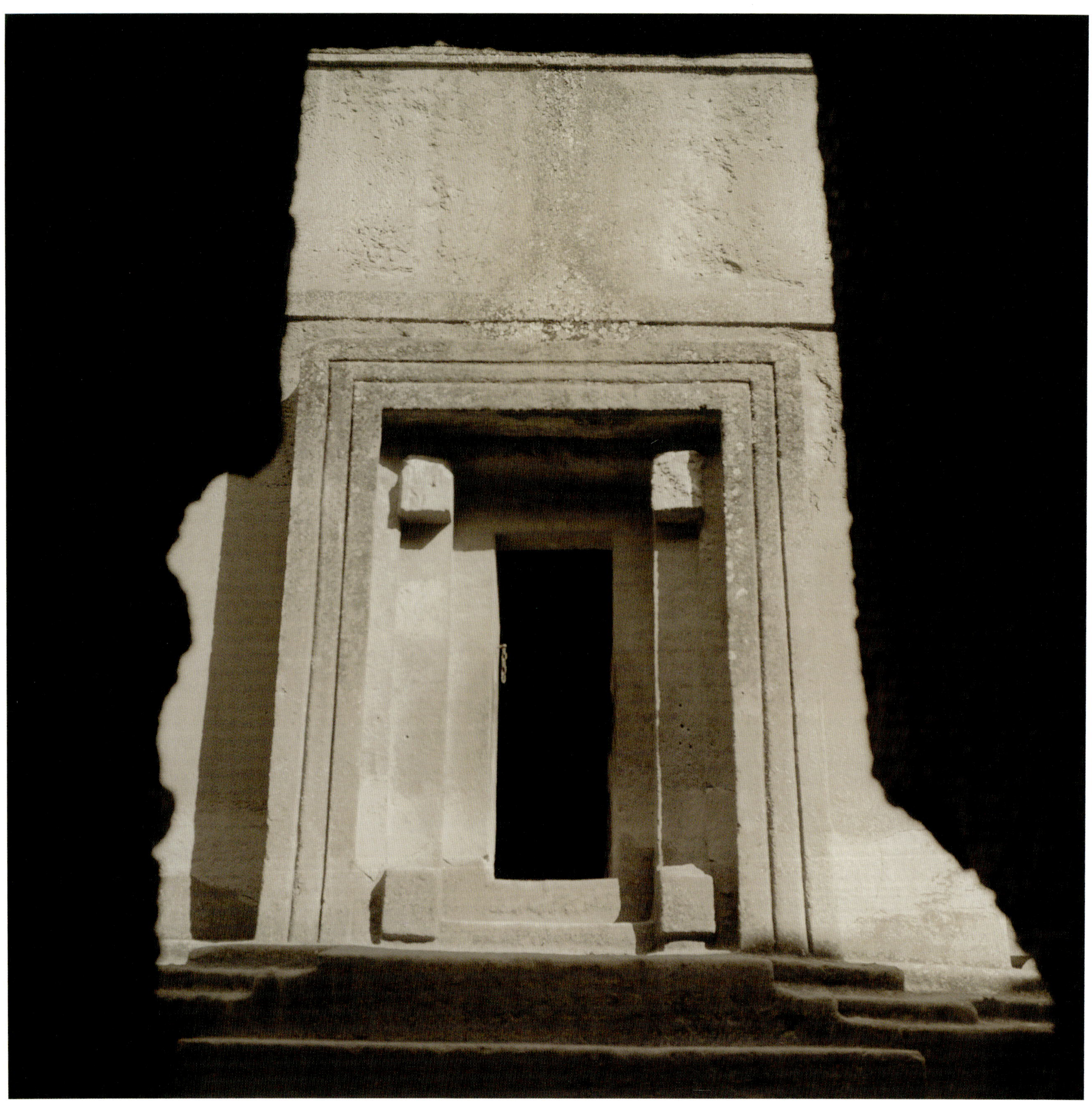

starry heavens above and the darkness of the underworld below. These gateways between dimensions commanded great respect and fear while determining the siting and other qualities of their jungle pyramid complexes. Thus, humans created their own power points, which integrated and resonated with the god-made power points inherent in the world.

The forests of Mayan temples that reach up into the sky in Central America were conceived as sacred mountains, and the entrances into their interior spaces represented caves leading to the heart of those mountains. Inside these caves grew the sacred World Tree—the Mayan cosmos—which united the underworld and "Skyworld" with the world of men and which completed the sacred trilogy of mountain, cave, and tree.[5] Much like the ancient ancestor and nature worship of the Balinese people, the surviving Maya Indians still re-create the sacred landscape of the cosmos in miniature out of leaves, vines, flowers, and with indentations in walls or hills.

The Mayan worship of the sacred jaguar was also transferred from jungle to cave, as the jaws of the jaguar symbolized the feared entrance to the underworld.[6] The seven caves of the Mayan origination mythology were where their ancestors came into being, departing into the vast and overgrown Mesoamerican jungles while their spirits remained to be venerated in the caves. Later replicated in sacred temples, caves evidently played a central religious role in cultures on many continents. Indeed, petroglyphs and cave paintings in many sites across Guatemala echo the paintings of the much earlier Paleolithic caves in France and Spain.

The Vision Caves of Lascaux and Pech Merle

Along the western edges of the Massif Central and the northern slopes of the Pyrenees in west-central France are hundreds of limestone caves that were inhabited during Upper Paleolithic times. Although many of the caves in this area were inhabited as early as 35,000 years ago (as determined by radio-carbon-dated bones and primitive tools found there), the most famous cave at Lascaux is of a different order altogether. In 1940, after squeezing through an opening that had narrowed over the millennia, four teenage boys discovered thousands of images that had been painted onto Lascaux's high, vaulted limestone ceilings by participants in a powerful shamanic culture. While remains in the cave are dated at the beginning of the Magdalenian Age 17,000 years ago, the art is similar to paintings from 15,000 years ago.

The imagery of Lascaux, which cover hundreds of feet of wall surface, is extremely beautiful, but the mind boggles imagining what is must have been like so many thousands of years ago to see by

OPPOSITE: Church of Bet Giorgis, Lalibela, Ethiopia, 1997

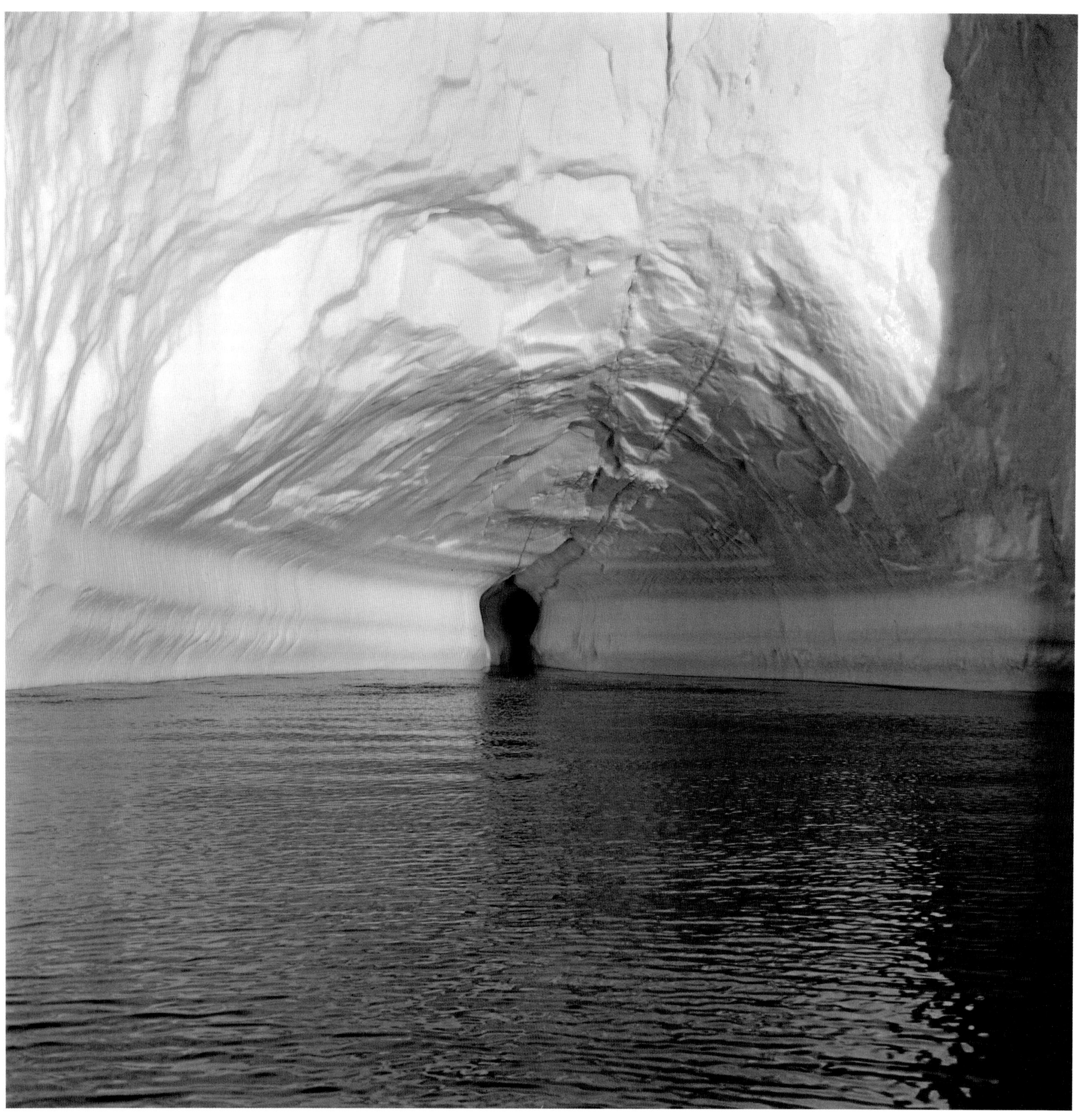

torchlight the most vivid representational art of the time: huge Ice Age bison cavorting across the rock walls, and strange geometric patterns of lines, like nets or starbursts. Such places were clearly initiation sites where these early humans kept records of their hunts, journeys, totemic animals, and mystical aspirations. Naturally, their mysteries were about death and the dynamics of the hunt, acknowledging a symbiotic relationship to the game animals upon which they depended for food, clothing, and other necessities. They also celebrated the animals that terrorized them, such as cave bears and lions, displaying them on their walls for the likely purpose of propitiating their spirits.

Graham Hancock points out in his book *Supernatural* (2006), that the first people to create the art at Pech Merle cave in France represented a gigantic leap in humanity's development, because the previous 100,000 years of Neanderthal and 25,000 years of Cro-Magnon evolution saw virtually no significant changes in habits, tools, or biology.[7] What is all the more extraordinary is that this time of cultural expression in cave paintings lasted for a period of 12,000 years—more than six times longer than the history of Christianity.[8] Hancock is quite obsessed with particular figures he found in many caves in France, Spain, and South Africa that portrayed a *therianthrope*—a human wearing a ceremonial bison head—which he identifies as a sorcerer or shaman. In early shamanic religions, the leader or sorcerer would take on the identity of the totem animal that the tribe believed held the key to their survival and would participate in ritual ceremonies within these caves. When we enter caves—or even architectural replicas—we immediately tap into their profound, sacred symbolism.

The fact that Paleolithic cave art is found all over the world indicates that the evolution of humanity occurred across the globe, not just in one isolated location. We carry a cellular memory of this development in the deeper and more formative recesses of our mind and spirit. The sacred dancing figures on the cave walls clearly demonstrate that these ancient shamans and initiates understood their relationship to their environment, to the cave, and to the world. To Hancock, however, they also mean much more. He posits that the imagery in the caves shows powerful religious experiences that arose from the ecstatic states attained by early shamans and that the caves were the site of these experiential mysteries. Even in modern times, certain hallucinogenic substances are known to re-create these prehistoric rituals in our minds, lending credence to the idea that the lives of our ancestors are encoded in our DNA.

It is this ancestral legacy that makes caves mysteriously sacred and womblike to us. Just as the sacred mountains, with their phallic quality and appearance of upward striving, were primarily associated with heavenly, mostly male entities, caves carry resolutely feminine associations as wombs burrowing into the earth, celebrating the birth of consciousness, if not of humanity itself.

OPPOSITE: Iceberg, Disko Bay, Greenland, 2000

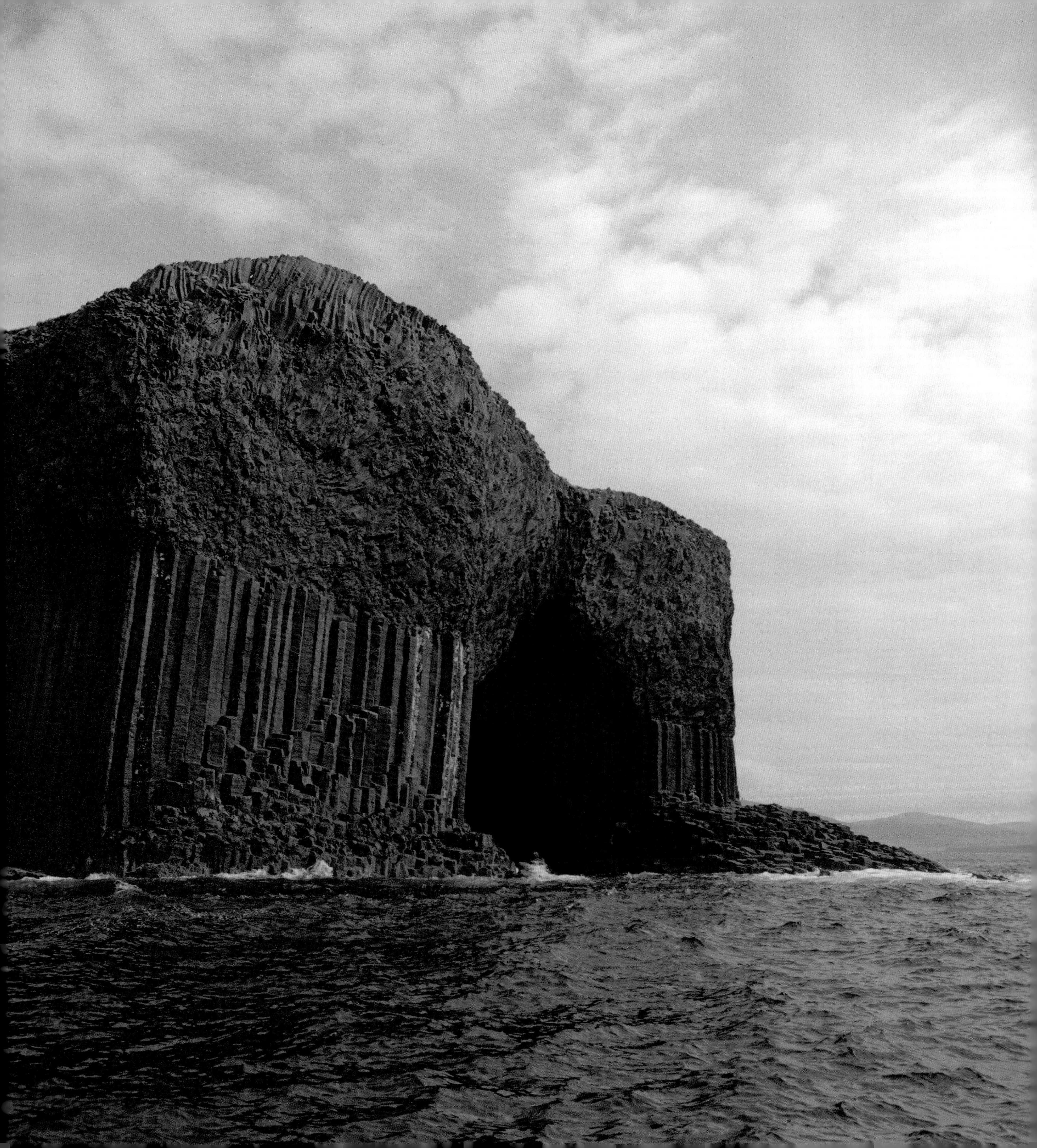

Delphi and Psychro

The sanctuary of the oracular god Apollo at Delphi is set dramatically in the Boeotian mountains as one winds westward along the Gulf of Corinth on mainland Greece. The roads and paths of access to this sacred site are labyrinthine and dangerous, and in ancient times it would have required mounting steep slopes, crossing waters with rushing currents, and passing over rocky clefts. After countless turns in one direction and then the other, you reach a gigantic cleft in the barren mountains. Researcher Vincent Scully sets the scene in his book, *The Earth, the Temple, and the Gods* (1962):

> As the way mounts the shoulder of the mountain across from the summit, two opposites come into view at once: a hitherto hidden and unexpected lake far below to the south, and the whole rocky bulk of the summit itself, a great domed and pointed mass with a single outcropping like a rhinoceros horn jutting from its north face. Directly underneath the vertical cliff of the horn the temple of Apollo was placed.[9]

Looming above Delphi, Mount Parnassus is, by some accounts, the Greek mythic equivalent of Mt. Ararat. As the Greek "Noah," Deucalion and his wife landed on its slopes after Zeus sent a great flood that drowned all other inhabitants of the first world age. Like Ararat, Parnassus was considered to be the "navel," or center of the world.[10] At Delphi, the significance of this place of prophesy is indicated by a blunt, rounded *omphalos* stone. "Delphi" has a similar meaning to the word "womb" in Greek and is linked with Gaia, their earth goddess. The association of this most famous oracular place of ancient times with the female cavern is further illustrated by a cleft in the rock, over which the pythias (priestesses of Apollo) sat and inhaled the strange gasses emanating from underground before going into their prophetic trances.

Though dedicated to Apollo, Delphi's numerous semantic and physical connections to the feminine reveal the site's original purpose as a shrine to the dragon goddess Python. In antiquity, serpents, snakes, or dragons were considered vehicles and familiar spirits of the feminine, embodying the twin mysteries of the feminine spirit: sexuality and time. Representations of Athena, patron goddess of Athens, often depict her with a snake at her feet, as if paying respect to the former "great goddess" era that preceded her. As Scully notes, "Delphi must therefore have seemed to the Greeks the place where the conflict between the old way, that of the goddess of the earth, and the new way, that of men and their Olympian gods, was most violently manifest. There can be no doubt whatever that it was the landscape itself which gave rise to this belief and which dictated the presence of the shrine."[11]

As with other sacred sites in Greece, like the healing temple complex of Epidaurus, and Zeus's reputed Cretan birthplace of Psychro Cave, priests and priestesses of Apollo required that cult participants

OPPOSITE: Fingal's Cave, Scotland, 2006

undergo a series of great physical hardships even to reach this remote sanctuary.[12] Indeed, before being admitted to the presence of the Apollonian shrine, it was necessary for visitors to cleanse themselves in the nearby Castalian Spring.

The journey to the Lasithi Plateau in eastern Crete is arduous, with winding switchbacks seemingly going up into the sky. Upon reaching the sacred plain high above sea level, we immediately taste divine fury with the extremely variable, late-afternoon patterns of lightning, flash rains, thunder, and winds, as sights of eagles soaring above punctuate the sublime landscape. Zeus's symbols clearly abound here, so it isn't surprising that this plateau is the site of some of the earliest cult rituals in all of Greece, stretching back to the Minoan civilization. Although Mount Olympus was primary site where the god Zeus was worshipped in the north of Greece, the sacred Psychro Cave is where Zeus was supposedly born to Rhea and raised in secret by the goat-nymph Amalthea, so that his jealous father, Kronos, would not discover him. As Rhea is an earth goddess, the cave obviously represents the birth canal through which Zeus and, by symbolic extension, all the gods and goddesses were born. Traces of early civilizations abound in this huge, underground grotto, where they were venerated for millennia until the entrance was obscured by fallen rocks. Strikingly, there is a rocky outcropping at the bottom of the cave that resembles the image of Kronos in profile, creating a mythical gloom that permeates this ritual site.

Caves of the Precious Master

In Tibetan Buddhism, there is a long tradition of caves as places for meditation and retreat. The most famous example of this tradition is found in the story of Padmasambhava, also called Guru Rinpoche ("Precious Master"), who appeared in the eighth century CE as an eight-year-old child birthed from a lotus blossom floating in Lake Dhanakosha within the kingdom of Uddiyana (present-day Pakistan). He came into the world with such a profound and sacred blessing that he is considered a second Buddha by the Nyingma school, as the widely known Buddha Shakyamuni had left clues hinting at Padmasambhava's arrival. Padmasambhava demonstrated the miraculous deeds and levels of realization of a bodhisattva, achieving the most profound state of *samadhi* (right concentration) in the cave of Yanglesho in the Kathmandu Valley.

There are many legends about the mysterious tantric rituals Padmasambhava performed with his main female consort, Yeshe Tsogyal, to achieve the transcendent state of *nirvana* in the caves of the Himalayas. He blessed many sacred caves and hermitages that later became monasteries and he would often withdraw from the world to receive the highest teachings of the Buddha in such places.

Padmasambhava also hid many religious treasures (*termas*)—including the notable funerary text known as the Tibetan Book of the Dead—for future generations of *tertöns* (spiritual seekers) to discover in lakes, caves, and forests in the Himalayas, and he founded a number of monasteries in and among the caves of Pakistan, India, Nepal, and Tibet.[13] As a result, caves all over the region are associated with this Buddhist master.

The Yungang Caves at the foot of Wuzhou Mountain in the western Chinese province of Shanxi are a famous treasure house of sublime fifth-century Buddhist sacred art. In this sacred locality, thousands of stone carvings within numerous caves depict events in the life of the Buddha Shakyamuni, such as his enlightenment under the Bodhi Tree and other stories from Buddhist spiritual lore.[14]

As was shown in Chapter 3, the Inca also venerated caves, regarding them as places of origin, or *paqarina*, from which their ancestors emerged. Many bones have been found in caves near Cuzco, Peru, where ancient ceremonial burials took place. Later, these caves were regarded as shrines, and remain so to this day.

The connection of cave to underworld remains a primary ancestral memory for us, and thus, caves remain formidable places. Their influence carries on into the major world religions as part of the pilgrimage paths taken and revered by followers. The cave becomes abstracted as a catacomb, a ritual cellar, or a temple cut from rock, that replicates the hardship and hazardous entry of the early cult caves, but remains an integral, symbolic component of essential rituals.[15]

PAGE 74: Terracotta warriors, Xi'an, China, 2001

PAGE 75: Buddha wall, Yungang Caves, Datong, China, 2001

PAGE 76: Cave tombs of the Achaemenid kings, Naqsh-e Rostam, Iran, 2001

PAGE 77: Stalactites and stalagmites in the Luray Caverns, Virginia, United States, 1991

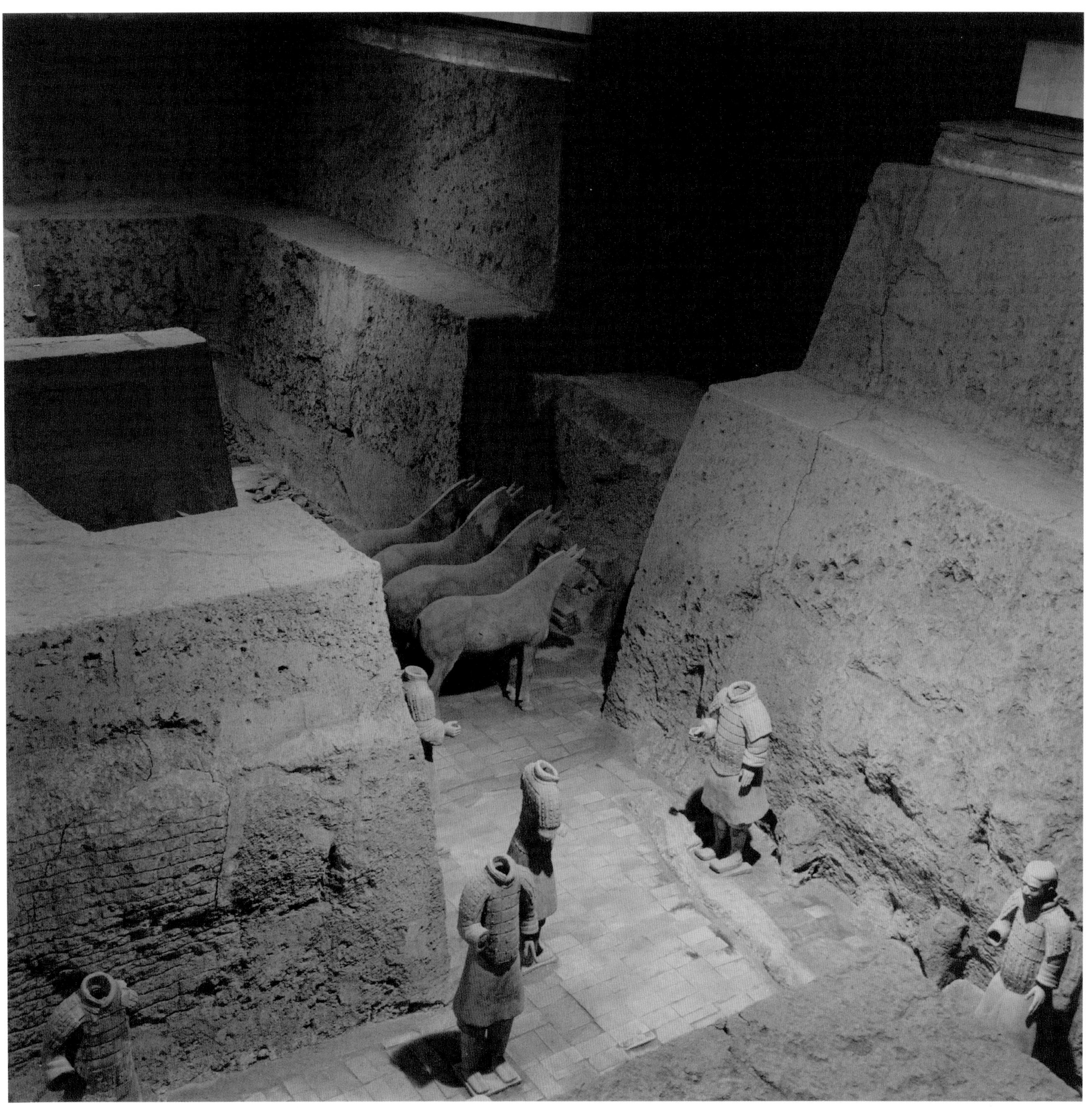

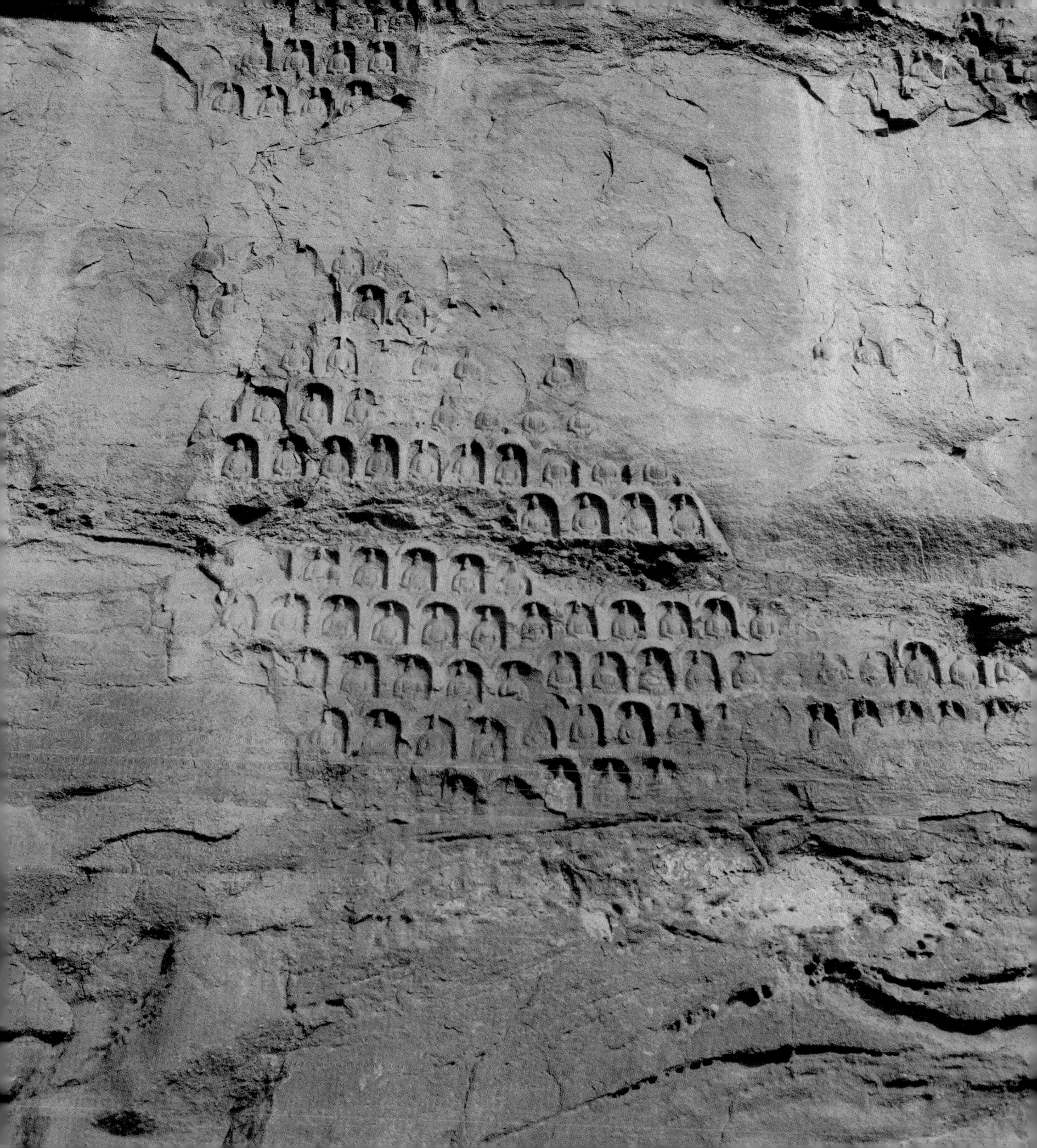

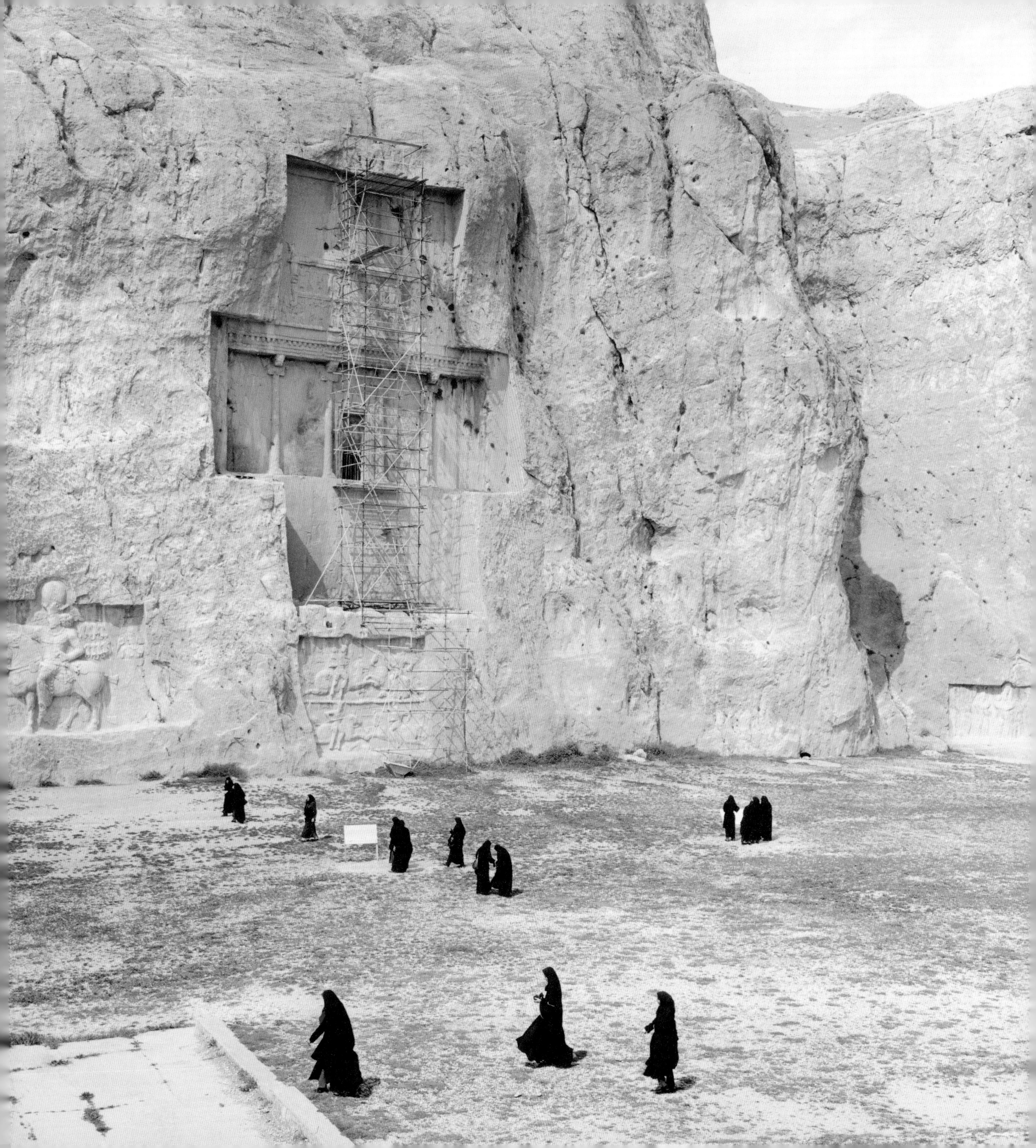

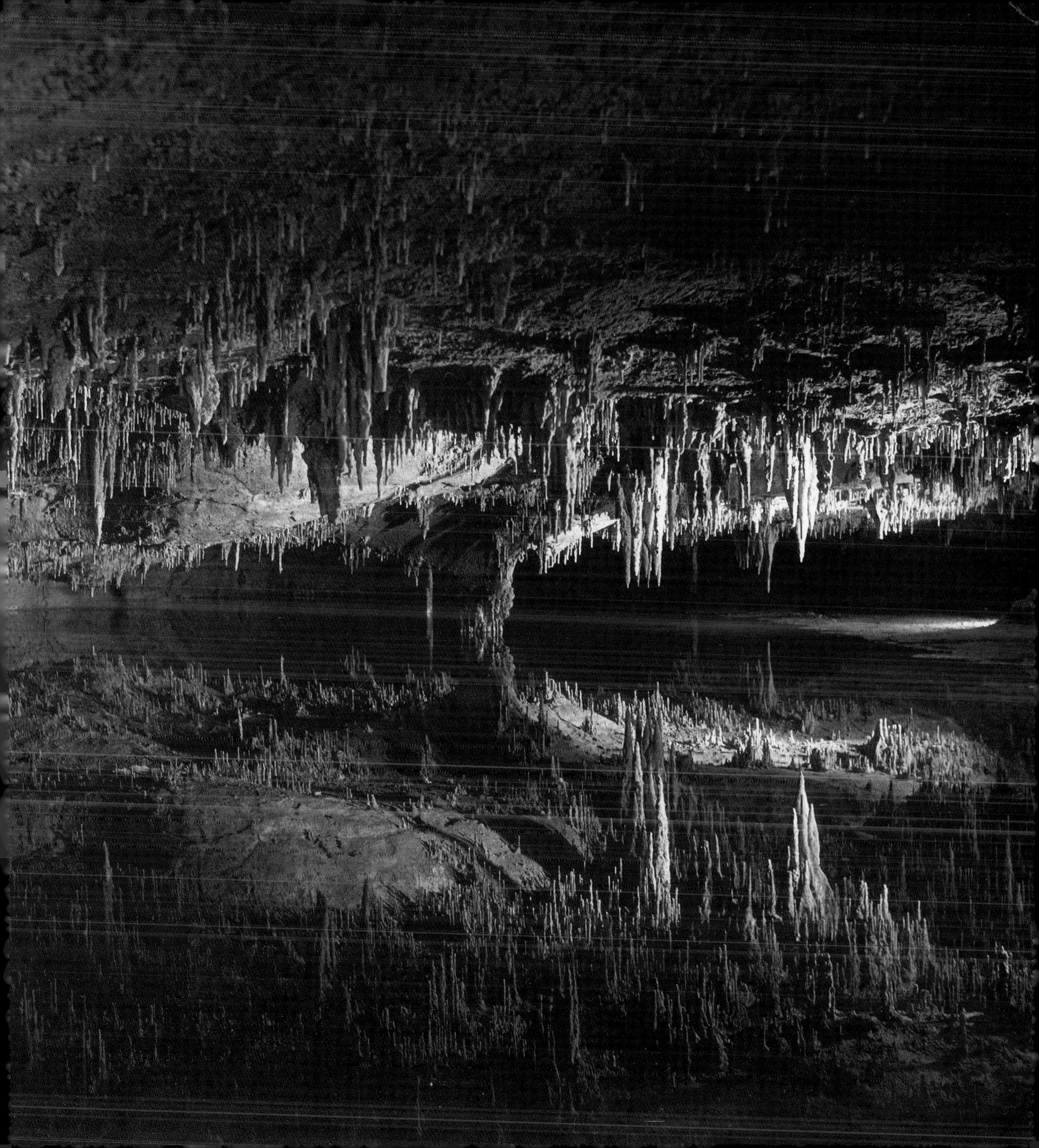

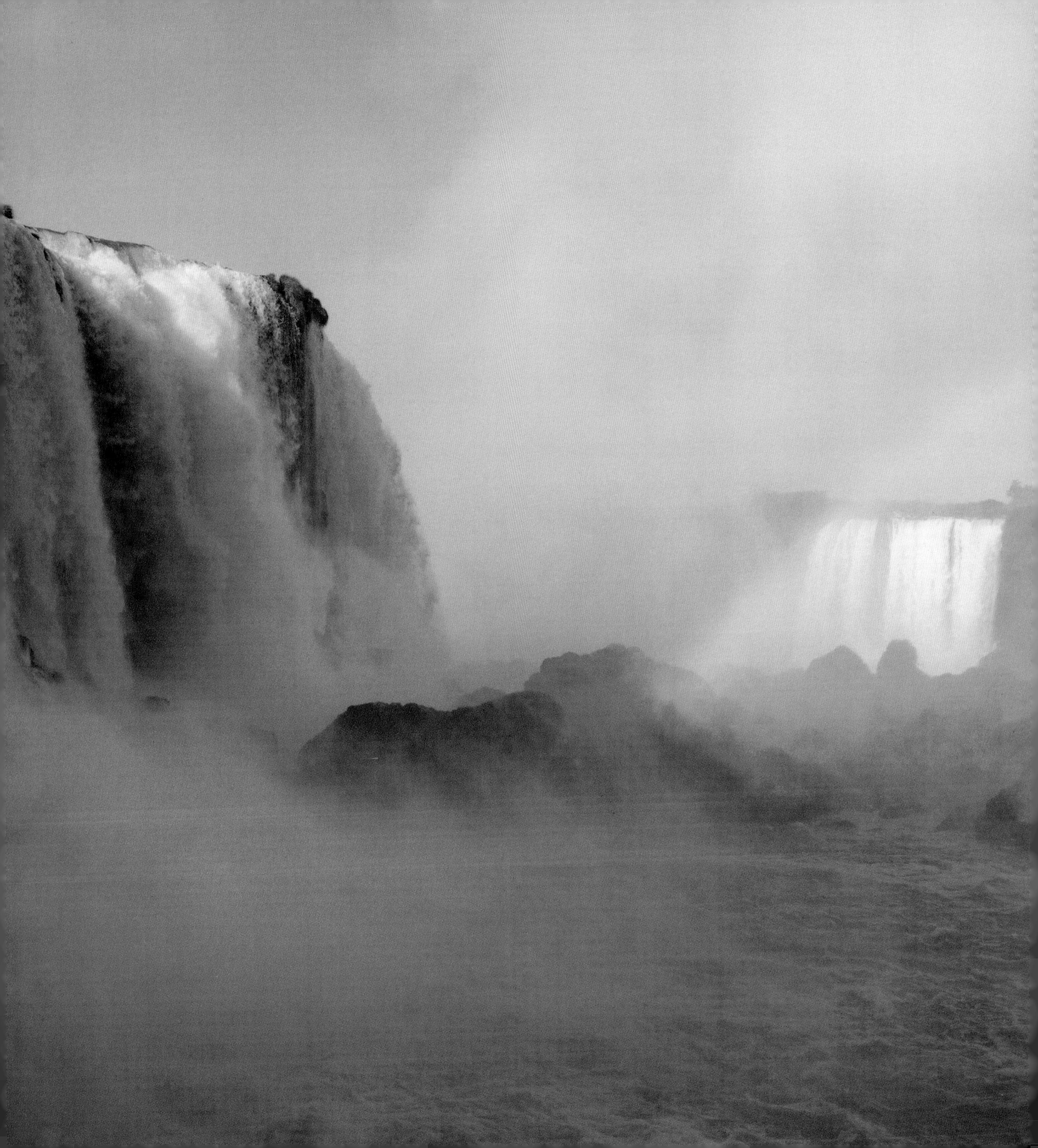

CHAPTER 5

Flow

O useful element and clear!
My sacred wash and cleanser here,
My first consigner unto those
Fountains of life where the Lamb goes!
What sublime truths and wholesome themes
Lodge in thy mystical deep streams!

~From "The Water-Fall" by Henry Vaughn (1621–95)[1]

Water is the substance of life both in the physical world and in our bodies. It allows for the growth of crops, it determines our climate and weather, and its movements are essential for transportation of goods around the planet. We humans must drink it and bathe in it to maintain a healthy life. Water is also a mysterious and magical substance associated with the feminine, emotions, and tidal changes. Additionally, it symbolizes the amniotic fluid of the womb, and its flow is analogous to our dream life and soul.[2] When we live on or near the water, we can't help but be deeply affected by its rhythms, sounds, and overall presence. As water moves, so does time, and we talk about the inexorable flow of time, one of life's greatest mysteries and a governing principle of our lives.

Eastern philosophies such as Hinduism, Taoism, Confucianism, and Buddhism regard flow as a central component of spirit and health, as do Native Americans, shamanic religions, and many other spiritual creeds.

In sacred landscapes, flowing water is an activating substance. Every continent has a major mountain chain that gathers water and sends it toward distant seas, through a series of rivers that permeate the land and feed the great oceans. These rivers are the agricultural lifeblood of the continents—blood vessels of the earth, essentially—bringing vitality as they wash away toxicity and waste.

OPPOSITE: Iguazu Falls, Brazil, 2008

Water signifies regeneration, a washing away of sinful wrongs, and the ultimate mystery of death and rebirth. At the Castalian spring above Apollo's oracular shrine at Delphi, ceremonies were held in veneration of nymph goddess Castalia. The spring, located in a deep ravine near the sacred spot where Apollo killed the Python, is used for the purification of the pilgrims who came to the site. The immersion of newborns or the newly converted in water in the later Christian rite of baptism similarly represents a purifying cleansing as well as a return to a purer state—perhaps even an intrauterine state before birth in the world. Taking the metaphor further, myths about a great flood (such stories exist all over the world) imply a collective regeneration—more explicitly, destruction by water of a prior generation of humanity and other life forms, leading to a fresh start.[3]

> *A stream crosses the sky: a stream of souls, of waters, of the dead, of subtle substance. It is the Milky Way. It runs from one end of the sky to the other, then flows on upon the earth. Earth and sky are the two banks of one great river, and it would be hard to find the place where that river passes from the celestial to the terrestrial bank. Where is the meeting point? It was the Himalaya. Thus, flowing down from the mountaintops, the Milky Way becomes the Gangā. . .*
>
> —Roberto Calasso, *Ka*[4]

In a 2002 PBS interview, Coleman Barks, well-known translator of the poet Rumi, recounts how the iconic Persian bard explored the nature of water in many of his poems, like the one below:

> Take us down to the river.
> The face of peace, the sun itself,
> No more the slippery cloud-like moon.
> Give us one clear morning after another.
> The one whose work remains unfinished, who is our work as we diminish,
> Idle though occupied, empty and open.[5]

Reflecting on this particular poem, Barks said, "There's something about water that's like the substance of the soul. We carry it around in little containers, he says, but what the water really wants is to become part of the ocean again."[6]

The Sacred Ganges

Creator god Brahma is the first of the Hindu triumvirate, which includes Vishnu the preserver and Shiva (or Sivā) the destroyer. In the beginning, Brahma is alone and asleep, and as he awakens from the lotus flower that blossoms from the navel of Vishnu, the universe comes into being. Brahma is the First Thought that emerges from the pure generative heat. Like the flow of electrons from negative to positive poles, the flow between these gods sustains universes from creation to destruction. They govern the formative processes of the world because they *are* the world.

The sacred river Ganges is believed to be the generator of all life, since it flows through god Shiva's curled hair. This is because when the river goddess Ganga came down from heaven, the weight of the water was so great, Shiva heroically took the full force of it on his head, thus shielding humanity from potential destruction. "From his long hair, so black it is almost blue, drips the Goddess, now Ganga. They rarely speak to each other. But Ganga is witness to everything Shiva does. She is present at his embraces that have no end. Yet she is never jealous. She flows—that's all."[7] The Ganges is not only the longest river in India, but it is also seen as the prototype of all other rivers and bodies of water. On ritual occasions, cisterns all over India are filled with water in recognition of its generative power.

People access the Ganges at the holy city of Benares (Varanasi) by *ghats*, or a series of steps that pass down into the waters. When you look out at the river during certain parts of the year, you see the tops of many temples on lower levels completely submerged. When the river falls, these temples are swept out, repainted, and restored to their prior state, before the monsoon floodwaters return and cover them once again. Hindus believe that those who die near the banks of the Ganges achieve redemption, and they gravitate toward Benares as they near death. The poorer and sicker visitors sleep closer to the river, so walking down to the water at night is like entering the land of the dead—especially as the nearby *ghats* are used for burning the dead, shooting flames that cast a hellish light against the darkness.

Wind and Water

In the Chinese art of feng shui ("wind and water"), *ch'i* is the flow of vital energy, or life force, circulating within our bodies, between us, and in nature. It is the alternation of light and dark, open and closed, that creates flow. Light, electricity, and even the storage ability of computer memory are all products of the flow of electrons. For example, keeping circuits connected allows electricity to move continuously from electrode to electrode, but when the connection is broken, this flow ceases. It is the same for us, metaphorically. When we accept and create flow, change, and movement around us,

PAGE 82: *Ghats* along the Ganges, Varanasi, India, 2007

PAGE 83: Partially submerged temple, Varanasi, India, 2007

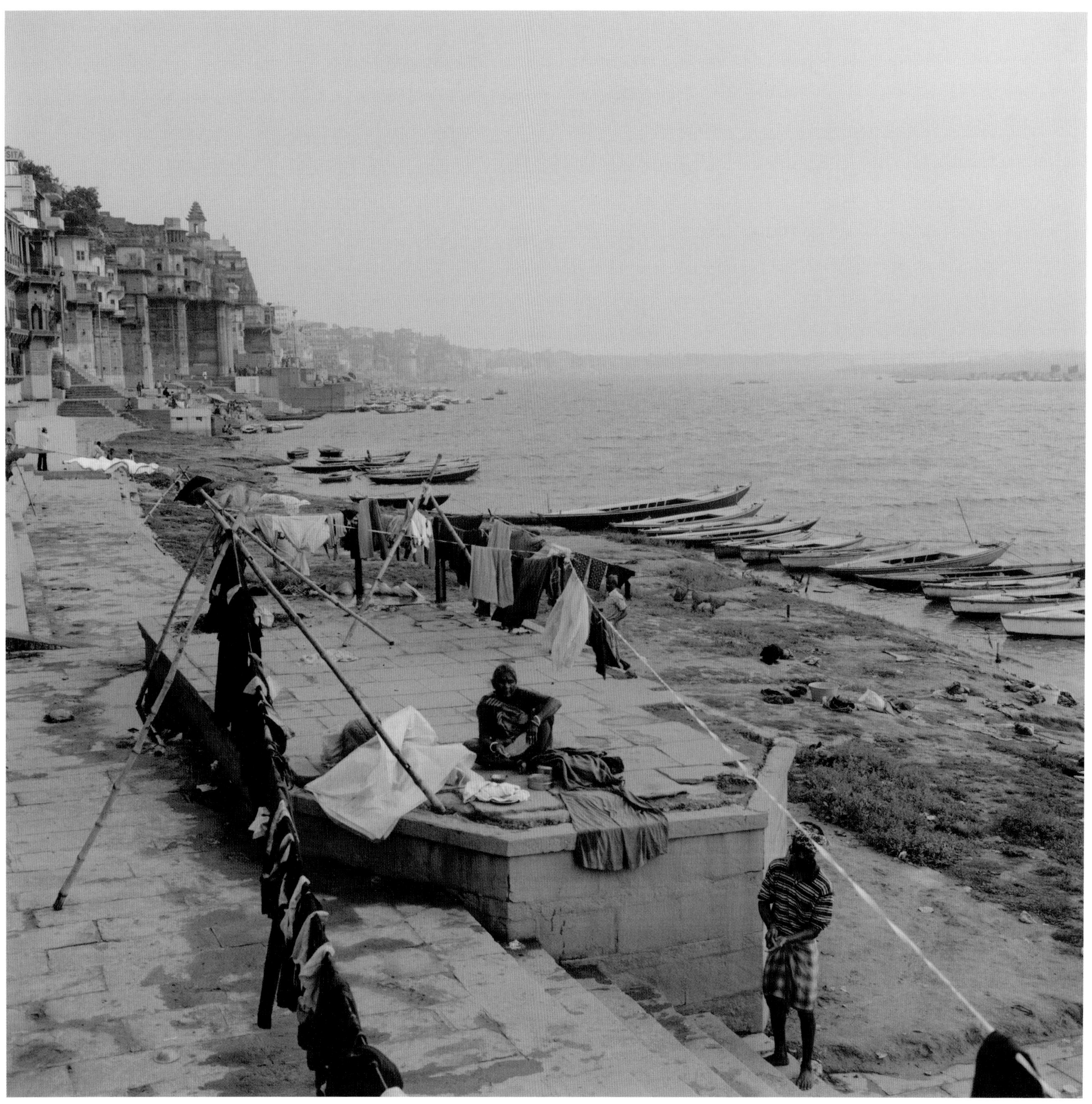

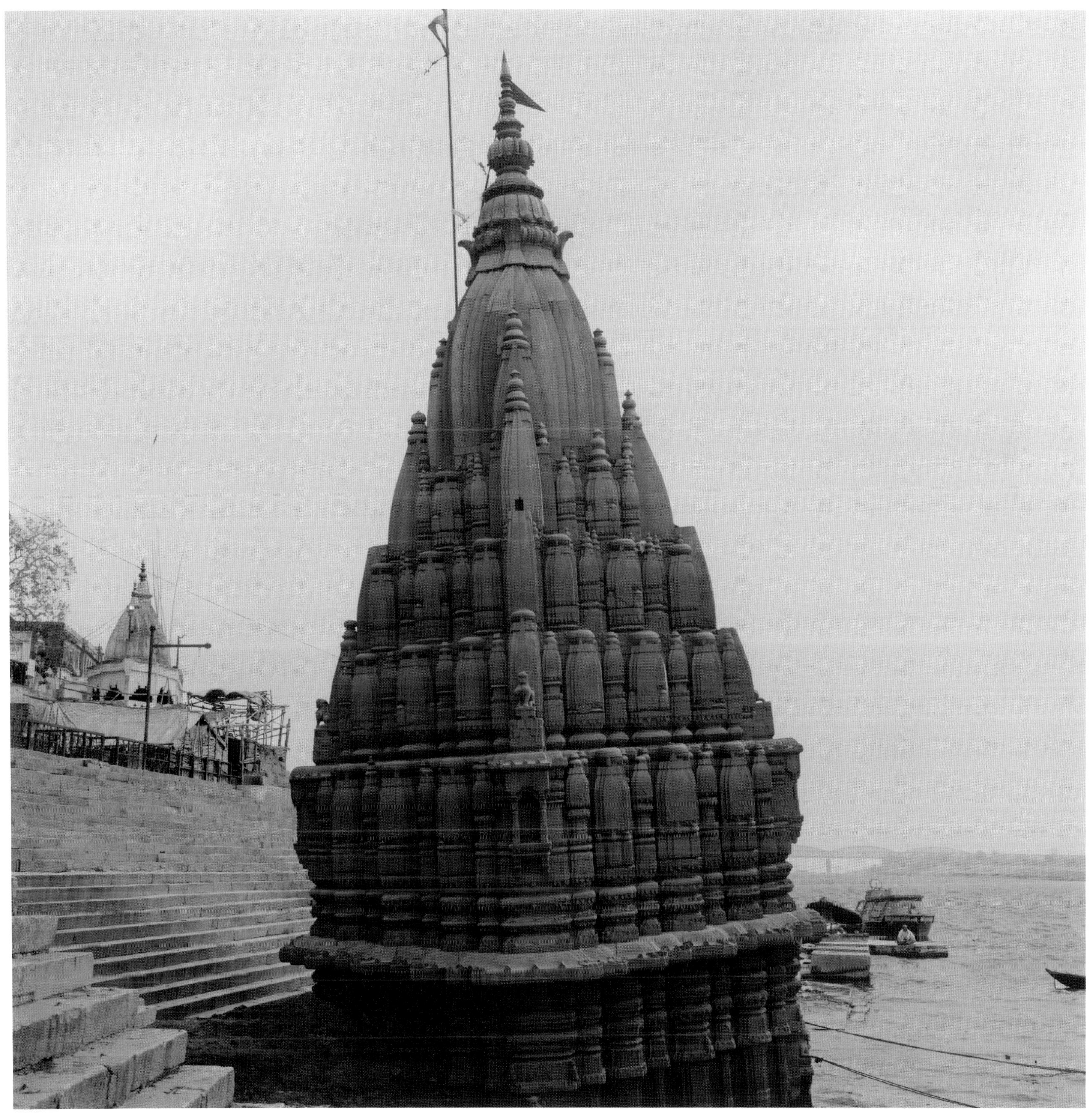

then money and health follow naturally. Conversely, when we restrict or resist flow, we will likely find ourselves at a dead end or will discover difficulties and constrained behavior that have crystallized into patterns that are damaging to our health, sexuality, and financial well-being. It is therefore necessary to learn to recognize flow and to enhance conditions that support it, so everything we encounter moves through life with great fluidity.

These same principles apply to any environment, but especially to sacred landscapes, where the earth energies are at their most powerful. A characteristic of high mountains is that moist air moves freely and often violently around the summit, nourishing life on the mountain and generating air currents that carry moisture to the surrounding regions below. Water from the fertile landscape is then carried up by the wind and released onto the mountain, creating an abundance of negative ions, which are known to produce healthful qualities. This process accounts for the incredibly fresh air at higher elevations and represents one of the most potent cycles in the continuation of life on earth.

Valleys and Lakes

Our current understanding of landscape attributes the formation of fertile valleys to powerful, flowing rivers. Waters come down from the sky to become snowcaps, glaciers, or mountain streams. These waters join, collect energy, and move downward, always getting stronger. The river valleys on earth were created over millennia by water flowing through rocks and soil, eroding the silt on the surface, and carrying it all toward the sea.

Some early traditions focus on the generative properties of great, standing bodies of water. In Buddhist legends, the Kathmandu Valley in Nepal was a vast lake, and at the center bloomed a resplendent lotus. From this thousand-petalled lotus shone a light that illuminated the entire valley.[8] This luminescence was called the *Swayambhu*, or "self-sprung." This magnificent lotus did not escape the notice of the bodhisattva Manjushri, who vowed to serve humanity by draining the lake and thus making the lotus accessible for worship. He flew through the air and landed on a Himalayan mountain peak at the edge of the lake. Holding aloft his sword, which symbolized wisdom, he cut a gorge through the mountain range that separated Nepal from India. After the original lake drained away, a fertile valley remained.

OPPOSITE: Three Gorges, Yangtze River, China, 2001

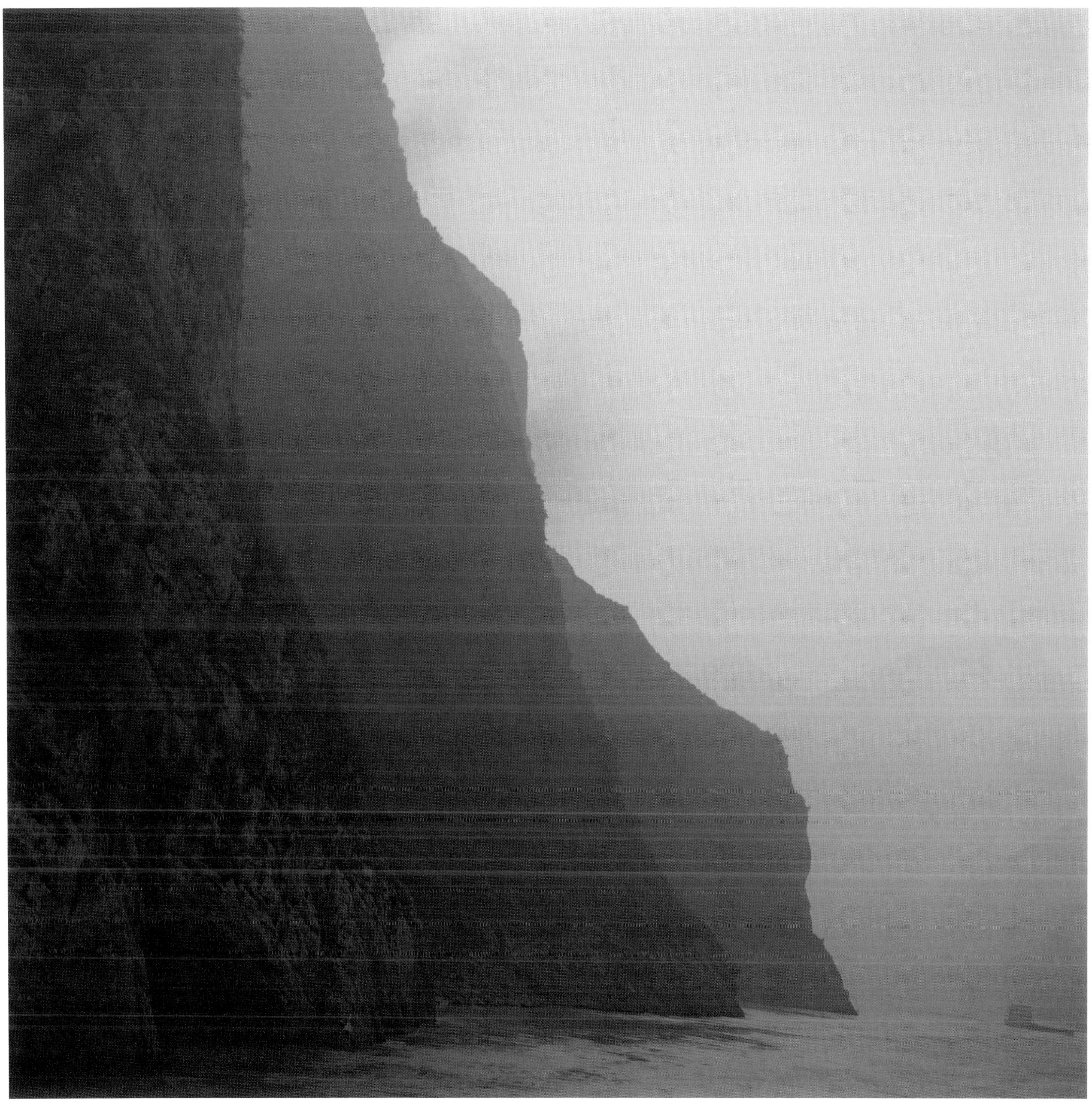

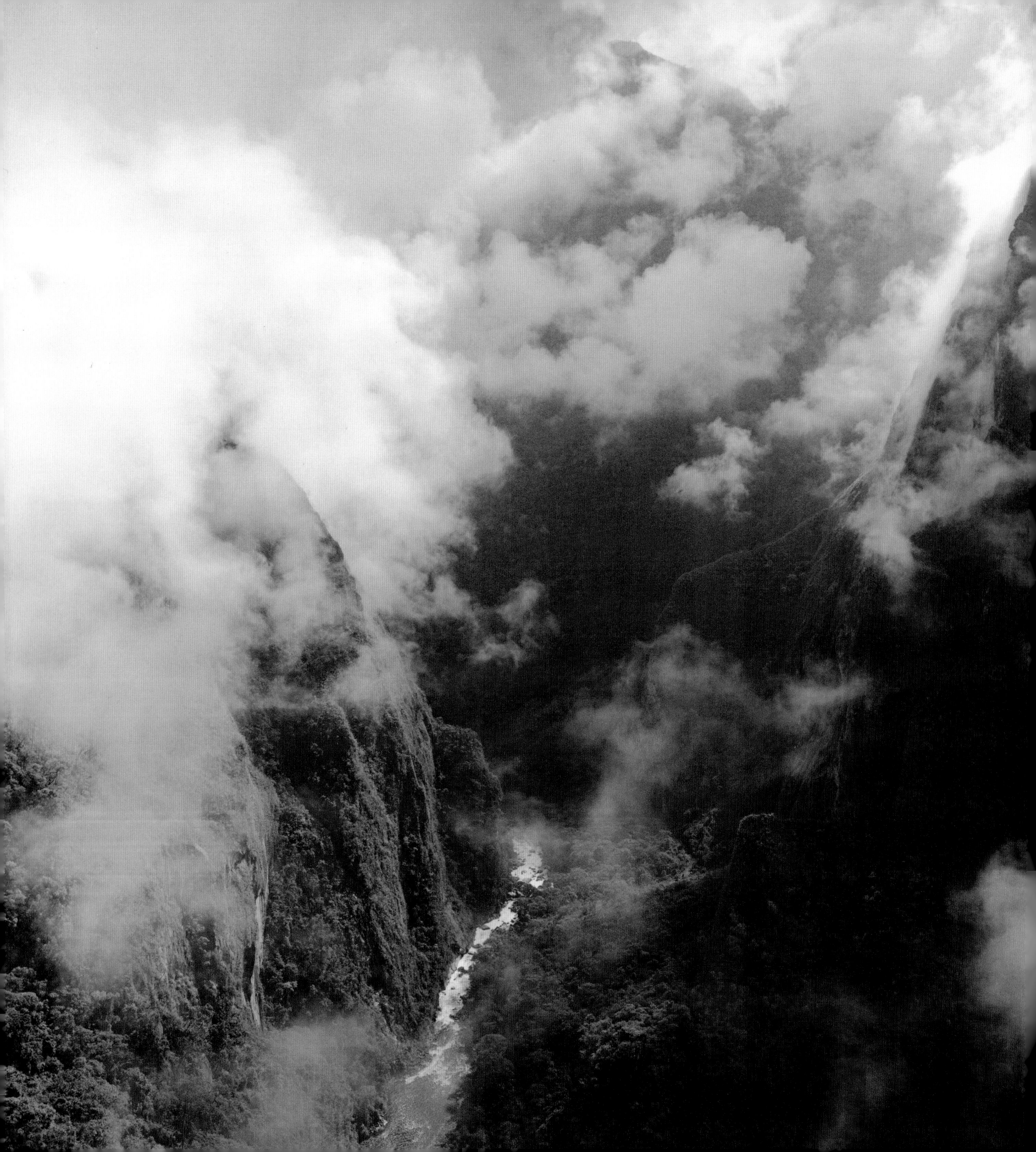

The Magic of Flow

Throughout history, water has been venerated for its "magical," healthful properties. Take, for instance, the rushing Urubamba River that snakes around the peaks of Machu Picchu. The great Inca emperor revered this river and the accompanying *aguas calientes* (hot springs), where he and his followers bathed, partaking of the magnetic qualities of the special water that arises from the depths of the Andes.[9]

In alchemy, water is a mysterious and powerful medium for sacred magic. The ultimate symbol of alchemy is the pagan god Mercurius.[10] Associated with mercury, the "water of life," he is slippery and evasive but also the cosmic spiritual being. The tenth-century Persian alchemist Avicenna writes, "He is the spirit of the Lord which fills the whole world and in the beginning swam on the waters. They call him also the spirit of Truth, which is hidden from the world."[11] Mercurius is also considered a metaphor for the experience of the divine in nature or in the unconscious. According Emma Jung's *The Grail Legend,* Mercurius's dual nature unites Christianity with earlier, darker qualities associated with the legendary magician Merlin and the mysteries of the Holy Grail. A poem attributed to the sixth-century Welsh bard Taliesin, a reputed companion of Merlin, illustrates the link between the divine and the natural dynamics of the pagan world, which we have since lost:

> I have been in many shapes before I attained a congenial form.
> . . .
> I have been a drop in the air;
> . . .
> I have been a shining star;
> . . .
> I have been a bridge for passing over three-score rivers;
> . . .
> I have been a boat on the sea;
> . . .
> I have been enchanted for a year in the foam of the water;
> there is nothing in which I have not been.[12]

Describing himself as a godly entity capable of self-transformation, Taliesin evokes Mercurius's divine yet slippery nature, which in turn echoes the power of water's transformative properties.

In the mystical tarot, the suit of cups signifies water, and when a cup is turned up in a reading, it brings emotion and unconscious forces into play. The cup is a container of our emotions, but our emotions are also what fill the cup. Therefore, we can either identify with our emotions, defining and containing them, or we can be an open vessel that accepts whatever is brought to it. The way we frame emotional situations affects our overall emotional security, as emotions by their very nature are fluid, flowing, and changeable. Water and emotions are associated with the moon's phases, its light and darkness, and its identity with the soul.

OPPOSITE: The Sacred Valley of the Urubamba River, below Machu Picchu, Peru, 2000

Metaphysically or astrologically, water signs (Cancer, Scorpio, and Pisces) symbolize primal emotion, the psychic domain, depth, changeability, the mother's womb, and the emotional structure of the family system. Water dissolves and abolishes form, and thus removal from water signifies individuation. The process of manifestation, from formlessness to the world of form, requires separation from water:

> After the earth, as solidity and consciousness, had been separated from the sea, the surging, fluctuating unconscious, the soul came into being as if arising from the water. Is it not her who the ancients worshipped as Aphrodite, the foam-born, and who is still called up today as Stella Maris? [13]

As mentioned above, water is associated with the feminine and the mother goddess. An early Sumerian goddess gives birth to Heaven and Earth, and is shown as an ideogram of the sea. The Virgin Mary likewise takes her name from the Latin *mare*, which means sea. Sigmund Freud identifies the "oceanic" feeling of limitlessness, eternity, and the unbounded, and associates it with subjective, spiritual feelings that are often seized upon and incorporated into religion. We therefore see primal experiences of the sacred co-opted by religion, as evidenced by the multitude of primeval and natural symbols built into religious structures.

Subterranean Currents

Water has an obvious and potent role in sacred landscapes as rivers, streams, oceans, seas, but also in less familiar forms of geysers, wells, underground springs, waterfalls, glaciers, and icebergs. All these forms are spectacular and dramatic, and as a result they often carry strong associations in our collective unconscious.

The well is a major influence in Scandinavian mythology. In the *Prose Edda*, an early myth attributed to the bard Snorri Sturluson, the well from which Mimir gains his prophetic wisdom is under the roots of the World Tree. One of the seminal stories tells of how the prophetic god Odin gives up one of his eyes in order to receive the wisdom of the well water. Odin's eye allegedly remains in the well, and since the well is full of the stories of all gods and men, it unites the twin skills of prophecy and storytelling.[14] Thus, by tapping into the lifeblood of the earth, wells transmit the magical and prophetic powers of water to humankind.

Another less visible form of flow in the landscape is the movement of water currents below the surface. This is analogous to our unconscious emotional and psychic life, which exists just below the surface of consciousness, always ready to emerge in unusual and unpredictable emotional situations. In the 1970s, I moved to London and became associated with two organizations that were active in related fields. The British Society of Dowsers (BSD) is composed of people from all over the United

OPPOSITE: Stepped Tank, Royal Center, Hampi, India, 2007

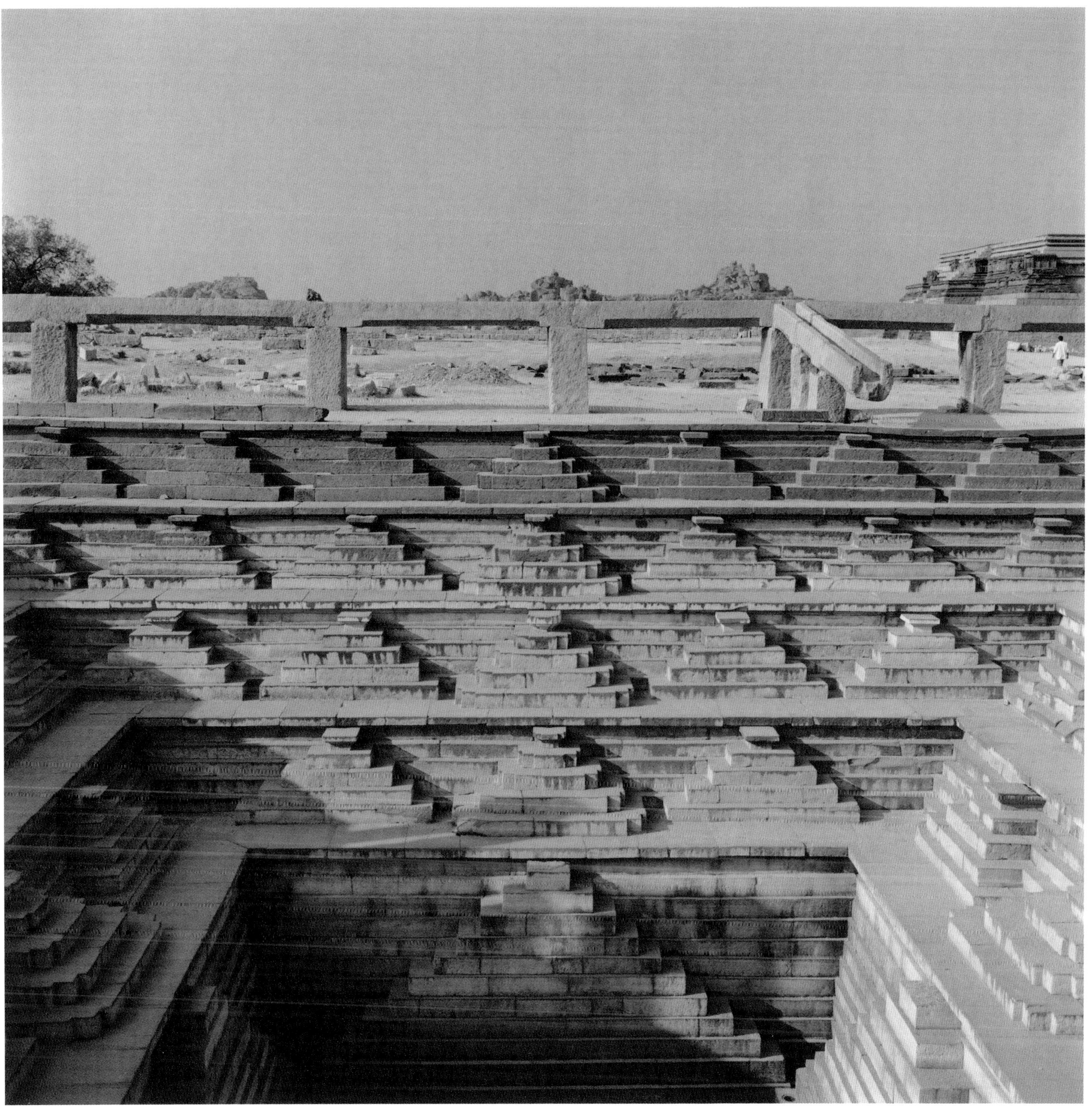

Kingdom and Europe who use rods, willow branches, pendulums, or other instruments to detect earth energies, underground water, or other substances beneath the surface of the earth, and who explore the invisible effects of these mysterious forces on people. Surprisingly strong currents of underground water pass from high ground to lower ground in the rolling hills and mountainous regions. Such underground channels interweave and crisscross, and when they pass under houses—especially bedrooms—they can create health problems. Moving water generates a strong electromagnetic current that interrupts the body's electromagnetic field in unpredictable and occasionally disastrous ways. Similar to static interrupting the transmission of a radio or television program, it disturbs the natural communication channels within our body. Commonly called geopathic stress, this phenomenon can be measured and its effects are known about and recognized.

At BSD meetings, dowsers would present their analysis of sites explored with such earth energies in mind. In the process, it became clear that virtually all sites of standing stones like Stonehenge or Avebury (and there are hundreds of such sites throughout Western Europe), churches, cathedrals, town square crosses, and Neolithic mounds such as Silbury Hill or Glastonbury Tor have prominent underground watercourses in and around their vicinity. These watercourses often form unusual shapes, like outward-flowing spirals or multiple concentric spirals, as the underground water and associated energies create a vortex. Since most of these sites are at least four or five thousand years old, it became clear that sacred or religious monuments were placed there as a way of identifying such earth energies. Underground water is dangerous to residences because of its electromagnetic currents, but when such waters accumulate in sacred places they are ritually contained and transformed into powerful healing energies by the geometry of stone circles, monuments, or sacred architecture.

The Research Into Lost Knowledge Organization (RILKO) was founded in England in the early 1970s and devoted to arcane discoveries about the many sacred sites in Europe, as well as about their history, mythology, orientation, mythology, and geometry. It was a known truth that these sites were always potent energy centers and vortexes of underground water in the much earlier landscape. For instance, Chartres Cathedral, west of Paris, was built in the twelfth century on top of a much earlier Druidic mound temple to the Black Virgin (originally Isis) and still retains an underground chapel for this worship under the main altar.[15]

Creation Lakes and Waterfalls

OPPOSITE: Angel Falls shrouded in mist, Canaima National Park, Venezuela, 1992

Crater Lake in the Cascade Mountains of Oregon is sacred to the Klamath tribe. They believe that in an earlier era of creation, the chiefs of the Underworld and the World Above fought each other, and the lake

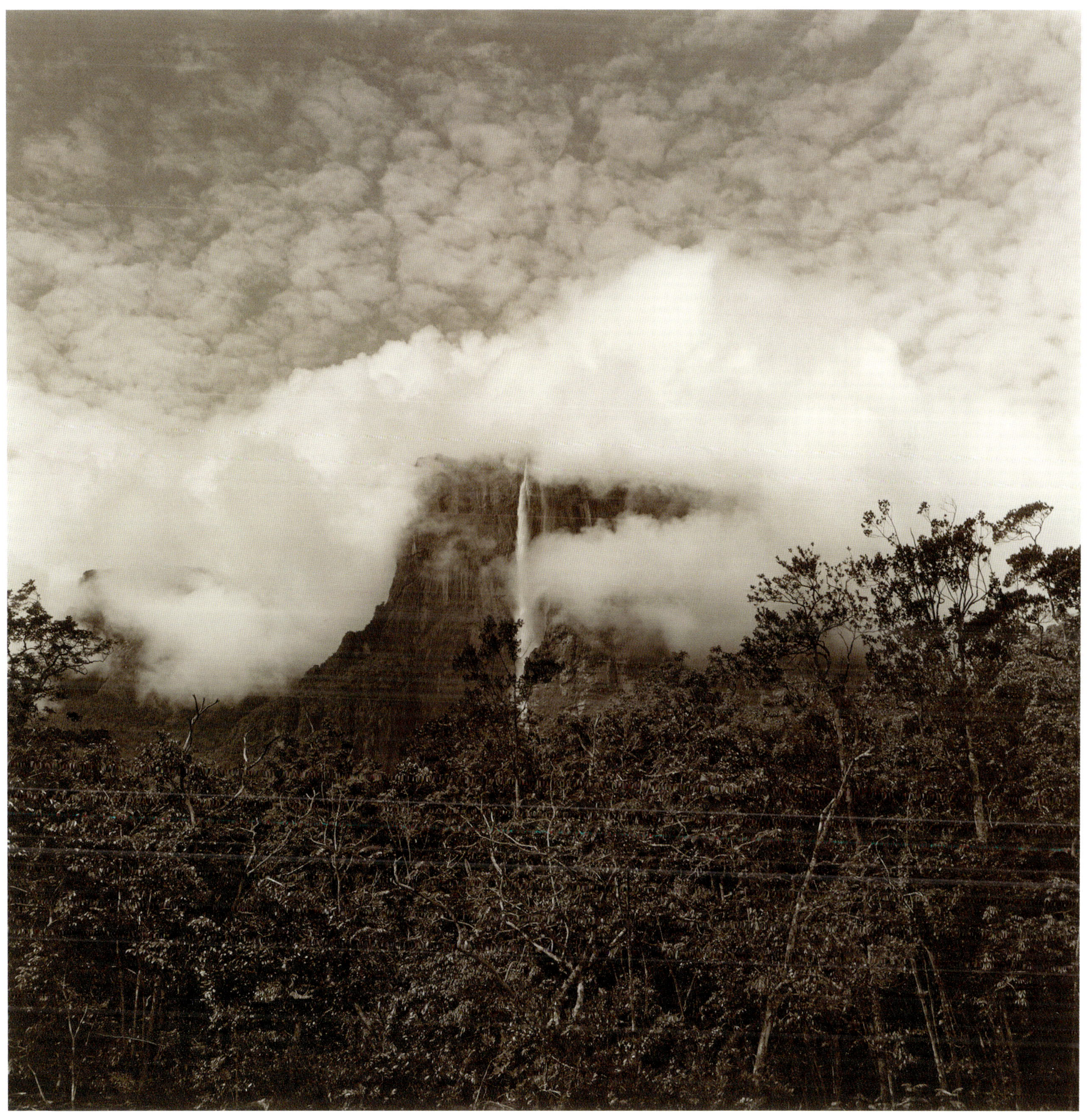

was the result of their pitched battle. This is fascinating, as the lake was formed over seven thousand years ago when the volcanic Mount Mazama exploded—apparently forty times more powerfully than Mount St. Helens in 1980—and some of its upper reaches collapsed back into the remaining crater that is now filled with crystal clear water. The story is appropriate because part of the message is that the chiefs are culture transformers in Klamath tradition, "teaching subsistence techniques, and generally preparing the world for the myth age humans."[16] The Indians regard the lake with fear and awe, and many vision quests have taken place there. Like many sacred mountain lakes, the way up the mountain is dangerous and steep, and the lake itself is thousands of feet deep in some places. It is a site where many Native American shamans were required to swim at night to communicate with the spirits in the depths of the lake, and to this day, it carries enormous power.

For anyone who has been on the Maid of the Mist tour boat at the foot of Niagara Falls, it is easy to understand how these Thundering Waters are the most powerful symbol of the Iroquois people. The sheer amount of water pouring across this huge arc—and its accompanying steady roar—is certainly intimidating. The Iroquois believed that the spirit of the waters looked after them only when respected adequately, and until the mid-eighteenth century they held a yearly ritual sacrifice of a maiden. Decorated with flowers and fruits, she was sent over the brink of the falls in a white canoe. A sorrowful propitiation of the god of the falls, it was considered a great honor for the girl and her family.

To the Huron Indians, Niagara Falls is the "place where thunder strikes."[17] Legends tell that the spirit of Lake Ontario is a serpent, and when it once tried to leave the lake, the Creator struck the serpent so violently that, even today, the serpent spirit of the lake roars at the mere memory of the blow. As the blow was given because the Creator considered the snake's energy vital to the lake's ecological balance, the myth reveals a powerful environmental awareness among these early Americans.

The magnificent, nearly 360-degree horseshoe of Iguazu Falls that separates Brazil and Argentina dwarfs Niagara Falls and covers a length of almost two miles, at a height of more than 210 feet. According to the Guarani people, the river was inhabited by a giant snake god that loved a beautiful, young Aboriginal woman named Naipí, but their union was interrupted by her mortal lover Tarobá, who kidnapped her and paddled away down the river in a canoe.[18] In a jealous rage, the snake god snapped his giant body and destroyed the riverbed, creating the waterfalls. The condemned pair of lovers was never heard from again, however the Aboriginals believe that they were transformed into a palm tree and a rock at opposite ends of the falls. From the mouth of the main waterfall, known as the Devil's Throat, the river snake watches the palm tree and the rock to make sure that they never meet again. The pair does manage to join together on occasion, however, on sunny days when a rainbow stretches from one to the other in memory of their union.[19]

OPPOSITE: Iguazu Falls, Argentina, 2008

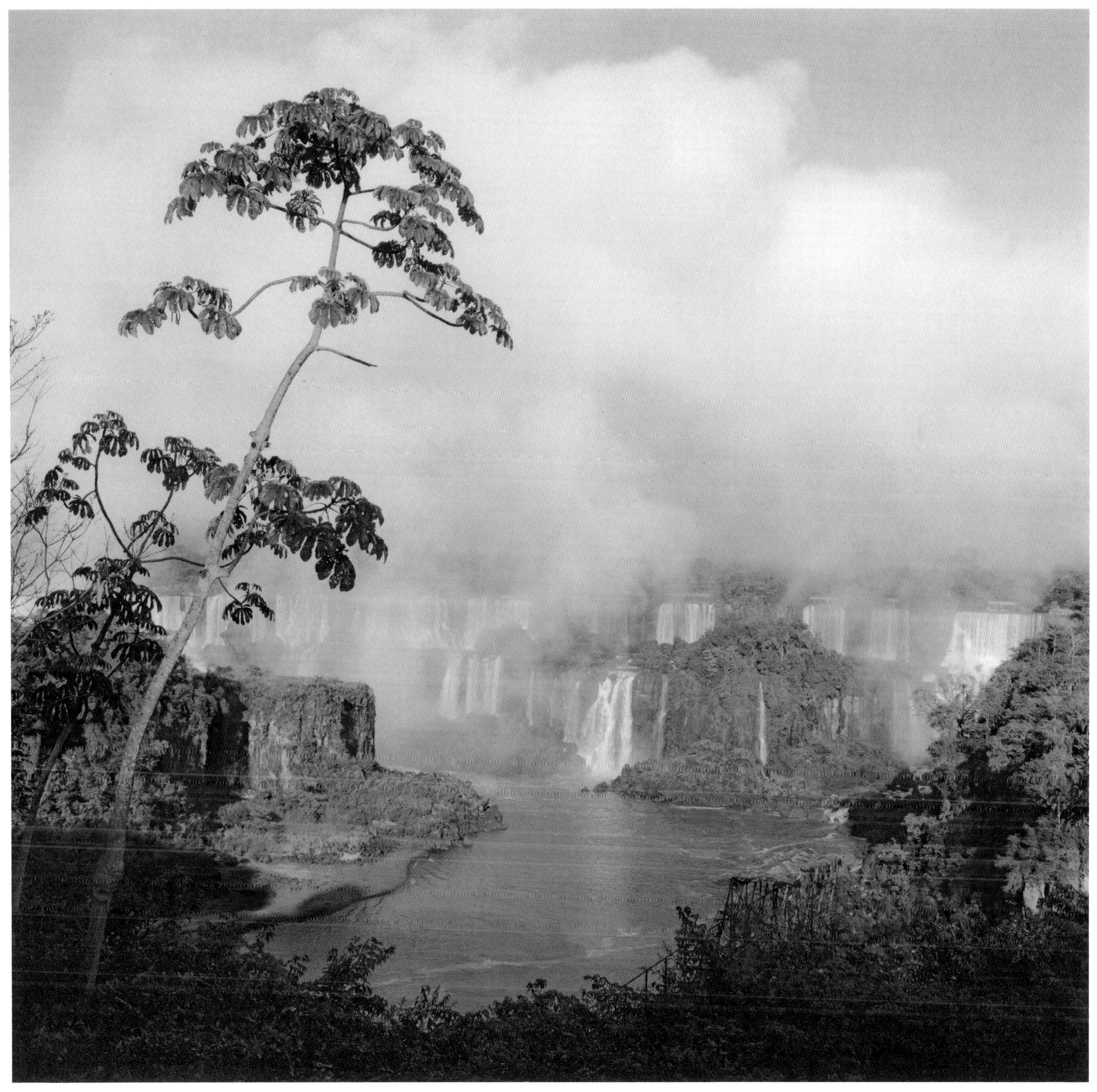

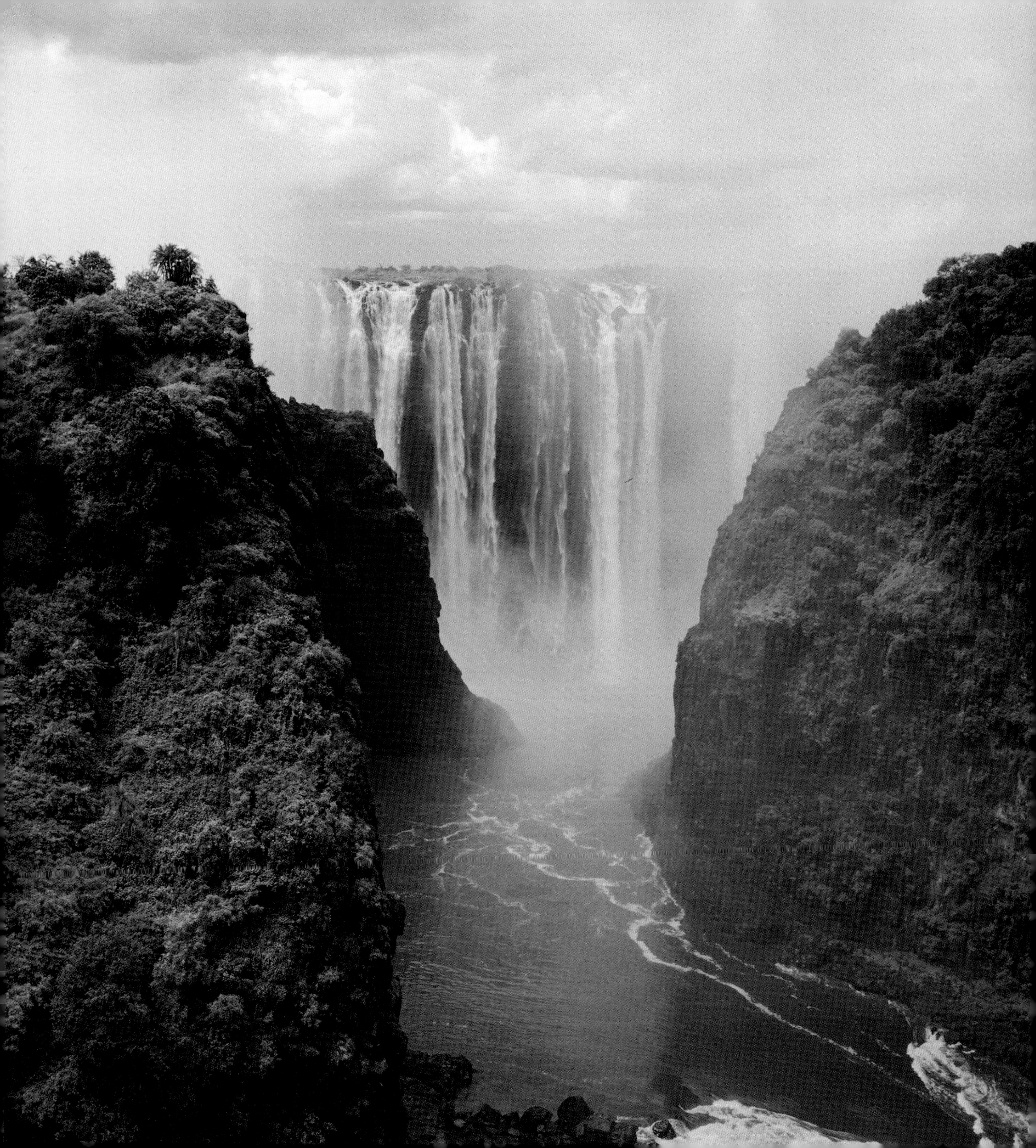

Flow as a Solid

While rivers and waterfalls are the most dramatic expressions of flow in the sacred landscape, there are other forms that convey similar feelings yet do not move at all. The lava flows in Hawaii, or anyplace with volcanoes, appear to be frozen in stone when they cool down. Beautiful and inspiring, they cascade around the islands and are considered sacred to the native people, who worship Pele, the fiery, vindictive goddess of the earth and volcanoes. Folk legends say that anyone taking bits of hardened lava as souvenirs risk taking the curses of Pele home with them.

Agung and Batur, two volcanoes on the island of Bali, are said to be pieces of the peak of the sacred Mount Meru as well as the thrones of the grandson of creator god Prajapati and the water goddess Danu. (Prajapati is an emanation of the Hindu god Shiva and therefore represents the physical creation of the world.[20]) The Balinese use the volcanic stone from Mount Agung's most recent eruption to create temples and altars, and the stupas that surmount the altars represent the sacred volcano. These ceremonial representations of the sacred mountain serve as protective icons, linking the people's fates with those of the gods and goddesses. Much of Bali's water originates in the lake that fills the crater of Mount Batur and is harnessed through the amazing terraced farmlands that stretch far into the distance. The entire precinct is protected by Danu, who preserves the water, lakes, and fertility of this island paradise.

The mythic landscape of Dreamtime is evident in the topographic features of the continent of Australia, which represents a divine being lying on his back, with Uluru as his navel. Inside the body is the snake Wunggud, who is responsible for the creation of all life, as well as for the sacred rivers and waterholes. One Aboriginal myth tells of the beginning of the Dreaming, when the gigantic sea serpent Wunggud swam inland, burrowing into the ground and creating fissures and tunnels in the bedrock, which imploded to form deep valleys and gorges. The water that flowed in from the ocean in Wunggud's wake became the rivers, and pools of water that formed between her coils when she came to rest became sacred water holes, now called Wunggud places.[21]

We have already seen that the Australian mountain Uluru, powerful in its display of smooth, flowing shapes created from weathered sandstone, is sacred to the Aborigines through its connection to their Dreamtime myth. The Aborigines believe that in the time of formation of the world, when the "earth was soft," their ancestors took on flowing forms in the landscape to remind them forever of the Dreamtime.[22] Reflecting on the encoding of the myth into the mountain as well as the surrounding myths and streams, James Cowan, author of *The Aborigine Tradition*, declares, "This myth cycle is embalmed in stone at Uluru." There are rock holes that identify where a god died, and the rainwater that flows down its slopes symbolize his blood.[23] The flowing, mythic language of the Aborigines allows

OPPOSITE: Victoria Falls, Zimbabwe, 1998

PAGE 96: Lava fields, Hawaii, United States, 2005

PAGE 97: Mound, Palmyra, Syria, 1995

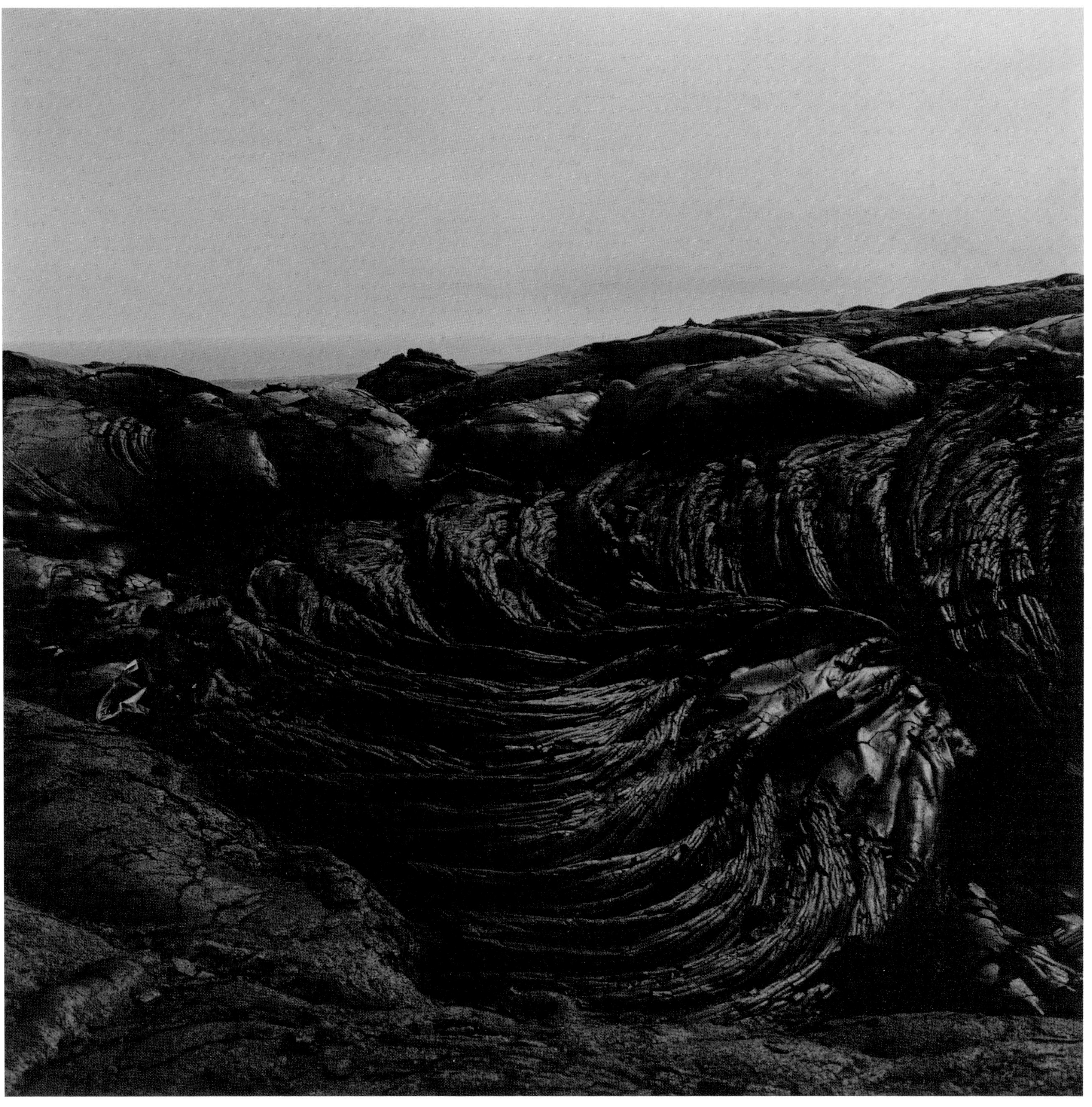

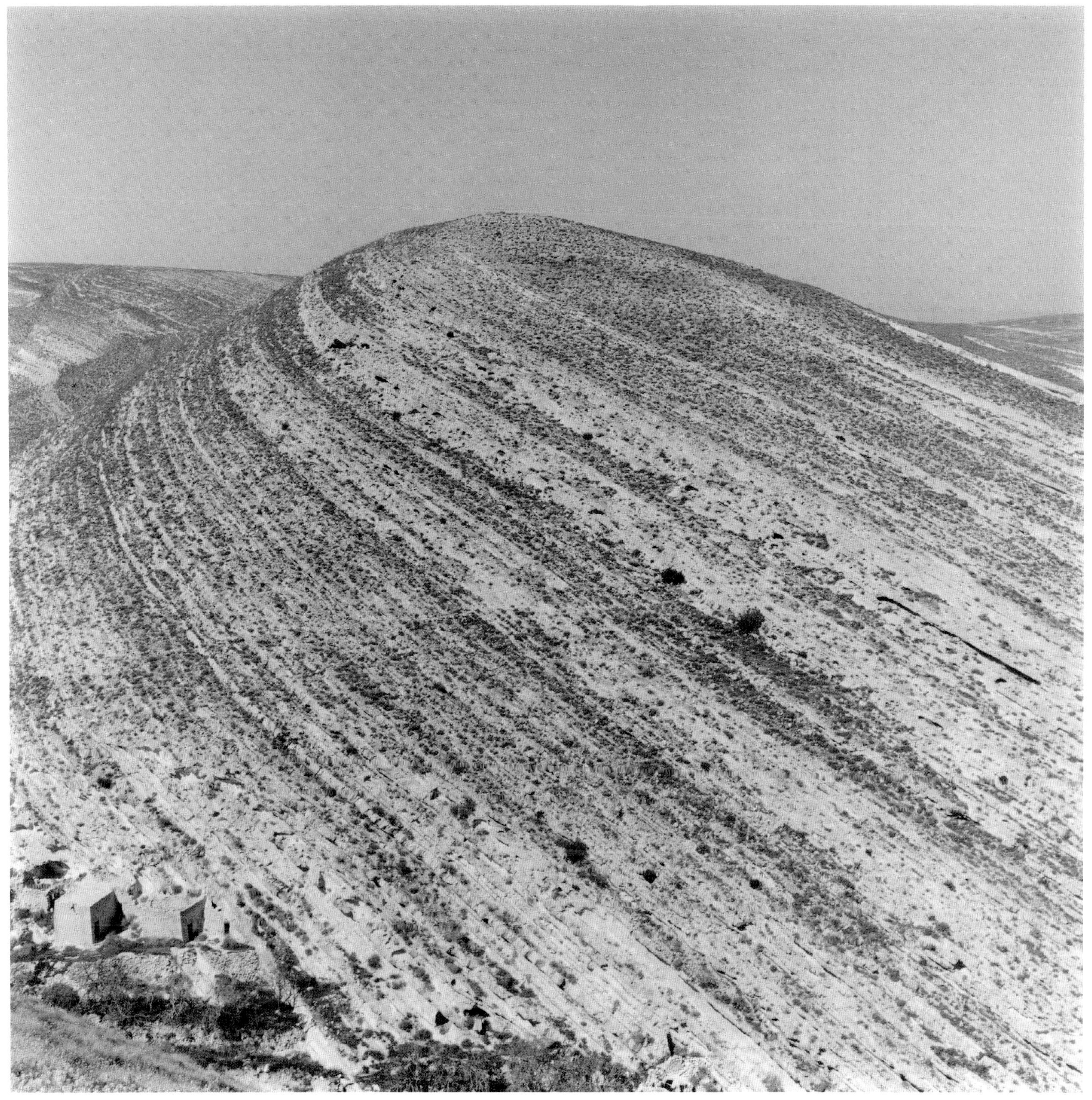

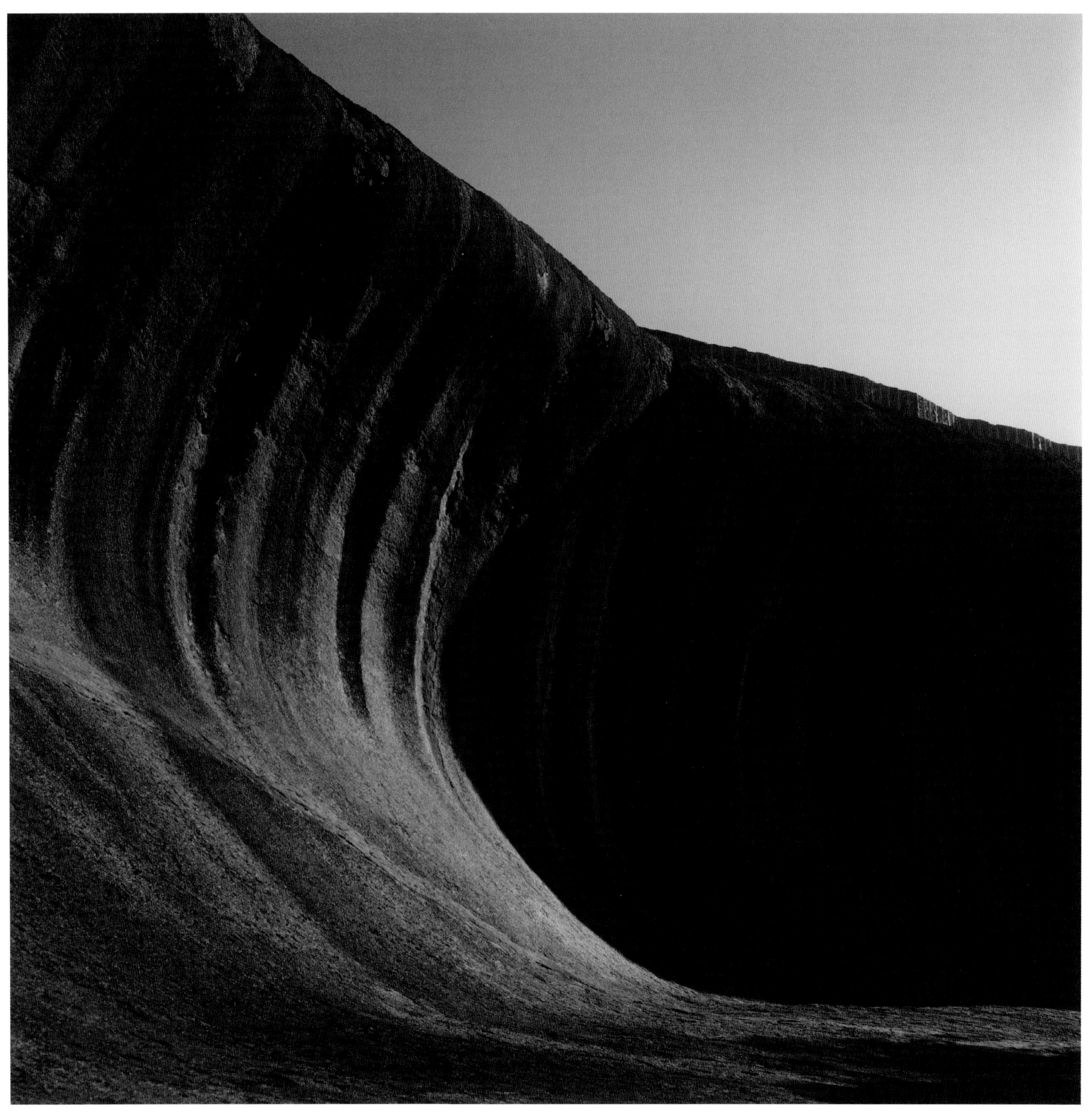

them "to range free over a realm of the imagination which belongs to the Soul of the universe. For it is clear that the Dreaming represents just that: a supreme interworld of archetypal images which themselves partake of the revelation."[24] The beautiful Wave Rock of Western Australia is another granite inselberg formed hundreds of millions of years ago—a testament to pure flow in as solid a form as you could find.

The Dynamics of Flow

Austrian naturalist Viktor Schauberger (1885–1958) was a pioneer in the study of the form and movement of subtle energies in nature, specifically the movements of water. His discoveries directly challenged the perceived thinking about how we utilize, control, and move water, both in nature and in our bodies. His primary finding concerned the shape of the rivers and streams that usher water around our planet, as well as the dynamics of this movement and their effect on our bodies. Much of his work involved how water moves through riverbeds and streambeds and the patterns that this motion creates.

Schauberger's thinking was that all life is in motion, and yet this movement is rarely, if ever, in straight lines. Rather, the movements of nature tend to be spirals or spiraling vortexes, like the shape of spiral galaxies, the movements of planets around their suns, the spirals of sunflower seeds within the flower, and the position of branches as they spiral around a stem. Spiral movements can be confined to one plane or may move between planes, like the double helix of the DNA molecule. The movement of gases, water, turbulent air, water vapor, and even blood, follows these spiral paths.

What is true in the physical, visible world is also true in the invisible world, and thus electromagnetic, electrical, and even atomic energies also move in spiral patterns, following what Schauberger called "cosmic breathing."[25] For example, as water flows along a streambed, with its continual s-bends, at each bend the water molecules spin around. Through left-hand bends, the water spins in a counterclockwise direction, and then through a right-hand bend, in a clockwise direction. This gives water molecules a perfectly spherical shape, and the spiraling energies provide water with exceptional buoyancy and purity, including the ability to cleanse itself and carry nutrients to plants and animals. He realized that when water passes through pipes with right-angle bends—as is the case for water delivery in virtually all buildings and homes—the water molecules crash against the right-angle bends and the molecules become broken and toxic, losing their nutritional and energetic qualities. The water becomes essentially damaging instead of life-giving. This affects our health in profound ways, and most of us are entirely unaware of the phenomenon.

The spiral movement of water in streambeds also creates and maintains many layers of water vortexes at different temperatures, which in turn energizes the water and enables the molecules to carry

OPPOSITE: Wave Rock, Hayden, Western Australia, 1991

the healthy minerals that they absorb along their winding paths. In line with his theory, Schauberger even created special vortex filters that purified water without the water passing through a screen of any kind, as he believed that such a screen breaks down the integrity of the spherical water molecule. Recent work by Japanese scientist Masaru Emoto supports Schauberger's ideas.[26] Photographing spring water with an electron microscope, Emoto discovered a crystalline structure that reflects the purity and healing power of the molecules. The shape and purity of such crystals were also found to reflect not only environmental quality, but also emotions and thoughts. The purest water is formed when the water is either blessed or taken from a holy well or fountain. When water is damaged or impure, the energies of the water shoot out from the molecule in a jagged and fractured form, in contrast to the regular, geometric, or spherical form of pure water. Thus, the structure of water seems to echo not only what is in it, but also what is around it.

Where the wandering water gushes
From the hills above Glen-Car,
In pools among the rushes
That scare could bathe a star,
We seek for slumbering trout
And whispering in their ears
Give them unquiet dreams;
Leaning softly out
From ferns that drop their tears
Over the young streams.
Come away, O human child!
To the waters and the wild
With a faery, hand in hand,
For the world's more full of weeping than you can understand.

—W. B. Yeats, "The Stolen Child" (1889)[27]

The intimate and profound interconnections between humanity and water show us that flow is as essential to us as it is to our planet. Water all over the earth rises and falls in rhythm with the moon and tides, and these rhythms affect us profoundly, as well. In this sense, sacred wells, rivers, lakes, and oceans are repositories for the memory and energy of all of humanity.

OPPOSITE: The Great Enclosure at Great Zimbabwe National Monument, Zimbabwe, 1998

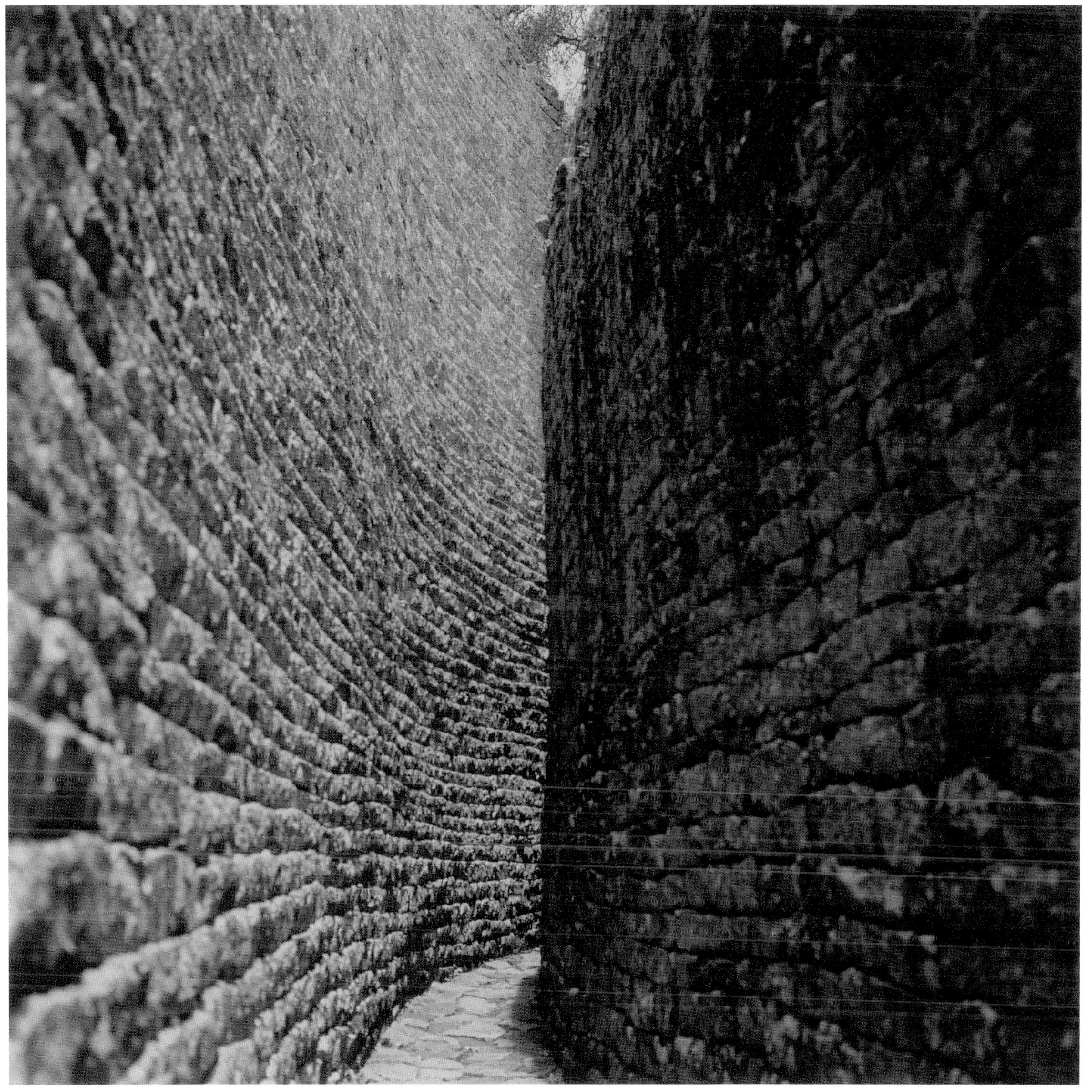

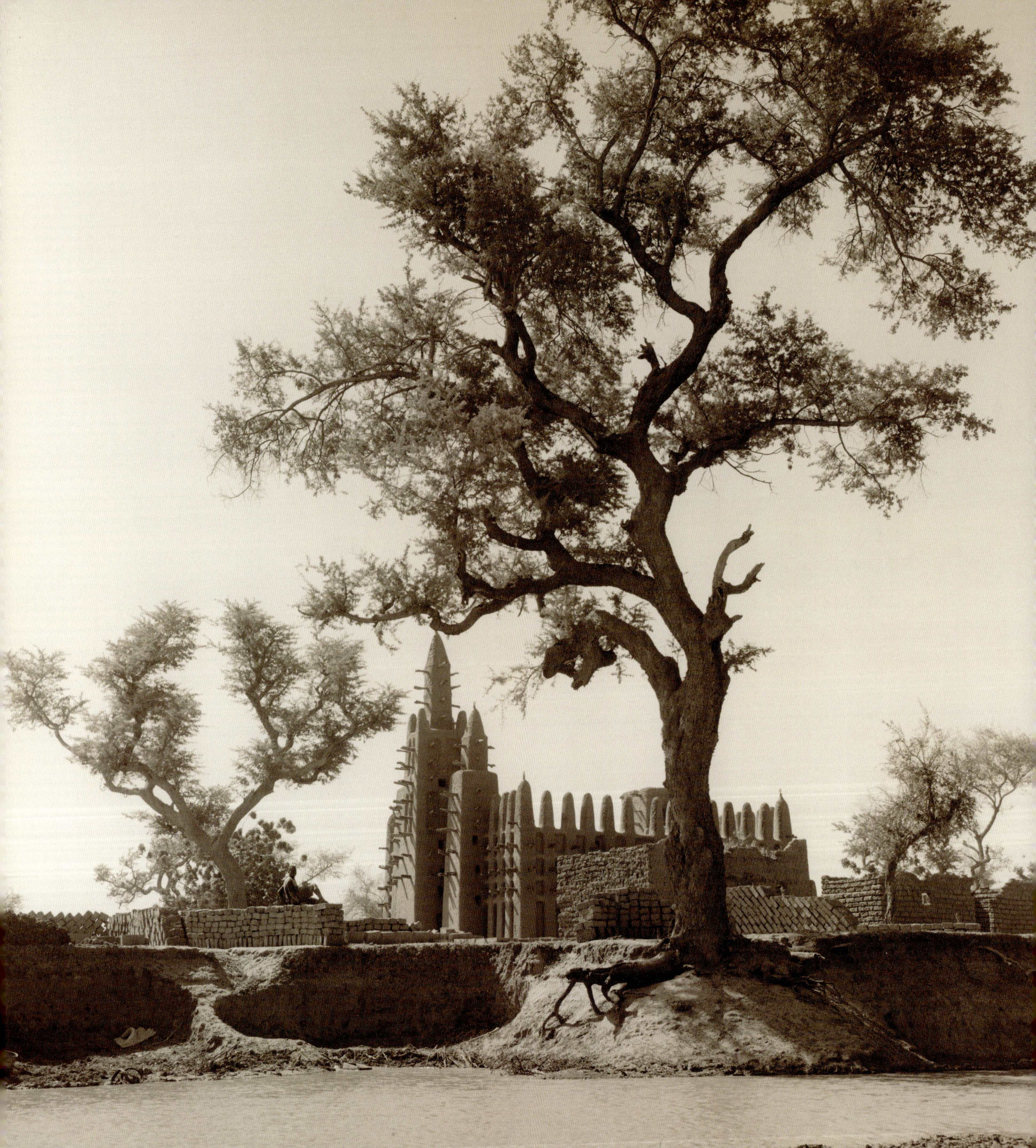

CHAPTER 6

World Tree, Cosmic Axis

Then, in one moment, she put forth the charm
Of woven paces and of waving hands,
And in the hollow oak he lay as dead,
And lost to life and use and name and fame.
Then crying "I have made his glory mine,"
And shrieking out "O fool!" the harlot leapt
Adown the forest, and the thicket closed
Behind her, and the forest echoed "fool."

—Alfred, Lord Tennyson, *Merlin and Vivien* (1859)[1]

We tend to underestimate the great tangible value trees have for the world, even as they provide us with houses, books, furniture, ships to sail the oceans, implements to work in the fields or garden, axe handles, gunstocks, baseball bats, newspapers, and even the very oxygen we breathe. It is therefore not surprising that trees are among the most sacred living things and an essential component of virtually all early creation myths, legends, and folk tales. They inhabit our inner world and unconscious mind simultaneously and are potent symbols of the living contents of the personality and a prototype of the self.[2]

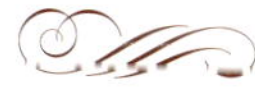

A sacred mountain is considered an axis of the world (*axis mundi*), and trees perform the same function in creation myths. Balancing their visible upper halves with the invisible root systems that hold them firmly in the soil, the leafy canopies symbolically reach up to the heavens as the roots penetrate down into the underworld. Thus, it is not surprising that the mythic "Tree of Life" remains with us today as a powerful esoteric symbol.

The biblical Garden of Eden was centered on two trees: the Tree of Knowledge of Good and Evil and the Tree of Life, the first of which harbored the notorious serpent that tempted Eve into eating the fruit that led to human expulsion from paradise. There are many artistic representations of the seduction

OPPOSITE: Mosque of Djenné, Mali, 1997

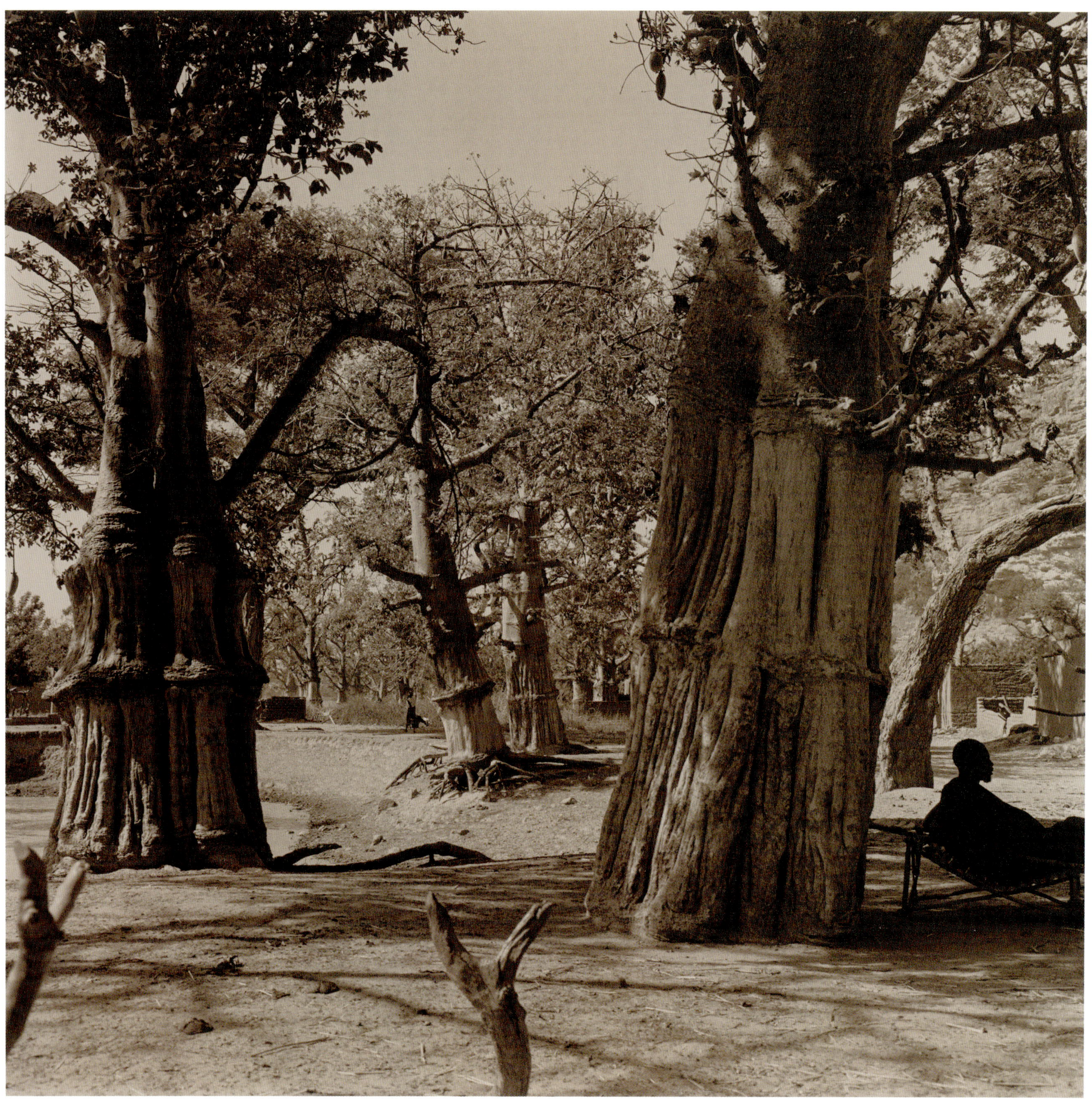

of Eve, and Michelangelo's fresco painting "The Fall" in the Sistine Chapel shows a serpent with a woman's head curling around the Tree of Knowledge. The link between the cold-blooded snake and the female sex is not surprising if you view the biblical story as showing that the twin temptations of women and sexuality are the causes of the fall of humanity. Exploring this connection even further, the story of Adam and Eve is likely the residue of earlier Middle Eastern creation mythologies, in which the serpent or snake is the primary symbol of the great mother and the eternal feminine. As the bearers of life, women were also understood to be responsible for the inevitable death that follows life, and this dual nature of the feminine is nowhere as prominent as in the lineage and understanding of trees.

Buddha and the Tree of Life

There are many significant trees in the life of the Buddha: Prince Gautama was born under a Sorrowless tree (*Saraca indica*) and later attained enlightenment on the banks of the Niranjana River under the Bodhi tree, which the Buddhists call the Tree of Enlightenment.[3] After seven days he went to a banyan tree and resumed his illumination. Finally he found the "Tree of the Serpent King, Muchalinda" as a fierce storm gathered. The cobra god enwrapped him in his coils and protected him with his hood. The banyan tree became known as the Eternal Wisdom Tree, and there are reputedly descendants of this tree at the site today. In this legend, the tree is a powerful symbol because trees enact the yearly cycle from winter barrenness and death to spring growth and resurrection, illustrating the central Buddhist concept of impermanence.

Towns and cities all over the world identify their history and fate with grand trees that seem to have lived forever—trees alive since before the time of Muhammad, Jesus, and the Buddha. Forests of cedar trees in Lebanon that were used to build King Solomon's Temple in the tenth century BCE still exist.[4] In *Ancient Trees* (2002), authors Anna Lewington and Edward Parker discovered nearly one hundred species of trees that are more than a thousand years old, and they speculate that there are probably many more. They report that there is a lime tree in England that is known to be 6,000 years old and a common yew in Scotland that may be 9,000 years old.[5] Colonies of aspen trees in the western United States are unusual in that they share a massive root system and identical genetic structure, making all apparently individual aspen trees technically the same tree. Therefore, a single aspen colony can occupy hundreds of square miles, making it the largest organism alive on our planet.

To many cultures, the sacred tree is a world axis around which the stars and planets circle in the domed vault of the sky. For example, the Lakota regard the World Tree as a sun pillar, sacrificial post,

OPPOSITE: Dogon village, Mali, 1997

and axis mundi. This central pillar, which appears to connect our earthly domain with the Pole Star above, is where the divine energies enter the world for us to partake of them. In Scandinavian mythology, the wondrous Yggdrasil ash tree branches upward toward the heaven of Valhalla, where warriors slain in battle are chosen by the female Valkyries and find rebirth in Asgard, the crown of the great Tree of the Worlds,[6] and the ash tree roots extend deep into Hel (from which we derive our word for this realm), where the three female Fates spin the lives of all living beings. Forming the vertical, central axis that links the underworld with the realms of the humans and heavenly entities, the tree represents the entire cosmos.

In Mayan cosmologies, the World Tree was at the very center of the universe. The underworld below—Xibalba—was darkness and unseen, yet it transposed itself onto the sky above at sunset every night, becoming the firmament. The World Tree, or Wacah Chan ("six sky" or "raised up sky"),[7] linked the heavenly and hellish worlds to the middle plane of human existence. However, this world tree looked like no tree anyone had ever seen because its branches seemed to emerge from double-headed serpents. The Vision Serpent deity was intertwined throughout and around the body of the tree, and the Celestial Bird deity was perched on its apex. To the Maya, the branches of the monstrous tree represented the universe, while the roots of the tree were its rear head. It was therefore the very center of the cosmos and also the primary channel for communication between the upper and lower world.

The Nature Myths of Merlin

In the traditional Arthurian legend, Merlin is treated as a vain old man who is easily seduced by a lovely and scheming enchantress named Vivien (also known as the Lady of the Lake). She charms the sorcerer into teaching her the secrets of natural magic and, once satisfied, extracts from him the ultimate spell, using it to encase him in an oak tree—a Druidic symbol—forever.

However, Merlin is more than a peripheral figure in the legends, since he and many of the other participants have characteristics that are distinctly part of nature and cosmological myths rooted in sacred landscapes. Merlin embodies an age when nature was seen as feminine and in the realm of the goddesses, who grant power to Merlin and other important figures. For example, King Arthur received Excalibur, his magical sword, from the Lady of the Lake and later returned it to her. Merlin's entombment signifies the profound shift that occurred when mother worship passed out of power. As towns and cities developed, patriarchal dominance became the norm in political and social spheres, while nature began to be devalued and ignored. As so frequently occurs, outcasts need and attract each other. In this way, perhaps, those vestiges of female power that had not been usurped by male domination became

OPPOSITE: Temple of Apollo, Didyma, Turkey, 1995

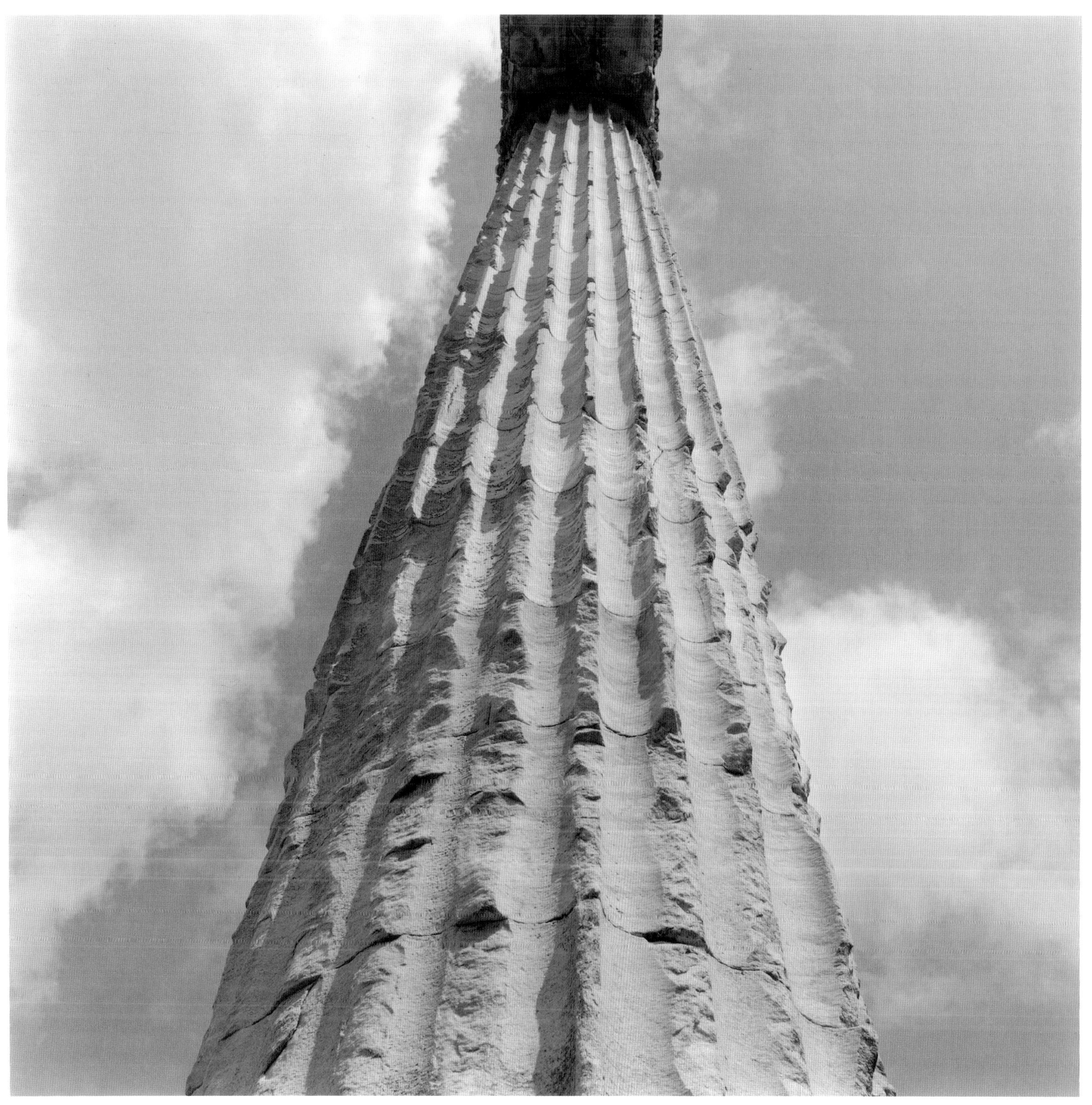

WORLD TREE, COSMIC AXIS

relegated to the increasingly insignificant world of nature. Vivien may seem all-powerful in her triumph over Merlin, but she was consigned to a prison of nature, a world "modern" men no longer respected. The story of Merlin and Vivien depicts the transition from the pagan, "magical" vision of the world to a more rational—but not necessarily healthier—worldview that followed hundreds of years later.

The Arthurian legends are shamanic and deeply mythic, yet years after the historical Arthur lived, his struggle to unify Britain was transformed into "a story of a mystic brotherhood of Christian knights and a chivalric code of pure romantic love."[8] Incidentally, many scholars believe that the Round Table itself was a zodiac embedded in the landscape around the town of Glastonbury, and this was indeed discovered in the 1920s and made public in 1935 by Katherine Maltwood. It is what remains of prehistoric land art so colossal, it can only really be appreciated from the air. Some sources even suggest that this unusual prehistoric earthwork was discovered centuries earlier than this, by the famous Elizabethan scholar and magician Dr. John Dee.[9] While researching the images of an ancient manuscript she was illustrating, Maltwood realized that the area corresponded to the Isle (or Vale) of Avalon mentioned in the adventures of the Round Table knights. This landscape zodiac is a magical area full of sacred symbols, such as the sacred mountain of Glastonbury Tor, a monumental pagan earthwork surmounted by a Christian chapel; Glastonbury Abbey, which is sited, proportioned, and designed based on the *vesica piscis* (two intersecting circles that also represent Christianity); the Chalice Well, a baptismal font and magical spring with a cover displaying another vesica shape; and even the famous Glastonbury Thorn, which, by some legendary accounts, sprouted from Joseph of Arimathea's cane, when he brought certain relics associated with the Holy Grail[10] to England after the Crucifixion and forced the cane into the ground near Glastonbury Abbey. At the Glastonbury site, Joseph founded what is reputed to be the world's first Christian church. Thus, we see that Christian legend, pagan sites, and sacred landscapes are so intimately intertwined that it is nearly impossible to separate them or determine which is dominant. Nevertheless, these mysterious traces are surely emblematic of a passing of ages.

R.J. Stewart wrote two books that were published in 1986 about the mystical life and prophecies of Merlin, with much of the material based on the twelfth-century manuscript *Vita Merlini*, where history, myth, psychology, and legend all combine within the natural landscapes of England and Wales.[11] Merlin was, above all, a dark, wild man of the woods. Trees abound in these works, as symbols for both Merlin and the Druids who inhabited the same territory. Some believe that the character of Merlin (Latinized from "Myrddin") could be based on an ancient figure who was worshipped at Stonehenge as an original sun god,[12] partially because the legends all have a distinctly astrological character and are certainly part of the Druidic cosmology that is a backdrop for the Arthurian legends.

There are many references in the original legends to Merlin riding horses or centaurs. These evoke the sign Sagittarius. The leading of herds of goats echoes the symbolism of Capricorn. Similarly, the women of the Arthurian myths are associated with both Luna, the Roman goddess of the moon, and Venus, the Roman goddess of love.

The Celtic legend of King Arthur is very old, and some versions of it suggest earlier customs of rulers marrying earth goddesses. In fact, the ancient kings of Sumeria could rule only if they married a high priestess, who was considered a vehicle of the goddess.[13] The deeper significance of the romance of King Arthur and Guinevere is alluded to in the medieval poems and stories.[14] Arthur was both born of and married to the goddess of the land, in the form of Guinevere. The name Arthur means "heavenly bear" and the name of his father, Uther Pendragon, means "head of the dragon," both of which refer to the Pole Star. Surrounded by the constellations Ursa Major (the Great Bear), Draco (the dragon), and Alpha Draconis (the head of the dragon), this star is the magical (and astronomical) center of the world and pointer of the Earth's axis. The myth of Arthur's magical succession thus describes the precession of the equinoxes as the position of the North Pole star shifts from the dragon to the bear. We see this again and again in civilizations across the globe; seemingly primitive sacred landscapes are, in reality, sophisticated maps of the Heavens brought down to Earth and sanctified. Like the Angkor temple complexes in Asia that map the Hindu-Buddhist mythological cosmos, astrological maps of Britain, such as the Maltwood Zodiac, are still a source of information and wonder today.

Magical Groves

Around the middle of the first millennium, Roman Catholicism began to spread among Germanic tribes, who assimilated and Christianized their nature gods and goddesses. The Germanic Yule tree and the winter solstice became the Christmas tree and Christmas. Early Germanic myths and stories continued to be told, although they became seen as the historical poetry and old sagas of a prior era instead of spiritual texts.[15] "Both urbanization and Christianization brought about increasing separation and psychic distance from the wilderness world of forests, heaths, and mountains. It was easy for the missionaries to portray those who lived in the country, separated from the social and religious life of the cities, as pagans lacking true religion."[16]

The Druids were among the only inhabitants of Europe who developed their own schools and education, although they were run in the "old ways." In their alphabet, a different tree represented each letter, and the Druids depicted these characters with runes resembling branches of the various trees that could be found in nature. Caesar remarked that the Druids used Greek letters for their formal messages, but a secret runic alphabet for their more sacred or hidden communications. This "Ogham" alphabet was in existence for many hundreds of years.

The worship of the oak tree in groves by the Druids of Wales was a migration of a potent Roman symbol, as the oak tree was sacred to Zeus. The first Olympic Games were a commemoration of Zeus's emasculation of his father, Kronos (time), an act connected with an early oak-king cult that often worshipped within stone circles. Robert Graves, author of *The White Goddess*, argues that the oak cult was incorporated into later barley and wheat cults.[17] In these mysteries, Hercules (the sun)—often referred to as the "green Zeus"—was symbolically cut into twelve pieces and eaten as a Eucharist, or ritual feast celebrating the sun. During the first Olympic Games, the sacred event was a race between fifty priestesses of Hera for the privilege of being the new chief priestess, and near the major city of Corinth, where such celebrations took place, was a stone circle. Thus, we find evidence that tree cults covered most of Europe for millennia.

The Tree of Life

The universal image of the Tree of Life is an alchemical motif as well as a central one in many creation myths, including the biblical account in Genesis of the Garden of Eden. In some alchemical manuscripts, the tree is shown inverted, with its branches penetrating the earth. Sometimes the tree represents the pagan god Mercurius. According to alchemist Basil Valentine, the apple tree's sap reputedly has magical, regenerative properties that compare with the properties of human blood, and whoever eats its fruit never goes hungry.

In the Jewish alchemical tradition, the Tree of Life is described as a "golden tree with seven branches," each putting forth blossoms. These seven branches may have astrological significance, representing the seven planets of ancient astrology that lend their names to many alchemical substances, figures, and processes. The golden branches may also correspond to the seven major chakras, or energy vortices in the body.[18] In early Middle Eastern iconography, there were many tree goddesses who possessed extraordinary power, and indeed they are often represented as having women's bodies or, as in Michelangelo's depiction of the guardian of the Tree of Knowledge in the Sistine Chapel, as a serpent wrapped around a tree.

These tree goddesses were potent and had a powerful hold on the spiritual imagination of the ancient world. Astarte and Ishtar, the tree goddesses of the early Semites, were worshipped in sacred

OPPOSITE: The Temple of Olympian Zeus, Athens, Greece, 2008

PAGE 112: Temple of Athena, Delphi, Greece, 2008

PAGE 113: The Porch of the Caryatids, Erechtheion (end of fifth century BCE), Athens, Greece, 2008

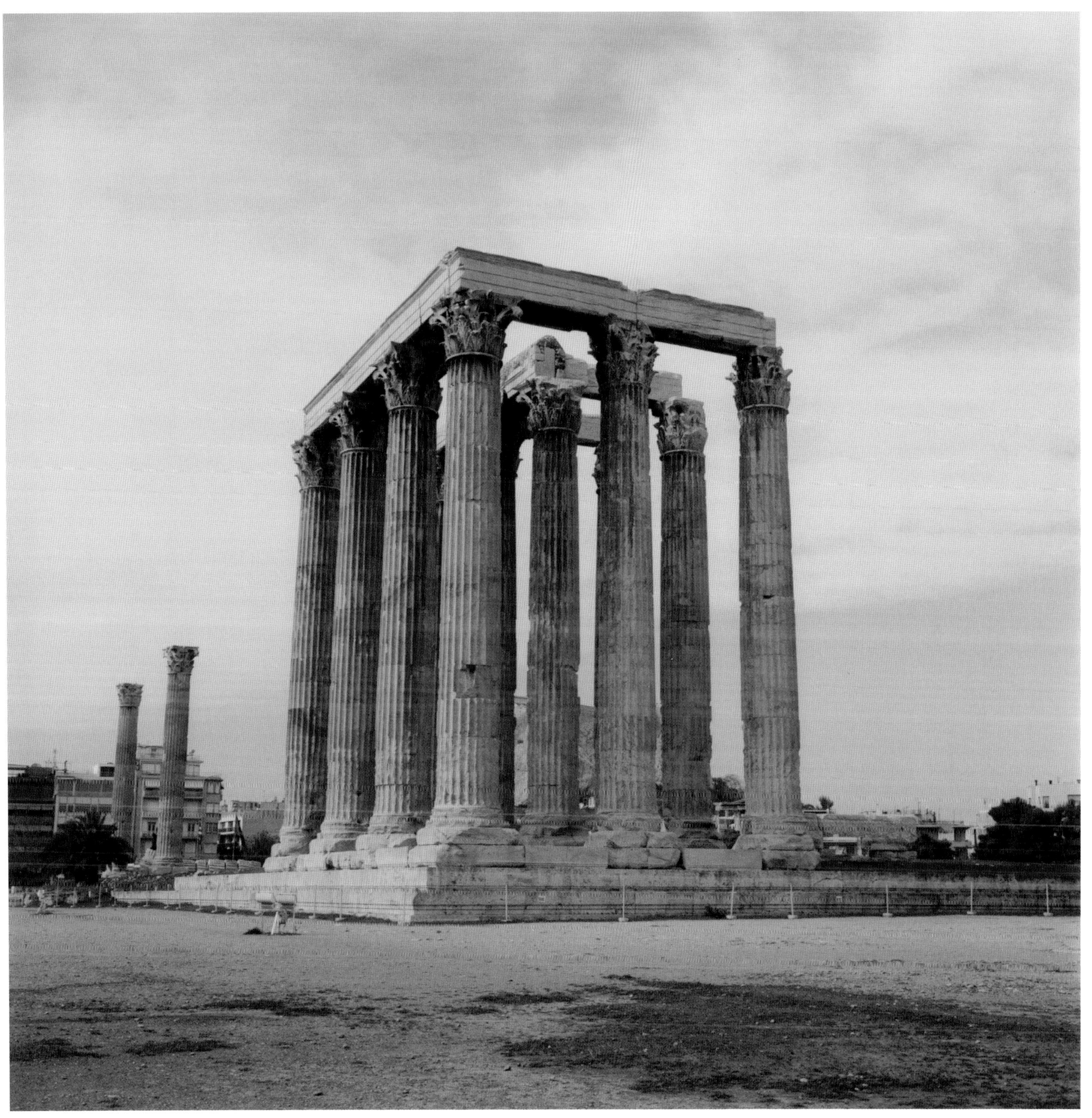

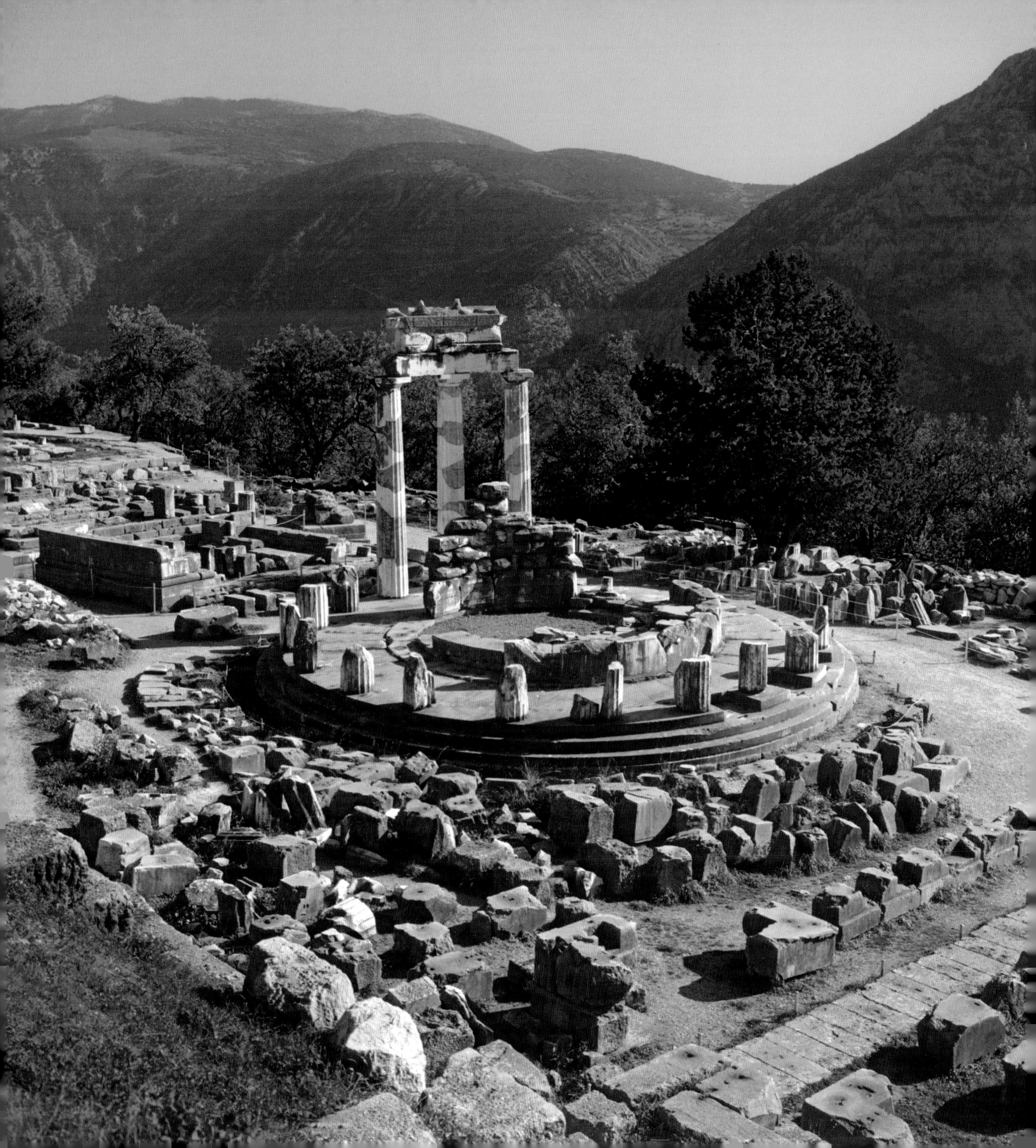

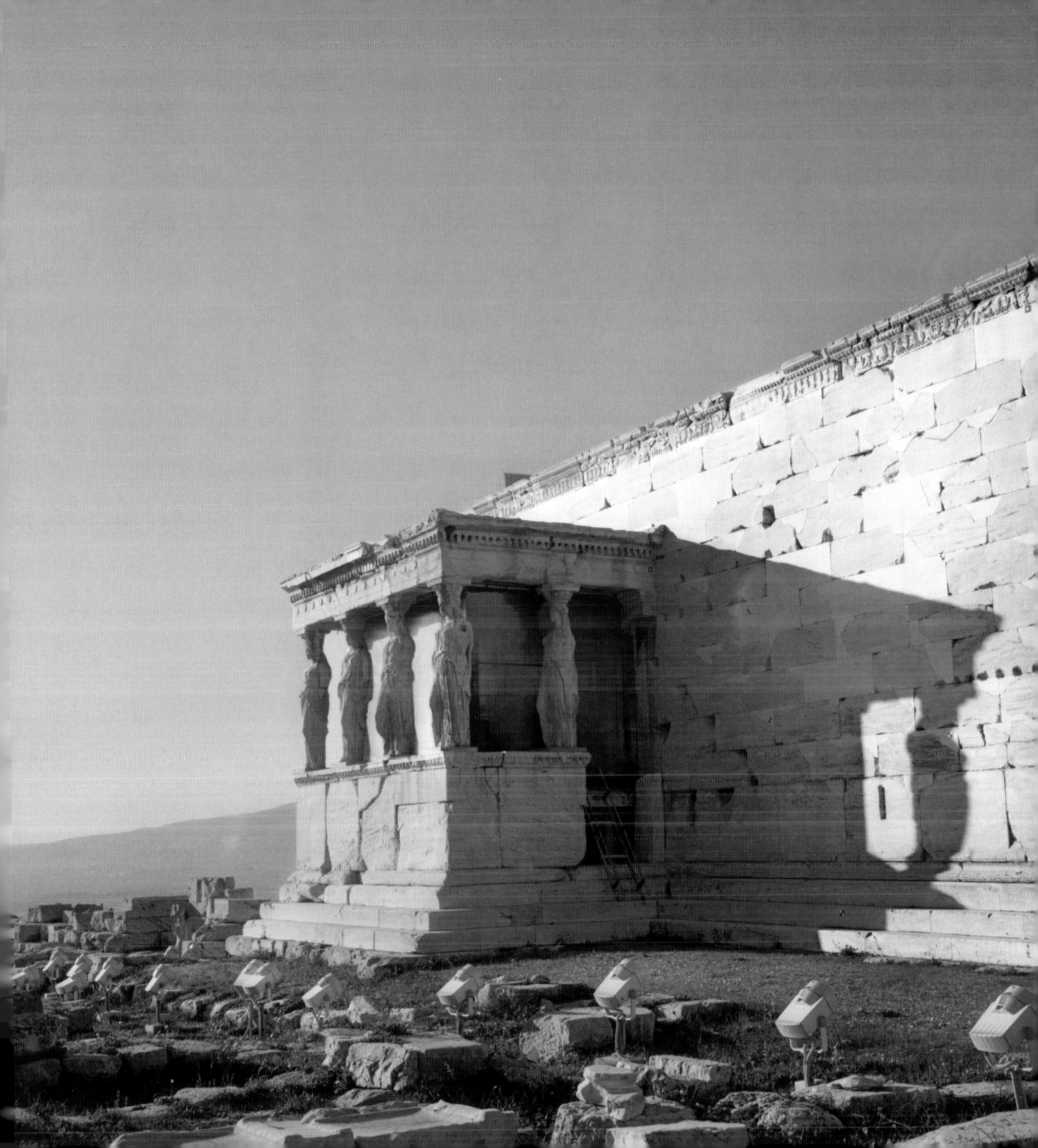

groves, paying special homage to the acacia tree.[19] The Hebrew Bible illustrates the ongoing battles between the newer, patriarchal beliefs and the prior, matriarchal tree goddess cults, which often re-emerged during times of hardship or strife. Many view this schism as the primal seed that led Western civilization to eventually turn away from the realm of the sacred feminine landscape, regarding it as the immoral domain of wanton goddess worship.

Gather the fruits, for the fruit of this tree led us into the darkness and through the darkness.

—Pseudo-Aristotle, *Theatrum Chemicum Britannicum V* (c. 1660)[20]

Noting the central significance of the sacred tree to Native American belief, Sioux chief Black Elk explained the symbolism of one of their most important rituals, the Sun Dance: "The circle helps us to remember the Great Spirit, who, like the circle, has no end. There is much power in the circle . . . In setting up the Sun Dance lodge, we are really making the universe in likeness . . . each of the posts around the lodge represents some particular object of creation, and the one tree at the center, upon which the twenty-eight poles rest, is the Great Spirit, who is the center of everything."[21] The central pole from the cottonwood tree in the teepee represents the Tree of Life and is also a sun pillar that "rises from the altar of the navel of the earth, penetrates the world door and branches out above the roof of the world."[22] When the Sioux enter the sacred circle, they access the axis of the world and accomplish a renewal.

The sacred tree symbolizes the world axis that connects heaven and earth, yet it is much more than that. Its antiquity means that cultures all over the world and throughout history integrated the sacred tree into their belief systems and religions as places of worship and shelter. Trees served as a source of fuel and a material from which to make practical objects, weapons, and sacred ritual objects. Justly, the tree is a primary symbol of the sacred in nature.

OPPOSITE: Saanaheit Pole, Sitka National Historical Park, Alaska, United States, 1999

PAGE 116: The Nympheum, Hadrian's Villa, Tivoli, Italy, 1993

PAGE 117: Tetrapylon, Palmyra, Syria, 1995

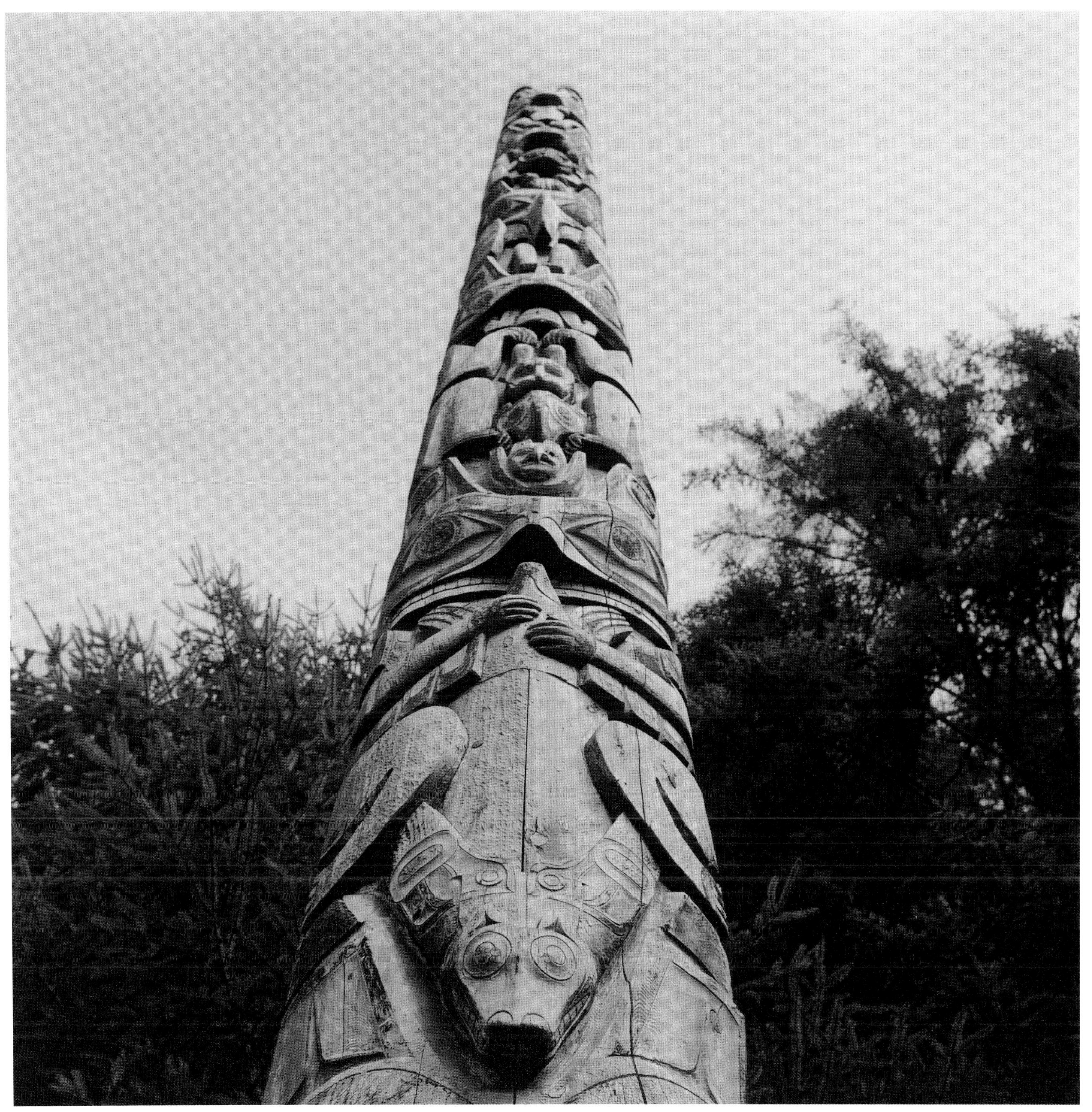

WORLD TREE, COSMIC AXIS

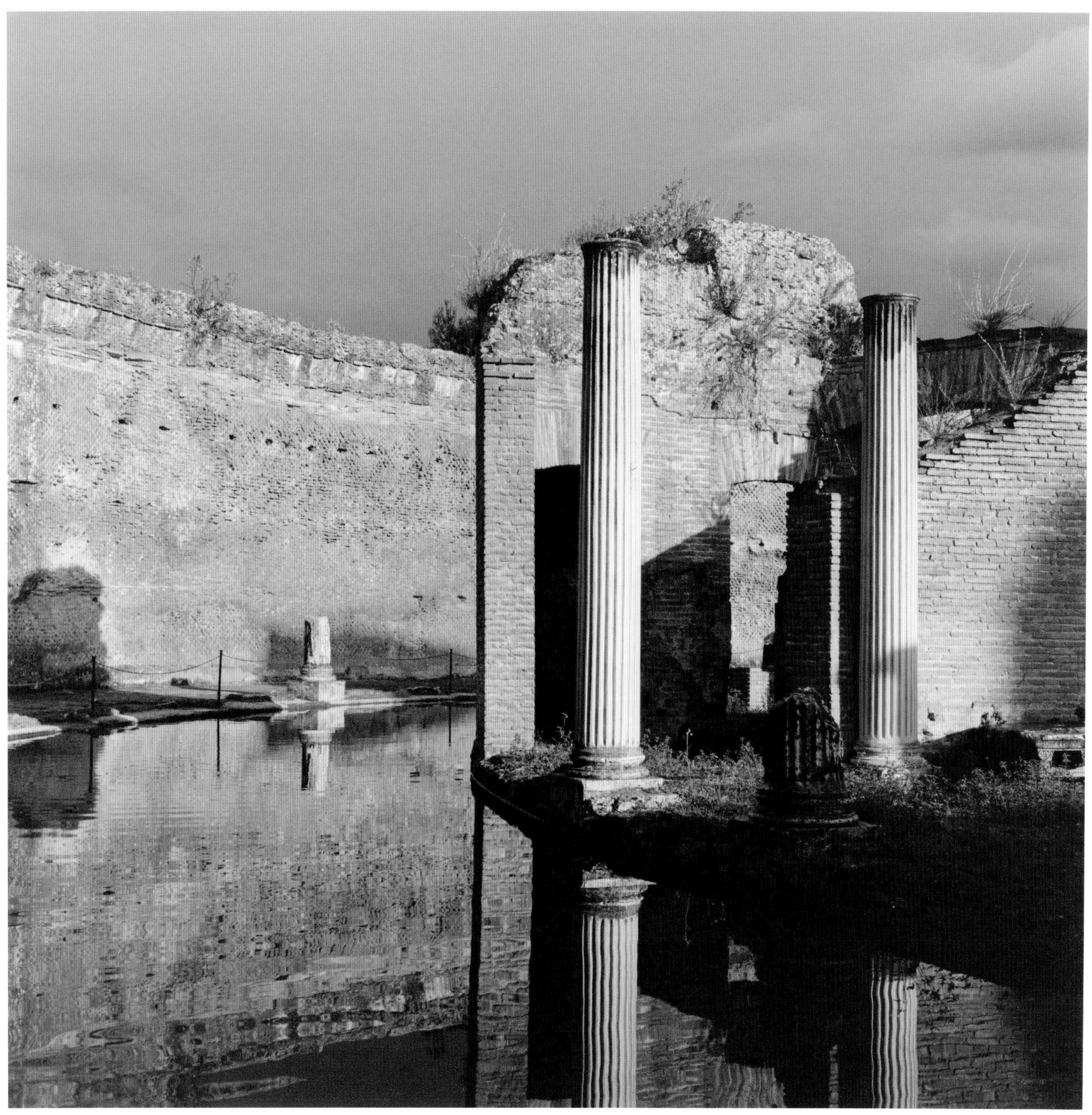

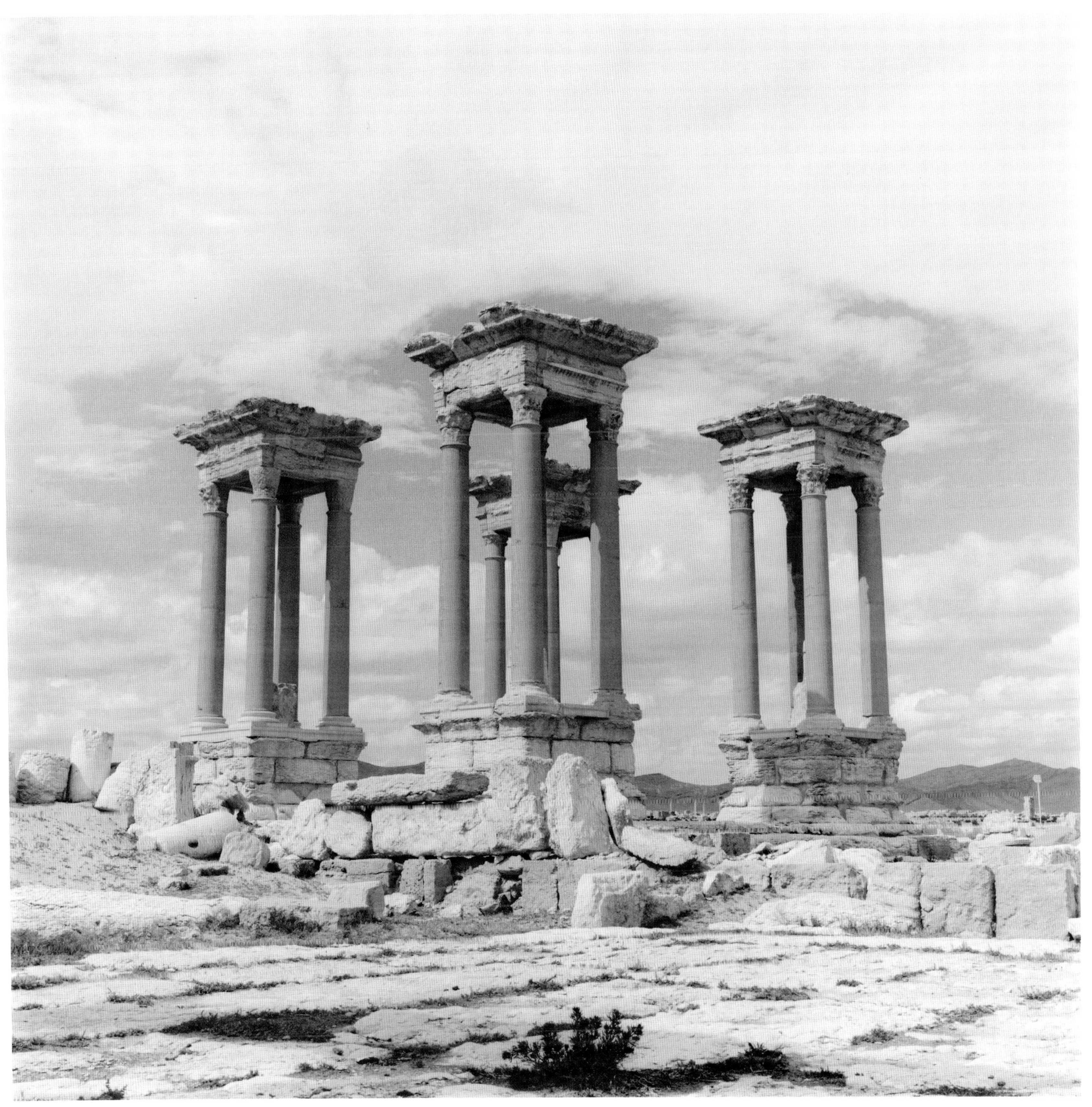

CHAPTER 7

The Elements

The altar cell was a dome low-lit
And a veil hung in the midst of it;
At the pole points of its circling girth,
Four symbols stood of the world's first birth,
Air and water and fire and earth.

~Dante Gabriel Rossetti, *Rose Mary* (1881)[1]

The classical elements are Fire, Water, Earth, and Air, which are joined in Chinese philosophy with Wood and Metal (in place of Air). They are considered aspects or powers inherent in the nature of the physical world, rather than what we now know as the elements of the periodic table, which are pure chemical substances with unique atomic numbers. Each classical element also has its own vocabulary of qualities, forms, and shapes. Through time, various cultures abstracted, stylized, and represented the elements in their landscapes and buildings: blue tiles represented water, columns were trees, and domes were heaven, for instance, as the universal vocabulary of sacred forms came into existence.

Not only do the elements have obvious forms, but they also have symbolic forms. The upward-pointing triangle is Fire, which replicates the flame and stands for masculine energy. Similarly, the opposite element, Water, is a downward-pointing triangle resembling the vulva, signaling the feminine. The hexagonal Seal of Solomon is the integration of fire (upward) and water (downward), or masculine and feminine. In landscapes, we therefore see the elements represented literally and symbolically. We can see that water penetrates down into the underworld of the earth. Likewise, any upward-pointed shapes, such as angular mountains, signal fire. Air is ethereal and vaporous, permeating the domain above and considered magical, because it cannot be seen.

Additionally, air is the essential breath of life, and, indeed, breath was associated with spirit in earlier times. Wood is anything living and generating, producing fruit and symbolizing vitality. Wood also

OPPOSITE: Pagoda, Yangtze River, China, 2001

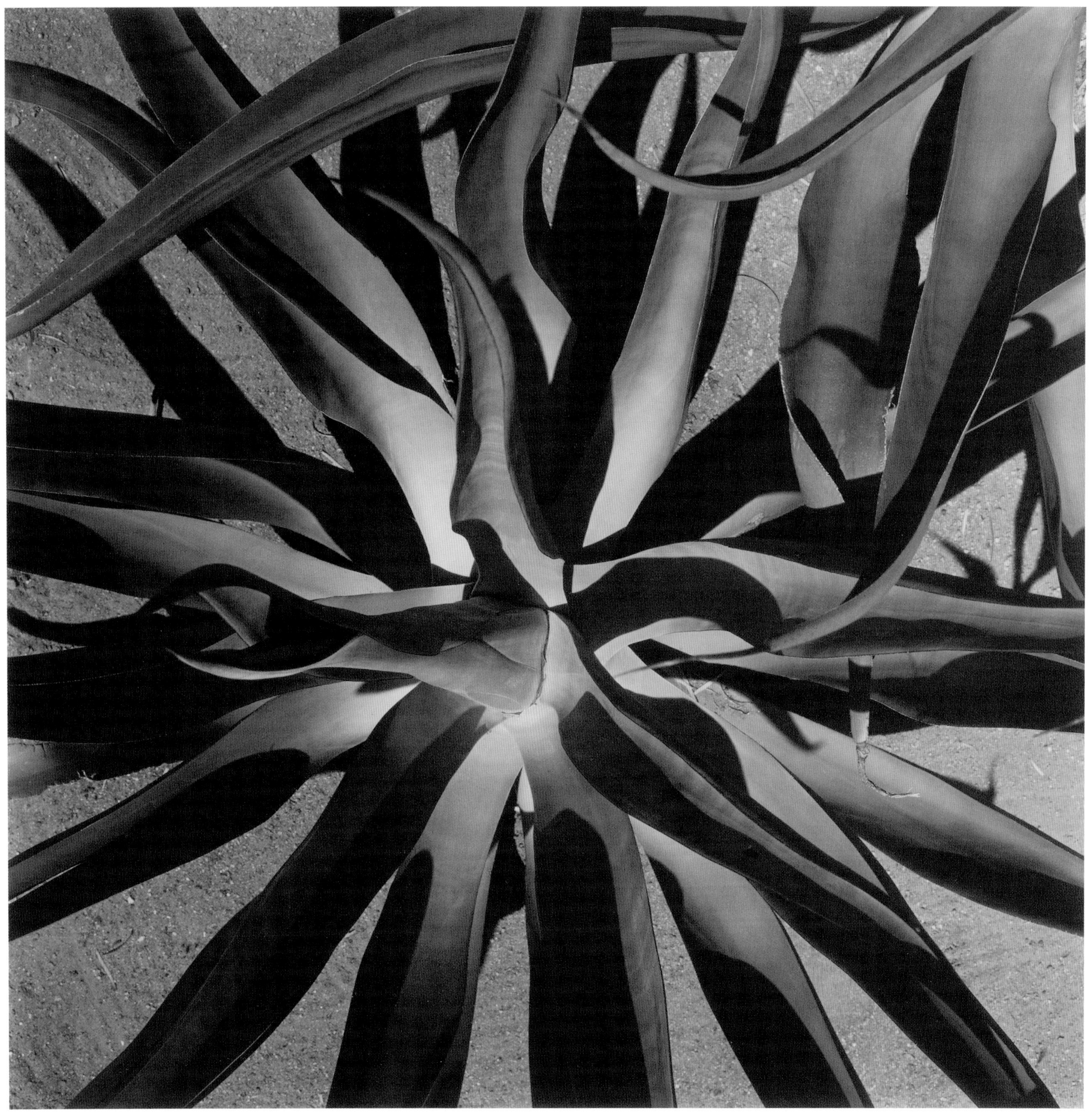

requires the existence of Earth, Air, Fire, and Water. Water and air contain oxygen, carbon, and hydrogen. When combined with the sun's fiery energy, they transform into nutrients through the process of photosynthesis. Metals contained within the minerals in the soil also provide nutrients that are vital to the growth of trees. Similarly, we require that all the elements be in the right balance in order to be healthy.

The four elements common to Western mysticism and the five associated with Chinese geomancy (feng shui) and religion are positioned around the environment and within us psychologically, emotionally, and physically. Sacred places include sites where there is a predominance of one element, where two or more elements meet and interact energetically, or where various elements are in balance. For example, solid earth and flowing water meet at the seacoasts and at mountain springs, while air and earth seem to join atop mountains.

Fire: Magic, Passion, and the Forge of Creation

The element often connected to creation mythologies and also associated with qualities of the world axis is Fire. Fire resonates with the energy and power of the sun. The primary ways earthly element Fire manifests are lightning strikes that ignite forest fires or that burn woodlands, lava emitted from active volcanoes, and bonfires created by humans. One of the primary foundational myths involving fire is that of Prometheus, who, according to Greek mythology, brought fire to humanity by hiding it within the stalk of a fennel plant. In the myth, fire is much more than simply the element that warms, cooks, consumes, and burns; it also includes the symbolic gifts of intelligence and clairvoyance—qualities that make us uniquely human. They are also associated with what are called the mantic arts—astrology and divination. In *Cosmos and Psyche,* Richard Tarnas points out that Prometheus helped Zeus overthrow the dominance of Kronos (time) and then give humanity fire, which he stole from Zeus. This earned Prometheus a place as the wisest of the gods as well as the gift giver of the arts and sciences. In some myths, he is even credited as the creator of humanity.[2] The symbolic actions of Prometheus are acts of passion, especially the securing of humanity's freedom from the power of the gods and the liberation from the dominance of time. He is a catalyst for breakthroughs, fomenter of revolutions, and creative spark of new things. As such, astrologers associate him with the quality of rebelliousness associated with the planet Uranus. The source of the fire Prometheus stole is generally thought to be the volcanic Mount Mosychlos on the island of Lemnos, which was the forge of the blacksmith god Hephaestus.[3] Of course, in the Roman iteration of the equivalent god, Vulcan (hence the term "volcanic"), his forge was within Mount Etna, in Sicily. Curiously, in Greek mythology the women of Lemnos were known for performing

OPPOSITE: Cactus, Tucson, Arizona, United States, 1994

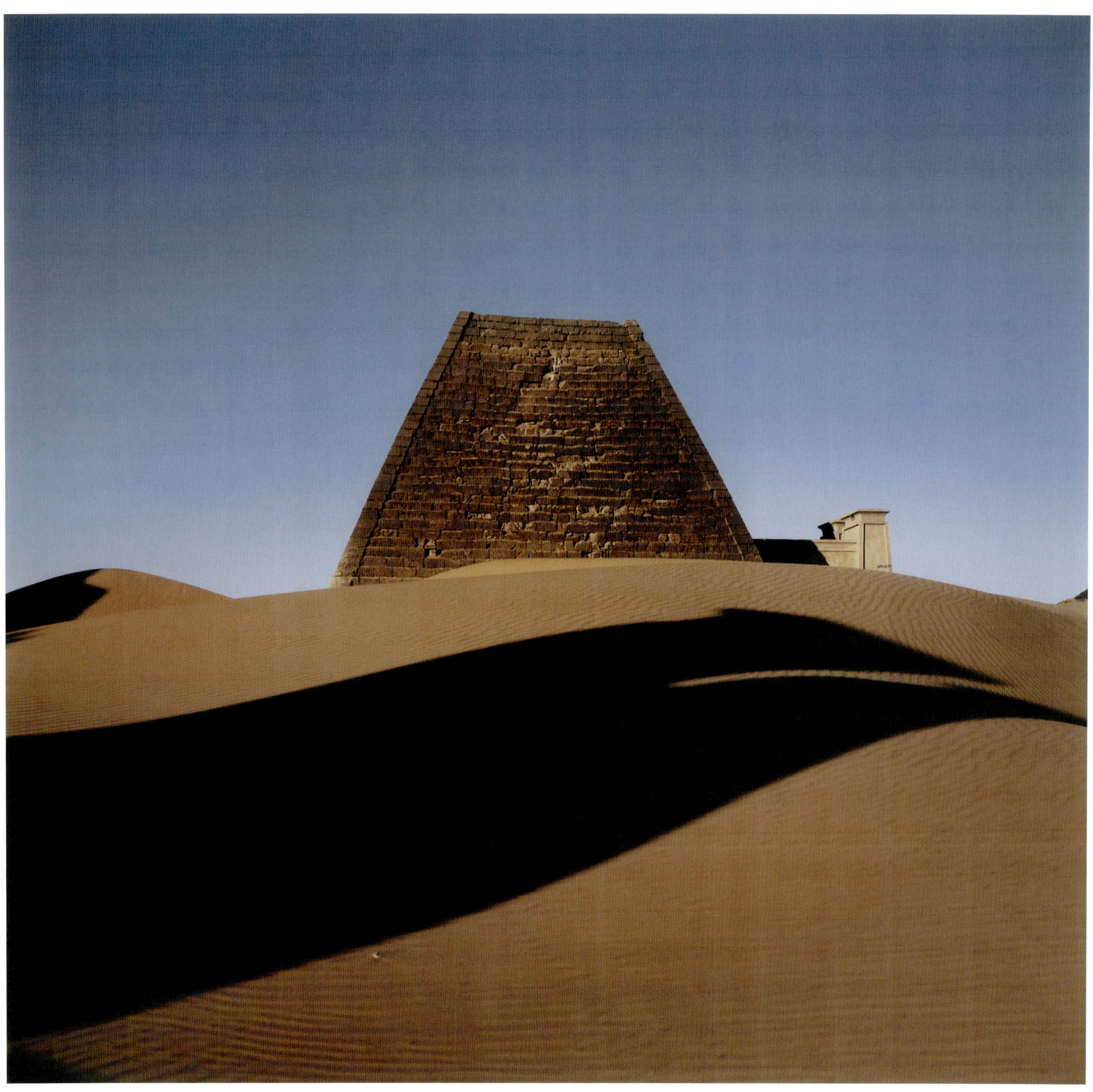

rituals to subterranean deities. Since these rituals often entailed putting out all fires, the sacred fires of Delos needed to be transported back to Lemnos to enable the residents to resume their daily lives.[4]

Associated with the play of different elements in sacred landscapes are various creatures called "elementals." In the fire mythology of Prometheus, the Kabeiroi are twin stewards of the fire within the earth. These dark, dwarfish creatures supposedly made beautiful things out of metals mined from the heart of the earth, and in some mythologies they are thought of as having been sown into the ground like seeds.[5] Prometheus and his brother god Hephaestus were believed to be fathers to the primordial Athenians, which demonstrates, once again, the intimate connection between origin myths and sacred landscapes—in this case, the volcano.

Ethnobotanist R. Gordon Wasson and others point out the presence of the fiery core and nearby magical gardens in these early mountain myths. Examples of such myths include the fate of Prometheus's brother, Atlas, who became the pillar between Heaven and Earth in the garden of the Hesperides and, in a later myth, was transformed into an actual mountain. Another example is Shiva, of Hindu mythology, who allegedly resides on Mount Kailash in the Himalayas, dances the creation and destruction of the world, and bears on his left hand the Fire element that annihilates the body of creation.[6] These mythological axes mundi are magical regions through which sacred, spiritual energies flow upward to heaven and downward to the lower realms. It is as though impulse comes from the patriarchal light or the fire gods above, and true generation from the goddess realms below. Taken together, this composite imagery echoes early beliefs about conception and birth, which were seen as the true mysteries.

The things that are in the realms above
Are also in the realms beneath.
What Heaven shows is often found on earth.
Fire and flowing water are contraries,
Happy is thou if thou canst unite them.

—From the *Twelve Keys of Basil Valentine* (1599)[7]

The Garden of the Hesperides is associated with sunset, as Hesperus is the name of the Evening Star, which is actually the planet Venus as it sets after the sun. Eos (the Morning Star) is the planet Venus when she rises in the morning, preceding the sun, and to make love in the morning hours before sunrise was, therefore, considered a guarantee of fecundity. In many other mythologies we find that the west, where the sun sets, is the sacred land of the dead, while eastern orientations are associated with conception, birth, and the land of the living.

Since archipelagos like the Hawaiian Islands in the Pacific and the Canary Islands in the Atlantic are volcanic in origin, fiery deities are held in very high esteem among their inhabitants. In Hawaiian mythology, the goddess Pele lives within Kilauea, one of the most active volcanoes on earth. Quite naturally, Pele myths typically involve her amazing temper and her sister's continual attempt to suppress

OPPOSITE: Meroë, Sudan, 1998

her fiery expressiveness by pushing her underground. Pele is much like Shiva, in that both are gods of the dance as well as the fire of creation and destruction of worlds.

Indonesians make very practical use of the volcanoes' sacred character—many temples on Bali and Java are built from volcanic stone and solidified ash. Volcanic stone is strong yet light and very porous, making it durable, malleable, and easy to transport. The gigantic Buddhist temple at Borobudur in Eastern Java is entirely made from this material, and it is still a powerful monument twelve hundred years after its creation. This stone evokes fire, smoke, and the black and gray colors that permeate these sacred, tempestuous landscapes. The presence of this material all around the coast of India and at Cambodian temples like Angkor Wat and Angkor Thom provides clues about the vibrant natural histories of South and Southeast Asia.

Unborn and imperishable
Is the original mind
Earth, water, fire and wind
A temporary lodging for the night
Attached to this
Ephemeral burning house
You yourselves light the fire, kindle the flames
In which you're consumed.

—Bankei Yotaku, "Song of the Original Mind" (1653)[8]

Water: Blood of the Earth

Water is an important element in Mayan cosmology as the substance upon which the world floats.[9] In *A Forest of Kings*, authors Schele and Freidel even describe water as the substance in which all actions in the world take place. The Maya also connect water with the mouth of the underworld and, by extension, death and its mysterious processes. It seems the soul flowed into the underworld at death through this watery gateway.

The Maya were geniuses in harnessing water, constructing a network of stone waterways that provided every house with flowing, pure, and clean water. They also understood that water was the lifeblood of all humanity, and the glyphs for water and blood are very similar, both with circular and spiraling curlicues alternating in bands with straight parallel lines. These glyphs demonstrate the Maya's awareness that the placid surface of water often masks its active nature, as in the flow of tides beneath a deceptively still ocean. In this sense, the way the Maya pictorially represent water corresponds to the later discoveries of Austrian naturalist Viktor Schauberger, who noted that the movements of

OPPOSITE: Rock wall, Zion National Park, Utah, United States, 1991

PAGE 126: Northumberland Strait, Gulf of Saint Lawrence, Canada, 1994

PAGE 127: Victoria Falls, Zimbabwe, 1998

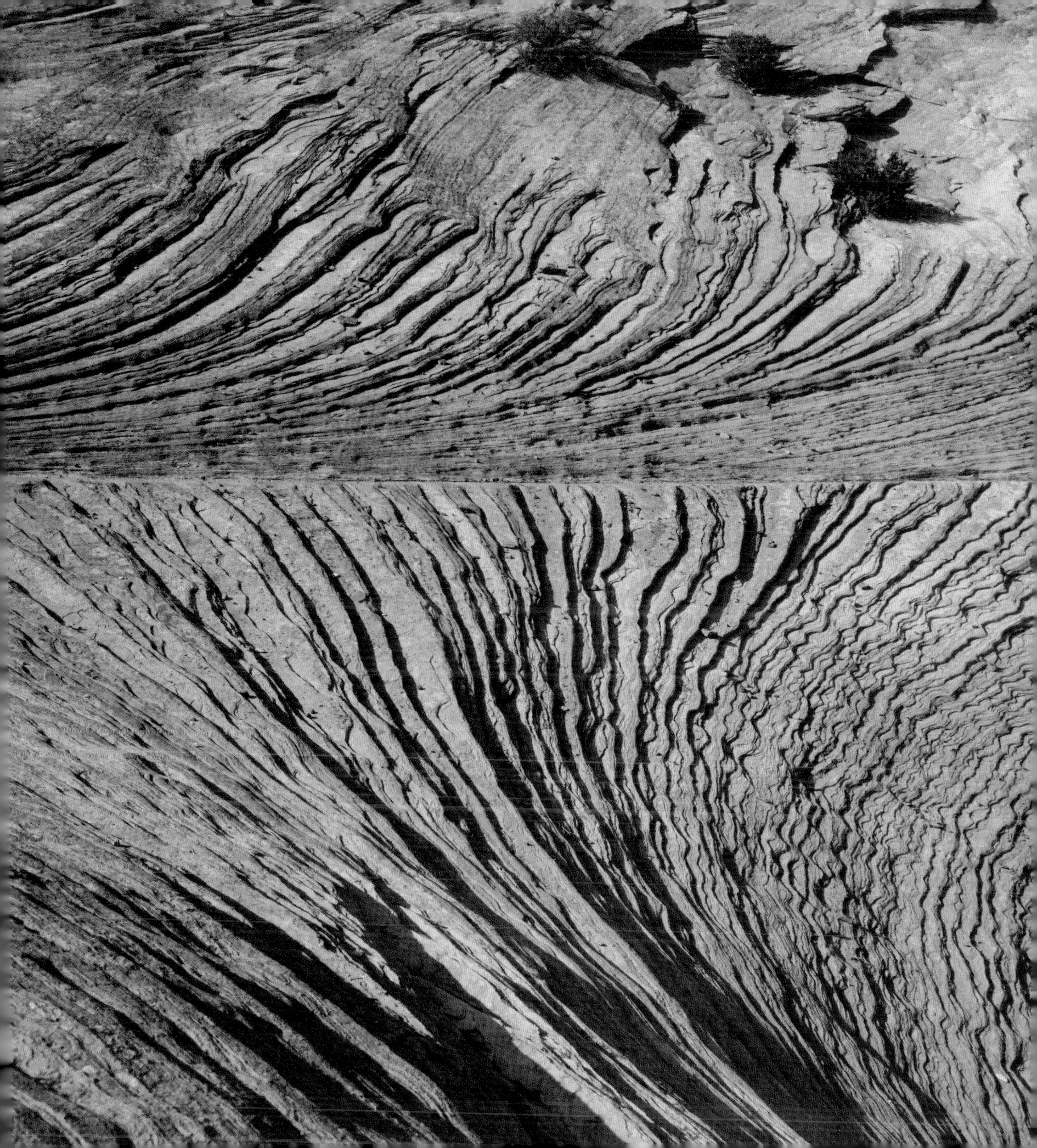

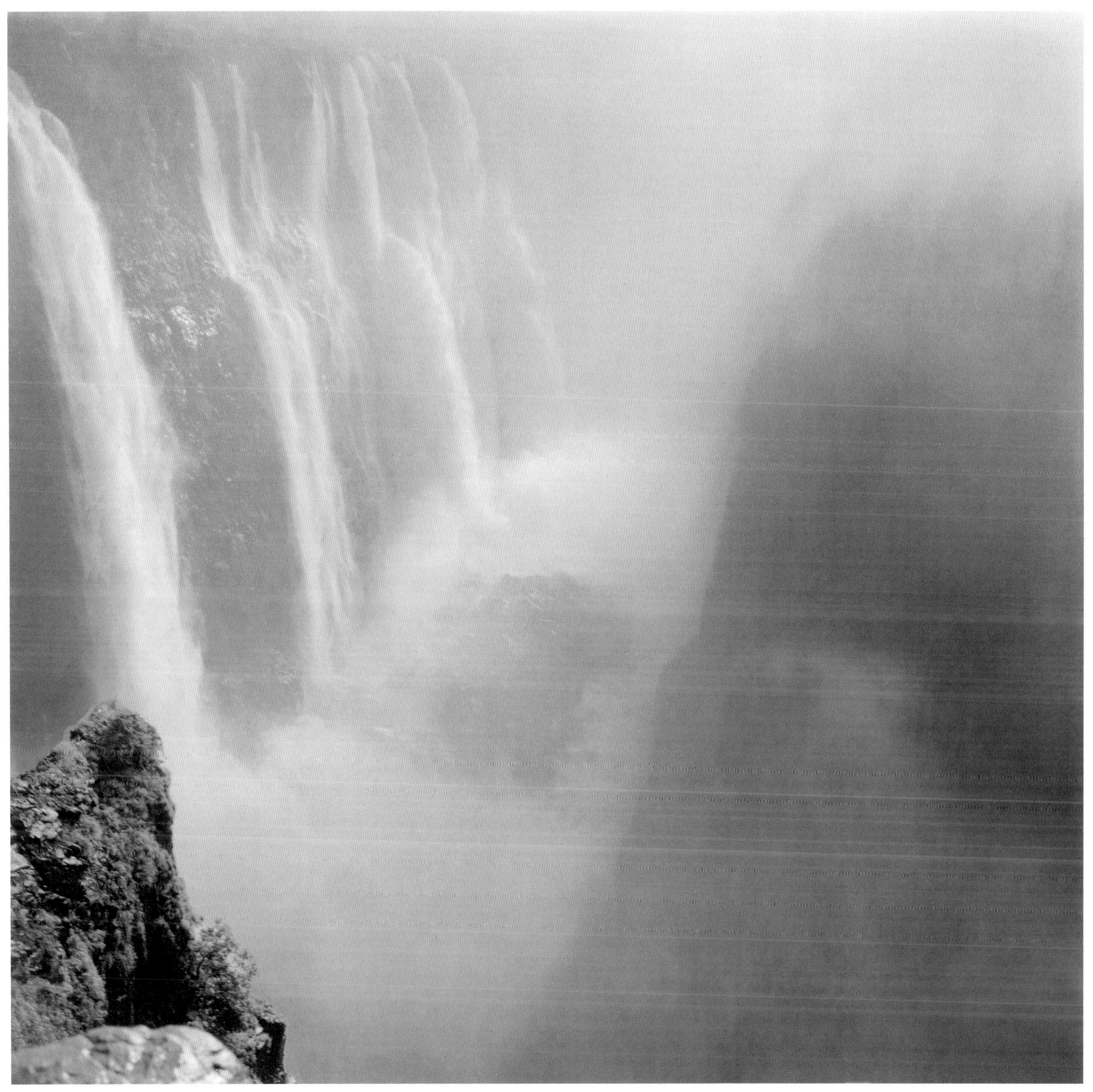

nature—particularly fluids and gases—resemble spiraling galaxies. Thus, these "primitive" Mesoamerican beliefs about water recur in modern scientific theories.

Earth and Stone: Foundations, Permanence, and the Hub of Life

The element Earth carries and symbolizes all that is solid, unchangeable, stable, and permanent in our world. Earth signifies the unmoving center, provides the foundation for our buildings, and stands for our body—the ultimate ground for our actions and life. According to a Pacific Northwest Okanogan Native American creation story, creator-goddess Old One fashioned the earth out of a woman:

> You will be the mother of all people, he said. Earth is alive yet, but she has been changed. The soil is her flesh, the rocks are her bones, the wind is her breath, trees and grass are her hair. She lives spread out, and we live on her. When she moves, we have an earthquake.[10]

Magnificent stones at places like Stonehenge, the Great Pyramid, and Machu Picchu evoke great reverence, and, indeed, the stone serves as the foundation of many sacred landscapes. One sees important stones in Japanese Zen gardens representing the Buddha, in Neolithic landscapes of northern Europe, and in Viking burial sites along the coasts of Scandinavia.

The brilliant psychologist Carl Jung found that stone was so central to his life that he often spent days carving stone at his second home called Bollingen, down the lake from Küsnacht, Switzerland. Bollingen, which Jung himself constructed entirely out of stone found in the local area, was sited at a rocky place by the lakeshore where he would often sit and meditate. Construction began near the time of his mother's death and was finished a year after his wife's death, thirty-three years later. Jung considered Bollingen a shrine to his inner guide, Philemon, a winged spirit based on a Hellenistic figure who, according to Ovid's *Metamorphoses*, hosted the gods during "a ruthless and godforsaken age."[11] Reflecting on the importance of his private place, he remarked, "Without my piece of earth, my life's work would not have come into being."[12]

Jung found a cubic stone at one point, carved faces in it, and then placed it in a special spot in his garden. Likening this sacred stone to a world navel, or gateway to a timeless realm of origins, he wrote, "the air around the stone is filled with harmonies and disharmonies, with memories of time long ago. Of vistas into the dim future with reverberations of a faraway, yet so-called real world into which the stone has fallen out of nowhere."[13] To Jung, the stone not only represented the magical, alchemical stone, but also a vessel containing traces of a bygone age that echo within us and imprint themselves on our collective unconscious, reminding us of the great mysteries that continue to guide our psychological development.

OPPOSITE: Machu Picchu stones, Peru, 2000

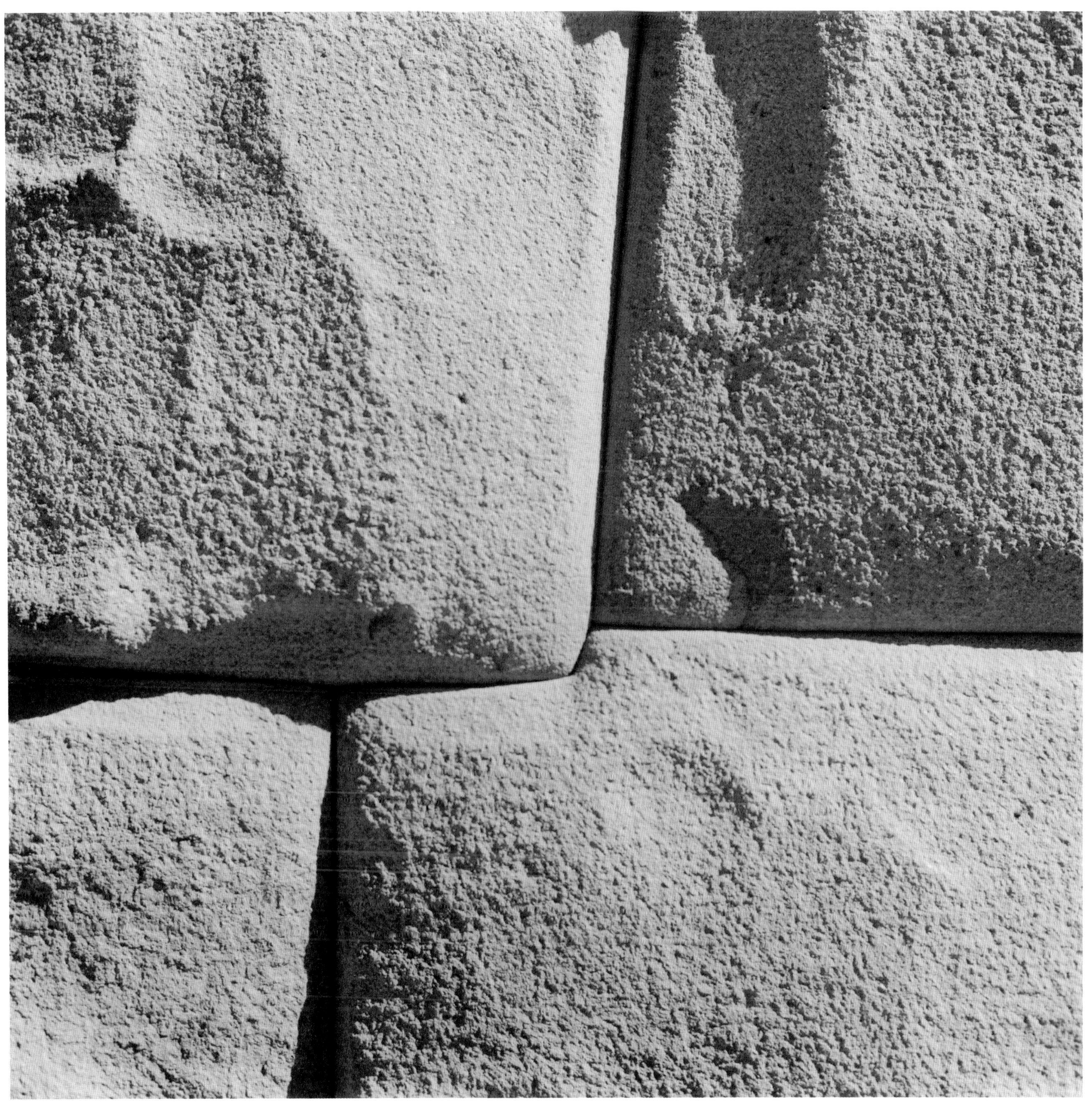

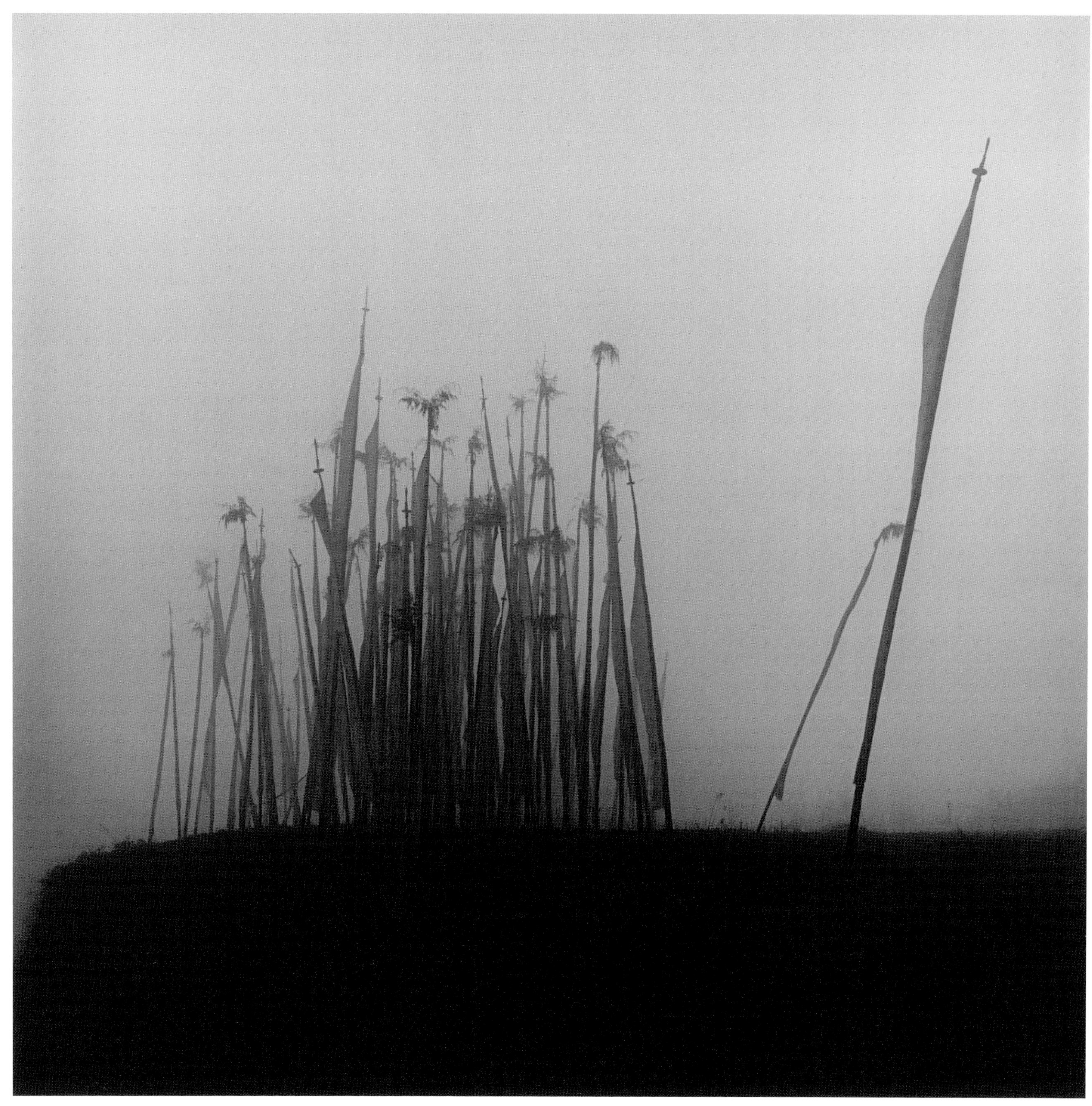

Just as we engrave messages in stone on graves and monuments, so the quality and endurance of earth and stone remind us of the impermanence of our own lives. This may be why stone monuments such as the city of Machu Picchu and the pyramids of Egypt evoke ancient energies, reminding us of ages long past and of mysterious civilizations of which only traces remain.

Air and Sky: The Celestial Backdrop

Air is a mysterious, invisible, and ubiquitous element and the original ceiling for sacred places was the sky. The movements and illuminations of the sky were the eternal backdrop for many early altars and sacred sites, so it was natural to replicate this celestial hemisphere on the interiors of subsequent sacred monuments. It is even believed that the inner surfaces of the early Hebrew temples—tents that were movable and that traveled with their nomadic worshippers—were decorated with stars and images of dark heavens.[14]

Sky is a ceiling, dome, and vault. Since the sky—particularly the night sky—was originally seen as a solid shape, we naturally find domed ceilings and star patterns in many of the great European cathedrals, in mosques such as the Hagia Sophia in Istanbul, and in temples in China, India, Tibet, and Southeast Asia. At Borobudur in Java, carved panels depict the seven stars, or the seven planets, together with the Buddha. In ancient Egypt, sky took the form of barrel vaults with magnificent starry heavens. On the ceiling at Dendera, a temple to lunar goddess Hathor, whose image is a cow with horns resembling the moon's crescents, was a complete star map of the heavens. This map now resides in Paris at the Louvre. One of the most beautiful and highly symbolic images of Egypt is that of sky goddess Nut, whose long, arching body is shown against a field of stars. Carved representations of Nut show within her arched body glyphs and symbols depicting the Egyptian view of creation, which indeed happened under the guidance of these stars.[15] Similarly in Greece, many temple ceilings were decorated with stars and heavenly signs in concave coffers. Even now, in many cultures humans are believed to rejoin the stars at death, and it was common practice in ancient times to decorate the top of coffins with star patterns, so that one would lie under the stars for eternity.

Wood: The Totemic Element

As noted previously, Wood is one of the five elements in Chinese philosophy. This element is ubiquitous: furniture, books, and newspapers are just a few of the many products made from it. Besides signifying generation and the life force, it is a carrier of creativity.[16] Wooden totem poles celebrate the various

OPPOSITE: Prayer flags in the mist, Bhutan, 1992

animal deities of Native Americans in the Pacific Northwest, as their environment teems with gigantic cedar trees and other species. The images carved into the totem poles carry stories, legends, and myths of creation—both tribal and individual—and chiefs have their own poles that identify their animal clans and trace their family histories. These magnificent wooden sculptures represent the axis mundi and are roughly equivalent in meaning to the tent poles of the Plains Indians.

Wood is also associated with language and literature, as exemplified by the Celtic tree alphabet that Robert Graves discovered and popularized. In their worship of this element, which pervaded their natural surroundings, the ancient Druids founded colleges in woods and groves that employed a secret language where trees symbolized letters.[17] Graves takes the association of trees with language and education even farther by mentioning that the tree name "beech" is a common synonym for "literature" and is etymologically connected to the word "book."[18] Noting its historical use as a keeper of records, representation of the cosmos, and means of communication, Graves shows the totemic qualities inherent in this element that we all rely upon for shelter, transfer of information, and numerous other uses.

Integrating the Elements

Historically, we have often captured sacred landscapes in our architecture by abstracting nature; trees become columns, stupas symbolize mountains, fountains are rivers, and pools represent seas. The incorporation of natural elements into architectural structures helps balance the natural world with man-made edifices, integrating nature and culture. For instance, in many sacred buildings that have been left to decay and that have broken down over the centuries, only the columns remain, leaving the powerful impression of trees or even forests as markers of the sacred. Such sacred places demonstrate that growth and form are vital to our peace of mind and spiritual health. By rediscovering the vocabulary of sacred architecture, we come into balance with the natural world.

Stupas, and the multi-tiered pagodas of the Chinese, are evocations of the elements. There are four- and five-story versions in Hindu, Buddhist, Confucian, and other Eastern religious traditions, and they mark the landscape as a sacred place holder, orientation point, and local navel. Each part of a five-story stupa corresponds to one of five elements. The foundation is square and corresponds to Earth. Next is the sphere of Water, then the triangle or pyramid of Fire. Above this is an upward-facing half-moon shape representing the wind (Air), and at the top sits the gem-shaped symbol for Metal (corresponding to Ether or Air), which can also appear as a teardrop or pointed obelisk.
The stupa is therefore a symbolic representation of the elements in balance.

In the architecturally complex Islamic mosques, it is usual for all the elements to be present in symbolic form, particularly when the mosques are in desert lands, where there are few trees and few bodies of water. The way the materials and form of these mosques reflect the elements is both beautiful and sophisticated. As an example, the floor of the Great Mosque at Isfahan in Iran is made up of thousands of colored, randomly placed tiles, which embody the flow, fluidity, and beauty of the various multicolored reflections that make water so alive and enticing. In addition, columns are often carved to resemble trees, reeds, stalks, and plants. Indeed, the columns of the Lion Court at the Alhambra in Granada, Spain, resemble a forest of trees.

The mythological creatures known as elementals, touched on earlier in the chapter, are of four varieties. Gnomes are associated with the earth and the materials at its core, and they are a bit like the warrior Gimli of J. R. R. Tolkien's *The Lord of the Rings*, whose dwarf race lives underground in deep caves, mining and forging metals in addition to hoarding gold and precious minerals. Like the Nibelungen of Wagner's "The Ring Cycle" operas, gnomes are guardians of hidden treasure. The undines are water sprites or spirits, primarily feminine in gender, and especially beautiful and enchanting. They inhabit waterfalls, streams, forest pools, and mountain lakes, and when we experience water in any form—especially moving water—we come in contact with the undines.

Salamanders are primitive fire spirits that exist in the air ether and are required for flame and fire to function. In medieval times, it was believed that fire would not start under any circumstances unless a salamander was present as catalyst. When incense is burned, salamanders allegedly congregate and make their presence known. Last but not least, sylphs, according to sixteenth-century Swiss-born alchemist Paracelsus, are beings of the air and mediums of sight, sound, smell and other stimuli that traverse the invisible substance. Sylphs are additionally known as the instigators of the mantic arts of prophecy, of which they are also guardians. All of these invisible, elemental spirits were traditionally believed by early people to inhabit the world around us, particularly those landscapes regarded as sacred.

In our current shift toward monoculture, or growth of a single crop on agricultural land, we lose the variety and balanced integration of plants, animals, and textures of the natural world. Our modern landscapes perfectly exemplify the ease with which we subject our natural environment to commercialism and its attendant toxic agents, just as many of us subject our bodies to pharmaceuticals and chemicals that cause more harm than good. By surrounding ourselves with a variety of textures and natural environments, and by exploring the play of light and shadow, permanence and the ephemeral, we integrate nature into our daily lives and find spiritual shelter there.

PAGE 134. Friday Mosque (Abbasid dynasty, eighth century CE), Isfahan, Iran, 2001

PAGE 135: Tile floor, Friday Mosque, Isfahan, Iran, 2001

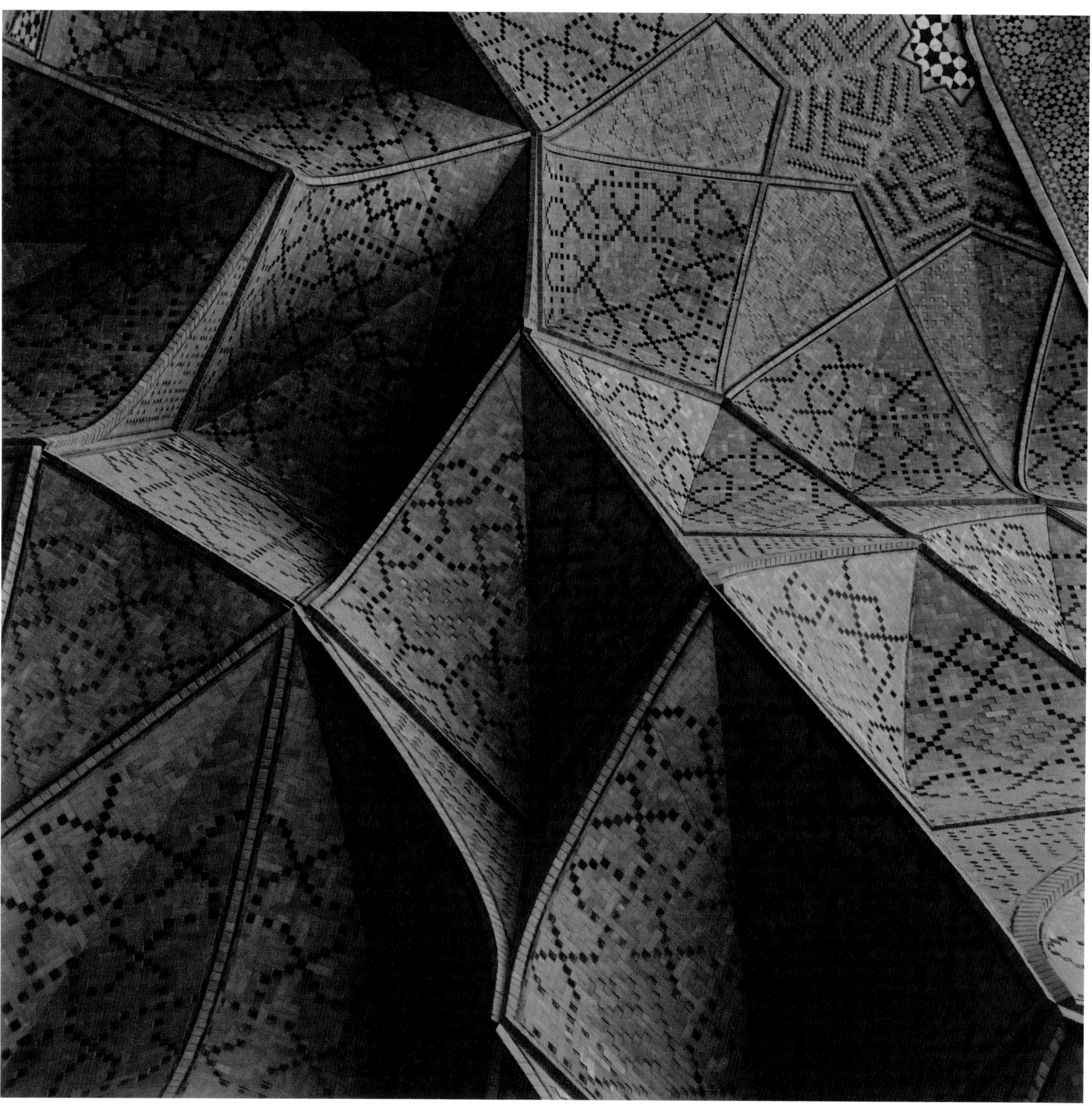

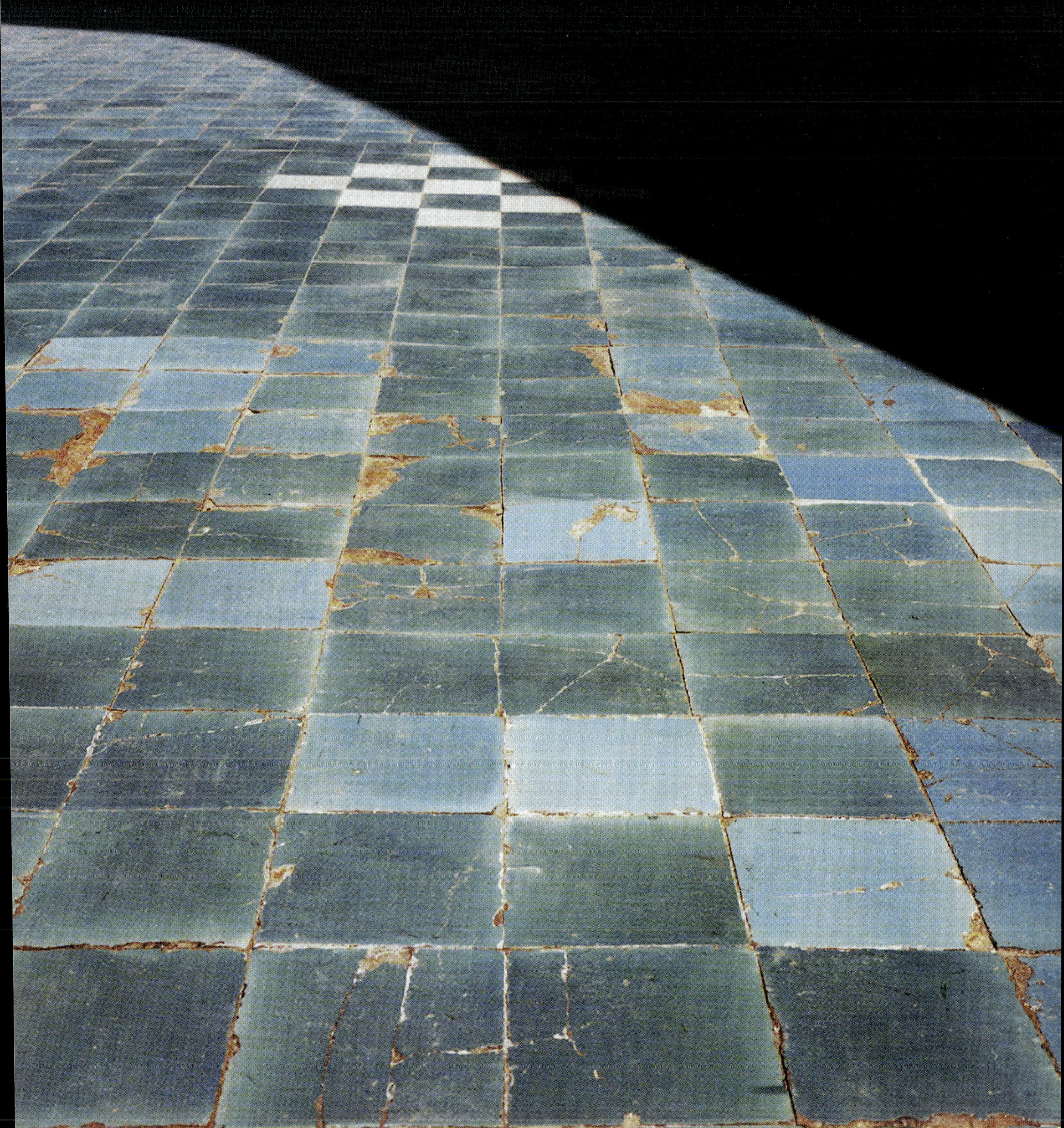

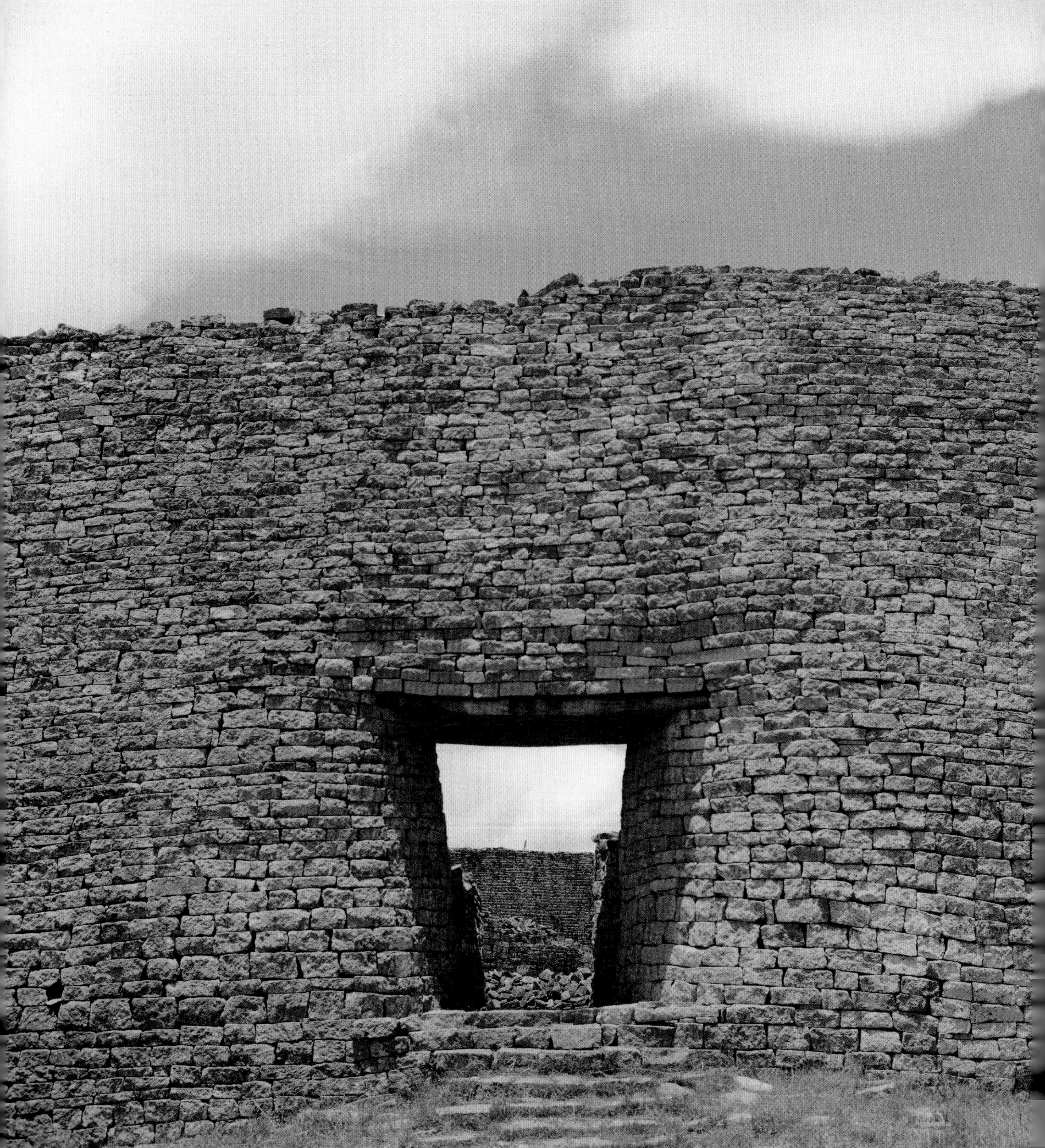

CHAPTER 8

Gateways and Boundaries

The Mysterious Gate has many names. Although it is given different names by the three religions, it is nonetheless the same thing. In Confucianism, when this gate is opened, the sage emerges. In Buddhism, when this gate is opened, the Buddha emerges. In Taoism, when this gate is opened, the immortal emerges.

~Nineteenth-century commentator Shui-ch'ing Tzu on the *Tao Te Ching*[1]

A culture's landscapes powerfully reflect the people's attitude toward the sacred as well as the relationship of the individual self to nature. When the landscape contains numerous boundaries and gateways, the typical individual is often inhibited and the culture is highly structured. The more communal and open a culture's landscapes, the more individuality and liberty are celebrated. For instance, early Native American cultures had no private property and no ownership, utilizing natural boundaries and gateways exclusively to frame their journey through life and the world. Thus, the entire natural world served as an entrance in their initiation rituals.

In many cultures there is a ceremonial path that crosses the land and transports the pilgrim or worshipper toward the goal of enlightenment. In some cases, this goal requires a test of strength and perseverance, and the path thus takes on the form of a passage or an initiation. Pilgrimages reflect and enact our collective nomadic heritage and have been an essential process of the evolution of consciousness throughout history. We still find traces of ancient, sacred trails today, although the rituals that accompanied them have, for the most part, been lost. The gateway is also a metaphor for the *yoni* (Sanskrit for "birth canal"), and represents the hidden passage of the creative powers of the gods and goddesses that preceded formal religions. In this sense, the gateway is comparable to the cave, a protected region where the mysteries originate, where life begins, and where the holy relics are kept. Biblical Solomon's Temple marked off a sacred sanctuary containing the mysterious Ark of the Covenant that was believed to have held Moses' Tablets of the Law, and successive gateways within the Temple protected the holy

OPPOSITE: Gateway at the Great Zimbabwe National Monument, Zimbabwe, 1998

relic to such an extent, no one really knows what treasures were actually within the Ark. Similarly, the mysterious Black Stone, which allegedly fell from Heaven and indicated to Adam and Eve where to build the world's first temple, is guarded within the cubic curtain of the Ka'aba in Mecca, the most holy city of Islam. The rituals of the Freemasons also utilize the symbolism of the veil to protect the sanctity of the tabernacle, which is based upon the original, portable Hebrew tabernacle that was supposedly built under Moses during the Hebrew exodus from Egypt. These holy sanctuaries are all gateways that identify boundaries between the mundane world and the domain of the sacred.

The shape of the archetypal gateway is usually one of two forms: a rectangular opening with an arch above it, integrating Earth (the rectangle) and Heaven (the arch), or a *vesica piscis*. A *vesica piscis* is a shape formed by the interlocking of two circles. Carrying the proportions of the Golden Ratio, which defines order and equilibrium in the natural world, it is a profound symbol of generation, creativity, and the feminine. Many European cathedrals and churches use both arches and the *vesica piscis* in their architecture, and even in the layout of the lands around them, to represent the gateway between Heaven and Earth.[2]

Eleusis: Passage Between Worlds

In their wonderful book *The Road to Eleusis: Unveiling the Secrets of the Mysteries* (2004), scholar-scientists R. Gordon Wasson, Albert Hoffman, and Carl A. P. Ruck explore the Eleusinian mysteries that were practiced in the ancient Greek city of Eleusis for a nearly uninterrupted period of two thousand years and annually celebrated at the autumnal equinox. When the specially determined initiates joined the ritual to Dionysus, they journeyed beyond this world as they "paraded on ceremoniously through the narrow entrance of Plouton's cave ['Plouton,' meaning wealth, is another Greek name for Hades], down into the subterranean labyrinth, across the aquifer, perhaps in Charon's boat to regroup, as in the myth of Er, on the plains of Elysion."[3] The initiates relived the original Greek creation myths of death and rebirth, where Hades, god of the underworld, tricked the Olympian goddess Persephone, daughter of grain goddess Demeter, into eating the fruits of a pomegranate tree. This mythic act forever made humanity part divine, while also describing the cycle of the natural year, with Persephone allowed to join her mother Demeter for the spring and summer months—during which the air warms, the earth quickens, and plants grow.

The Eleusinian initiates kept the secret of what exactly went on during their rituals under pain of death, so there are no written records of the substance of the mysteries. However, the sacred path remains, although, as the authors state, "There is nothing sacred today about the Sacred Road except

OPPOSITE: Arch, Bagan, Burma (Myanmar), 1993

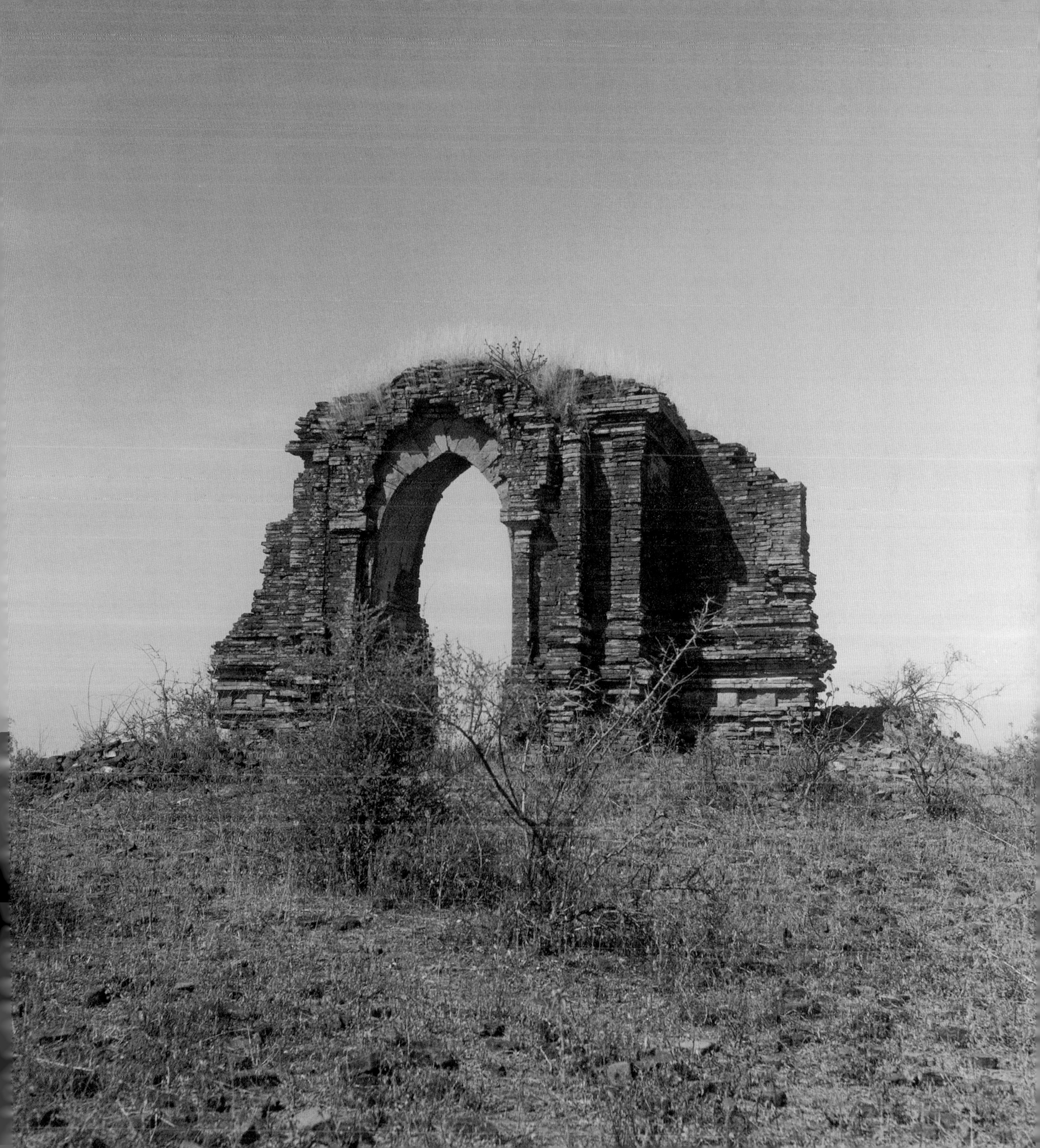

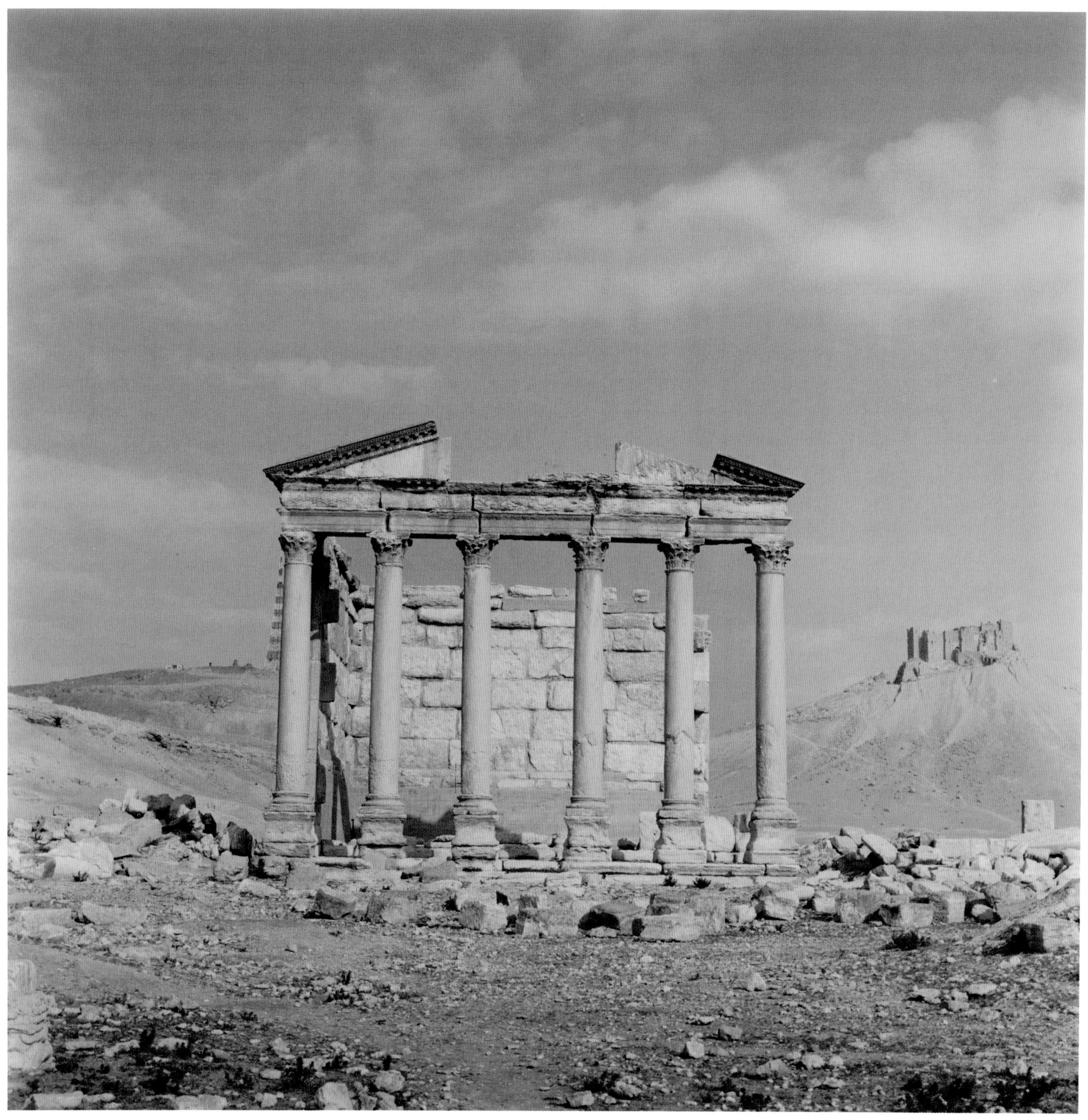

its name."[4] This statement is true for many sacred pathways of ancient times. In this case, the entire pathway between Athens and Eleusis is one of the densest industrial areas in Greece, with hundreds of oil tankers unloading into massive storage facilities on the shore. While we celebrate those sacred places that are in wilder and less urban areas, many ancient sacred sites were overtaken by civilization and overrun by technology, and as a result, their magic has vanished.

It is clear from the few descriptions or reconstructions of what may have happened on these sacred journeys that many elements of the sacred are integral to the path. Dionysus, god of the vine, likely led the carefully chosen initiates to meet Demeter and daughter Persephone. They would find and pass ceremonial graves, wells, and sanctuary gates, all united in a dance throughout the night. "And with them in their dance would dance also the starry sky and the moon and all fifty of the daughters of Ocean, rising out of rivers and from the sea."[5] Once reaching the sacred Telestrion, a dark, rectangular sanctuary akin to the womb or germination place for all life, they would partake of a sacred potion from the Kykeon vessel. This drink was almost certainly made from the wheat sheaf sacred to Demeter and the ergot fungus introduced into it,[6] allowing for the transport of the initiates into the hallowed state of enlightenment.

Yin-Yang and the Gateway to Emptiness

Such ritual paths are common around the world, and most sacred landscapes include such an entryway, which is often signaled by symbolic landscape elements such as mountains, streams, waterfalls, great trees, caves, and more. The Chinese used the yin-yang symbol to protect and to identify their sacred places, tombs, and architecture, as well as to represent their view of healing. An alchemical text attributed to Lao Tzu but written seven hundred years later, early in the Christian era, explains the significance of the *wu-chi* diagram—a black-filled circle that represents the Void—within this universally recognizable Taoist symbol: "Read from the bottom up, the *wu-chi* diagram describes the process of transformation through internal alchemy, or the return to the Tao. The empty circle at the bottom is the Mysterious Gate or the Valley Spirit. *Gate* means 'opening,' and *Valley* refers to 'Emptiness' or 'Void.' On the physical level the Valley Spirit lies in the Life Gate on the spinal column (an area on the spine between the kidneys). . . . On the spiritual level, the Valley Spirit is consciousness emptied of sensations, emotions, and thoughts."[7] As our ancestors were acutely aware, our movement through such gateways of emptiness in the sacred landscape reflects our individual quest for balance, health, and enlightenment.

OPPOSITE: Temple, Palmyra, Syria, 1995

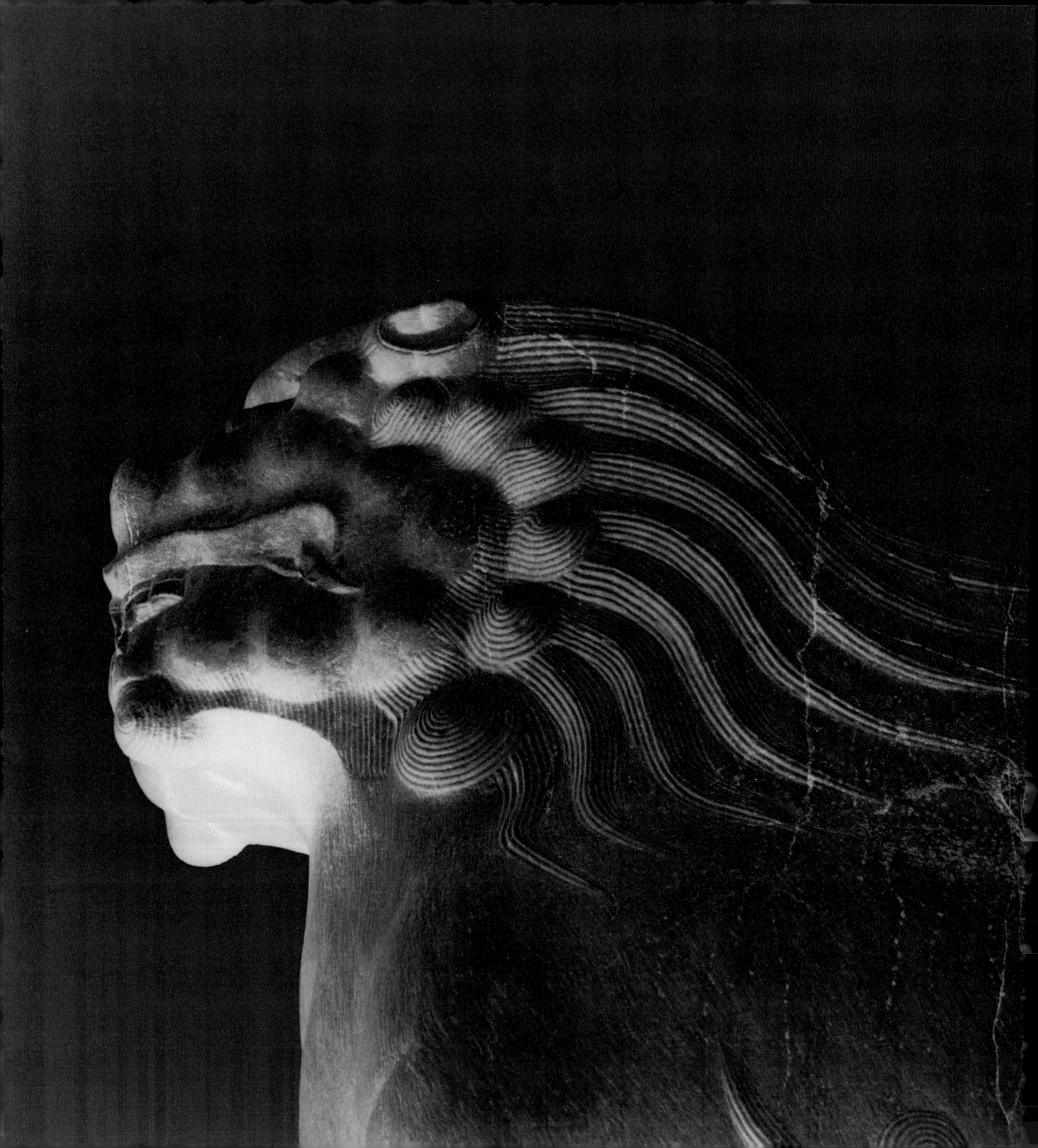

Celestial Animals: Guardians of the Landscape

There are many animals associated with and appearing in sacred landscapes that act as gateway guardians, most notably lions, dragons, serpents, birds, dogs, bulls, eagles, elephants, tigers, and, in Egyptian symbolism, falcons, ibis, and cats. These animals occur as constellations in the sky, as well, and therefore they function on many levels: as totem animals, as guides between the worlds, as protectors and guardians of sacred domains, and also as gods or goddesses with animal forms on earth that correspond to their starry form in the heavens.

Enwrapping the Pole Star like a serpent, Draco is a significant constellation in many cultures. Most cultures that have projected imagery onto the stars by grouping them into constellations identify either a dragon or serpent constellation in the identical location. Arabian astronomers called it the "Poisonous Dragon," and the Egyptian city Thebes was called the "City of the Dragon" in honor of the star Gamma Draconis within this constellation.[8] In Greek mythology, Draco also represents the escape of Zeus in the form of a snake, together with two bears (the constellations Ursa Major and Ursa Minor) from his father, Kronos. Because of the proximity of the three circumpolar constellations and the common use of the orientation of the Great Bear to determine the yearly cycle,[9] the snake or serpent has always been associated with the progression of time, and the orientation of Draco or its equivalent was considered an indicator of the seasons of the year.

Scientists are able to calculate the position of Draco at different periods in history using computer analysis and a phenomenon called the "precession of the equinoxes," which refers to the very slow rotation of the Pole Star over a period of 25,920 years. Twelve astrological ages occur during this period, in backward order, corresponding to the position of the twelve zodiacal constellations at the spring equinox every 2,160 years or so. One such precessional period, the Age of Aquarius, has even found its way into popular culture as a reference to the hippie heyday and New Age movement of the 1960s and 1970s.

It is known that many sacred places are also calendars, including Stonehenge in England, Newgrange in Ireland, the Great Pyramid in Egypt (see page 146), the many stone pyramids in Central America, Serpent Mound in Ohio, Machu Picchu in Peru, and many others. Via these magnificent gateways, ancient civilizations all over the world tied their culture to the stars and to the zodiac.

OPPOSITE: Sacred Way of Xiaoling, Eastern Qing Tombs, outside Beijing, China, 2001

PAGE 144: Horus statue, Temple of Horus, Edfu, Egypt, 1989

PAG 145: Ramses II, Great Temple of Abu Simbel, Egypt, 1990

The Serpents of Angkor and Uxmal

One of the most profound sacred places in the world is the region of Cambodia where the temple of Angkor Wat and the city of Angkor Thom are located. These magnificent temples, which were

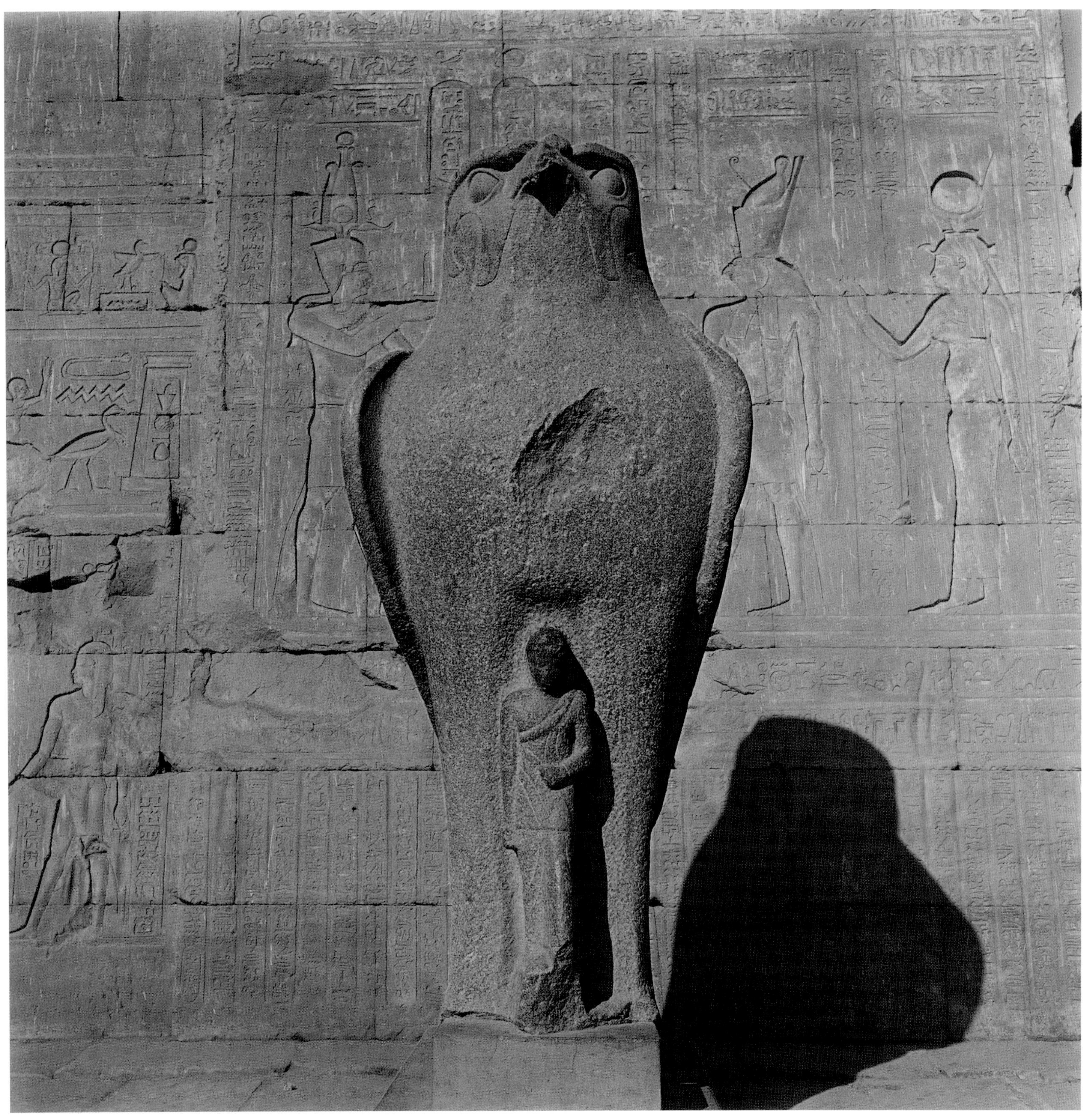

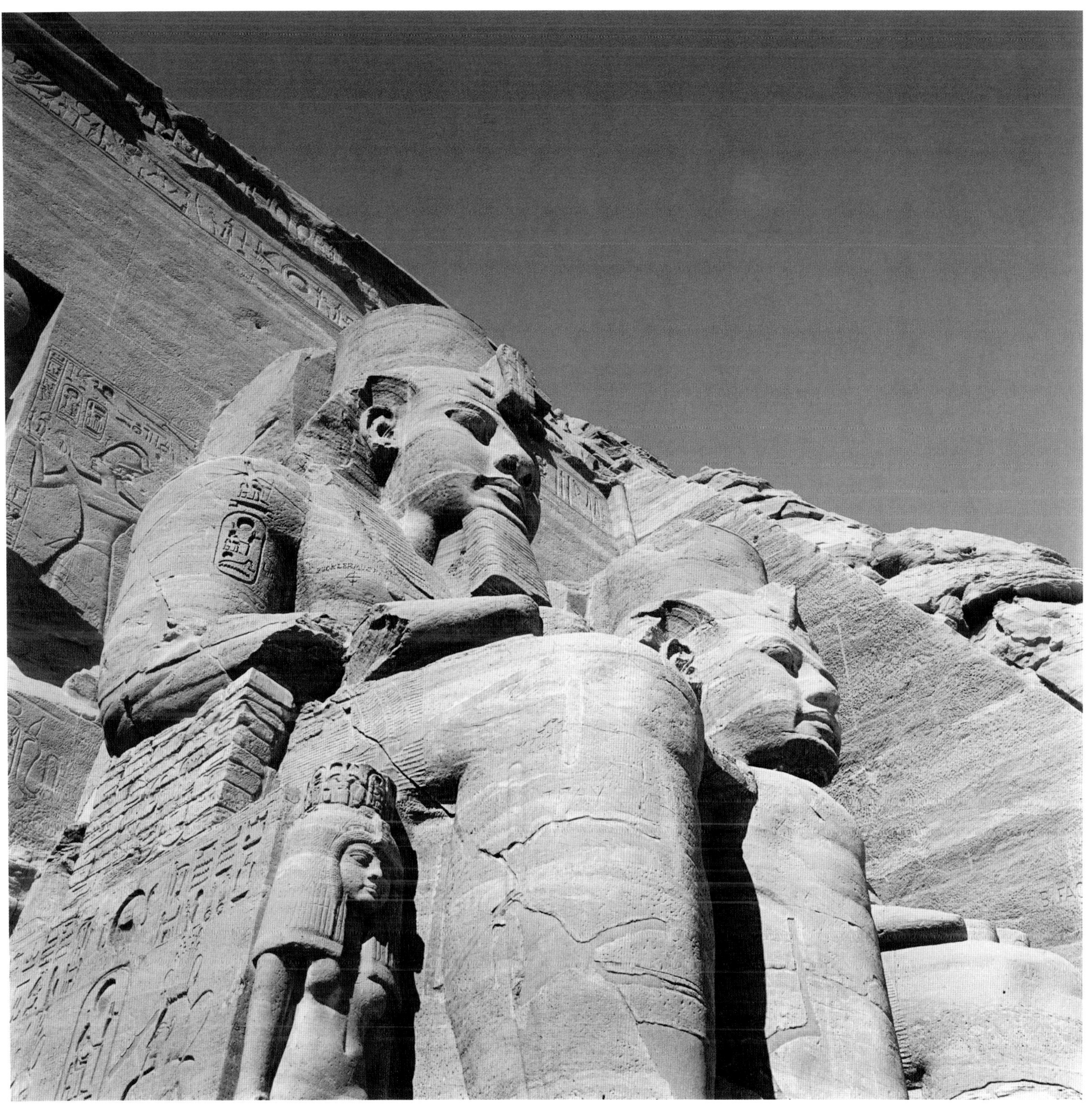

constructed between 900 and 1200 CE, represent masterful gateways and boundaries. The entire complex of monuments is oriented to the cardinal axes, with miles of ritual paths connecting the buildings. Each individual building appears as a mandala—a meditation diagram known to promote peace and equilibrium—when seen from above. Gateways in the centers of long walls, as well as lion guardians and symbolic dragons, protect these sacred temples, which also reflect the four cardinal directions. Atop each of the four entryways of the Bayon temple at Angkor Thom, for example, are Buddha heads that face north, south, east, and west.

Astonishingly, the principal temples of Angkor are positioned to reflect the constellation Draco (the Dragon) as it appeared at the spring equinox in 10,500 BCE.[10] This discovery was suggested by journalist Graham Hancock and photographer Santha Faila in their book, *Heaven's Mirror: Quest for the Lost Civilization* (1999). Hancock asserts that the siting of the Angkor temples reflects a similar principle of orientation and placement to that of the three main pyramids and Sphinx at Giza in Egypt, which allegedly matched the position of the stars in Orion's Belt and the constellation Leo (respectively) at that same spring equinox in 10,500 BCE. These correlations imply that all these sacred sites are reflections of the firmament on Earth, bringing heaven to humanity.

What amplifies the mystery of Angkor is that at its latitude in the southern hemisphere it was not possible to see the entire constellation of Draco in the sky at any time during construction, since Draco is farthest north of all the constellations except the Pole Star. If we accept this premise, it means that if the builders of Angkor copied the layout and orientation of the constellation in the buildings, the complex must have been planned at a much earlier time, when Draco was visible on the horizon.

The elegant and majestic main southern gate for entry to the city of Angkor Thom is covered and surrounded by protective imagery. "The fifty-four divinities grasp the serpents with their hands, seemingly to prevent their escape. Above each gate are five gigantic heads of Buddha, four of them facing the cardinal points of the compass: the fifth head, brilliant with gold, holds a central position. On each side of the gates are elephants, carved in stone."[11] All of these imposing sculptures serve simultaneously to protect the inhabitants and also to mark the area as sacred landscape.

Much like Angkor, the pyramidal temples of Central America use serpent imagery to protect and sanctify the sacred landscape. In particular, the Mayan Pyramid of the Magician at Uxmal on the Yucatan peninsula, where landmarks feature the feathered serpent Quetzalcoatl in his various forms, exhibits this characteristic serpent energy symbolism. The temple steps are extremely steep and difficult to ascend, and the iconography on it is startling and highly symbolic, as is all Mayan architecture on sacred sites. John Stephens, who rediscovered the site in 1840, found a hook-shaped

OPPOSITE: Gate of Angkor Thom, Angkor, Cambodia, 1993

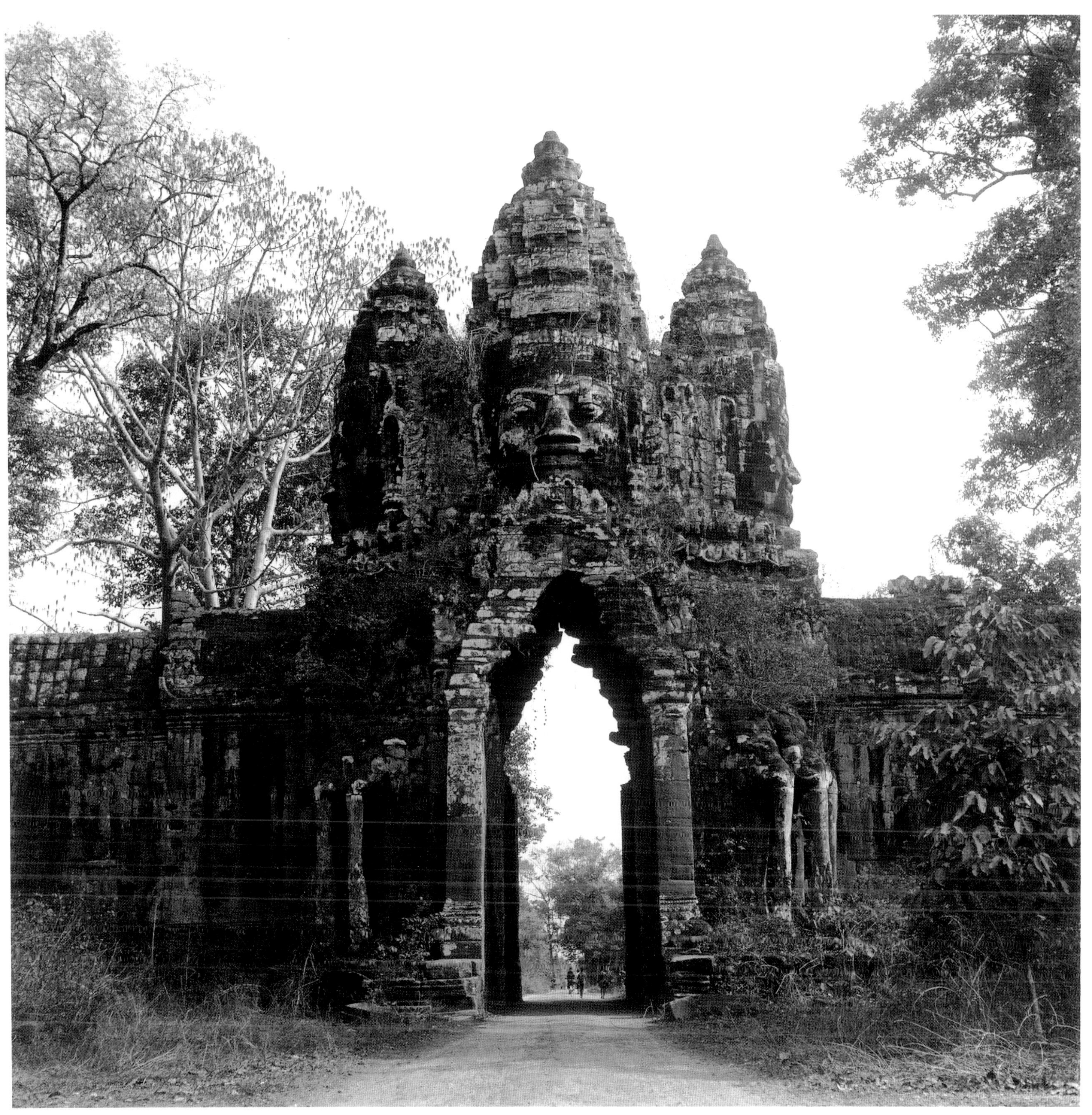

object on all four sides of the temple, which contained roundels reflecting the shape of the Big Dipper (Ursa Major), and showing, once again, how the Maya encoded astronomy and astrology into their architecture.[12] Coincidentally, the center of the circular *luo pan* Chinese geomantic device is often adorned with stars of the Big Dipper constellation,[13] leading some to suggest a common connection between Chinese and Mayan cultures, whose sites may be places where survivors of the destruction of Atlantis later settled.

Gateways have a literal function as entrances, but when they are decorated with symbolic animals, symbols, or natural elements, or when oriented in specific ways, they become much more. Representing the magical transition between the "real" mundane world and the world of the gods and goddesses, gateways across all continents create thresholds between worlds.

OPPOSITE: Iceberg, Disko Bay, Greenland, 1986

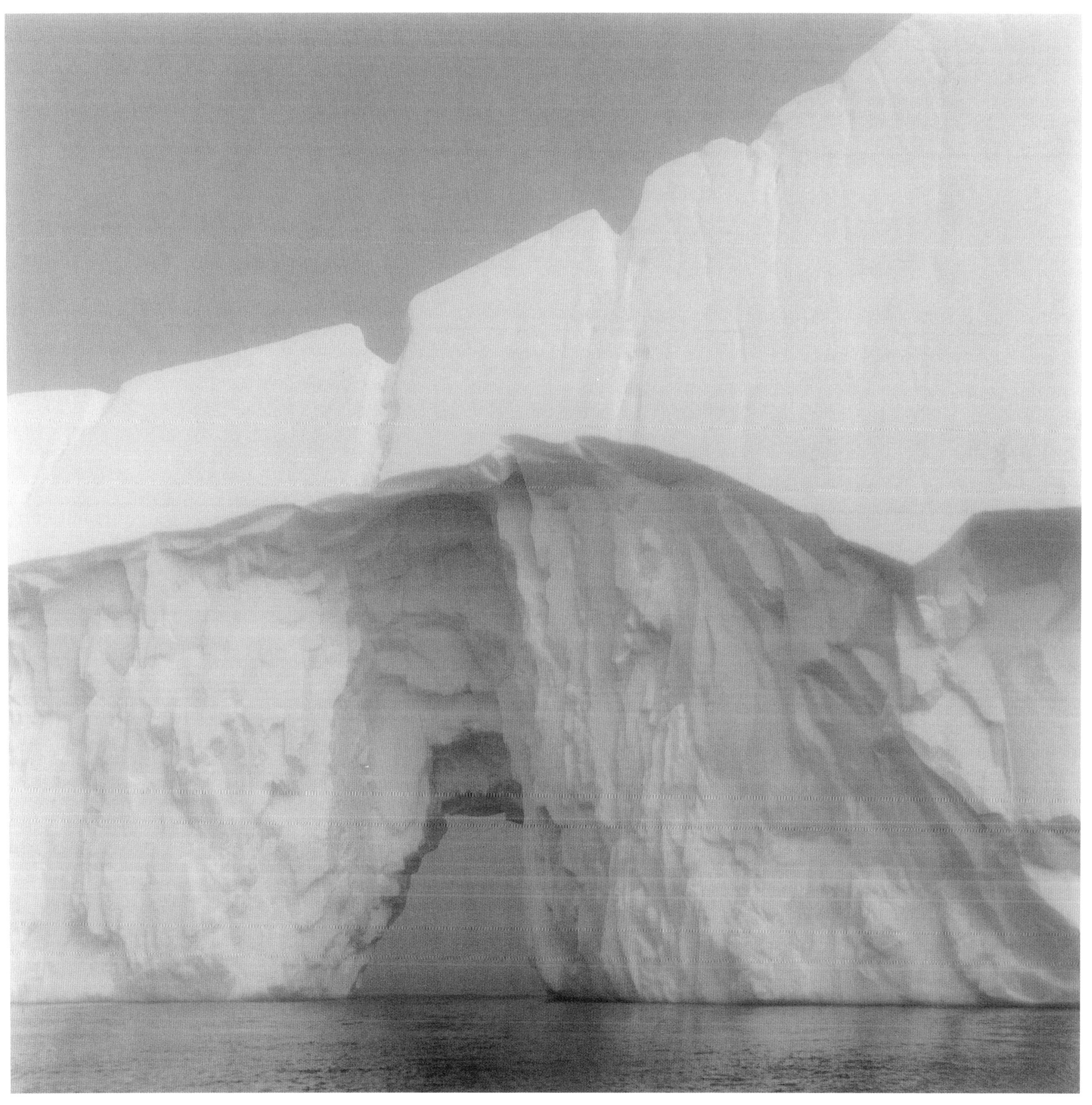

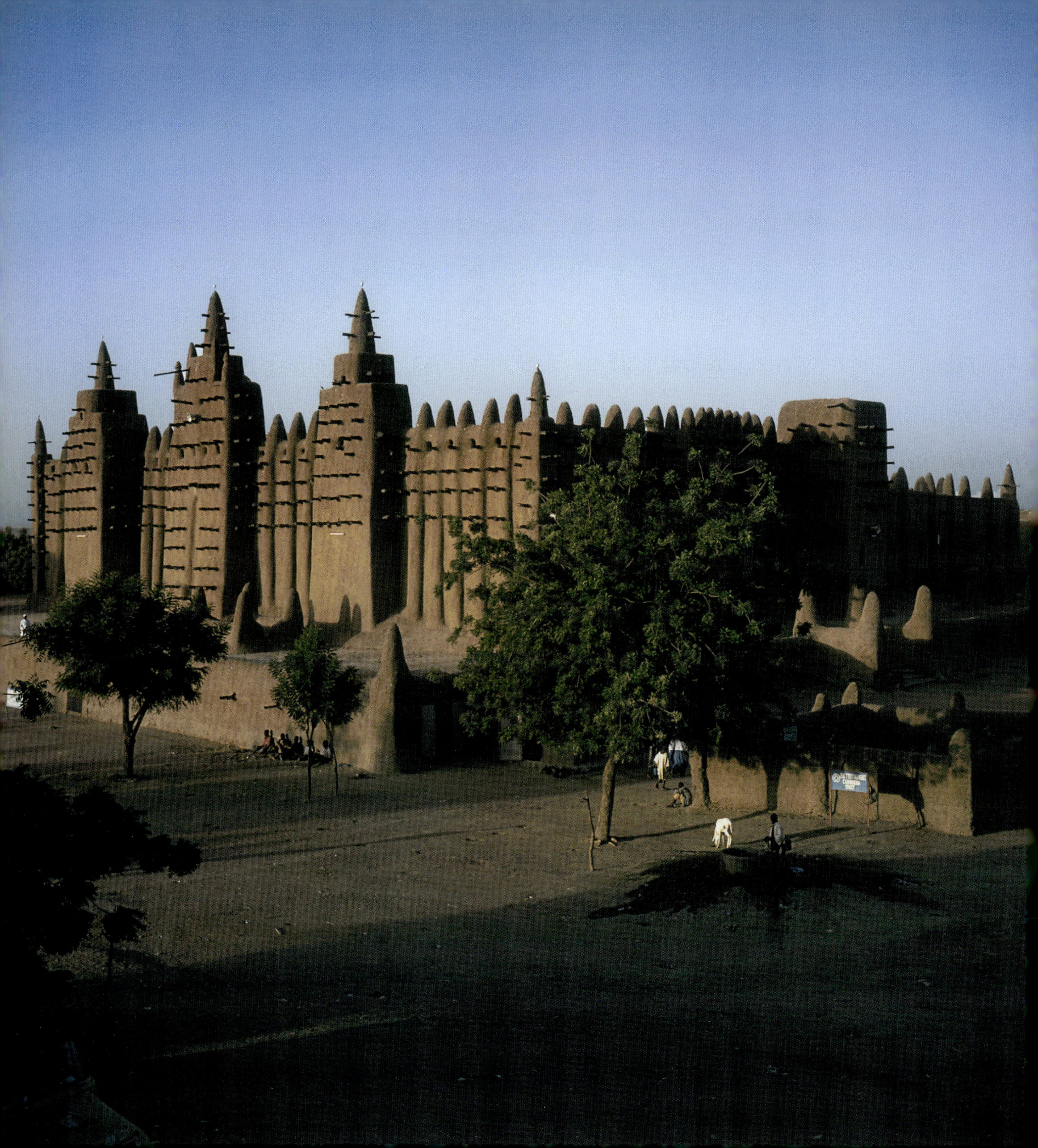

CHAPTER 9

Mythic Sacred Lands

In Xanadu did Kubla Khan
A stately pleasure dome decree
Where Alph, the sacred river, ran
Through caverns measureless to man
Down to a sunless sea.

~Samuel Taylor Coleridge, *Kubla Khan* (1798)[1]

While many tangible mountains and lands have been identified as sacred for millennia, there have been a succession of mythic sacred lands that may or may not have physical parallels or antecedents on our plane of existence. These go by names such as Shambhala, Shangri-la, Arcadia, Atlantis, Lemuria, the Fountain of Youth, Tolkien's Middle Earth, and, of course, the Garden of Eden. Some are fictional, others mythic with religious overtones, but in every case they are embedded in our collective imagination to the extent that some scholars and authors are obsessed with discovering traces of their existence.

With the immense worldwide influence of modern cinema, it is not surprising that the 1937 Frank Capra movie *Lost Horizon*,[2] based on James Hilton's book of the same name, was so compelling in its portrait of a hidden and inaccessible mountain community called Shangri-la. In this sacred locale, inhabitants lived many hundreds of years in peace. Although Hilton was thought to have invented it, or even misspelled the name of the Tibetan mystical kingdom of Shambhala (see page 152), there are many possible prototypes of such a magical and profound land where peace reigns and inhabitants live beyond many lifetimes. The name Shangri-la itself warrants close scrutiny because the word *shan* (mountain in Chinese) is included in the name of all the sacred mountains of China. Also, the valleys of Shangri-la evoke an area of China near the Gobi Desert called Kun Lun Shan, a chain of mountains more than a thousand miles long that many consider a Taoist paradise. According to legend, the first

OPPOSITE: Mosque of Djenné, Mali, 1997

mortal to encounter this ancient place was King Mu, who reigned in the tenth century BCE. There, he visited the magnificent jade palace of the mythic originator of Chinese culture, the Yellow Emperor, and consummated a relationship with the Queen Mother of the West[3]—an obvious remnant of the earlier matriarchal Earth Mother culture of pre-dynastic China. Chinese Buddhists also allege that within the Kun Lun mountains is the legendary center of the world, Mount Meru.[4]

Since the ever-popular movie of *Lost Horizon*, many other places have also been designated as potential Shangri-las, including northern Pakistan—the region currently favored by the Islamic militant organization al Qaeda—areas in Tibet and Nepal, Mongolia, as well as the mysterious and tiny country on the Tibetan border, Bhutan. All of these places, populated to a large extent by followers of Tibetan Buddhism, feature extraordinarily romantic and remote landscapes, representing the Shangri-la archetype of a domain that is sheltered from the outside world and governed by a benevolent and wise lama—a kind of paradise that probably does not exist anymore, though we all wish it did.

Shambhala Tantra Teachings

A great probability is that Shangri-la is a derivation of the much earlier legendary Tibetan Buddhist paradise called Shambhala. Descriptions of this mythic kingdom appear most notably in the teachings of the Kalachakra Tantra (Sanskrit for "Wheel of Time"), which were allegedly transmitted to King Suchandra of Shambhala by the Buddha and passed down for twenty-four centuries through a line of great kings. According to the teachings, Shambhala is a mystical land in the far north, where bodhisattvas reincarnate in the form of wisdom and compassion, venturing out from Shambhala—the "Pure Land"—to bring all sentient beings to enlightenment. Although Tibetan Buddhists believe that Shambhala is located somewhere on this planet, only those beings with pure minds and the highest karmic propensities can see it.

Considered by most traditions to be the very pinnacle of Buddhist teaching, the Kalachakra Tantra is also extremely controversial because the texts pit the Buddhist army of Shambhala against non-Buddhists during a future Armageddon and revival of the dharma (Buddhist canon), although most scholars agree that the war is symbolic of the struggle between enlightenment and ignorance. The teachings are considered especially important in this present degenerate era, and as they are associated with fostering world peace, Kalachakra Tantra initiations are given at large public gatherings, most notably by His Holiness the Dalai Lama.[5]

The descriptions of Shambhala are fabulous and may certainly account for other visions of such a paradise on earth. According to the tantra, Shambhala lies north of the Sita River, most commonly identified as the Tarim River in east Turkestan. Many therefore believe that Shambhala lies in what is now Mongolia. Shambhala is considered a land of tantric adepts, and its geography reflects this: as depicted in the various *thangkas* (mandala paintings) that represent Kalachakra, the country is shaped like a giant lotus with eight petals, rimmed by a circle of great snowy mountains.

In the legends, the capital of Shambhala is Kalapa. Its palaces are made of gold and silver, as well as turquoise, coral, pearl, emerald, moon crystal, and other precious stones. The light given off by the mirrors outside the palaces shines so brightly that night cannot be distinguished from day. Near the thrones, which are made from the finest gold, are crystal glasses that allow one to see far into the distance. On the ceiling are special circular crystal skylights that allow one to observe the palaces, gods, and hearts of the sun, moon, and stars as well as the rotating crystal celestial spheres and even the zodiac. These descriptions are beyond anything we can imagine, triggering deep emotions in the mind and heart.

But the great issue remains: Is Shambhala in world geography? Can we find it on the world map? If not, does this mean that Shambhala is nonexistent? Many of the greatest Indian and Tibetan masters have practiced the Kalachakra Tantra and were able to develop a genuine realization through its teachings, so one cannot say that Shambhala is nonexistent. As His Holiness the Dalai Lama noted in 1985 during a Kalachakra initiation in Bodhgaya: "Although those with special affiliation may actually be able to go there [to Shambhala] through their karmic connection, nevertheless it is not a physical place that we can actually find. We can only say that it is a pure land, a pure land in the human realm. And unless one has the merit and the actual karmic association, one cannot actually arrive there."[6]

Being exposed to the positive karma generated by the Kalachakra Tantra teachings is a gift in that this ancient wisdom is as relevant today as it ever was—and probably even more so.

The Garden of Eden

The Garden of Eden is a definitive yet paradoxical story. Fundamentalist Christians believe in its literal existence, and yet it remains a mythic place. On the one hand, Eden was a perfect paradise, as it was ordained and created by God and located at the center of creation. Above all, however, it is associated with "the Fall"—Adam and Eve's expulsion from Paradise—signifying the corruption of the intrinsic nature of humanity and our ancestors' loss of innocence. Interestingly, many people are interested in returning to Eden metaphorically, to our former integration with nature. This effort to overcome our current dissociation from nature became a clarion call during the 1960s that embraced a

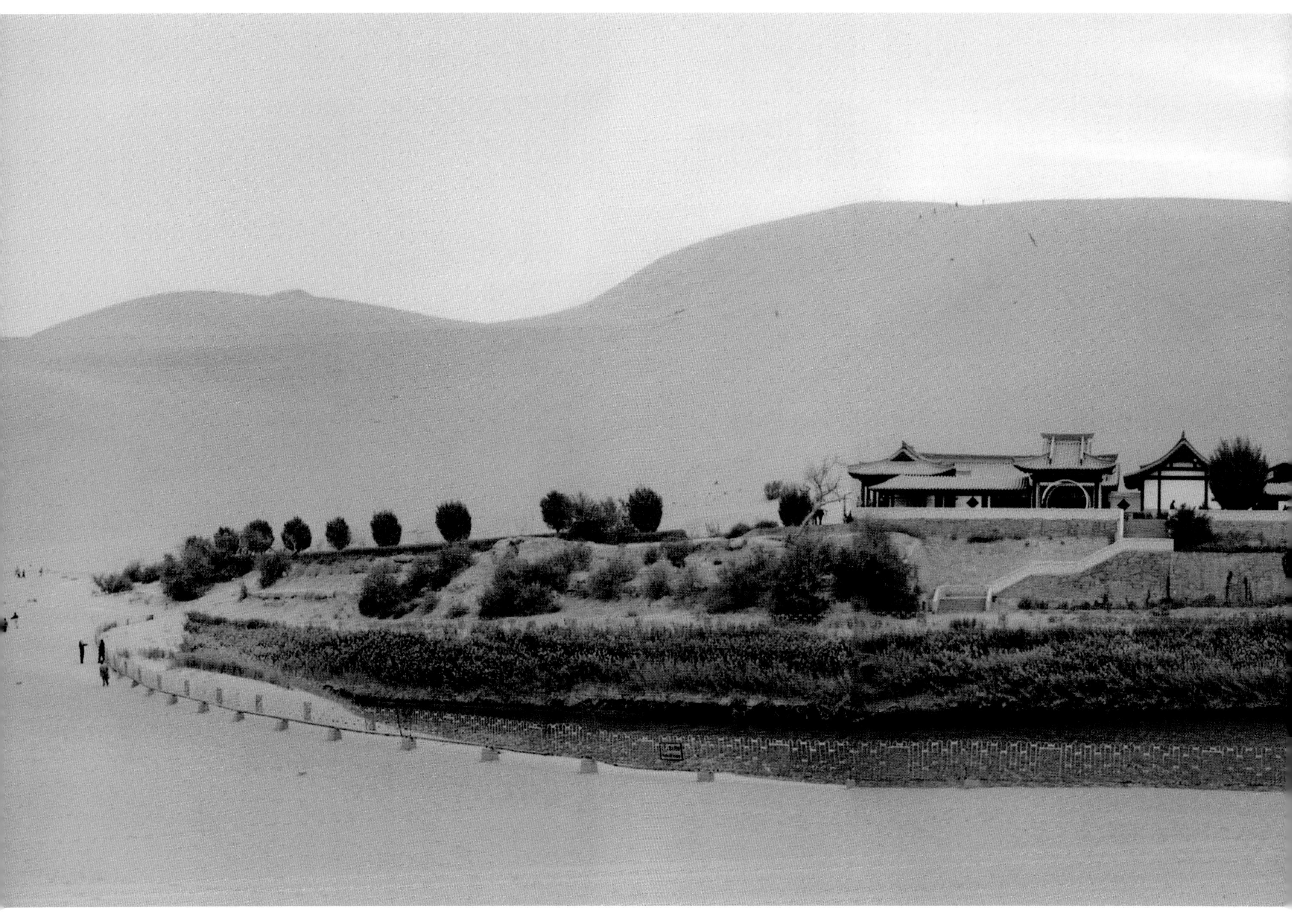

ABOVE: Crescent Moon
Spring, Dunhuang,
China, 2001

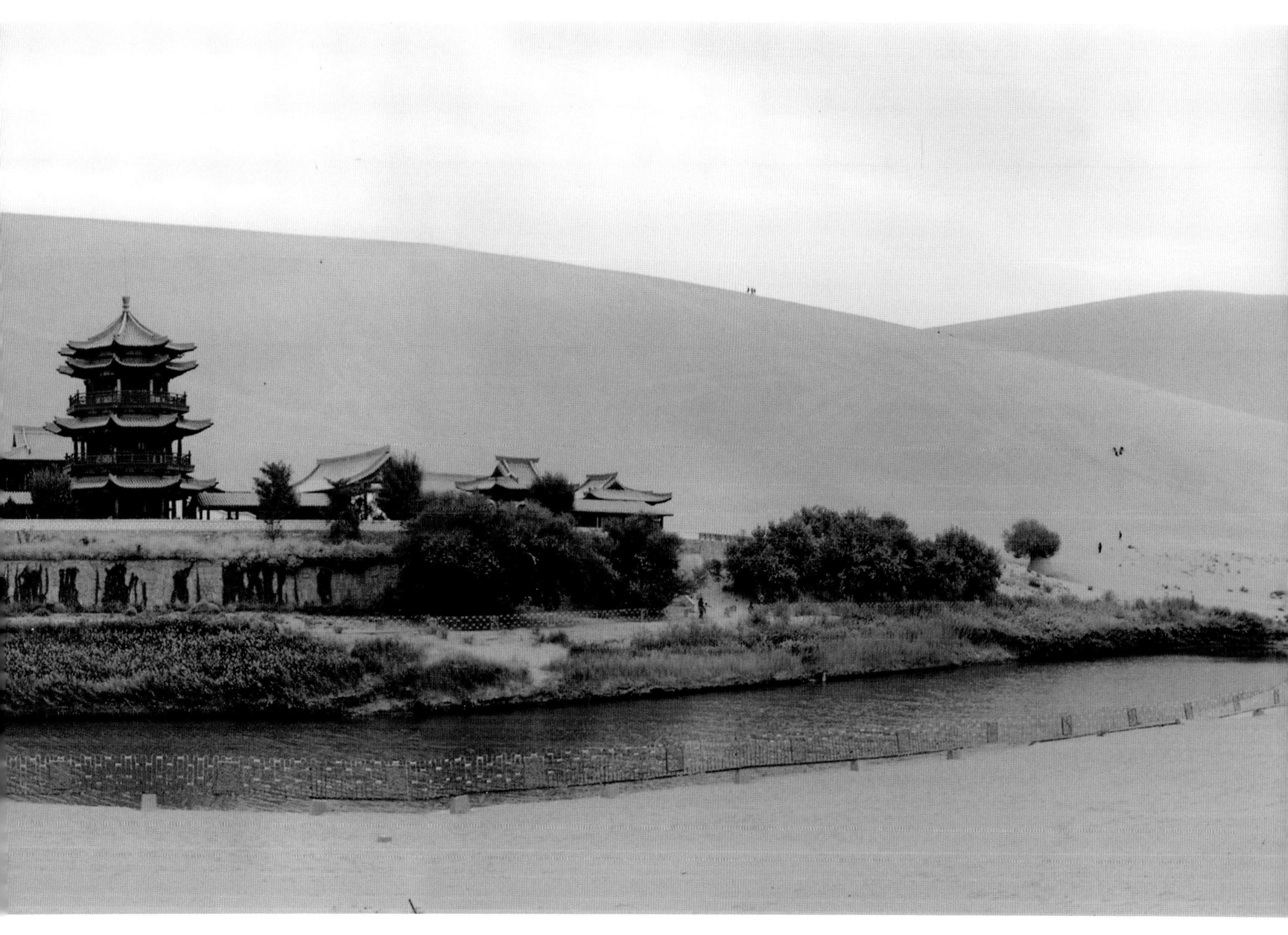

In the morning I bathe my intellect in the stupendous and cosmogonal philosophy of the Bhagvat Geeta, since whose composition years of the gods have elapsed, and in comparison with which our modern world and its literature seem puny and trivial; and I doubt if that philosophy is not to be referred to a previous state of existence, so remote is its sublimity from our conceptions. I lay down the book and go to my well for water, and lo! there I meet the servant of the Brahmin. . . . The pure Walden water is mingled with the sacred water of the Ganges. With favoring winds it is wafted past the site of the fabulous islands of Atlantis and the Hesperides, makes the periplus of Hanno, and, floating by Ternate and Tidore and the mouth of the Persian Gulf, melts in the tropic gales of the Indian seas, and is landed in ports of which Alexander only heard the names.

—Henry David Thoreau, *Walden* (1854)[7]

return to the land, the growth of organic gardening and farming, a revolution in eating habits, the increasing power of alternative and holistic healing techniques, and many other positive shifts that are more and more relevant as time goes on.

The Garden of Eden also embodies our changing views of gender and sexuality. The biblical Adam and Eve are, for many, a literal origin of humanity in the world and a primal archetype of the male-female relationship. From this perspective, the Bible serves as a prototype of patriarchal dogma, relating the story of a male god who creates the first man in his own image, as well as a secondary, inferior woman from Adam's rib. In *Sacred Sexuality* (1995), which I wrote with Jane Lyle, we explore the many ways in which the story of Adam and Eve is used to reinforce a dangerous and regressive viewpoint of female sexuality, but understanding this patriarchal myth of origin is important as a starting point to a more enlightened perspective.[8]

One fascinating, early source of biblical text is the Nag Hammadi codices, which were found in an Egyptian mountain cave in 1945 and include *On the Origin of the World*. This work presents an alternative creation story, combining Hellenistic, Christian, Gnostic, Hebrew, Egyptian, and Coptic philosophical themes, which suggests that Adam and Eve embody transcendent and sacred principles and that their creation and expulsion from Eden symbolize the split from an initial divine unity.

OPPOSITE: Temple on the Ganges River, Varanasi, India, 2007

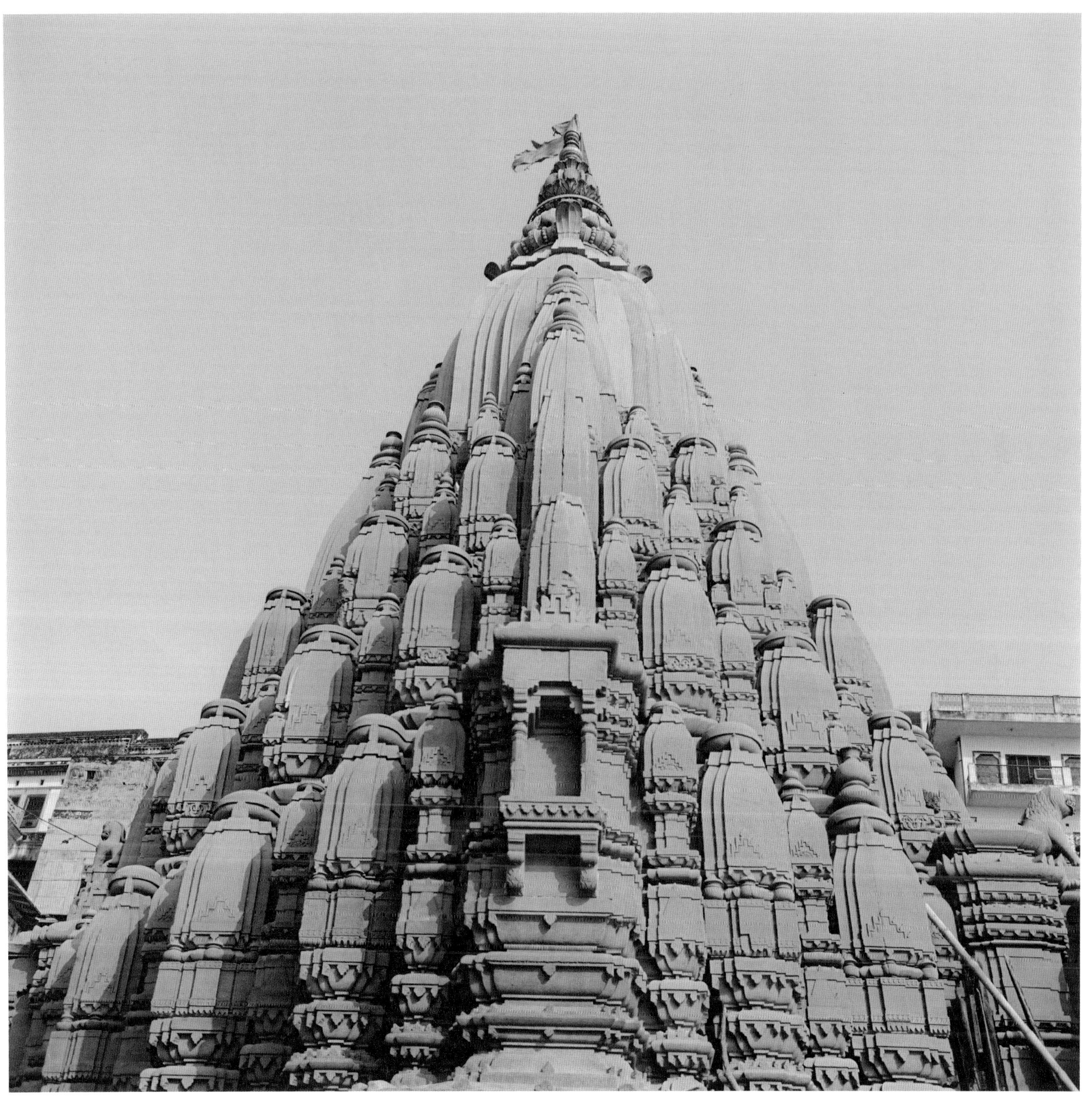

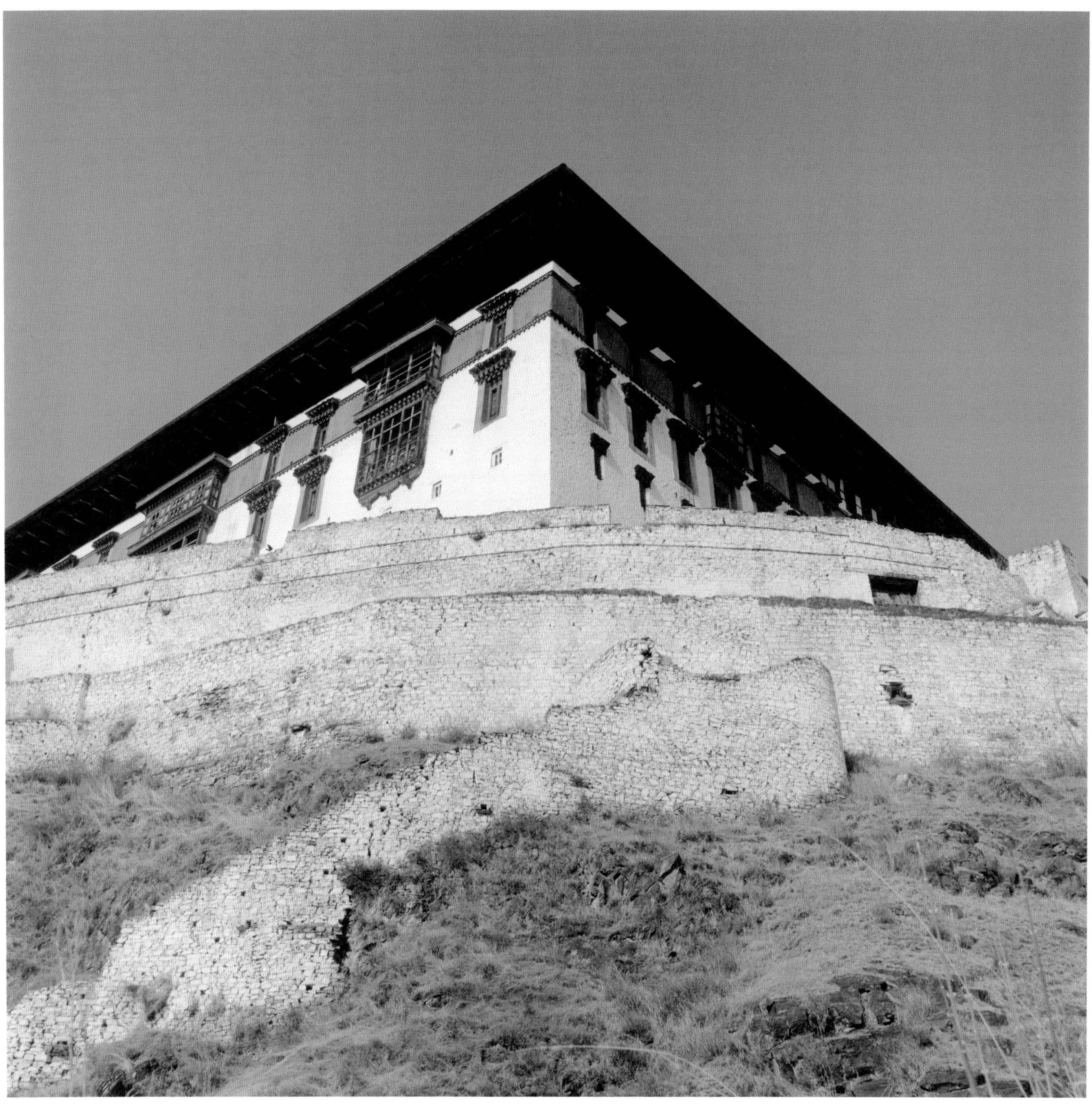

You are the tree of knowledge,
which is in Paradise,
from which the first man ate,
and which opened his mind,
so that he became enamored of his co-likeness.

—From *On the Origin of the World*, The Nag Hammadi Library (c. 100)[9]

Gnosticism was an early "outgrowth of the mystery traditions of antiquity" that were in turn an "outgrowth of the indigenous, Goddess-oriented shamanism of pre-Christian Europe."[10]

The Gnostic versions of Adam and Eve in the Garden of Eden are many and varied, and most are different from the traditional version of Genesis. *On the Origin of the World* reveals a doctrine of integration of the sexes, which existed in early Middle Eastern religions but was superseded by the ancient Hebrew leaders and then the Christian church in the centuries after Jesus, before it was eventually eradicated altogether. In this creation myth, Faith appeared as Sophia (wisdom) to veil the light of the cosmos from the void of chaos. She created the First Father, who was deluded into thinking that he was the sole creator. When Sophia gestated upon the waters, the first human, Eve, was created in Sophia's image.

The seven androgynous rulers—offspring of the First Father—feared that Adam would learn to rule his body, so he was born with no soul, but Eve breathed a soul into him. Adam arose and saw her and said, "You will be called the mother of the living, because you are the one who gave me life." The rulers were so disturbed, they taught Adam in his sleep that Eve had come into being so that she would serve him. The immortal Eve laughed at the rulers' false intentions and left a likeness of her body next to Adam, but her spirit entered the Tree of Knowledge, which she became. The rulers recklessly cast their seed upon the likeness, and this physical Eve bore the sons and daughters of man. Later, Eve and Adam ate from the tree and saw the distinctions between things, but they were forever cast out of Paradise.[11]

This tale presents yet another example of the early feminine goddess energy being overwhelmed by patriarchy. If, like the Gnostics, we view the supreme deity as a goddess embedded in the landscape rather than as a male creator god that reigns over Earth, then instead of identifying Eve as the snake encircling the tree—in paintings such as Michelangelo's in the Sistine Chapel—it becomes abundantly clear: the tree is Eve.

OPPOSITE: Rinpung Dzong, Drukpa Kagyu Buddhist monastery, Paro, Bhutan, 1992

PAGE 160: Pyramid, Meroë, Sudan, 1998

PAGE 161: Great Sphinx of Giza, Egypt, 1997

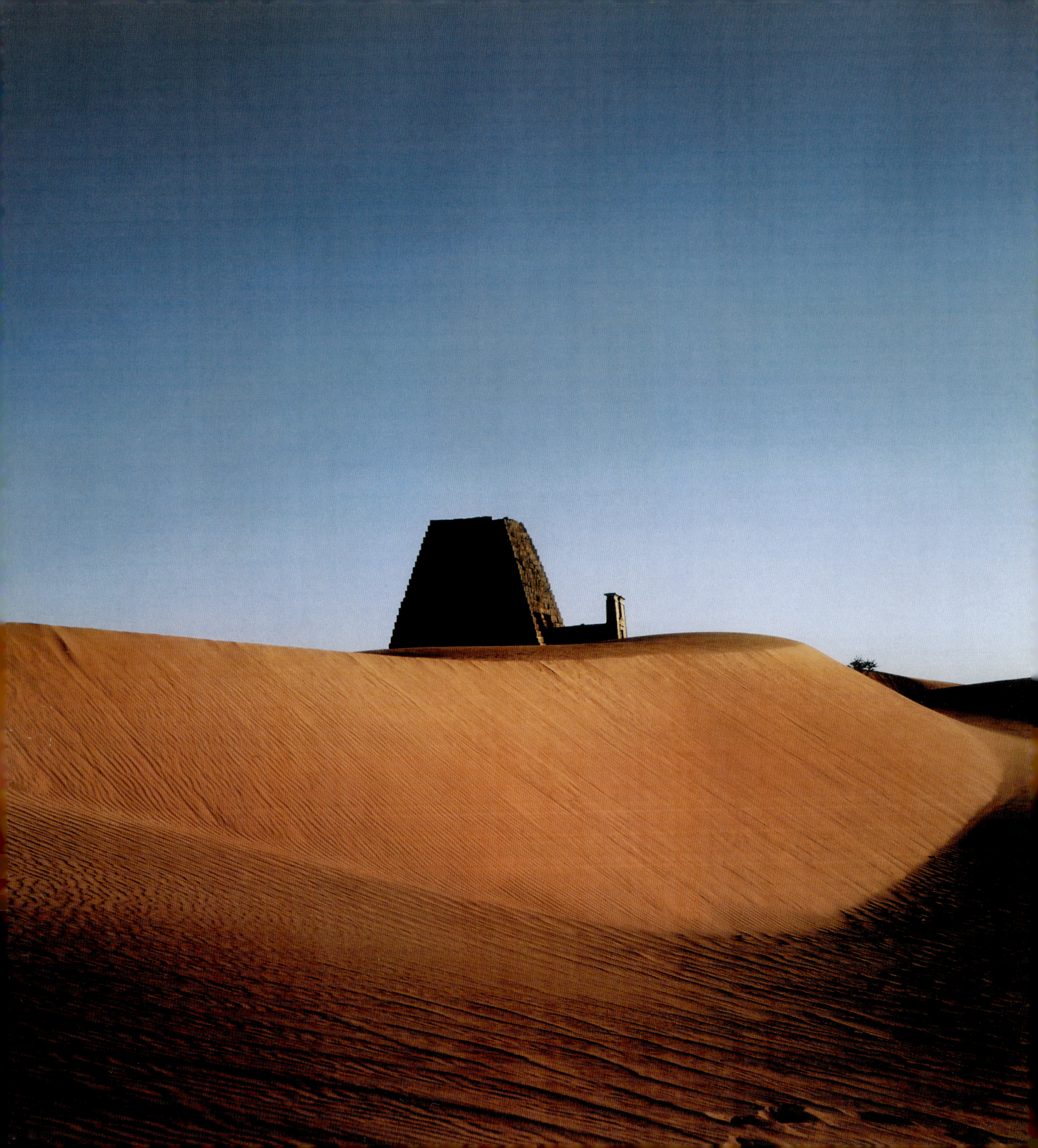

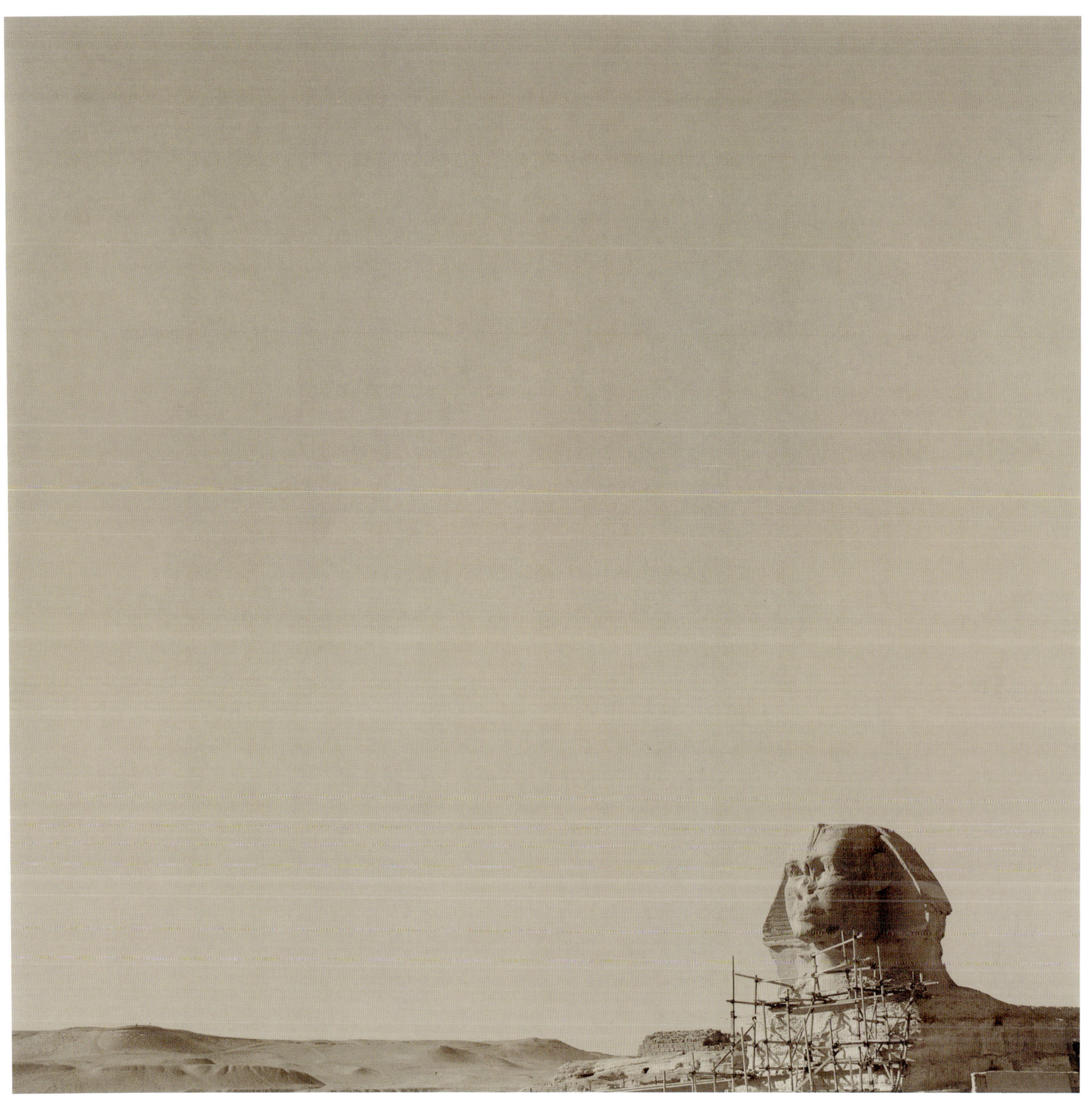

Atlantis and Its Colonies

The ancient mythic civilization of Atlantis was so named because European and Asian legends place it in the West, while North and South American legends place it to the East. In addition, Atlantis was assumed to be the acme of civilization of a previous world age that existed somewhere in the middle of the Atlantic Ocean. It was the prototypical precursor of civilization, the home of the gods, the Garden of Eden, Mount Meru, Paradise, and the "golden age" of humanity before the present era—all rolled into one. The scientific and historical establishments have never accepted the existence of Atlantis, but there have been an estimated twenty thousand books written about it nonetheless. Most, if not all, of the proof advanced is circumstantial, which it must be since Atlantis was a decimated former-world age civilization. The sheer number of commentators almost suggests that the principle of a previous golden age is ingrained in the human psyche as an archetype.

The earliest reference to Atlantis is also the most persuasive: the great Greek philosopher Plato described the extensive physical design, history, laws, agricultural practices, shortcomings, and virtues of Atlantis in his dialogue *Timaeus.* The destruction of Atlantis is partially described in *Critias,* but the manuscript ends in mid-sentence.

According to Plato, the story of Atlantis was told originally by the sage of Athens, Solon (640–558 BCE), who had heard it from Egyptian priests. Solon dated the fall of Atlantis approximately 9,000 years earlier, in the middle of the tenth millennium BCE.[12] Subsequent to Plato, many attempts have been made to locate the exact site of Atlantis and to trace its influence on human mythology, customs, art, and architecture. Due to the corruption, abuse of nature, and use of crystals to contain the sun, Atlantis was doomed to destruction, which happened when a series of catastrophic earthquakes led to the sinking of the entire island into the sea. Luckily, some Atlanteans left before or during the cataclysm and survived to colonize the remaining continents.

What is fascinating is that many of the sacred landscapes and sites in this book have been linked to Atlantis as colonies that were active in ancient times or were the result of Atlanteans fleeing the destruction of their island nation. Therefore, we see legends of Native Americans, Peruvians, Mexicans, Tibetans, Chinese, Japanese, Egyptians, Greeks, and even the African Zulus point toward connections with Atlantis. In my book *The Divine Plot*, I list thirty-nine countries around the world—on every continent except Antarctica—that have flood legends echoing the destruction of Atlantis and the worldwide deluge that resulted. There are myriad linguistic, symbolic, architectural, artistic, as well as mythic Atlantean parallels. This is especially profound, as there is no tangible proof that Atlantis ever existed.

The Grand Canyon is an important sacred space to the Southwestern Hopi, Navajo, and Paiute Indians, whose myths are cosmologies that regard the canyon as much more than a natural wonder. This great chasm in the landscape is allegedly supernatural and guarded by spirits. The springs of the Colorado River have souls, and even the various animals that the Indians hunted and killed were considered mentors and totem ancestors. The Hopi believe that the canyon was created by the Great Flood that had drowned the previous corrupt world, and that they had risen from this "place of emergence" as survivors of the flood.

The Return of Paradise

The great Elizabethan philosopher and statesman Francis Bacon (1561–1626) envisioned a dream shared by many of the Rosicrucian sages—a secret society of mystics formed in medieval Germany—which was a return to the principles of the ancient world of Atlantis. Bacon and his allies prepared for a golden age they called Arcadia, which they thought would be a time of concord and harmony. Their knowledge of ancient Atlantis was unique because it was always veiled in allegory, kept hidden from the masses, and only available to few scholars and churchmen. Bacon himself was renowned for playing and working with allegory as a way to protect himself from the profane and the authorities, so he was the perfect one to promulgate this theory.[13] According to scholar Peter Dawkins's *Arcadia*, Bacon and the Rosicrucians joined symbolism from Atlantis with what they knew of Egyptian mysteries and the legends of King Arthur, incorporating this utopian vision into their mysterious institution. In his early years Bacon was aided by the notorious alchemist Dr. John Dee, and he later taught and supported many of the major thinkers of his time in an effort to bring his dream to fruition.

A group of Unitarians at Harvard University founded the Transcendental Club of America in 1836. They were authors and poets Ralph Waldo Emerson, Frederic Henry Hedge, George Putnam, and George Ripley, who were soon joined by Henry David Thoreau, John Greenleaf Whittier, and Bronson Alcott and who later influenced Walt Whitman.[14] These American transcendentalists sought to reform the prevailing materialistic philosophy of their contemporaries by expressing idealistic social change that was suffused with spirituality from the Hindus, Greeks, Egyptians, and Persians, as well as Kant and Goethe. They even envisioned their own Arcadia in the United States, a group of shepherds and poets singing the praises of the pure environment and the power of nature.

The American transcendentalists talked about earlier British poets such as Carlyle, Coleridge, and Wordsworth and viewed them as inspirational supporters of their movement in England. They

PAGE 164: Granite buildings and terraces, Machu Picchu, Peru, 2000

PAGE 165: Marhubi Palace ruins, former home of Sultan Seyyid Barghash, near Stone Town, Zanzibar, Tanzania, 1997

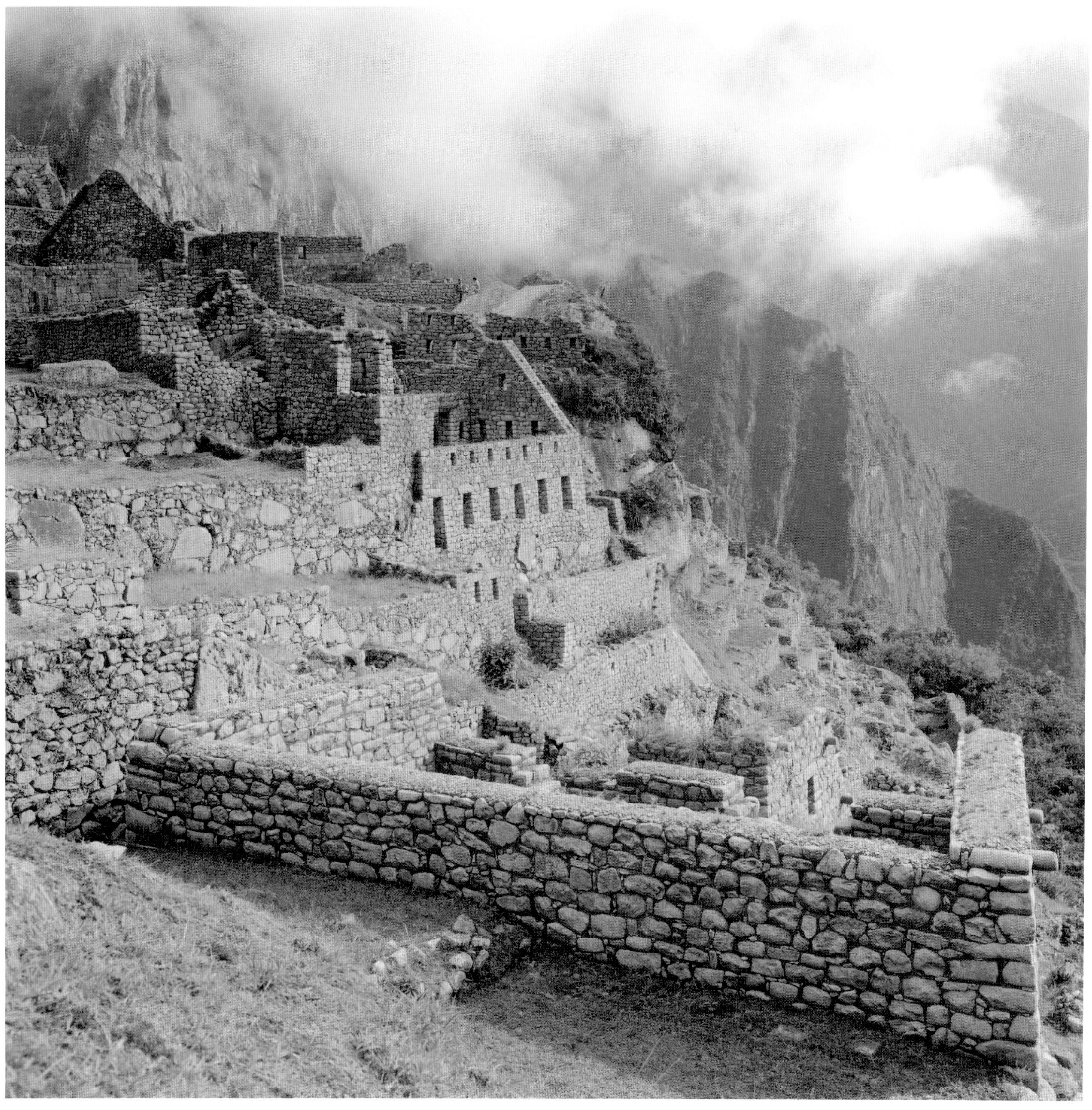

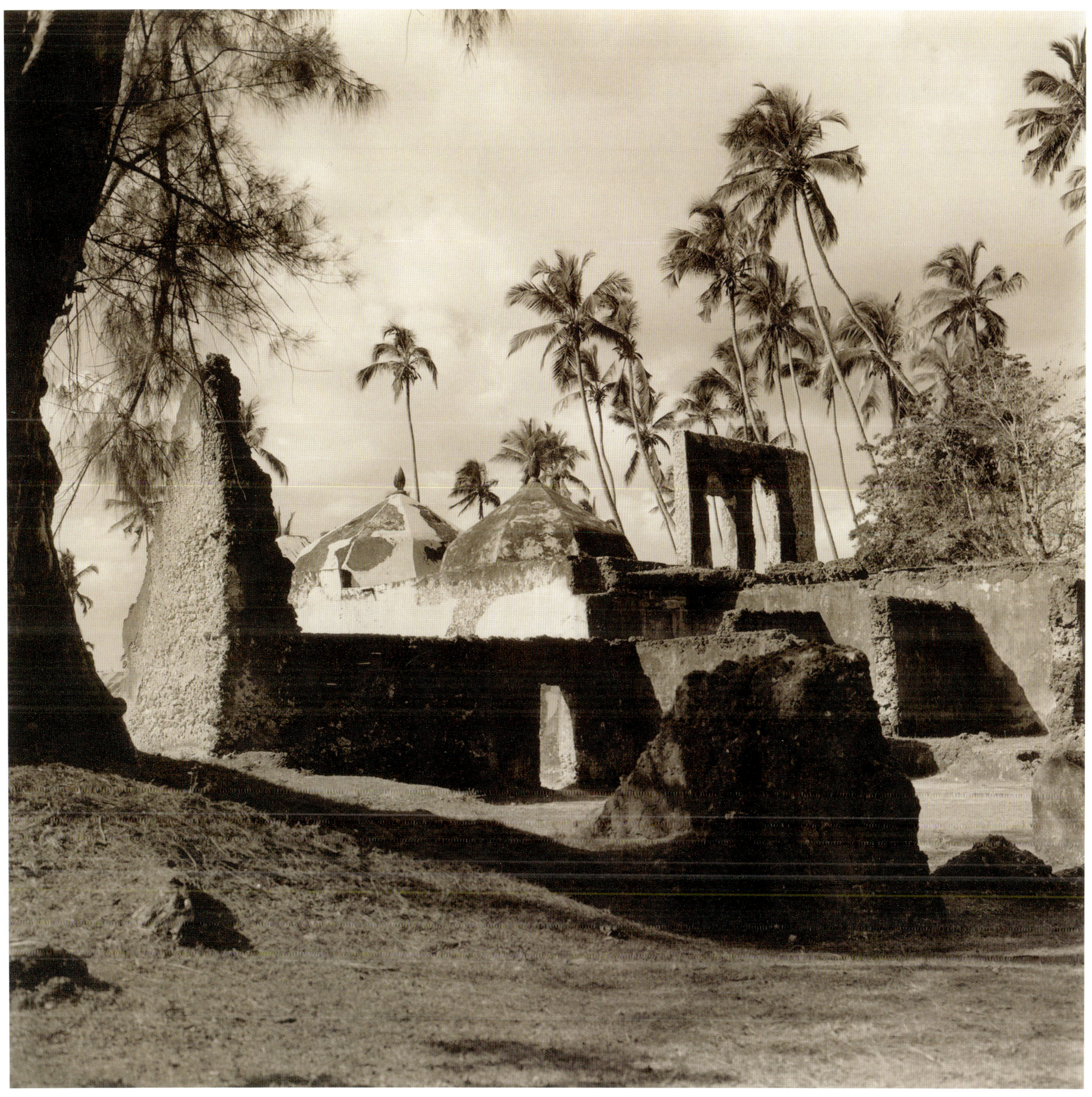

studied and translated Sanskrit classics such as the Bhagavad Gita, the Upanishads, the Vedas, and the Puranas. Thoreau wrote a meditation about the Bhagavad Gita and the Hindu gods in *Walden*, where he advocated a return to nature and to those cultures and religions that preached communion with Earth. This integration of Eastern and Western philosophies had a powerful effect on the work of all the transcendentalists. For example, an 1843 journal entry by Emerson posits reincarnation as central to his life philosophy: "Life itself is an interim and transition; this O Indur [Indra], is my one and twenty thousandth form, and already I feel the old Life sprouting underneath in the twenty thousand and first."

The landscapes of America have inspired generations of schools and painters, such as the Hudson River School of Frederic Edwin Church, Thomas Cole, and Sanford Gifford, as well as others who see the pastoral environment and landscape of heaven in their midst, just north of New York City. Indeed, a recent book by curator and art historian John K. Howat about these men is titled *American Paradise*.[15] Sometimes we find the mythic sacred lands in our imaginations and other times find them right on our doorstep.

OPPOSITE: Iceberg, Disko Bay, Greenland, 2000

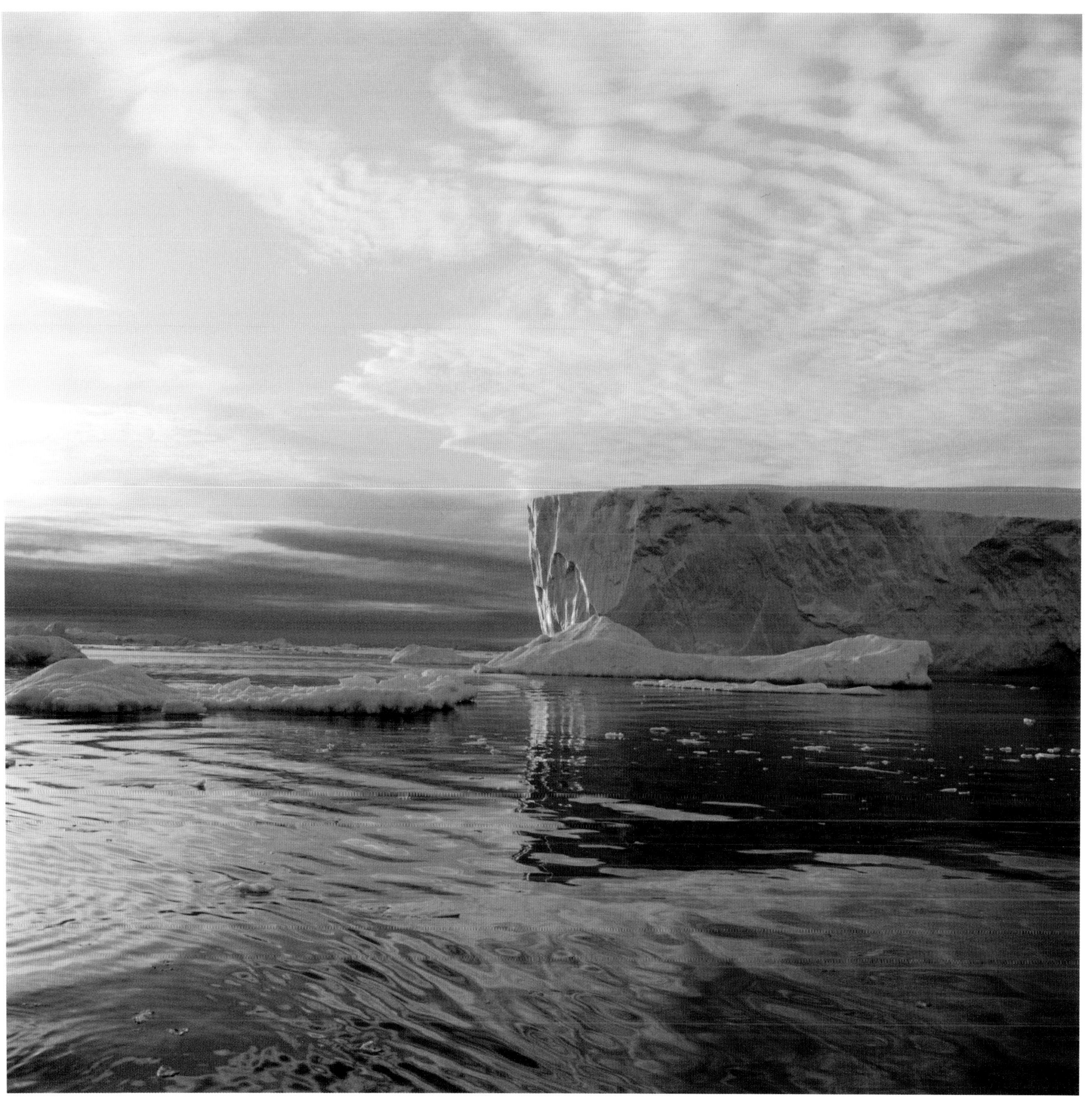

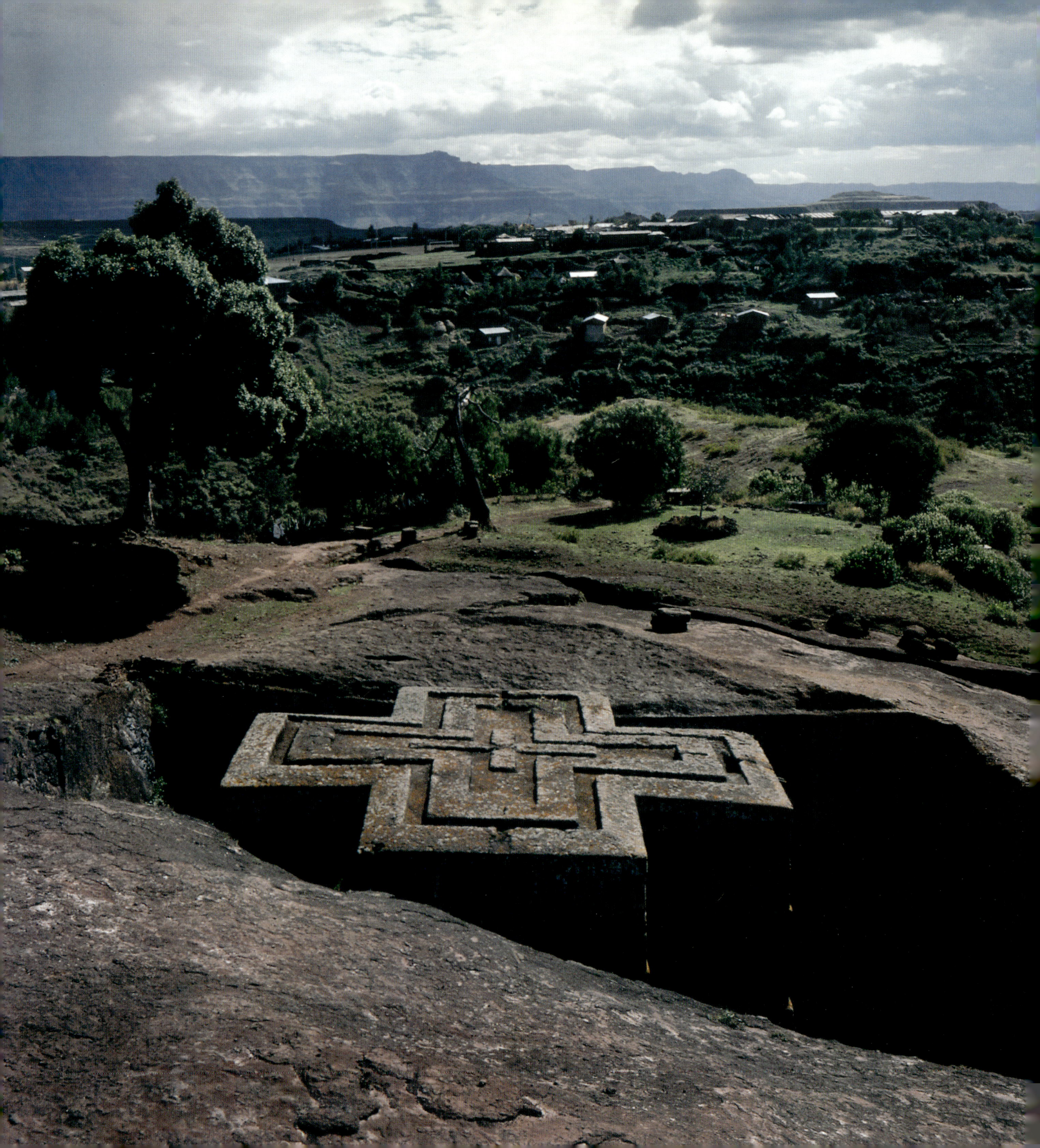

CHAPTER 10

Orientation

Landscape features as expressive of particular holiness . . . came about because of a religious tradition in which the land was not a picture but a true force which physically embodied the powers that ruled the world.

—Vincent Scully, *The Earth, the Temple and The Gods* (1962)[1]

The relationship of landscapes and buildings to the arc of the sun and moon and to the progress of days, nights, and seasons affects our awareness and our bodies in profound ways, but we easily neglect how we situate ourselves in respect to these natural patterns of life. The shifting of light and shadow continually modifies the landscape and plays with it. Our orientation in space and time is essential because it links our internal biological clocks with the natural diurnal patterns, or circadian rhythms, which are central to our health and well-being.[2]

As William Lethaby states in his wondrous book *Architecture, Mysticism and Myth* (1892), the "perfect temple should stand at the center of the world, a microcosm of the universe fabric, its walls built foursquare with the wall of heaven."[3] He acknowledges that the earliest human conceptions of the universe were cubic, as exemplified by the construction and orientation of foursquare Egyptian temples, Buddhist stupas, Mexican pyramids, as well as Greek and Christian places of worship. Indeed, this idea of the world is represented in the original Latin word for "paradise," which is derived from the original Iranian for "walled enclosure." Sacred buildings universally respect the four cardinal directions, and the positions of the sanctuary entrances and altars reflect the rising in the East and setting in the West of the sun, moon, and planets, which were seen in early cultures as messengers of the gods and goddesses.

There is much evidence that certain cultures watched, revered, and oriented their sacred places toward the sun or moon, as well as planets like Venus (the Morning/Evening Star) and various constellations. As shown in chapter 8, the three major pyramids of Giza are situated in the landscape to reflect the

OPPOSITE: Church of Bet Giorgis, carved from the bedrock, Lalibela, Ethiopia, 1997

PAGE 170: Mosque, Sudan, 1998

PAGE 171: Stone mandala, Lumbini, Nepal, 1992

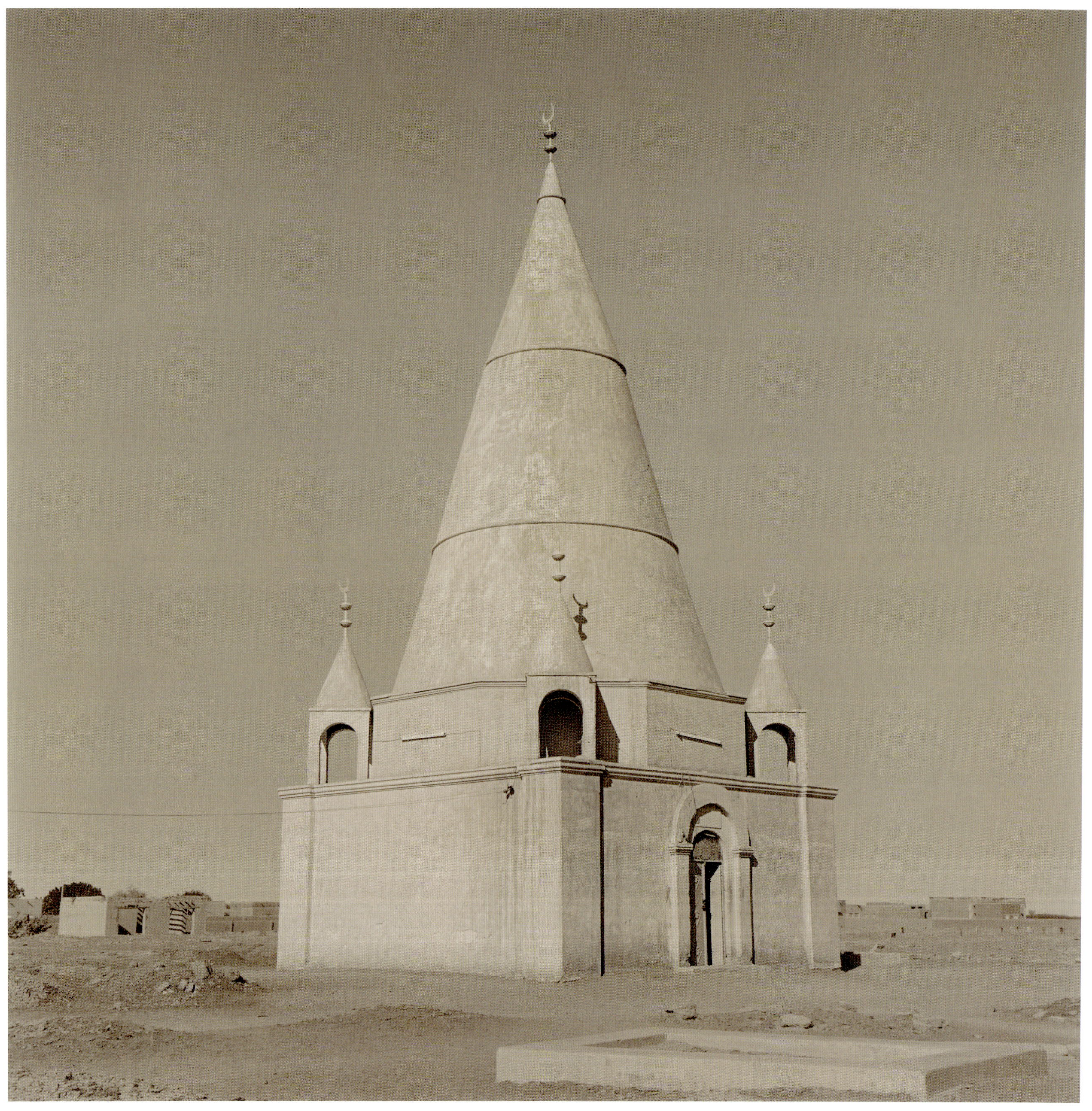

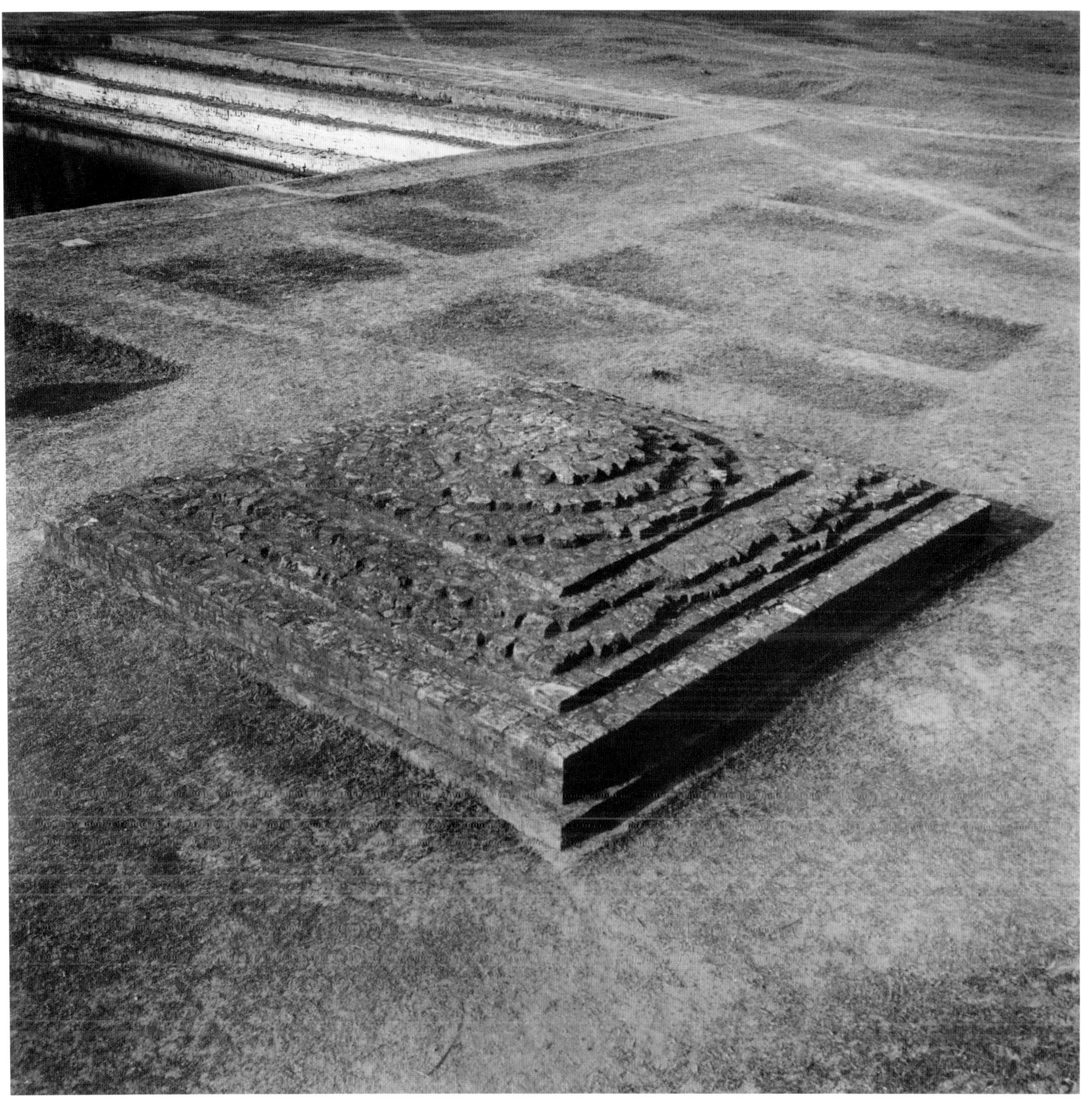

constellation Orion, and the placement of major temples at Angkor reflects the constellation Draco. Some even suggest that the Greeks worshipping Demeter oriented temples toward the auroras; and that the Dodona temples in Greece are oriented on the axis between the opposite constellations Leo and Aquarius.[4]

This theory of astronomical landscaping also links temples across Greece with their appropriate constellations; if the Parthenon is the navel of the Greek empire, then the sacred site at Delphi is equivalent to the Pole Star. Jean Richer, author of *Sacred Geography of the Ancient Greeks* (1994), takes the case even farther, suggesting that the entire structure of Athenian society was also based on this geometry manifest in their landscape. According to second-century grammarian Julius Pollux, "the Athenians (were divided) into four groups, each group into three tribes, and every tribe into thirty clans."[5] Each of these twelve tribes had a different hero, reflecting the magical number of twelve. Twelve was prominent in the Babylonian calendar and in the organization of astrology and astronomy—disciplines that, in ancient times, were the same thing.

The incorporation of celestial movements and mythological figures into ancient Greek landscaping animated these ancient sites, and many of the early Mediterranean landscapes were places where the sacred was alive. On the sacred island of Delos in the Aegean Sea, there was a sacred tree and altar made of goat horns, which signified the Cancer-Capricorn astrological axis. Later, these sacred landscapes gained temples and other ritual markers, but in the beginning their sacredness was based purely on their location as it related to the stars and planets. The Greeks also had an earthly equivalent of a solstitial axis—a nearby mountain peak, mountain crest, or island in the distance. These loci were considered gateways for the gods.[6]

The Mayan worldview is unique because the primary axis isn't north-south, but rather east-west, as determined by the positions of the rising and setting sun. As with many of the cultures we have seen, the Maya attributed colors, trees, animals, qualities and specific rituals to the cosmological quadrants overlying the human world. The east—always at the top of any image of the Mayan world—was where the sun was born.[7] However, the Mayan cosmological layout was also vertical, in that the physical world was complemented above and below by spirit worlds along the *wacah chan* axis that ran through the center of existence. "To the Maya the world was alive and imbued with a sacredness that was especially concentrated at special points, like caves and mountains. The principal pattern of power points had been established by the gods when the cosmos was created."[8] The power of this axis was verified by the king himself, through his visions.

OPPOSITE: Pyramid of Chephren, Giza (Dynasty IV, c. 2500 BCE), 1989

Likewise, Native American cosmological myths link the spirit of the sun, moon, and the Morning Star with the four cardinal directions, as reflected in ritual prayer to the elements of the sacred landscape for guidance and the assurance of good crops and hunting.[9] In some myths, the Coyote god identified

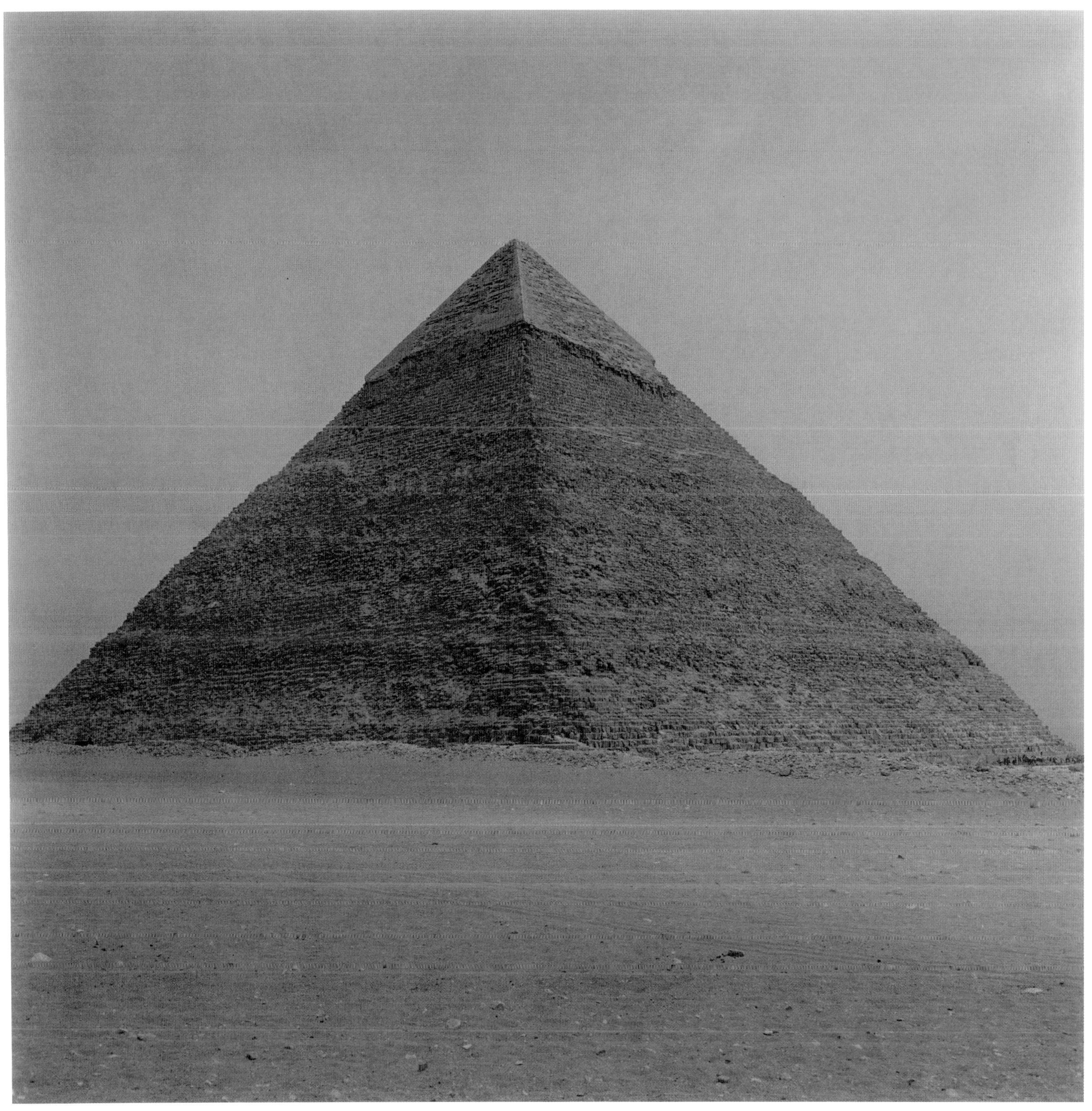

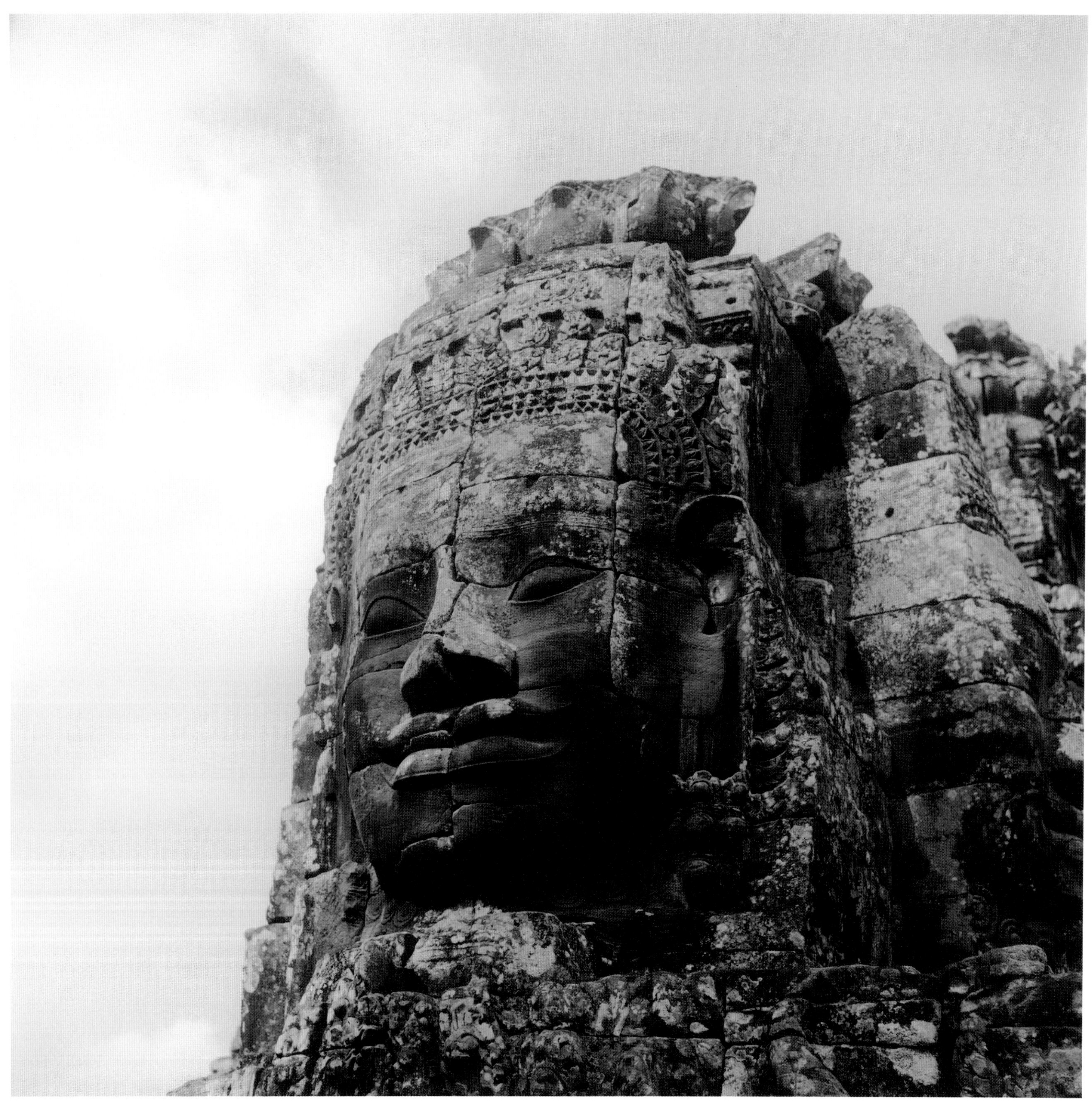

the Pole Star and the Great Bear (represented by the Pleiades or Seven Sisters) and then camouflaged them with mica dust thrown into the sky.[10]

The Neolithic Temples of Britain

The discoveries at Stonehenge in southwestern England by the astronomer and astrophysicist Gerald Hawkins (formerly of the Smithsonian Institution) are striking even today. For thousands of years, visitors have wondered what these magnificent stone circles could possibly have meant; they were thought to be a nature temple, a calendar, a place of sacrifice, a sun temple, a graveyard, a governmental symbol, and many other things. Hawkins's discoveries revealed that each of the rings of stones brought to the site and erected over a period of a thousand years had precise astronomical alignments. He also found that the exact siting of Stonehenge was determined mathematically and symbolically, and he claimed that its builders were familiar with the 54-year Triple Saros cycle, which is composed of three Saros eclipse cycles of 18 years, 11 days each.[11]

Hawkins came to consider Stonehenge a calculator or computer because of its unique geometry, units of measurement, qualities, and orientation. The earliest inhabitants to record their thoughts about Stonehenge naturally believed it must have been built by a race of giants from a previous world age, given the extreme size and weight of the stones and the fact that they were erected in a part of England that has no stone. Indeed, sarsen stones, averaging thirty tons in weight, were transported twenty miles from Marlborough Downs, and the smaller bluestones came from South Wales, almost 130 miles, as the crow flies, to the northwest.[12]

For years, many people wondered if there was some connection among the many megalithic sites all over the British Isles. During the 1920s, Alfred Watkins, an Englishman who traveled for a living, came to notice a complex criss-crossing web of lines that went straight through the landscape. These lines linked holy places and antiquities such as mounds, church spires, standing stones, crossroads, trees, moats, and wells that aligned perfectly with distant hilltops and mountain peaks.[13] He even noticed that sacred places where such alignments were discovered—Ley Hills or Ley Fen, for instance—often had names derived from the common language root "leigh" or "lea," which means pasture or enclosed field. Thus, he called them ley lines, and he subsequently observed them all over the British Isles and mainland Europe.[14]

John Michell was an early supporter of Watkins's ideas and at one point stated, "Anyone who has followed their paths across country will find that his life has been enriched, perhaps deepened, by the experience."[15] Michell knew that such a network of leys existed all over England and that traces of

OPPOSITE: Buddha head, the Bayon, Angkor Thom, Angkor, Cambodia, 1993

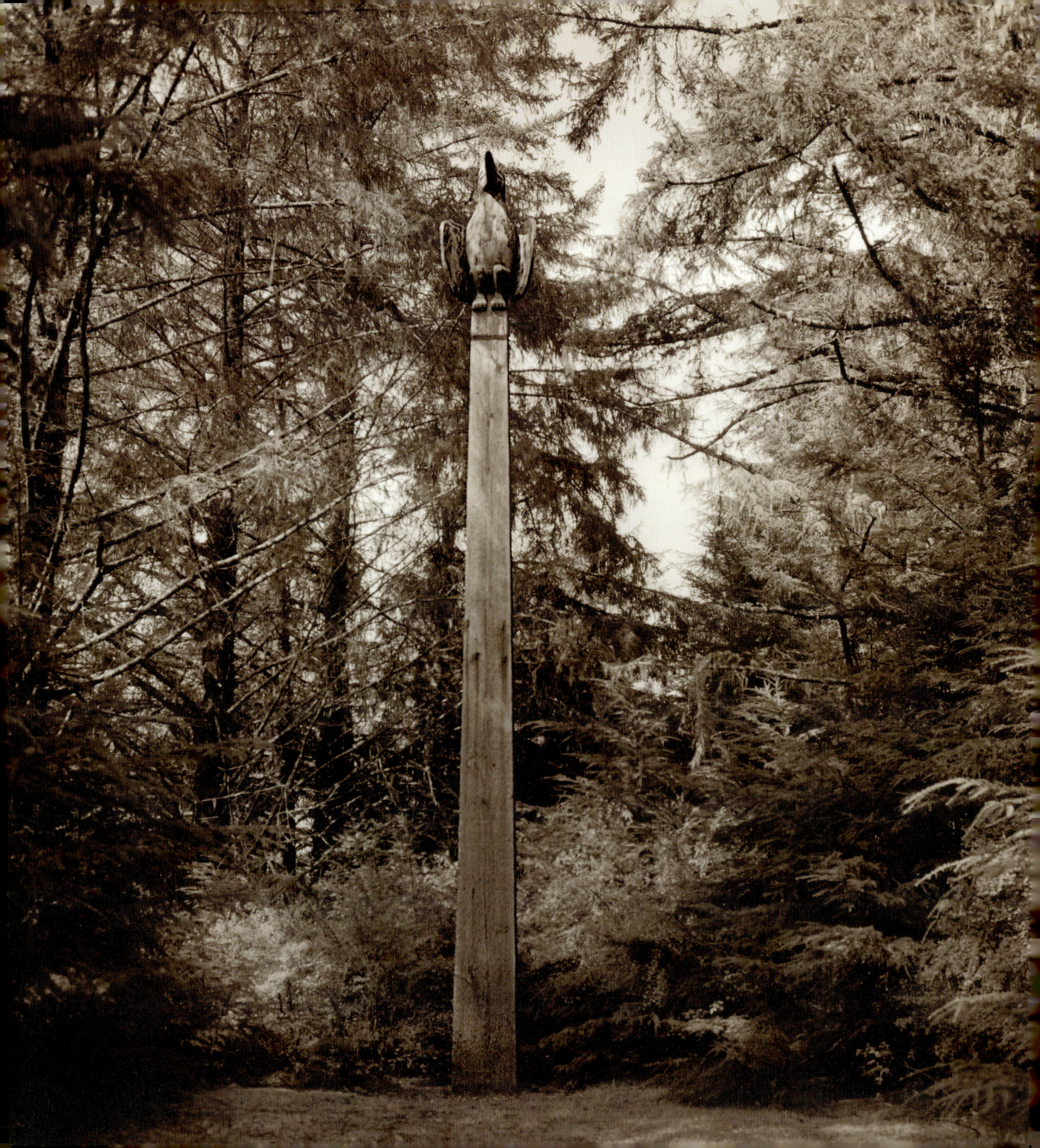

prehistoric leys also existed on other continents, including a Native American ceremonial path across New York State and Massachusetts. He also studied the plans of sacred cities in England, such as Glastonbury, and found that the layout of the buildings and special sites are not only on passing ley lines, but they also describe geometric shapes oriented in very particular ways to invoke and contain powerful spiritual energies from the surrounding landscape.

Michell mapped Stonehenge, Woodhenge, the church atop Glastonbury Tor, and many other sites and discovered repeating orientations and leys. He considered the sites cosmic temples and found that their geometries embodied special series of numbers related to numerology and utilized an ancient measurement system he called the "Canon."[16] This theory was influenced in part by Scottish engineer Alexander Thom's discovery of the megalithic yard—equivalent to 5.5 feet, or 1.7 meters in length[17]—which he linked with the royal cubit used for all sacred buildings in ancient Egypt.

The Mystery of Newgrange

Similar discoveries have been made at Newgrange and other Neolithic earth temples in the Boyne Valley, north and west of Dublin in Ireland. Artist and author Martin Brennan discovered that the 5,000-year-old carvings on these old mounds and their stones constitute an "entire cosmology, vocabulary of symbols, sundials, calendars, and other scientific tools of the oldest culture known in Ireland."[18] The ancient Irish kings reigned at the Hill of Tara, but they were all buried in the Boyne Valley on the plains of Royal Meath, within sight of Tara. Newgrange is the largest of the mounds in the Boyne Valley, the other major ones being Nowth and Dowth. They looked like small hills when they were discovered in 1699, but their orientation and relationship to each other were later found to have profound astronomical implications.[19] The long stone cavity in Newgrange, as well as the large stone near the entrance, are aligned with the winter solstice (on approximately December 21) sunrise, but there are many other orientation stones placed around the periphery of Newgrange that mark other important cosmic directions.

Four major alignments for all such monuments are common around the world: the sunrise and sunset angles on the summer and winter solstices, when the sun is farthest north and farthest south, respectively. The equinoctial points, as the name suggests, are halfway between the northernmost and southernmost positions of the sun.

Both outside and inside Newgrange are large stones lying supine on the ground, covered with strange and unique images that resemble hieroglyphs, with holes created in a number of very

OPPOSITE: Memorial column, Sitka National Historical Park, Alaska, United States, 1999

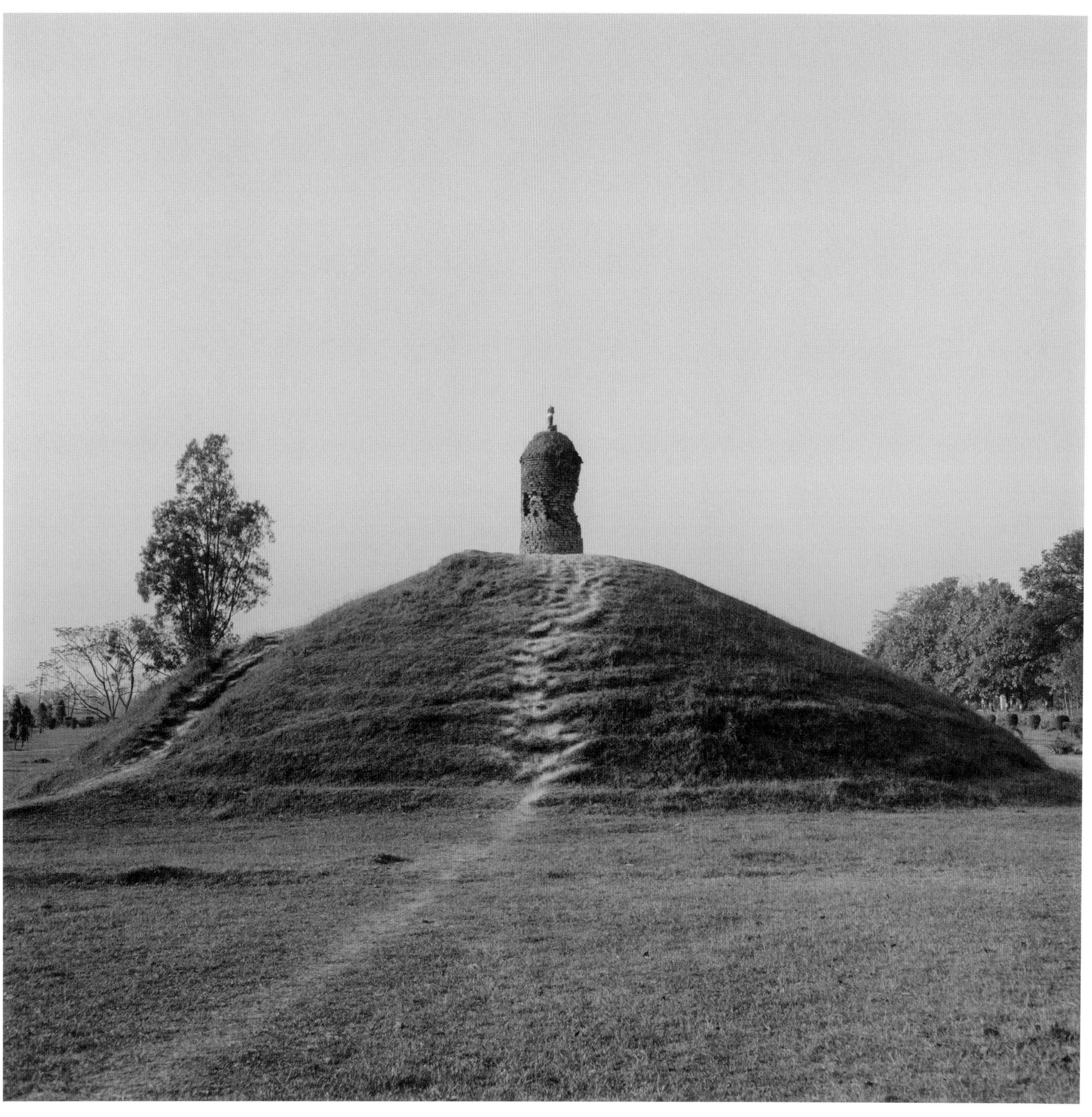

beautiful, symbolic forms. Some spiral out in clockwise and counterclockwise patterns, while others show a central "sun" with radiating sets of points emanating from them—the classic symbol for the radiant sun. Others are series of distorted triangles and rectangles in unusual patterns, almost like the ceremonial tattoos of certain African tribes. Brennan discovered a basic fact at Newgrange that has profound implications: "[I]n nature and in geomancy, where primary lines converge, the converging lines take a spiral course. Two opposing and equal forces form spirals on collision, as in water going down a drain."[20] The triangles of the Newgrange monument show the symbolic convergence of fire and water in the landscape, which resembles a Star of David, with an upward pointing triangle, symbolizing fire, intersecting with a downward pointing triangle, symbolizing water. The basic nature of water to sink down, and the tendency of fire to burn upward, together explain the relevance of these universal symbols that show up in sacred places all over the world. And, naturally enough, these sacred places are also positioned in places where the sun's path can be measured and where underground water moves in precise patterns.

The main geometry at Newgrange is formed by two crossings of solstitial points—which lie on the eastern and western horizons where the sun rises and sets on the winter solstice and summer solstice—that meet at the very center of the monument. At this precise intersection is an altar deep within the ground, and on this altar are stones that pinpoint where the sun's rays hit once a year, when the male sun god penetrates the earth goddess's womb. A configuration of stones above the entrance to the tunnel allows a pinpoint of light to enter at the significant times, and when those points are recorded and marked with carvings, they form amazingly beautiful spirals, like those at the entryway. Thus "the cross is the static union of opposites, while the spiral is the union of opposites in movement."[21] The spiral stone carvings at Newgrange depict the natural spiraling movement that water and earth energies often make, as in waterfalls and the meandering rivers and streams identified by Schauberger (see chapter 4). This offers a profound understanding of natural forces that existed thousands of years ago, when humanity was (supposedly) primitive.

Brennan speculates that the entire landscape of Ireland was surveyed five thousand years ago, which would explain why many cairns, stone circles, and standing stones are positioned according to the intersections of certain landscape lines. That such prehistorical tombs and burial places were used as a scientific instrument, rather like the Egyptians used the Great Pyramid, the temple at Luxor, and many other monuments, is a fascinating proposition. Many of the mounds form a huge circle around the Boyne Valley, almost twenty miles in radius, and could only have been sited so precisely if their builders possessed an amazingly accurate way of measuring both distance and time. Brennan even

OPPOSITE: Stupa ruins, Lumbini, Nepal, 1992

postulates that using Newgrange and its flattened geometry may have allowed the ancient Irish to realize that Earth wasn't a perfect sphere, but rather flattened at the poles due to geomagnetic energies and forces.[22]

Indian Observatories

While Stonehenge is an ancient device for measuring astronomical cycles, there is a younger landscape sculpture that doubles as a much more accurate, large-scale astronomical instrument: the Jantar Mantar in Delhi, India, created during the reign of the Maharaja Jai Singh II (1699–1743), who also built an observatory at Jaipur. He was ruler of the kingdom of Amber during the time when North India was ruled by the Mughal emperors and eventually became governor of the Agra and Malwa provinces. His people selected a perfect site for observation of the heavens, made models, and took measurements with their brass instruments for seven years, but when they found that these instruments were not accurate enough, they recreated them in masonry on a gigantic scale in 1724 CE. The entire architectural complex measures time and calculates the movements of celestial bodies with instruments that resemble massive sculptures. Fittingly, the name Jantar Mantar (Yantra Mantra), which means "calculation instrument," reflects the astronomical purpose of these enormous art forms. "Yantra" is an Indian term meaning a meditation diagram. Often composed of geometrical shapes, it is used for psychological or spiritual liberation.

Probably the most famous and iconic part of the observatory is the Samrat Yantra, a huge right-triangular building with a staircase on the diagonal that is aligned with Earth's north-south axis and that is surrounded on three sides with a reflecting pool of water. It is an equinoctial dial instrument, and its diagonal gnomon (like the triangular piece atop a sundial) makes an angle of 28 degrees and 39 minutes with the base—an angle that happens to be the exact latitude of Delhi. This instrument is flanked by two curved quadrants that are 50 feet in radius and marked in degrees, minutes, and seconds in both Hindi and English. In reality, the Samrat Yantra is simply an extremely accurate sundial, but only a sundial created with a superior geographic awareness would have the angle of its hypotenuse to the base the same as its latitude. In any event, this instrument can calculate the local time for Delhi, Indian Standard Time, the exact location of the Pole Star, and the declination of the sun, based on various other observations.[23] At any time of the day, the shadow onto one of the quadrants shows the exact hour, minute, and second, and when there is no shadow it is noon Delhi local time and 12:21 PM Indian Standard Time. At sunrise the exact time is read against the western quadrant, and

OPPOSITE: Gnomon of the great sundial Samrat Yantra, Jantar Mantar, Delhi, India, 2007

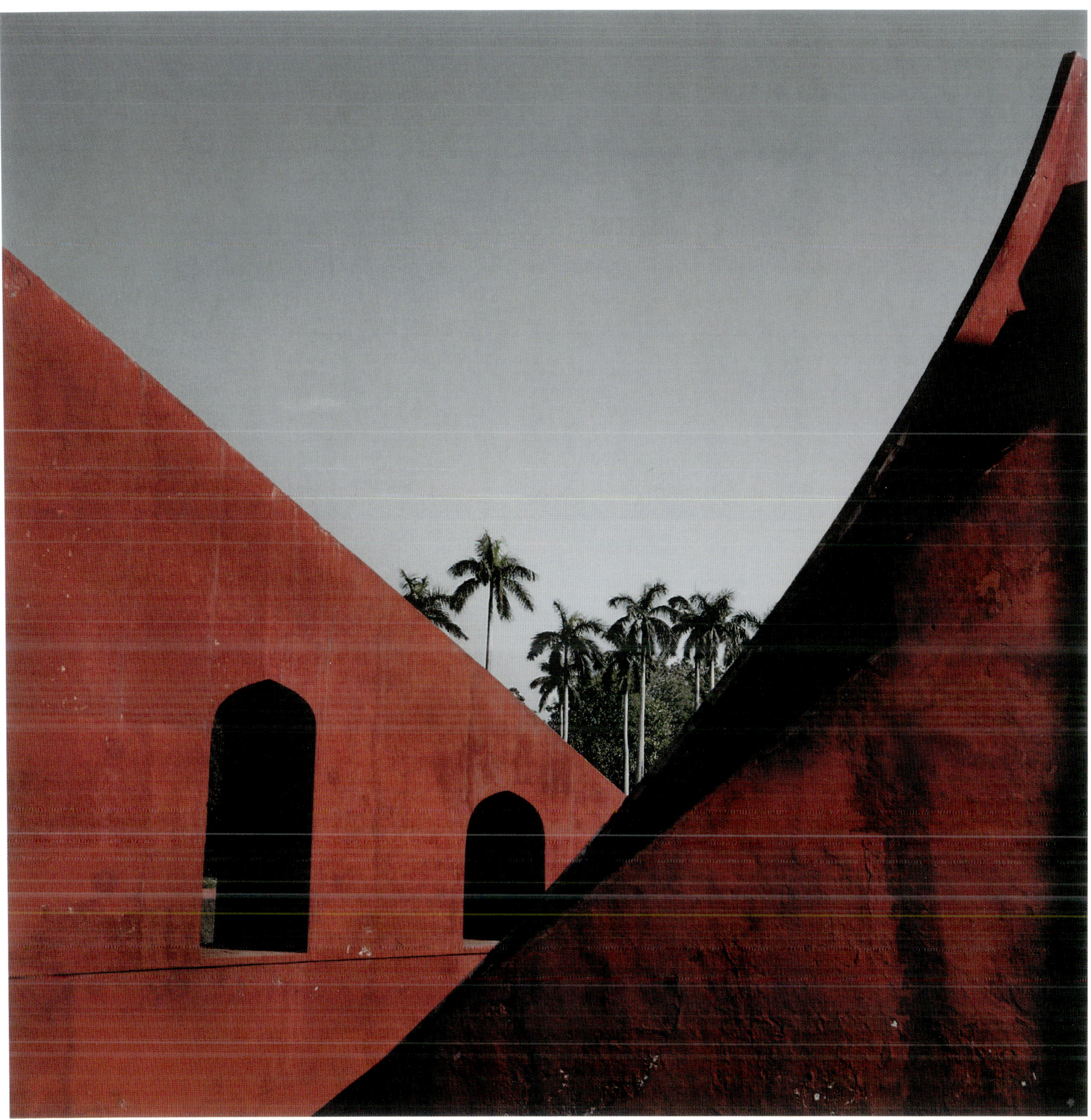

at sunset the time is read against the eastern quadrant. At night, the positions of known stars whose meridian times have been calculated allow the time to be known very accurately also.

The Samrat Yantra is derived from traditional sextants used by surveyors and by navigators at sea or on land; sextants have remained virtually unchanged until the advent of computers. In sacred landscapes, the sides of pyramids, the triangular pediments of Greek or Roman temples, Native American teepees, stupas, and even mountains can be used for the purpose of telling time when observations are made over long periods and are recorded with marks on the ground or on an equivalent of quadrants.

The Jai Prakash Yantra is constructed from two inverted hollow hemispheres with markings that reflect the visible sky as it would appear if it were turned upside down. By keeping an eye on the rising and setting times and locations of various planets or stars when sitting at night in the bottom of the bowl, it is possible to determine their exact positions. The two bowls alternate 15-degree sectors of masonry and open space and are inverses of each other; by using both bowls it is possible to know stellar positions in the entire sky, both day and night. This ingenious solution provides all the information necessary for a complete astronomical ephemeris, which includes the altitude, azimuth, declination, meridian, tropic, and zodiac engraved along the segments.

Other buildings in the Jantar Mantar allow the calculation of solar and lunar calendars and other planetary cycles, and one of the instruments allows the determination of planetary longitude, which is the distance a planet or other heavenly body is from 0 degrees Aries in the sidereal zodiac used in Vedic astrology. There is even a room on a platform used on two days of the year to predict weather based on the speed, strength, and temperature of the winds.

As miraculous and beautiful as the Jantar Mantar is, it appears in other forms in many cultures. Many such monuments for determining solar or lunar calendars or astrological ephemerides are either a part of the natural landscape or are built into important buildings. Often these are located at a place considered a sacred world center or, as the Greeks called theirs at Delphi, an *omphalos* (navel). During the Han dynasty (25–220 CE), the current Chinese town of Gao cheng zhen, located about fifty miles southeast of then-capital Luoyang, was considered the center of the world. More than two thousand years ago a gnomon similar to the Jantar Mantar was installed there so that time could be determined.[24] In the thirteenth century an astronomer built a pyramidal tower that had an angular "sky measuring scale" protruding from one of the walls to the north. In such instances pools of water are used, not only to see reflections of the heavens, but to provide an absolutely level plane for accurate observations. As the authority of the emperors of China depended upon their being considered sons of heaven, these observations supplemented their imperial power.

OPPOSITE: Mihrab, Friday Mosque (Abbasid dynasty, eighth century CE), Isfahan, Iran, 2001

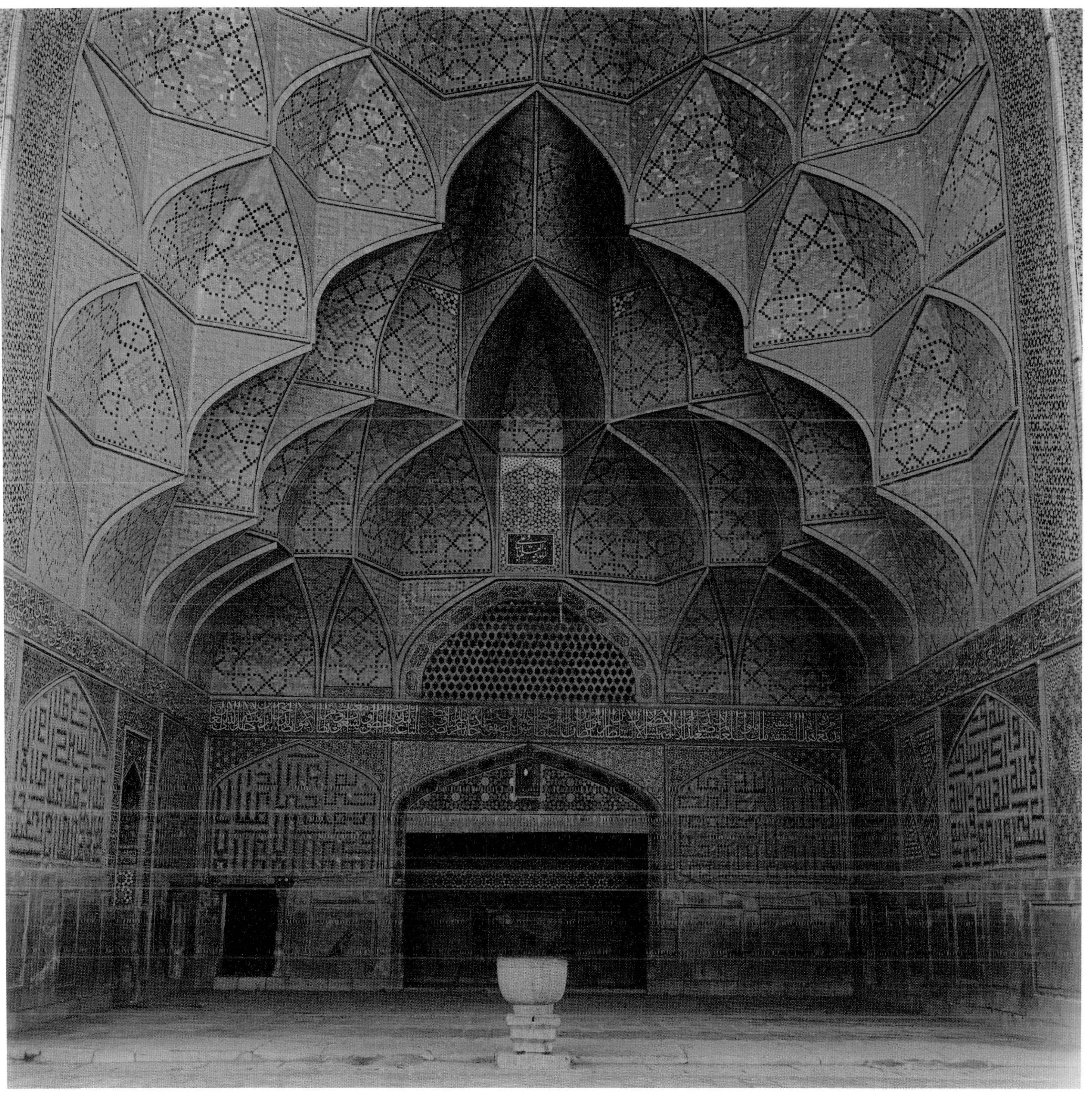

The mihrab is a central element in Islamic mosques because it directs the attention of the faithful to Muhammad, pointing the way toward the Ka'aba in Mecca. Its form is much like the entrance to a cave, and it is often decorated in beautiful ways that evoke a kind of geometric paradise. Ironically the same name designates private prayer rooms in Judaism, showing once again the deep relationship between these two Abrahamic religions.

Ancient America

Contrary to the mythology of Columbus discovering the primitive American continent, there are many places in the Western hemisphere—particularly in the western United States—where astronomical observatories have existed for thousands of years. Even as modern scientists refuse to acknowledge the presence of sophisticated astronomy in this hemisphere before the arrival of the Europeans, evidence continues to emerge showing that many different Native American cultures practiced calendrical and astronomical arts.

The extraordinary sacred landscape of Serpent Mound in Brush Creek Valley, Ohio, is the largest and finest serpent effigy in the United States. Its time of origin is in dispute, but radiocarbon dating suggests that it was almost certainly made hundreds of years before Columbus by the Fort Ancient culture and that it may even have been constructed as early as 800 BCE.[25] The mound resembles a huge snake or serpent curling through the landscape with an open mouth, appearing as if intent on eating an egg. The orientation of the coils of the serpent is in alignment with the summer solstice sunset and winter solstice sunrise, as well as with both equinox sunrises, meaning that it was almost certainly used as both a ritual site and an observatory for calculating the progression of the seasons and creating a calendar.

Serpent Mound sits within a gigantic meteoric crater five miles across and one thousand feet deep. The entire area is highly magnetic due to the buried remains of a meteor that 256 million years ago—when the Appalachian mountains were as high and as young as the Himalayas—collided with Earth at 45,000 miles per hour. Apparently scientists have found the very rare metal iridium embedded in quartz crystals 1,500 feet under the surface of the crater at a higher concentration than anywhere else on Earth—except its core. In fact, the edge of the crater is so prominent that various trees and crevices along the periphery could have allowed the mound's creators to determine places for aligning the rising and setting sun and moon times and positions. That this meteor-impact site is also magnetic and transmits powerful earth energy through the Serpent Mound basin evokes comparison with the meteor enclosed within the Ka'aba at Mecca, the central point around which participants of the yearly Hajj pilgrimages move in prayer, and toward which Muslims all over the world face during their daily prayers. It is not surprising that both of these "magnetic" places are considered centers of the world.

Evidence also indicates that the Maya observed solar, lunar, and planetary alignments from El Caracol, the famous observatory at Chichén Itzá. This monument, which incorporated the movements of the planet Venus into its layout, alignment, and architecture, was a cylindrical tower perched atop a pyramid. Within the building was another cylinder with four doorways not in alignment with the outer doorways. The purpose of this unusual layout was so that the positions of the rays of the sun or night positions of Venus, which penetrated through the narrow visual slots between the pairs of doors, could be recorded on the walls of the innermost room. The Maya of Chichén Itzá associated Venus with their primary god Kukulcan, identical to the Aztec deity Quetzalcoatl and one of the "crucified gods" of antiquity (in addition to Jesus and the Zoroastrian god Mithras). Various colors associated with the cardinal directions, which appear in the myth of Kukulcan, were likely painted onto the plaster-covered inside walls of the Caracol.

In fact, the entire sophisticated and precise astronomical and calendrical system of the Maya was based on the movements of Venus combined with that of the sun. In their society the high priest was essentially "He of the Sun," suggesting that, as in many other cultures, astronomical duties were an integral part of the priesthood.[26] Using their pictographic language and astronomical temples, they were able to calculate the appearance of eclipses to an amazing accuracy—something on the order of plus or minus one day in 4,500 years—which is astonishing. This beautiful and profound calendar also predicted the end of the world in the year 2012. The mythology, architecture, calendar, city structure, and mathematics of the ancient Maya were thus intimately correlated, demonstrating a high degree of cultural complexity that challenges our notions of what constitutes scientific knowledge and how it was attained in the past. To this day, the sacred landscapes of the Yucatan carry this mystery.

At Machu Picchu there are also ancient orientation devices that would be very easy to miss unless one understood the underlying dynamics of calendar arts and astronomy. The most obvious instrument, previously mentioned in chapter 3, is the Intihuatana. This strange sculpture was carved out of a single block of granite—astounding, as the Inca did not even know how to work iron to make tools. The way in which one of the hardest minerals in the world was worked to a completely smooth finish defies the imagination, and even more puzzling to scientists is how massive stones weighing many tons might have been transported up thousands of feet along paths barely wide enough to accommodate foot traffic.

The Intihuatana is a type of gnomon, or sundial, that is less than two feet high but that throws shadows onto its base, from which many subtle platforms protrude at odd angles. Because of the

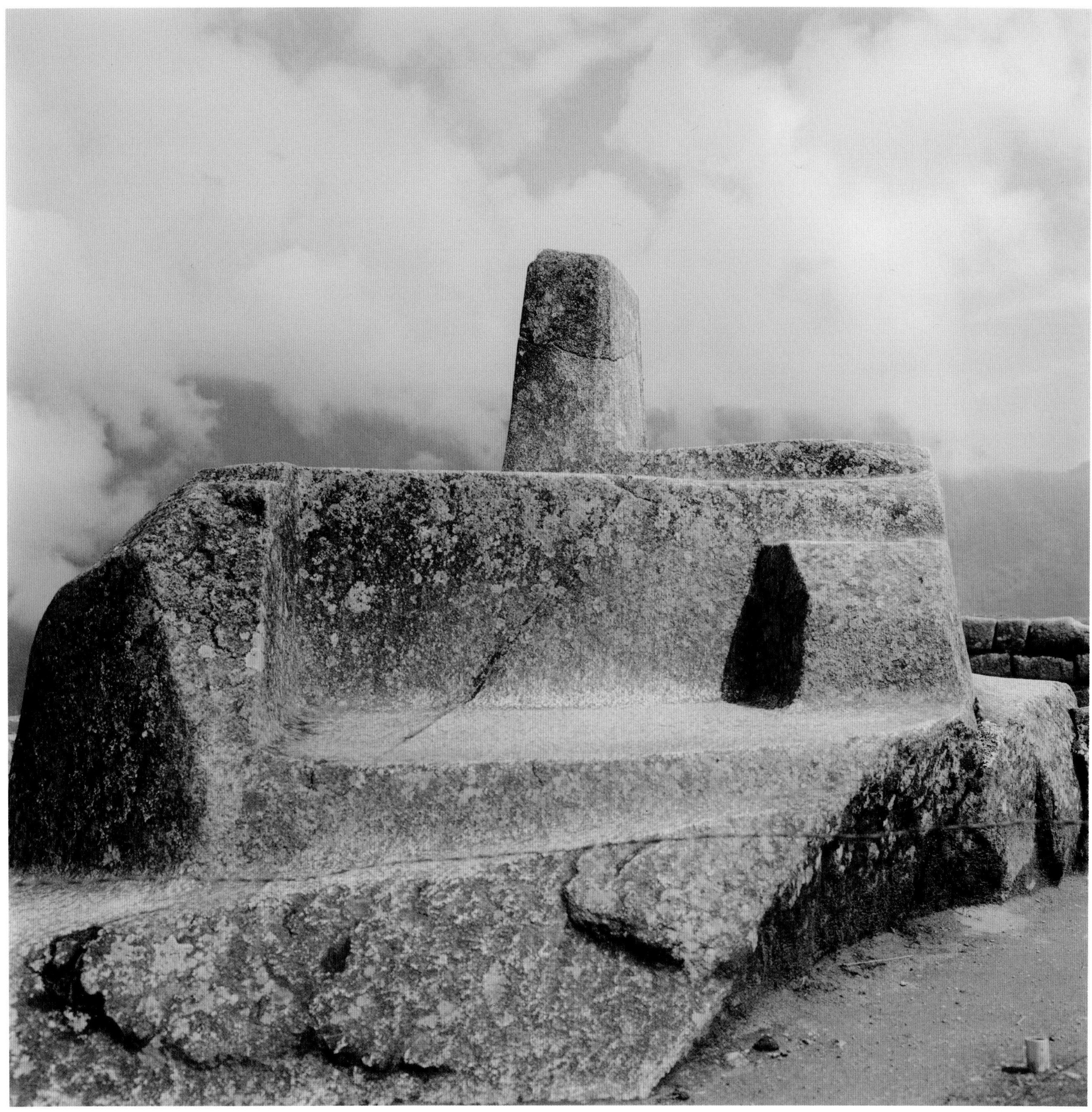

orientation and shape of the gnomon, it would have been possible to take very exact measurements based on the sun's position, as well as determine the exact times of equinoxes and solstices at the quarter points of the solar year. The Inca priests celebrated at these significant times of the year as a way to ritually control the sun, which they feared would move away from them to the north or south. Therefore, the probable purpose of the ritual was to "tie the sun" to the earth, or to ascend this "road to the sky" to the gods above. Since Peru is within 13 degrees of the equator, the sun would pass almost directly overhead twice in the solar year, at which times the Intihuatana would cast no shadows onto its base. At these precise moments—midday at the vernal and autumnal equinoxes—the Incas would decorate the gnomon and perform ceremonies in celebration of the sun's hitching to their sacred pillar.

The Incas also had their own equivalent of ley lines that emanated outward from the Sun Temple at the heart of Cuzco, and shrines and other monuments were located on these lines all across the extensive mountainous lands of Peru. They used these lines not only for astronomical or ritual purposes, but also to organize the entire nation politically and economically. Most of these monuments—especially the sun temples—were destroyed by the invading Spaniards, who never did find Machu Picchu.

Other buildings at Machu Picchu with windows looked out onto various rising and setting points of the sun and moon, and even the constellation of the Pleiades, which was worshipped as the center of heaven by the Chinese, the Lakota Indians, the Greeks, the Egyptians, the Mayas, and the Dyak of Borneo. In the Torreón at Machu Picchu, for instance, two windows were placed within a semi-circular building such that the sun and Pleiades constellation could be observed around the June solstice and zenith passages.[27]

Radiation, Form, and Sanctuary

A fascinating concept has great bearing on the form, location, orientation, and magic of temples and sacred places: Herbert Weaver discovered that the shape, form, and geometry of a building or element in the landscape carried a unique signal that either suppressed its energy output locally (within viewing range) or over long distances or enhanced it, making the structure either forbidding or inviting.[28] According to Weaver, these force fields of electromagnetic energy invoke an unconscious response from both animals and humans. Certain shapes in nature draw us in to them, while others we deem dangerous and consequently avoid. Further, he discovered that some buildings and sites signal us to approach, while other suppress their signals so that we do not enter their realm. For example, certain

OPPOSITE: The Intihuatana (gnomon stone), Machu Picchu, Peru, 2000

domed African tribal huts with small arched openings are considered dangerous by virtue of their form, so strangers or animals do not enter the space unless invited.[29]

Sanctuary was a critical requirement for early humanity. Safety involved being protected from the danger of animals or other humans. Early humans could sense the chemical or energy emanations of people and animals in a state of fear, and it was noticeably different from those of calm, secure, unthreatened beings. Although this awareness has since atrophied in modern humanity, early humans discovered ways to avoid detection by animals and others, protect their homes or caves, and cover their tracks. For example, Weaver claims that prehistoric cave paintings were intended to suppress vital signals and protect the tribe through the use of grids of intersecting lines drawn in front of and behind paintings of the animals they hunted. This, he postulates, shows how they forced herds of animals along narrow paths so that they could be more easily killed for food.[30]

Weaver collected and evaluated a wide range of objects and, through dowsing, found that certain patterns created particular reactions. For example, a law emerged that differentiated between odd-numbered groups of holes—which were vital for sending signals—and even–numbered groups, which suppressed signals over an extended area. Groups of sticks lying parallel did not suppress, unless there were four or multiples of four sticks in each group. When alphabets evolved, the letter signs also carried similar signals. Certain sacred vowels and names actually possessed energetic qualities that were either life-giving and vital, or deadly and suppressive. Furthermore, religious symbols were not only representations of gods or goddesses, but they also afforded protection. Circles only protected within their circumference, while a cross extended a radius of suppression beyond its visible limits. Even the rainbow symbol provided protection for beings within its arc. Some such forms were natural and obvious, while others were discovered through practice.

Weaver also found that the shapes of buildings and stone circles had specific effects according to their configuration. When joined by straight lines, groups of free-standing stones (e.g. Stonehenge) created wide-extent suppression and contained the energy of the circle within their boundaries. Ditches banked with soil, such as those found at Stonehenge or Avebury, tended to provide underground suppression. Domes closed a space aurally, visually, and magnetically. When walls turned back in on themselves, they provided greater protection than when they extend upward. These simple structural modifications could have made a difference as to whether hostile individuals or animals entered a space or not.

Safe sanctuary is a primary human requirement, and the first architecture reflected this need. Crosses, squares, four-multiples, and spiral shapes all suppress over wide distances, creating the most favorable conditions for protection and sanctuary. The structure of tents, wigwams, and hogans also provided the American Indians with protection, not only from animals and enemies, but from the influence of gods. Horns and antlers worn by warriors are decorative, but they also provide protective force fields that prevent chemical emanations from attracting distant foes.

Weaver's profound ideas strengthen the significance of certain shapes and patterns used by early builders, who kept a watchful eye on the rising and setting points on the horizon of the sun, moon, and planets as they constructed sacred centers and monuments. Aside from offering a method of measuring time, and in addition to providing sacred sanctuary, the orientation of landscape elements relative to each other and to buildings within the landscape reflects the ageless human quest to understand the universe—a quest that has continued throughout history, as later monuments and buildings constructed at these sites magnified and supported their sacredness.

PAGE 190: Virupaksha Temple, Hampi, India, 2007

PAGE 191: Washington Monument, Washington, D.C., 1994

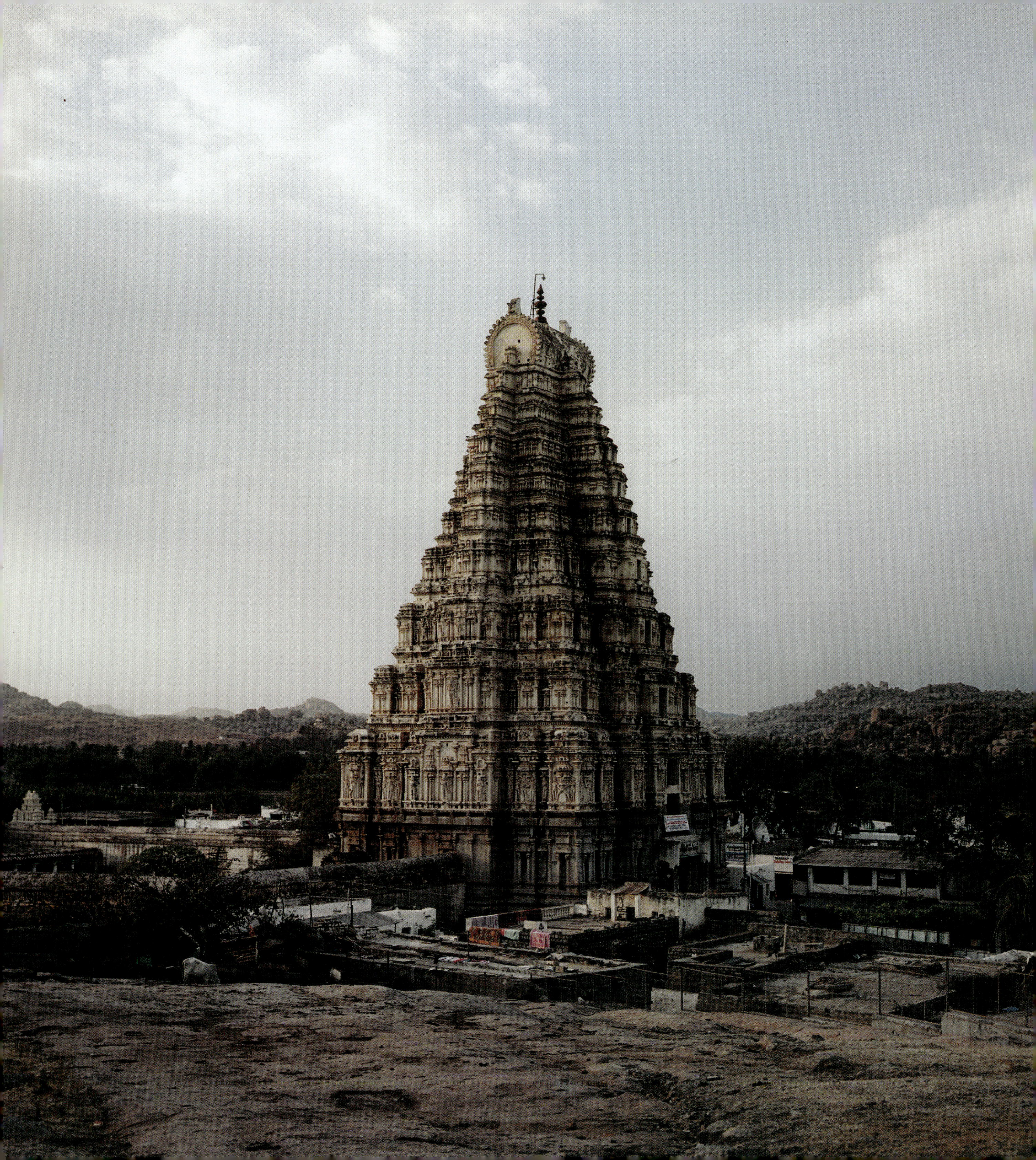

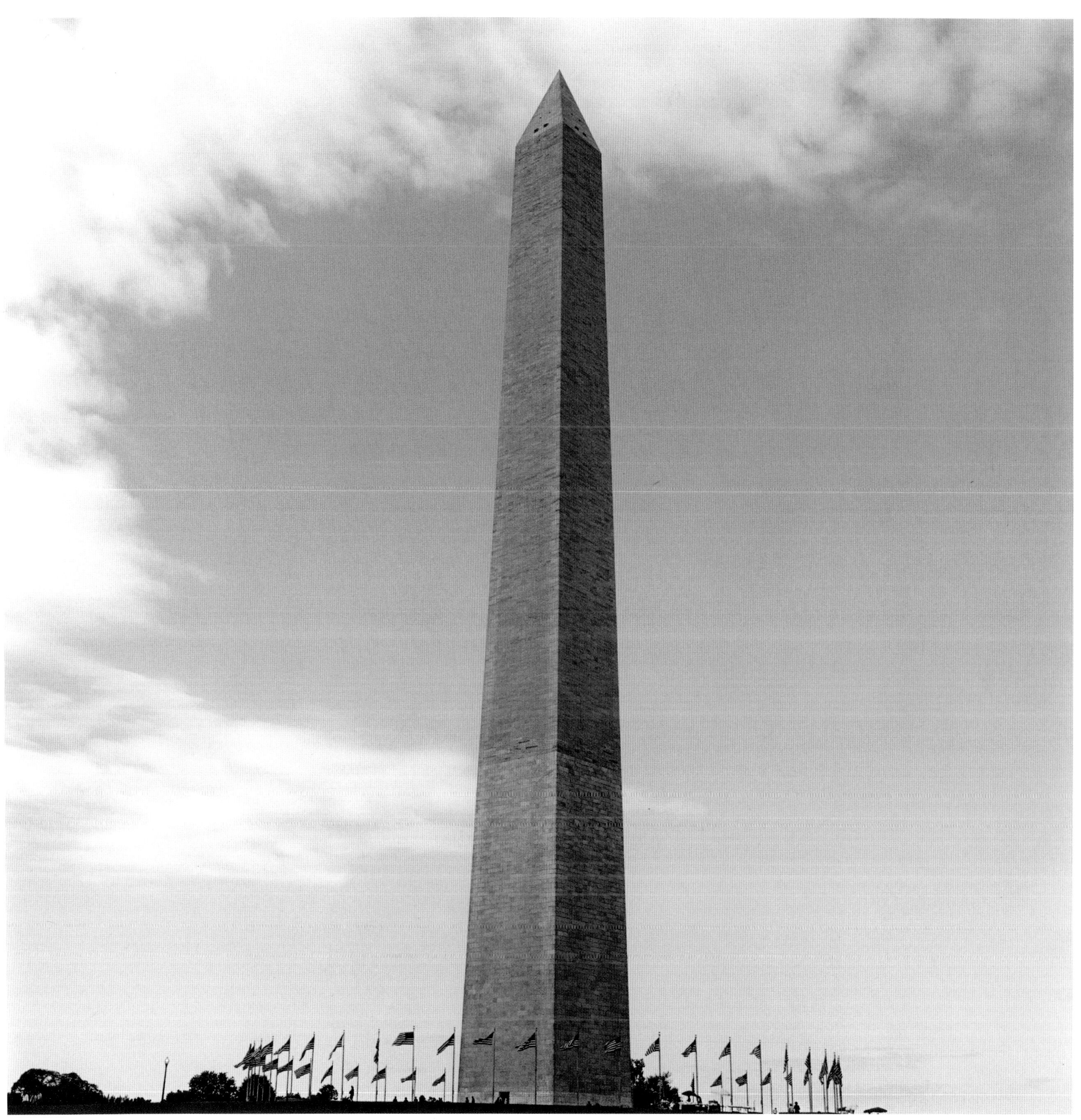

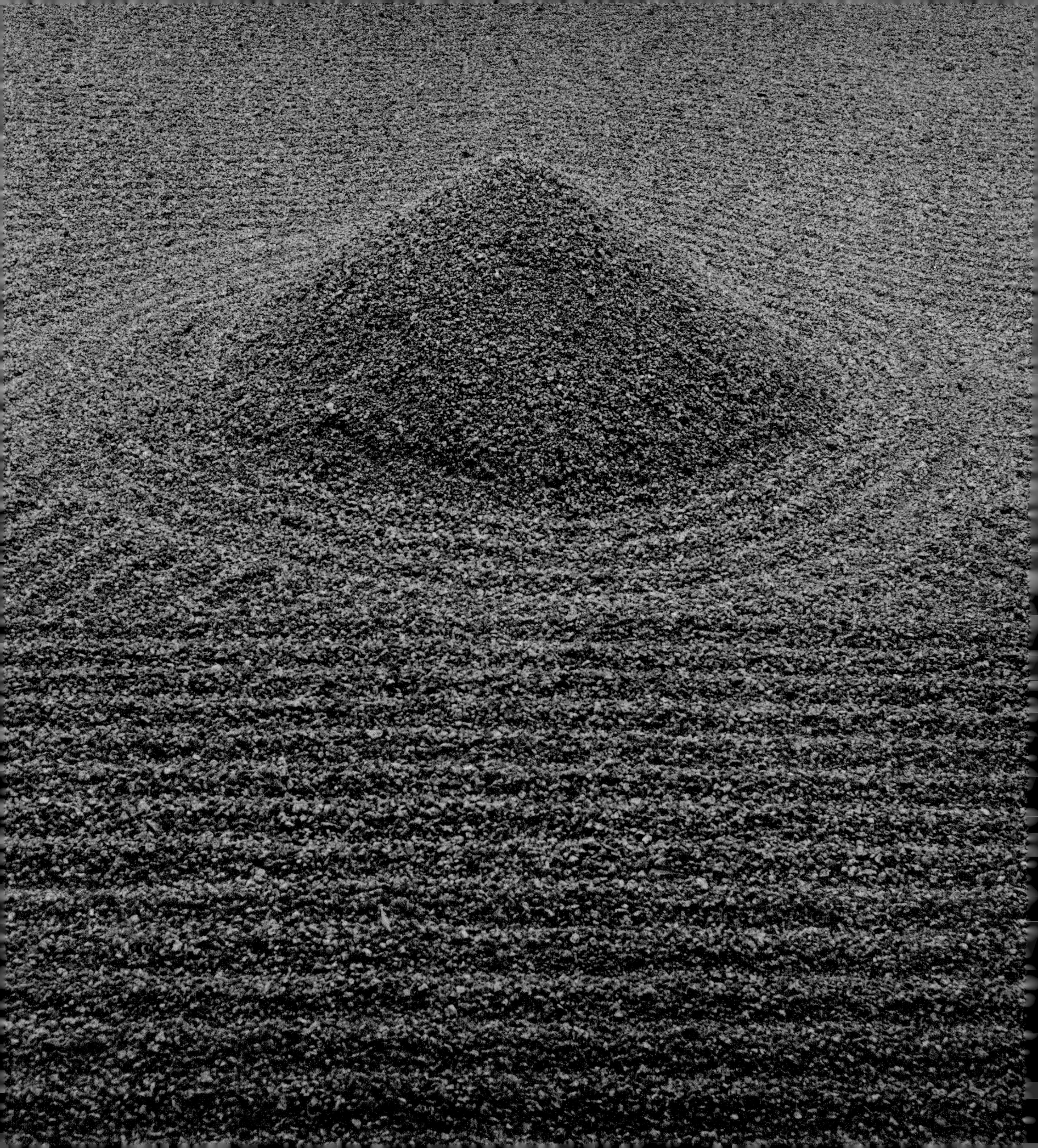

CHAPTER 11

Being and Nothingness

Cove and mountain; wind and moon—these are my tea and rice.

~Zen poet, calligrapher, and garden creator Ikkyu Sojun (c. fifteenth century)[1]

The tranquility and meditative qualities of Japanese Zen landscapes reflect a profound philosophy that originated in earlier Chinese landscape painting and design. Early Chinese landscape painters and landscapers wanted the landscape to appear largely untouched by man, but they found that achieving such naturalness required painstaking creation and attention. Zen landscapes reflect an evolution from the beauty and balance of the Chinese artistic tradition expressed in two-dimensional form to the creation of a literal Heaven on Earth. We can learn much from studying and creating such islands of balance in our sea of imbalance.

The south garden at the Zen Buddhist monastery of Daisen-in in Kyoto, a rectangle of empty river gravel raked into wave patterns suggesting the sea, is called "The Retreat of the Great Sages." Early in the genesis of this formless garden, an unknown monk placed two conical mounds of gravel, probably as a reserve pile, near one of the entrances. Over time these mounds became part of the garden and have elicited much comment and thought in the last four hundred years. To me, they represent the paradoxical nature of the Zen landscape garden: being and nothingness. The garden is beautiful to behold, but like a mirror that reflects the viewer, the very simplicity of the garden makes us consider our relationship to nature. It embodies the ancient and the beautiful, but it also embodies impermanence—a major doctrine of Zen Buddhism.

Kyoto became the sacred city of Japan in the eighth century, when its perfect feng shui qualities were discovered by Confucian geomancers. Essentially a valley surrounded by three hills and two rivers, Kyoto is protected by mountains that evoke qualities of the Japanese guardian spirits: the Azure Dragon on the east, the White Tiger on the west, the Dark Warrior on the north, and the Red Bird on the south. The city was laid out on a north-south grid that reflected the principles of yin and yang:

OPPOSITE: Raked gravel, Daisen-in garden, Kyoto, Japan, 1992

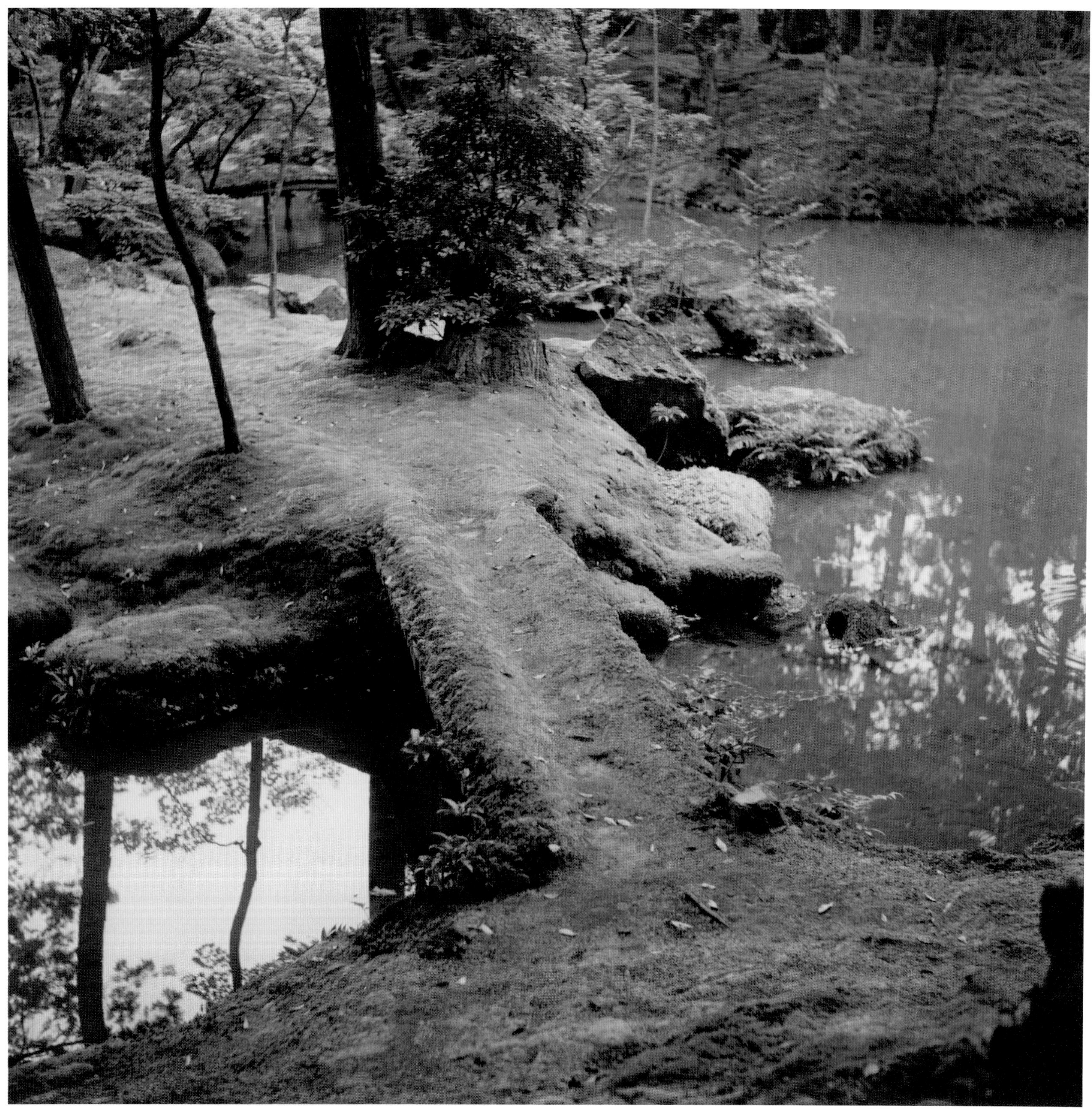

balancing the masculine and feminine forces in a harmonious whole. Indeed, given the influence of Chinese Confucianism on Japanese Buddhism, the city was to be a smaller-scale replica of the ancient city of Chang'an.

The temples for which Kyoto is now famous were created to the north of the city over the next four hundred years. These temples were oases reflecting the interdependence in Japan of aesthetics and spirituality. The first temples placed primary reverence on the mandala, the circular shaped cosmic diagrams so central to Indian and Tibetan Buddhism. The Japanese worshipped the four cardinal directions of the compass, which were reflected in the heavens, as well as the central element, which was a summation and synthesis of the earthly directions. The cardinal axes were considered by ancient cultures to be reflections of the world axis, which is embodied by the Pole Star. The symbolic central point was identified with the holy cosmic mountain at the center of the universe, Mount Meru. Thus, in many Zen gardens the central point was the holy mountain, represented as a mound or large stone, and the raked concentric circles—walkways one took to reach the center—were pathways through the celestial sphere, the ascent of which constituted a sacred process.

Gardens offered the noble court of Kyoto an opportunity to revel in the pleasures of nature, and for these pleasure gardens they selected the most beautiful components of the natural world—wondrous and rare trees, flowering shrubs, stones, bridges, and gateways—placing them around artificial lakes with picturesque boats. Streams meandered through the gardens, diverted from nearby mountains and hills to complete the enclosed scenes. Although the nobility delighted in their beautiful gardens, the various elements lacked any deep symbolism or content. Rather, these pleasure gardens were as contrived, superficial, and shallow as the man-made lakes within their confines.

During the Muromachi era (1392–1573 CE) great gardens were built around the residences of the samurai and the Zen monasteries they sponsored. Primary influences on the new form of garden, where the central building was the residence of the Zen abbot, were the earlier generations of Chinese Zen architecture, garden design, and landscape painting. While they appeared more naturalistic than previous gardens, they were painstakingly created to appear exactly this way. In addition, a new dimension was embodied in the gardens—they became spaces in which contact with the sacred, rather than the worship of an emperor, was the central function. In these sacred gardens, Buddhas and bodhisattvas were represented as trimmed hedges, formations of rocks or stones, or geometrically shaped islands of dry sand.

The structure of most of the famous gardens of the period is axial—probably a gesture to the earlier Tendai Buddhist forms. Major elements were grouped around a central north-south axis: the entrance gate, a lotus pond, the main gate, Buddha hall, lecture hall, bathhouse, and toilet. The abbot's quarters

OPPOSITE: Saiho-ji (Moss Temple) garden, Kyoto, Japan, 1992

PAGE 196: Iceberg, Disko Bay, Greenland, 2004

PAGE 197: Garden, Beijing, China, 2001

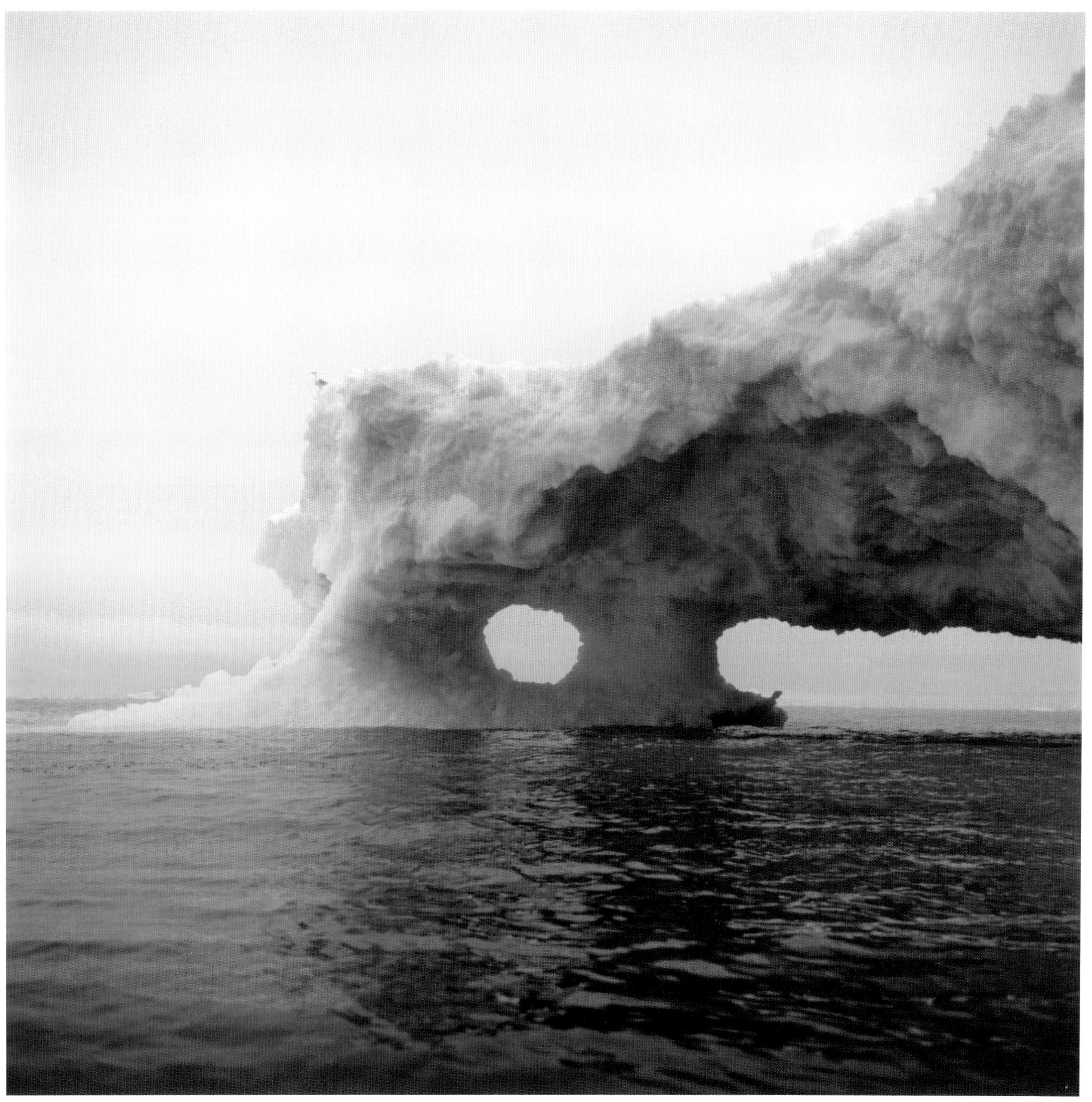

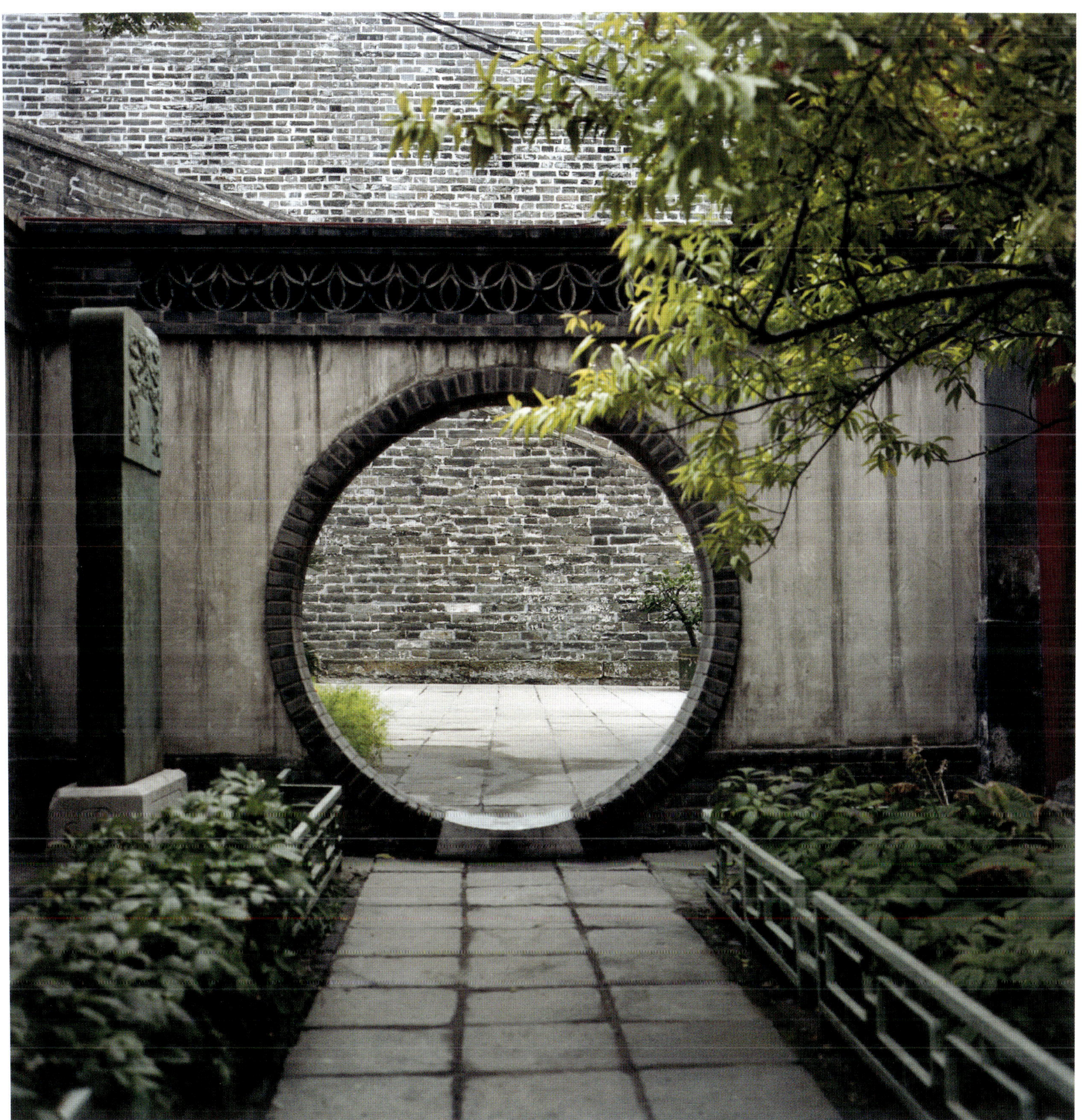

lay to the north of the entire complex, and sub-temples founded by notable monks were placed almost randomly around this unifying axis. In contrast to the much wilder and more romantic Chinese models, which were open to nature, high walls surrounded the temples within temples. Even higher walls surrounded the entire complex, separating the monks from the outside world. This isolation was not only characteristic of the mentality of the period, but also a metaphor for Zen meditation itself.

What Is Zen?

Zen Buddhism emerged in sixth-century China as a blend of Taoism, native Chinese religions, and Mahayana Buddhism imported from India and Tibet. The essence of Zen is notoriously difficult to describe, springing from a pure state of being that exists before manifestation of form. It may be expressed through a movement, a force, a sense of awareness or immediacy, or wellspring, but it is not any of those things.[2] It may be found in a bamboo spatula, a wall, a fence, the sound of water, a blowing plum blossom, a bird, or the colors on a mountain, but it only exists in our perception of them.[3]

A defining feature of Zen is the belief that your conscious self is the manifestation of something unique that exists "prior to form."[4] Zen masters call this the "fundamental" or "formless" self. It emerges from a place that exists before form, before personality, before universe, before consciousness, before being. It is without form or characteristics, although it assumes characteristics and is animated by form, much like the archetypes of the collective unconscious that Jung describes, which precede manifestation but require manifestation to function. Because of these paradoxes, which speak to intuition rather than rational logic, "being Zen" is most easily understood through the actual experience of it. In Zen art or design, for example, emphasis is given to the expression of something profound and ineffable rather than the form itself.

Despite the emphasis on silent meditation, words are an essential part of Zen, as various literary and poetic forms became the most prominent way for masters to communicate with their disciples and others. And yet Zen originally sprang up as a response to the profusion of texts, treatises, stories, myths, records, interpretations, scriptures, and writings that accumulated in the many centuries of Buddhism in India, Tibet, and China. The most elusive forms of Zen literary expression—the freely created haiku poems and *kōans*—were subsequently refined and formalized into extensive literary works with vastly more critical analysis than text. Zen strives vigorously to address and minimize this tendency for content to become less important than form—a tendency that can easily water down or weaken every powerful religious tradition—and Zen is no exception.

OPPOSITE: Buddha, Yungang Grottoes, Datong, China, 2001

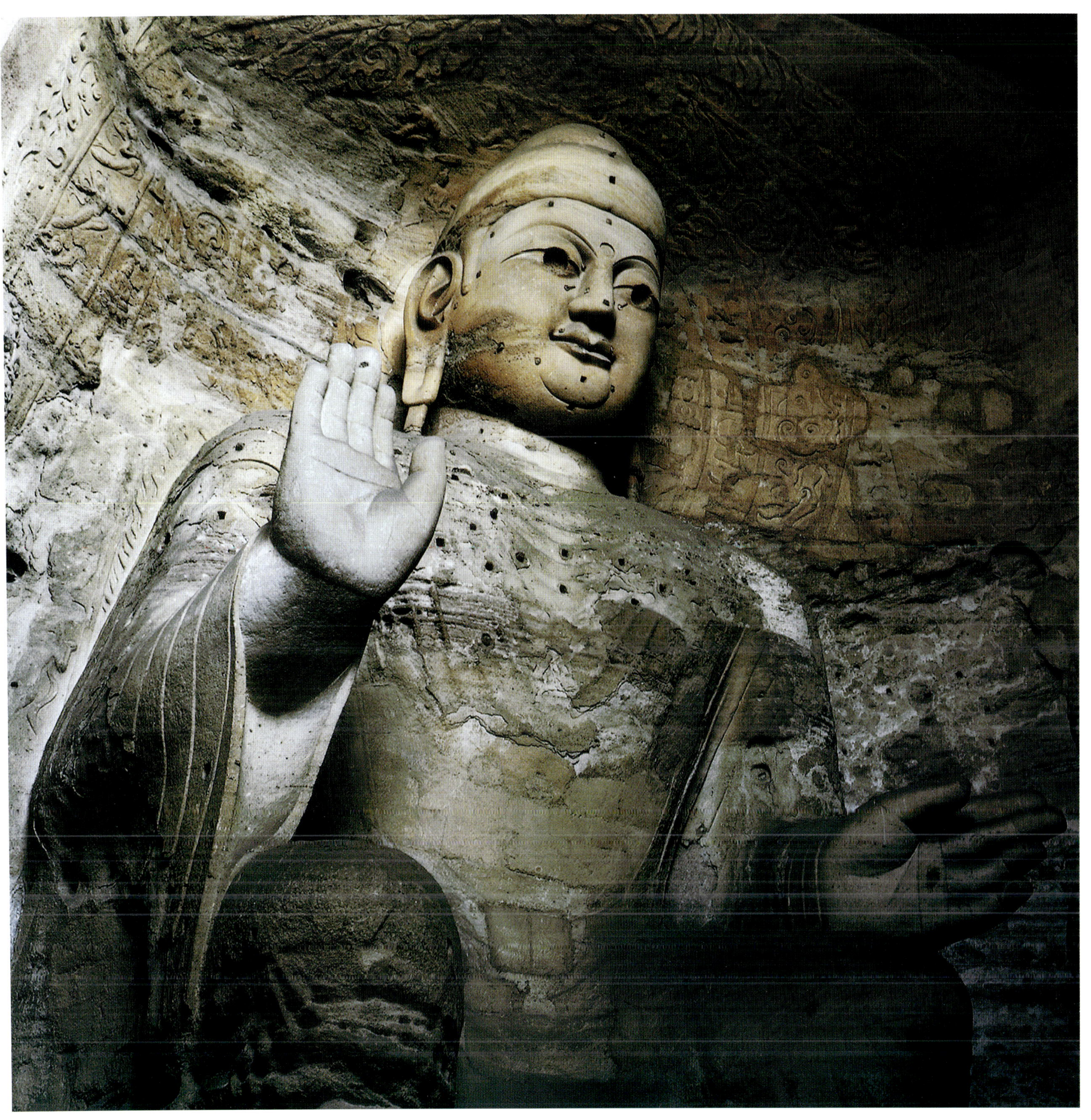

Space and Time

A fundamental difference between the Japanese and Western mind is the conception of space and time. In the West, time is seen as linear and absolute, due primarily to the powerful influence of the succession of Hebrew, Christian, and scientific worldviews. The Hebrew Bible measured time linearly from a specific time of origin into the present, and the Christian calendar recalculated this by measuring backward and forward from the birth of Jesus. Our modern civil calendar, which also used by scientists, is based on the linear Christian calendar. The Japanese definition of time requires the ideogram for the sun moving across the sky. This is a definition of time measured by the distance the sun covers during a given action or event. It is also measured by the space across which the shadow of a sundial moves, or distance around an analog watch dial. To the Japanese, time is this sense of flowing space, which suggests that time is essential in the human experience of space.[5] In Japanese architecture, these two dimensions are interchangeable. Space cannot be experienced without time, and vice versa.

In the West, space is understood as pure extension—an abstract void or vacuum into which objects intrude. In Japan, however, the character for "space" implies its heavenly origin: "ma" is a pictorial sign for "moon" under the sign for "gate." Thus, space is a shaft of moonlight streaming through a tiny opening in the entranceway.[6]

The movement through gardens is often modulated by the spacing and placement of stepping-stones. Movement can be effectively slowed down, speeded up, turned, or halted by their placement. As the sequence of the path governs our legs, so our eyes are similarly affected by this measure. This modulation, in turn, requires that we experience the sense of the garden subjectively—the feelings that arise either from our inner self being projected outward onto it, or some quality of the garden that we take into ourselves. Either way, the identity of a place is in the mind of the beholder.

This is in distinction to the Western view that positions the individual as self-contained and inherently separate from the surrounding world. In the West we have a boundary consciousness, and in the East a no-boundary reality. In his book *From Shinto to Ando: Studies in Architectural Anthropology in Japan* (1993), architect Günter Nitschke suggests that polarities of form and nonform, of object and space, of sound and silence, of action and nonaction, of movement and rest, and of human and society are joined in a total harmony in Zen works.[7] Thus we have, a priori, an eternal conflict of interests in the West and harmony in the East.

The word "ma" defines the continuum of space and time in Japanese thought in a way not conceptualized in Western science until the late eighteenth century. Eastern ideas about time and space as a continuum bring Western duality to a place of integration in the garden. In Zen Buddhism, "ma" also describes the concept of void or emptiness. This void exists before all individual experience and is accessible only to meditators or those in a state of enlightenment. Indeed, the void and the experience of the void are paradoxical and yet integral to Zen. In the dry rock gardens of Kyoto, the meditator sits on the veranda and eventually ceases to be aware that there is any difference between the garden of raked pebbles and the stones embedded in them, and between the stones and oneself. One is drawn out of oneself, out of time, and into the void. The outside reflects the inside and brings a renewed experience of consciousness that is not philosophical or aesthetic, but personal.[8]

A central idea in Zen gardens is the concept of capturing the landscape—finding and recreating a natural environment that appears to have formed on its own. For example, the bringing of distant views of mountains or the sea into small monastery gardens can be accomplished by framing the view with gates, windows, or other structures, so that the entire scene appears to be a painting on the wall. This type of design feature is most certainly inspired by the tradition of ethereal and beautiful Chinese and Japanese landscape paintings, which are typically composed with a central image surrounded by white (negative) space—space that inspires the mind's eye to fill the void with a frame. Framing a garden view serves to integrate urban places with the natural world beyond and is a wonderful vehicle for creating a sense of more space and closer proximity to nature. This powerful dynamic is a force for greater integration.

The Buddha said:
To meditate persistently on impermanence is to be guided by all the Buddhas.
To meditate persistently on impermanence is to be blessed by all the Buddhas.

—Patrul Rinpoche, *The Words of My Perfect Teacher* (1994)[9]

Impermanence is a fundamental tenet in the Buddhist understanding of reality; everything that comes into being inevitably grows old and dies, including universes, worlds, planets, animals, humans, gods, and even Buddhas. Watching the changing of seasons over the course of years vividly demonstrates to us this concept. Our desire for permanence is an illusion called *samsara* (Sanskrit for "continuous flowing"), which refers to the endless cycle of rebirth on the wheel of life. Only the Dharma—the path to understanding reality—endures.

We are surrounded by phenomena that remind us of the ephemeral nature of all things, but the landscape is our primary guide and teacher in this respect. We see trees sprout and blossom and then turn glorious colors and lose their leaves, becoming barren through the winter months. Similarly, in meditation we observe the flow of thoughts as one changes into another, and we experience the inherent emptiness of things. Thus, the changing landscapes around us, which are replicated in Asian gardens, teach us valuable lessons about the transient nature of all things (including ourselves), thereby encouraging us further on the path to an eternal, enlightened state.

PAGE 202: Iceberg, Disko Bay, Greenland, 2007

PAGE 203: Archway with mountain, Palmyra, Syria, 1995

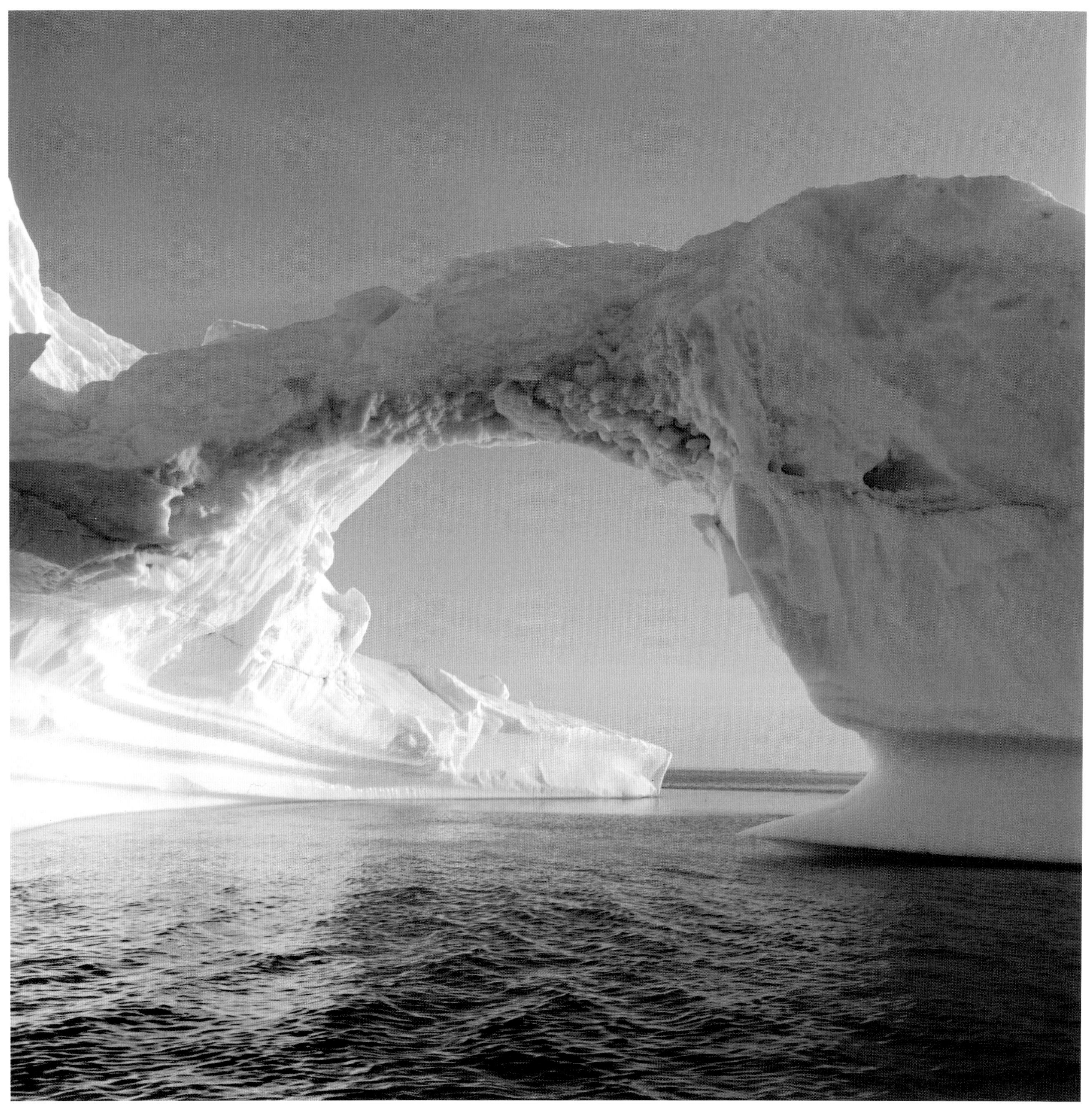

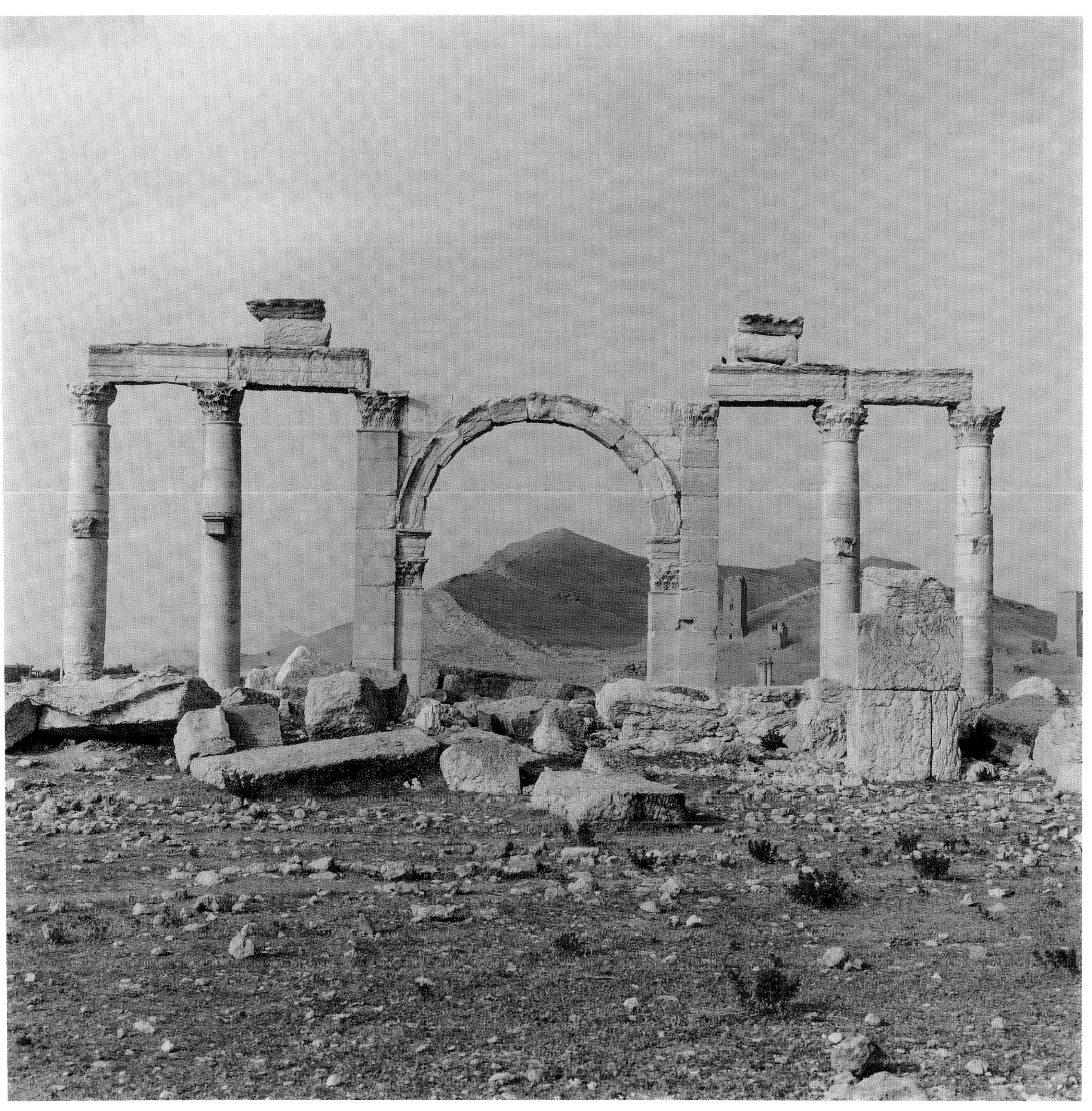

There was a time when meadow, grove, and stream,
The earth, and every common sight,
To me did seem
Apparell'd in celestial light
The glory and the freshness of a dream
It is not now as it hath been of yore;—
Turn wheresoe'er I may,
By night or day,
The things which I have seen I now can see no more.

—William Wordsworth, *Ode: "Intimations of Immortality from Recollections of Early Childhood"* (1802)[10]

OPPOSITE: Northumberland Strait, Gulf of Saint Lawrence, Canada, 1993

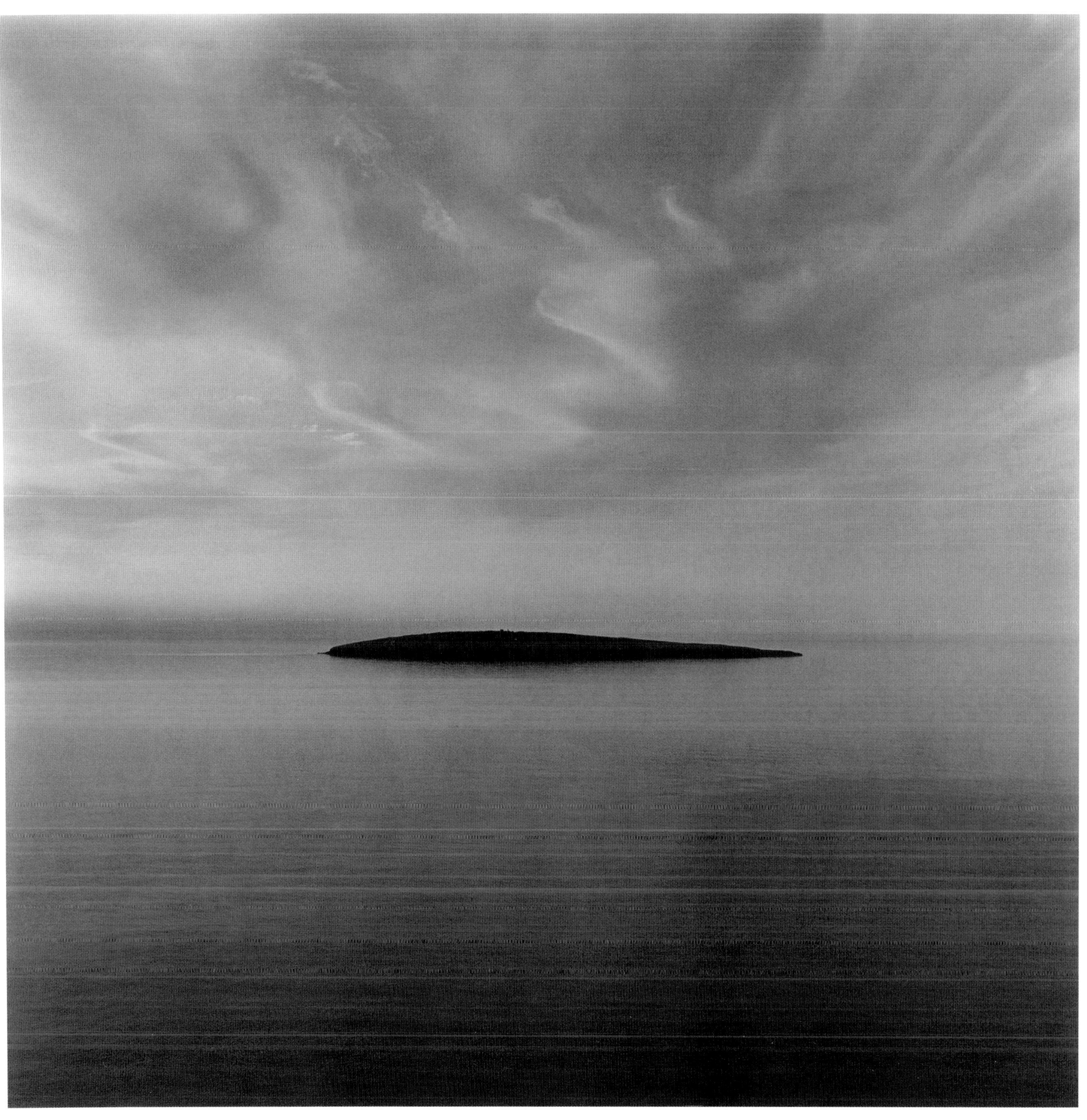

BEING AND NOTHINGNESS

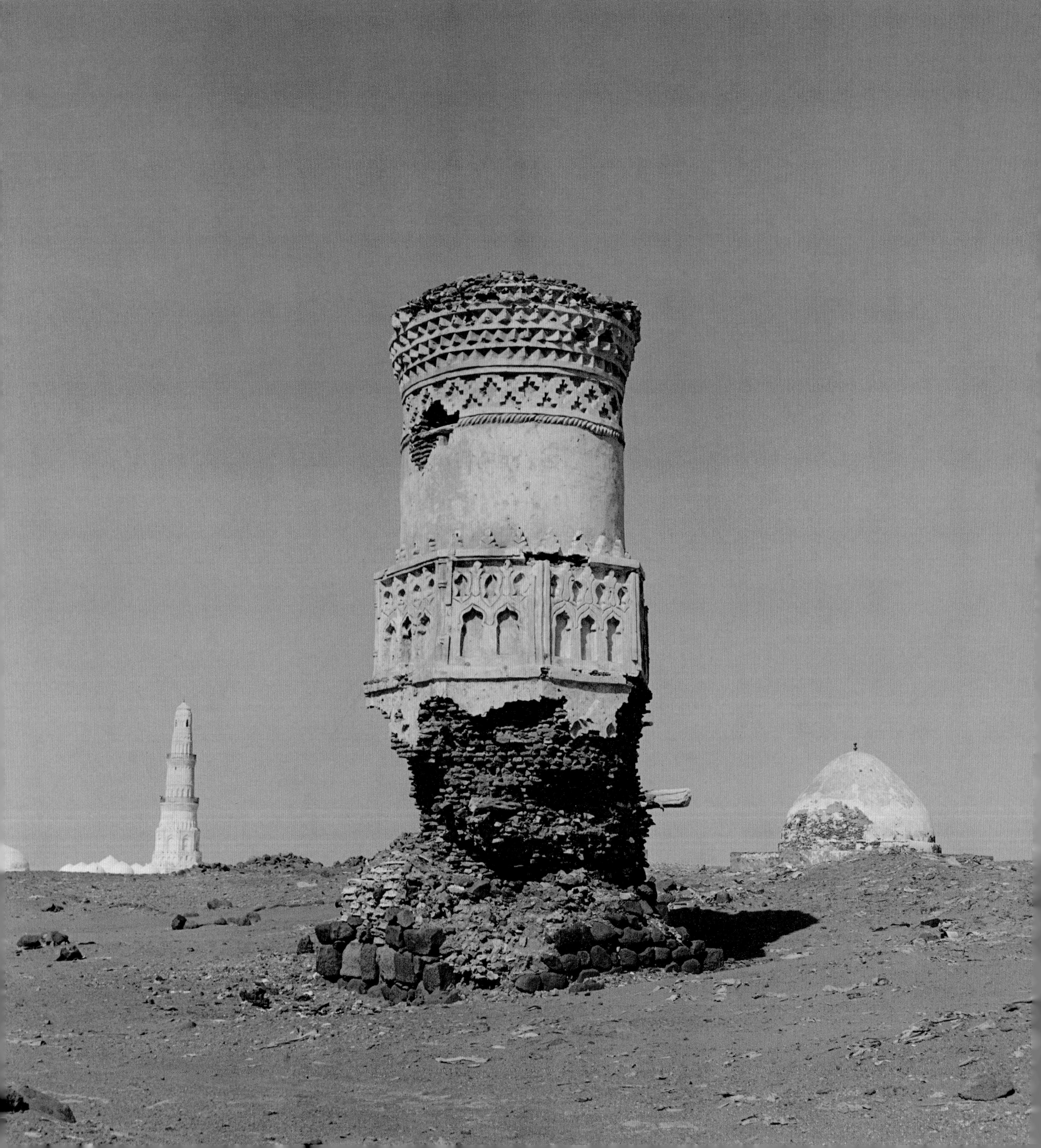

CHAPTER 12

The Vanishing Landscape

Sweet is the lore which Nature brings;
Our meddling intellect
Misshapes the beauteous forms of things:
We murder to dissect.

Enough of Science and of Art;
Close up those barren leaves;
Come forth, and bring with you a heart
That watches and receives.

~ William Wordsworth, from "The Tables Turned" (1798)[1]

An essential aspect of the natural world is that it frames the passage of time all around us. The rhythms of nature bring a real sense of the tenuous and profound balance between life and death, waking and sleep. Sacred places celebrate these natural shifts, incorporating them into their form. The beauty and power of many natural places is that they show how time gradually wears away even the hardest materials. Year after year, century after century, nature creates a continual and ever-changing play of colors and tones, imparting beauty on the landscape and its elements as it dissolves them, profoundly expressing the Buddhist doctrine of impermanence.

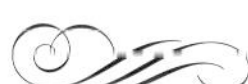

The ancients believed that those who lived eons ago, nearer in time to the creation of the world, were closer to the gods and to manifesting the universal order in their lives. The creator, triple goddess, divine king, great mother, and hero are all embodiments of a transcendent reality that the present world craves and that exists within us all, regardless of our beliefs. We search within the atom, in outer space, in the depths of the oceans, and on the highest mountains for the meaning and the origin of life. And somehow, in our desperate forage into all things remote, we neglect to search within ourselves and within the sacred landscapes around us.

OPPOSITE: Minaret at Mocha, Yemen, 1996

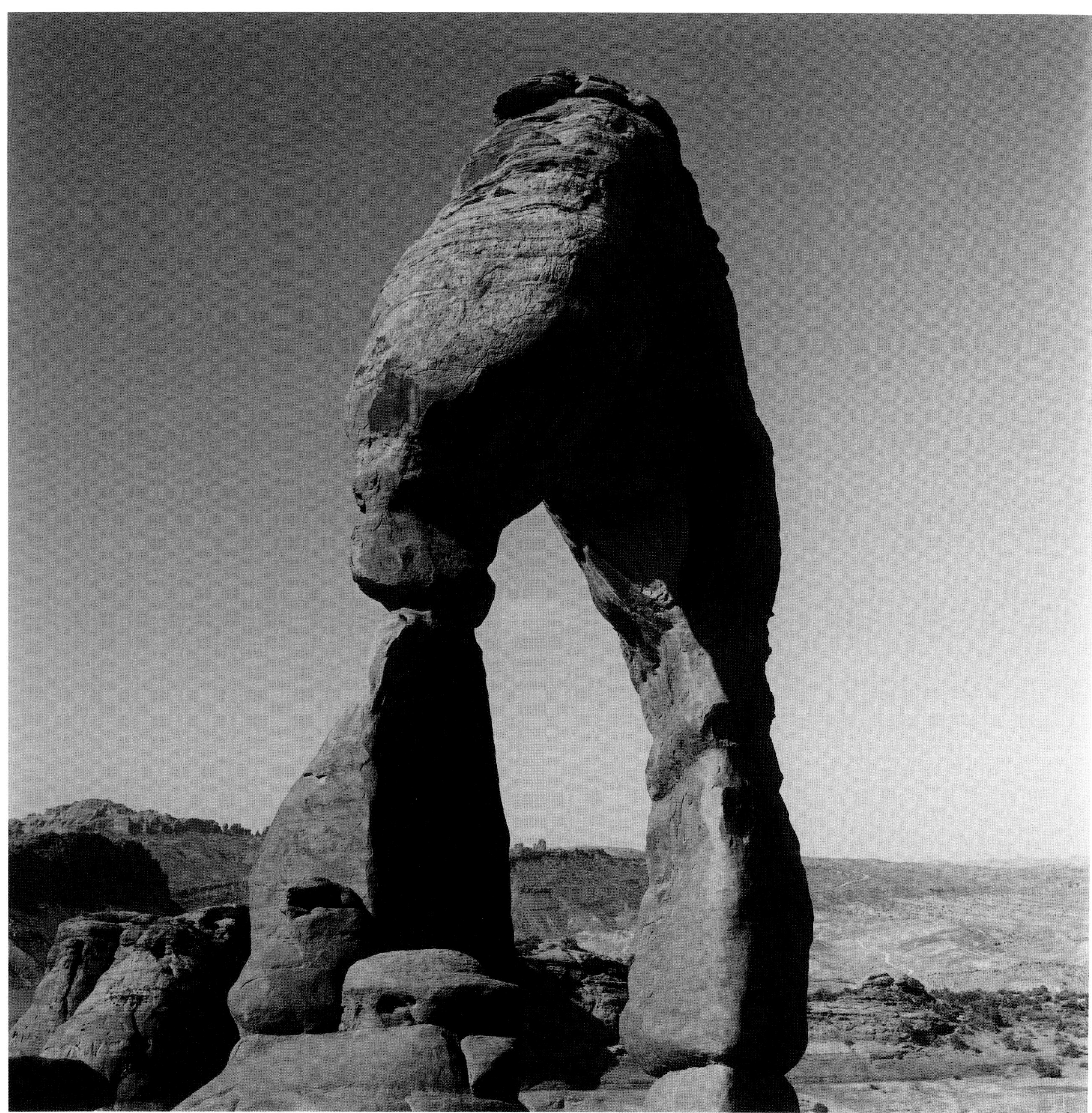

The nature of time—particularly the primordial time that is really beyond time—is the most profound mystery of all. Our historical approaches work backward into our collective past until our knowledge dissolves into myths, dreams, or fantasies. In very much the way that the seemingly irrational quantum world of particle physics and the realm of the psyche in psychology are mysterious and may never be fully understood, history, too, may never be completely uncovered. When we explore these realms, imagination, intuition, and the discernment of patterns are perhaps our only stepping-stones.

Due to the similarity of many myths across cultures, it is impossible to know how far back in time the original "mythic" event occurred. Each new retelling, rather than clarifying the mystery, renews its magic. According to German Nobel Prize laureate Thomas Mann, in early times "what concerns us is not calculable time. Rather it is time's abrogation and dissolution in the alternation of tradition and prophecy, which lends to the phrase 'once upon a time' its double sense of past and future and therewith its burden of the potential present."[2] Ancient myths generate strong feelings about the future, almost as though the earliest memories are simultaneously prophecies. Past events continually repeat until they are accepted as prototypical. This repetition suggests that not only is the past as mysterious as the future, but they are firmly linked, if not identical.

We are destroying the world's sacred landscapes at an alarming and terrifying rate. Speaking to *Common Ground* publisher Joseph Roberts in 2006, Coleman Barks, translator of the Persian poet Rumi, began with this insight: "I was thinking about the destruction of the Buddhist sculptures in Afghanistan, where Rumi was supposedly born. At first I was upset. Then I thought about the Tibetan monks doing sand paintings and brushing them all away afterwards. These beautiful sculptures are like three-dimensional sand paintings being brushed away by some fanatic's dynamite. Here we are just watching it all go by." The temples at Angkor Wat and the city of Angkor Thom wear battle scars that display the calamitous effect of human violence on sacred landscapes. The infamous war of the Khmer Rouge regime that began in 1970 saw the murder of tens of thousands of people and left these monuments abandoned for many years. Perceiving Buddhism as an enemy to the Khmer Rouge outlaw government, invaders destroyed the *apsaras* (protective deities that abound on the temple walls), shot bullets at the buildings and sculptures, and invited black market thieves to take and sell whatever they could find at the sacred sites.[3] Indeed, in all lands where there is little sympathy for earlier religions, sacred monuments face a dire threat.

Religious fanaticism is not the sole cause of this mass destruction, however. We can blame none other than our own uncontrolled appetites as carbon emissions increase, Earth's temperature rises, and the icebergs and glaciers of the high mountain, Arctic, and Antarctic territories melt. And while

OPPOSITE: Delicate Arch, Arches National Park, Utah, United States, 1991

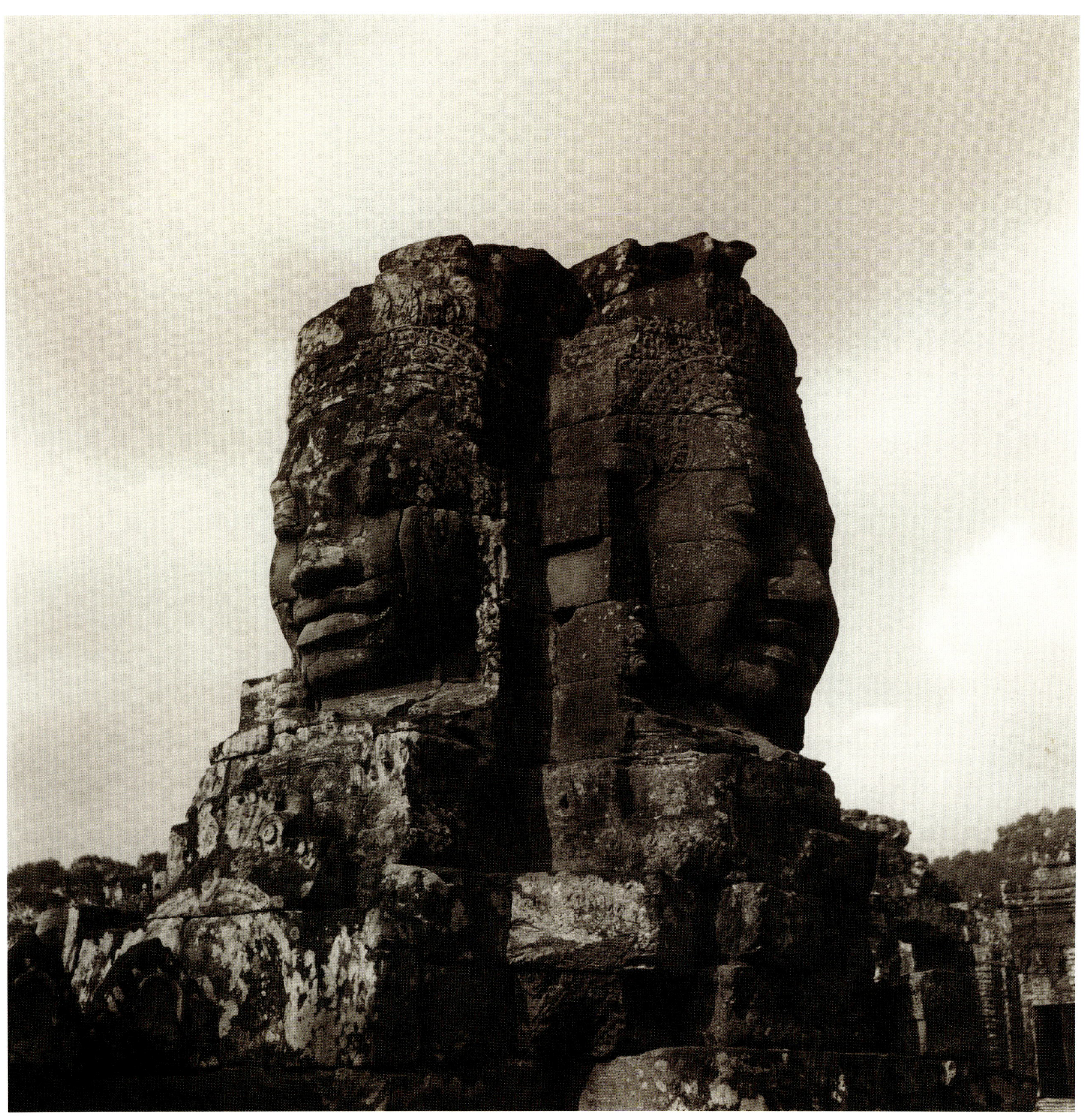

the obliteration of the Bamyan Buddhas of Afghanistan can be traced to the bigoted Taliban regime, tourism has also incurred damage on ancient landscapes and monuments.

Nature and the elements pose yet an even greater danger to sacred, man-made structures. In the midst of the Cambodian Civil War, the forests around the temple complex have encroached on the site, attacking the buildings in a variety of ways. Numerous aptly named strangler fig (banyan) trees have surrounded, penetrated, and grown over the fallen stone temples. Additionally, the complex was built on an unstable foundation of sand, which easily washes away, leaving the buildings at the mercy of subsidence. And as the buildings were themselves built of sandstone, which weathers badly (albeit it in a gloriously beautiful and romantic way), the stones themselves are extremely vulnerable to the ravages of time. One of the beautiful aspects of nature is that everything is eventually broken down and absorbed back into the body of Gaia. Rumi's poetry celebrates this dissolution, which echoes our spiritual need to allow the ego to dissolve so that our more profound being can shine through. Therefore, seeing Nature do its dissipative work on even the most exquisite landscapes or buildings is a teaching in itself, and a very strong yet strangely beautiful statement about the power of nature over humanity.[4]

Dissolving Icescapes

The polar regions of Earth have always been something of a fantasy, as most of us never have and never will see the sublime icebergs, ice floes, and mountains of Antarctica and the Arctic. Yet these immense regions are fast absorbing our awareness, since they represent the most obvious manifestation of the vanishing sacred landscape. Ice is disappearing at a much faster rate than even the most pessimistic scientists predicted years ago, as noted in *An Inconvenient Truth*, the powerful documentary by Al Gore, which finally brought to the public attention just how quickly these extraordinary landscapes are disappearing and the frightening implications.

One of the most intriguing facts about Antarctica is that, although its coastline has been buried beneath hundreds of feet of ice for thousands of years, mysterious maps that depict the terrestrial coastline exist as early as the sixteenth century. The Commodore Piri Reis map of 1513 showed in incredible detail the entire coastline of Antarctica, yet there is no way that it could have been viewed before aerial mapping techniques that were discovered in the last twenty years enabled scientists to see the land under the ice. Also, interestingly, we now know that the continents have drifted vast distances in the course of hundreds of millions of years—Antarctica was originally very close to all the other continents before eventually moving to the South Pole.

OPPOSITE: The Bayon, Angkor Thom, Angkor, Cambodia, 1993

PAGE 212: Ruined pagoda, Bagan, Burma, 1993

PAGE 213: Bam Citadel, Iran, 2001

PAGE 214: Via Appia Antica (The Appian Way), Rome, Italy, 1993

PAGE 215: Collapsed Pyramid of Amenemhet III, 12th Dynasty, Dashur, Egypt, 1997

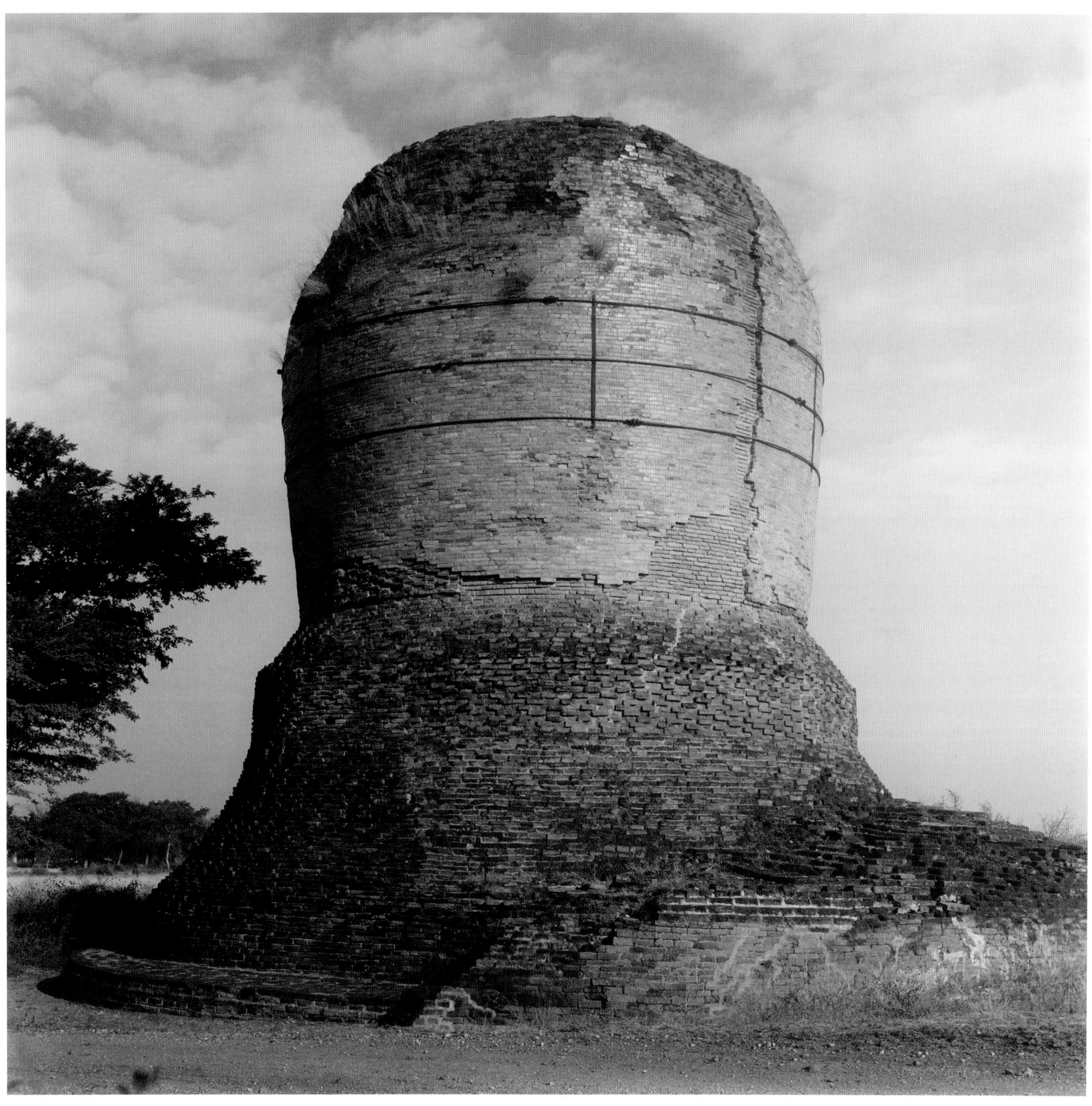

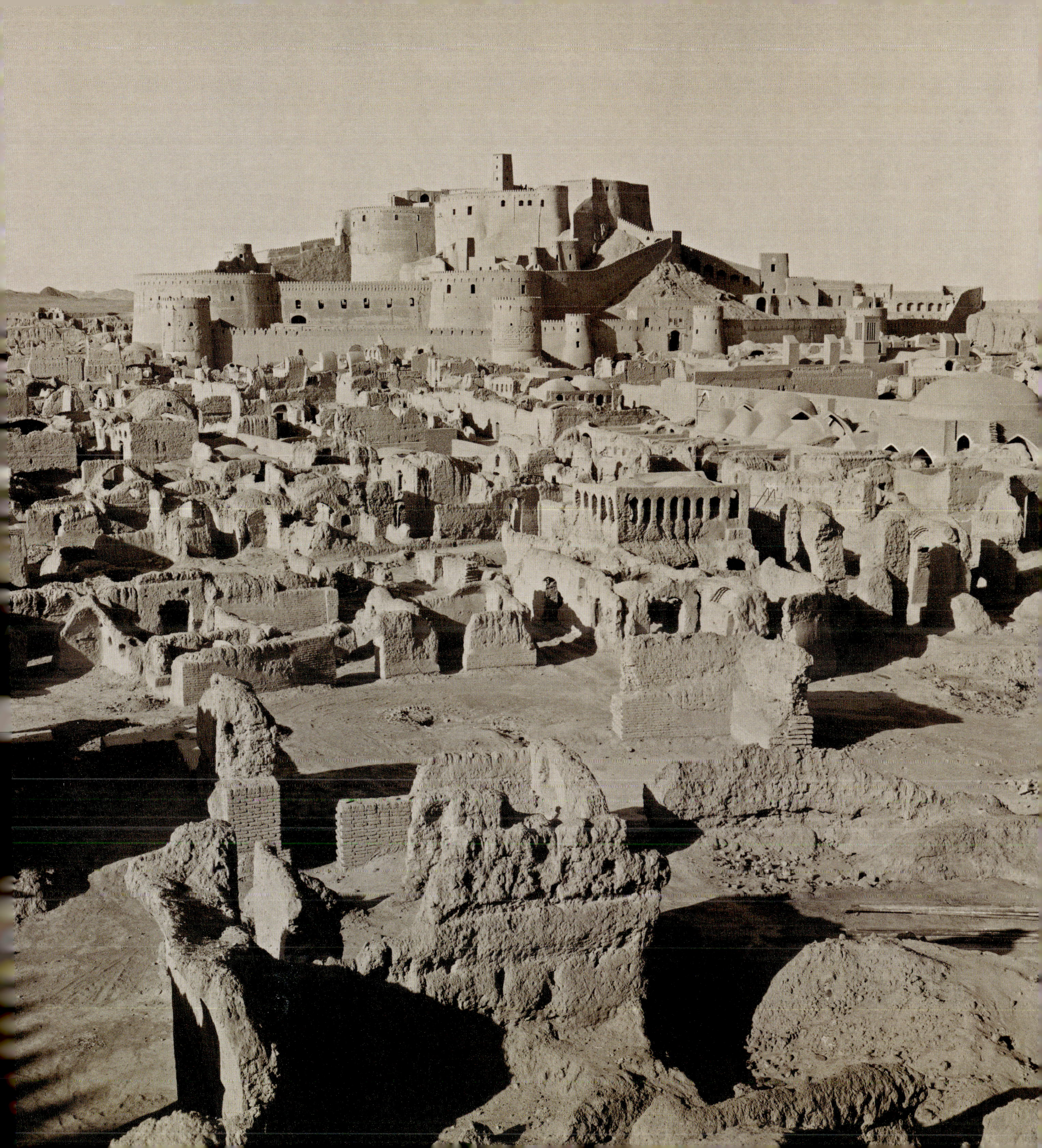

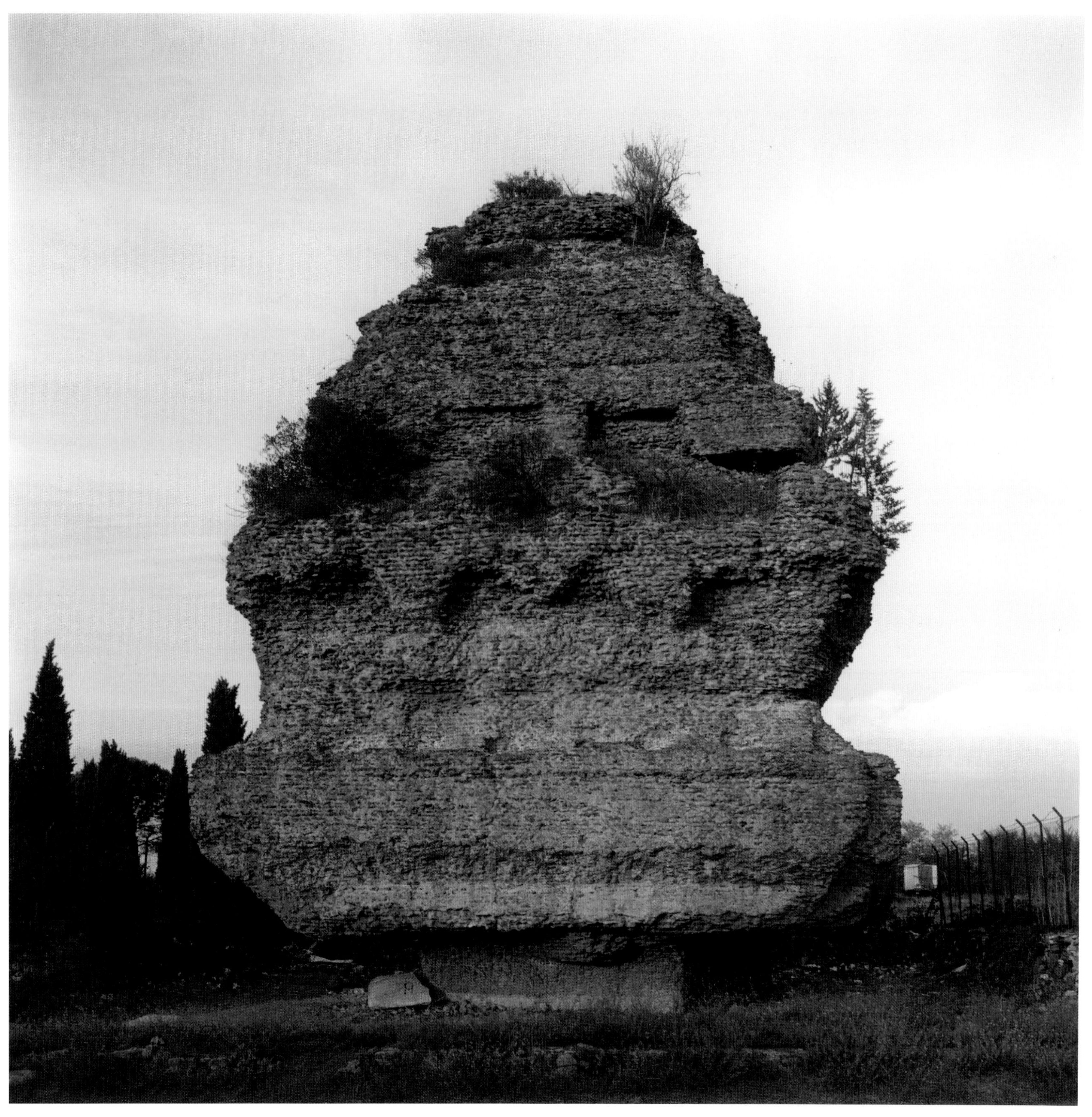

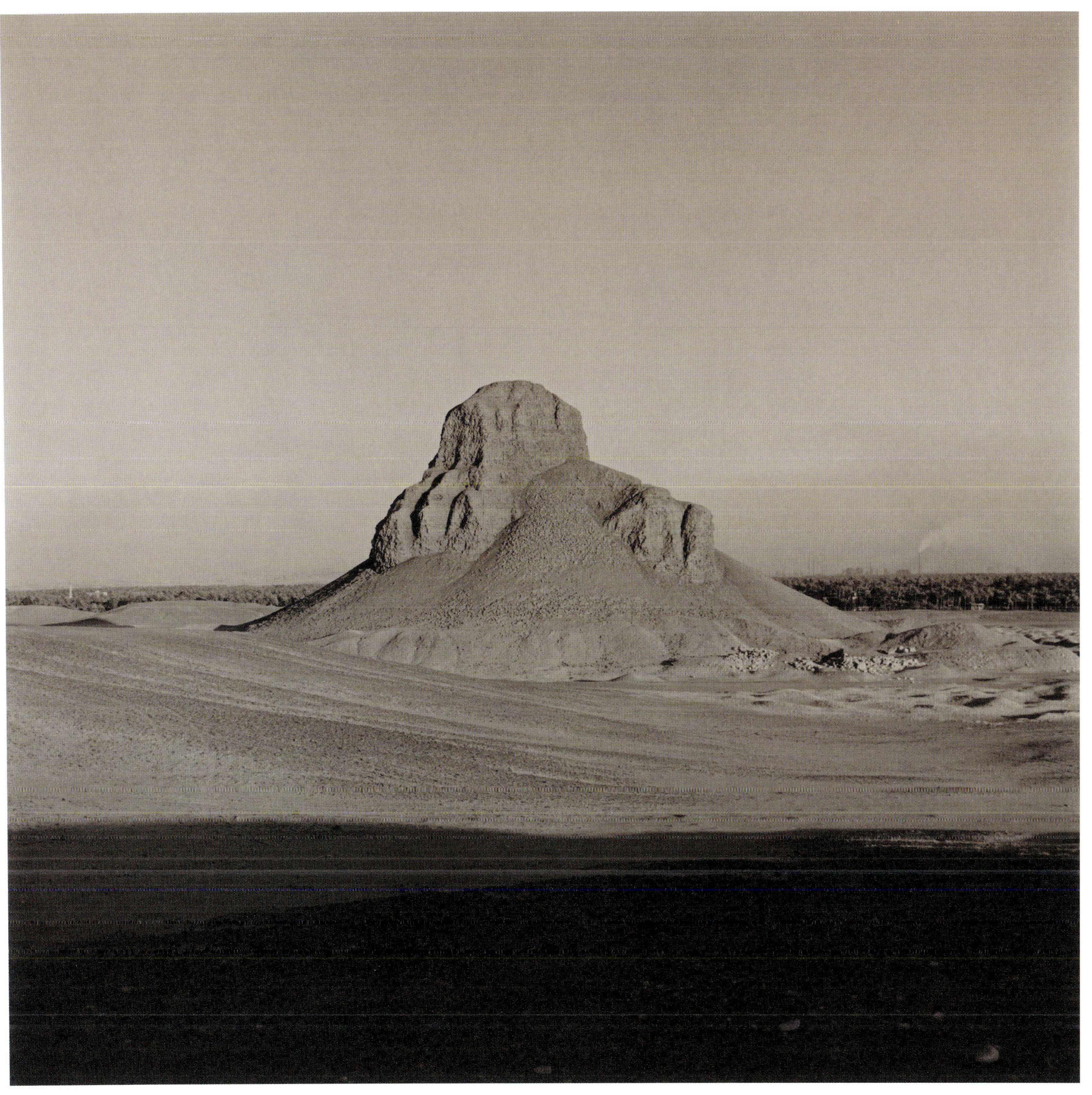

Northern myths contrast the potency and awe-inspiring beauty with the savage and unforgiving climate of the Arctic. The Icelandic Eddas, for instance, use grotesque, even violent imagery to depict the creation of the world. After the end of a previous world cycle, chaos resulted and out of this "yawning gap had given forth in the north a mist-world of cold and in the south a region of fire, and after the heat from the south had played on the rivers of ice that crowded down from the north a yeasty venom began to be exuded."[5] From these evocative formless beginnings a hermaphroditic, prone giant named Ymir appeared to be asleep, but as he slept he sweated, and a son was born from one of his feet and man and wife from his left hand. A cow condensed from the sweat to produce milk for the giant, and she in turn began licking the salty blocks of ice, carving away the first man. The man mated with others, and humanity appeared. His son, Borr, then married the giant's daughter and produced the first family, which proceeded to slaughter Ymir and carve his body into chunks.

> Of Ymir's flesh the earth was fashioned
> And of his sweat the sea;
> Crags of his bones, trees of his hair,
> And of his skull the sky.
> Then of his bones the blithe gods made
> Midgard for sons of men;
> And of his brain the bitter-mooded
> Clouds were all created.[6]

Midgard is the Scandinavian way of describing the earthly plane of existence surrounded by an impassable sea or ocean (the great mother), with Hel below and the heaven of Asgard in the world above. In this strange vision of the far north, the salty blocks of ice represent the earth as well as a creative engine for life. This runs counter to rational logic, as icy regions are relatively devoid of life compared to more temperate regions, yet the impending destructive trickle effect generated by the disappearance of the polar icecaps shows just how integral to life these forbidding ice-covered landscapes really are.

This myth of the sons killing and dismembering their father to create the world appears in other guises in many cultures, such as the castration of the Greek sky god Uranus, planned by his sons and carried out by Kronos, a symbol of Father Time, who is later identified with the Roman deity Saturn. Similarly, the dismembering of the Egyptian god Osiris by his brother Set—also a surrogate of Saturn and a god signifying time—was reenacted in a mystery ritual celebrating the annual harvest. Further, Osiris's thirteen severed parts were believed to represent the thirteen lunar months of the year. Since the mythological primal god is timeless and eternal, his dismembering can be thought of as the creation of time and of the year. Thus, we can see the progression from the timelessness of the unconscious into the domain of consciousness, which echoes the expulsion from paradise of Adam and Eve.

End-of-the-world legends of the far north depict a dramatic melting of the polar ice and its far-reaching implications. An example is the primary Norse myth, the Völuspá, which describes the end of the world, or *Ragnarök* ("twilight of the gods"), where an epic battle signals both the end of the world and the entire process of events, fate, and destiny. Giants, gods, and men fight on a battlefield one hundred leagues square. All actions are criminal and bloody, and decay reigns. The primary cause of this is that the gods begin to disregard their promises to men and to each other. Does this sound familiar? The tempo of downfall increases, the sun darkens, and storms rage over the earth. Demons imprisoned within the earth break loose and arrive to persecute humanity. A yellow eagle shrieks at the prospect of carrion, and the ship of death shatters its moorings. The world groans, mountains crash, the sky is rent, and the demons demolish the gods with their fiery swords. The stars vanish, smoke and fire abound, and the earth falls back into the sea. It is the end of the world, and it sounds like an ancient description of our current times.

However, even though men and gods die in the legend of Völuspá, the world does not disappear forever. The great fire of *Ragnarök* is followed by the terrible winter, and when it passes, the remaining gods raise the earth from the sea. Two people—Lif and Lifthrasir—survive, hiding in the forest Hoddmímisholt and eating only the morning dew. From them, a new race of men descends.[7] That this Scandinavian myth about cyclic time and the transition of one world to another is so resonant with what is happening around us today is certainly eerie. However, it also expresses a very optimistic realization that although we may experience a great world crisis, we will survive and start anew.

The icy landscapes of the far north are extremely beautiful, rich in subtle colors and amazing shapes. We discern sacred mountains, gates, boundaries, and flow. Further, the play of light and the crystallized aging process that the icebergs exemplify lend a magical quality to these massive monoliths. In some ways icebergs are like the spirit of the world, frozen in time but transformative in their exorable movement and warming. Similarly, the great glaciers all over the world—on the continents that abut the northern and southern poles and in the highest mountain ranges—are gradually accelerating in their disappearance. This is not only an unfortunate loss of their spirit and radiance, but it also means that their essential functions—providing water for the world and balancing the climate—will cease.

PAGE 218: Iceberg, Disko Bay, Greenland, 2000

PAGE 219: Ice floe, Disko Bay, Greenland, 2008

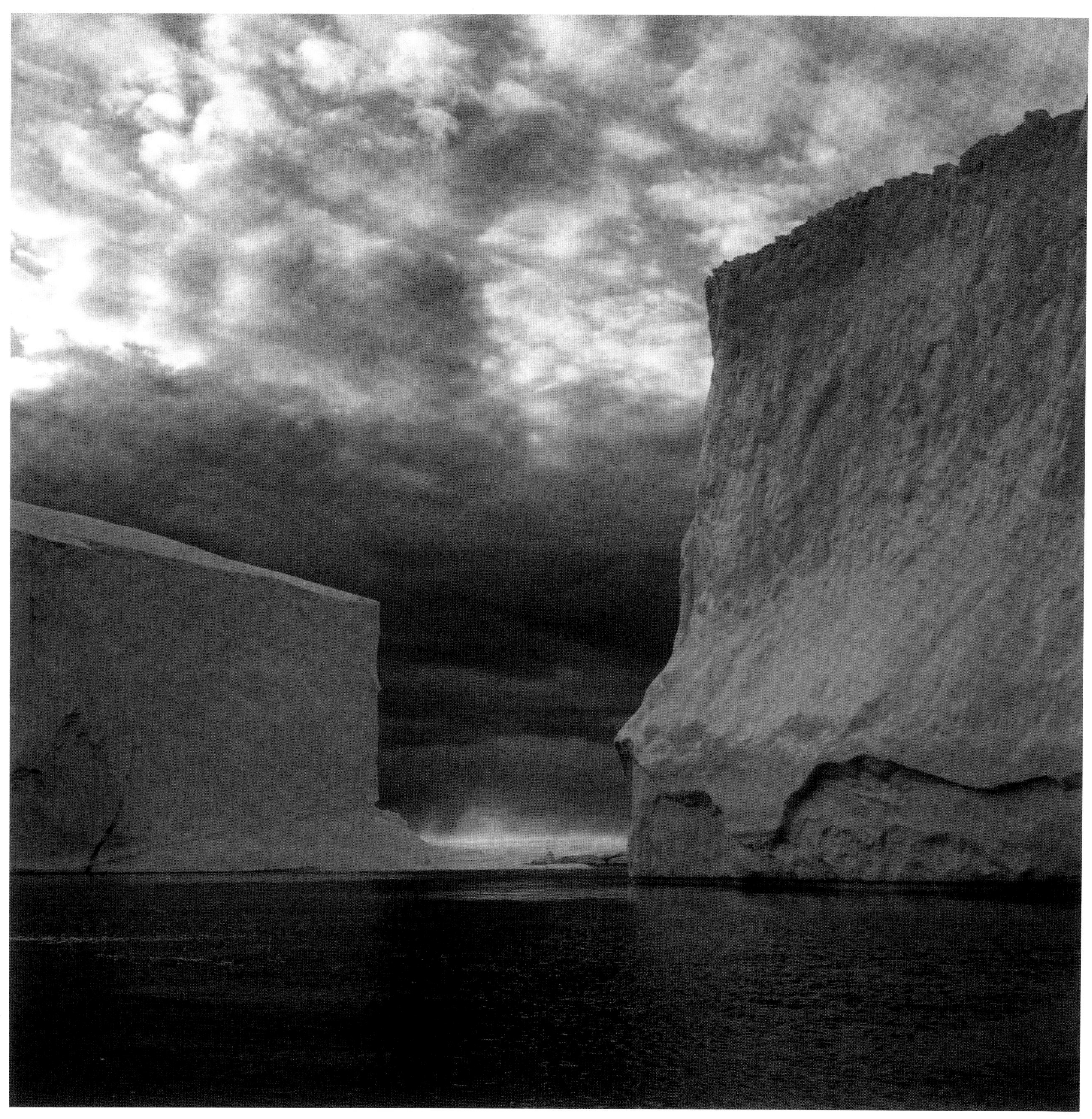

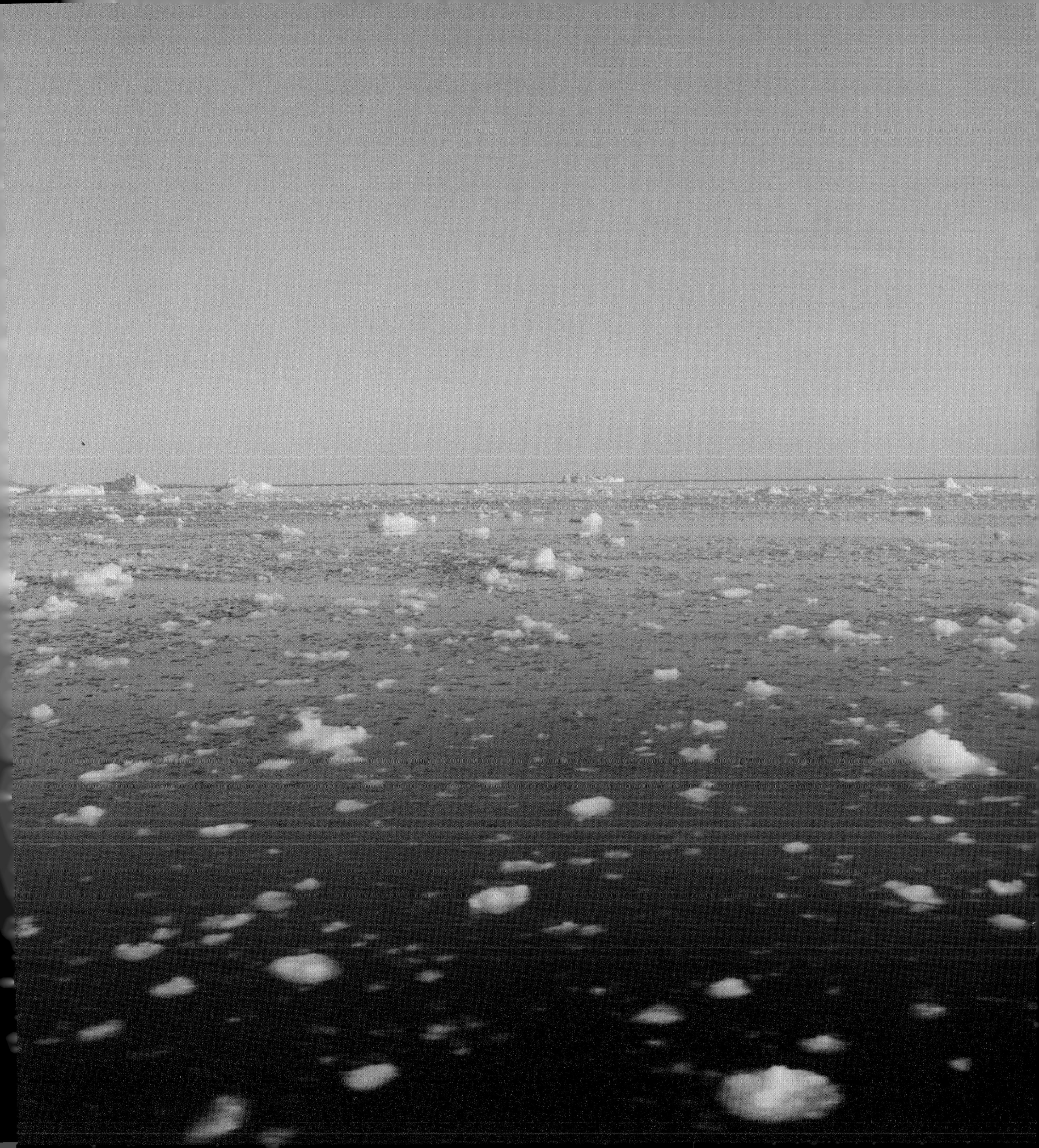

Afterword

Rediscovering the Sacred

Over hundreds of thousands of years, the forces of time and nature have worked their powerful ways on sacred places. This process often gives a new strength and beauty to the architecture or lands touched in this way and awakens in us feelings of nostalgia. And even today, there are still sacred landscapes to be discovered in strange and remote places. Not long ago, the ancient Buddhist temple at Borobudur in Java was rediscovered a thousand years after its creation because some Javanese people mentioned to then–colonial governor Sir Thomas Raffles that there was a mountain in eastern Java that had heads emerging out from it. When he finally explored the place he realized that these Buddhas were part of the gigantic temple that has now been restored to its former glory. Similarly, the tale of Hiram Bingham discovering Machu Picchu echoes the romance and adventure of finding a hidden city in the mountains. We can experience this romance in our own lives by exploring the Great Pyramid and the Sphinx, or the mysterious city of Hampi in central India, or the exotic and forbidden Mayan temples in Central America, which take us back into the mists of time to an era when the world was pure and the gods and goddesses reigned.

In our time of environmental crisis, we have demystified and desanctified our sacred landscapes. Such landscapes are alive: They flow, they produce a deep and powerful resonance that can be felt, and, above all, their power is often encoded in myths or stories that tell of ancient origins—mysteries that precede and influence the major world religions. There is no one true story, but rather a matrix of interrelated tales and myths that attempt to explain particular elements of a sacred place, or its coming into being, or the perceptions of various generations of inhabitants who lived in and experienced the place when it spoke directly to them. In this sense, these magnificent landscapes and the myths associated with them represent an older and deeper connection we share with our world.

Recycling and the lowering of dangerous emissions are important steps in the preservation of our environment, but technological efforts alone are not enough. Since storytelling is a primary way to communicate who we are and what we value, it is important to learn and retell the stories that are embedded in our landscapes. It is also essential that these stories remain known and that we pass their magic and mystery on to our children and their children. Faced with the daunting reality of rising oceans and the extinction of entire species, we must reanimate our landscapes and renew our understanding of their sacred qualities. Only when we achieve this universal, fundamental change in the way we relate to our environment can we hope to preserve the tenuous ecological balance of our only Earth.

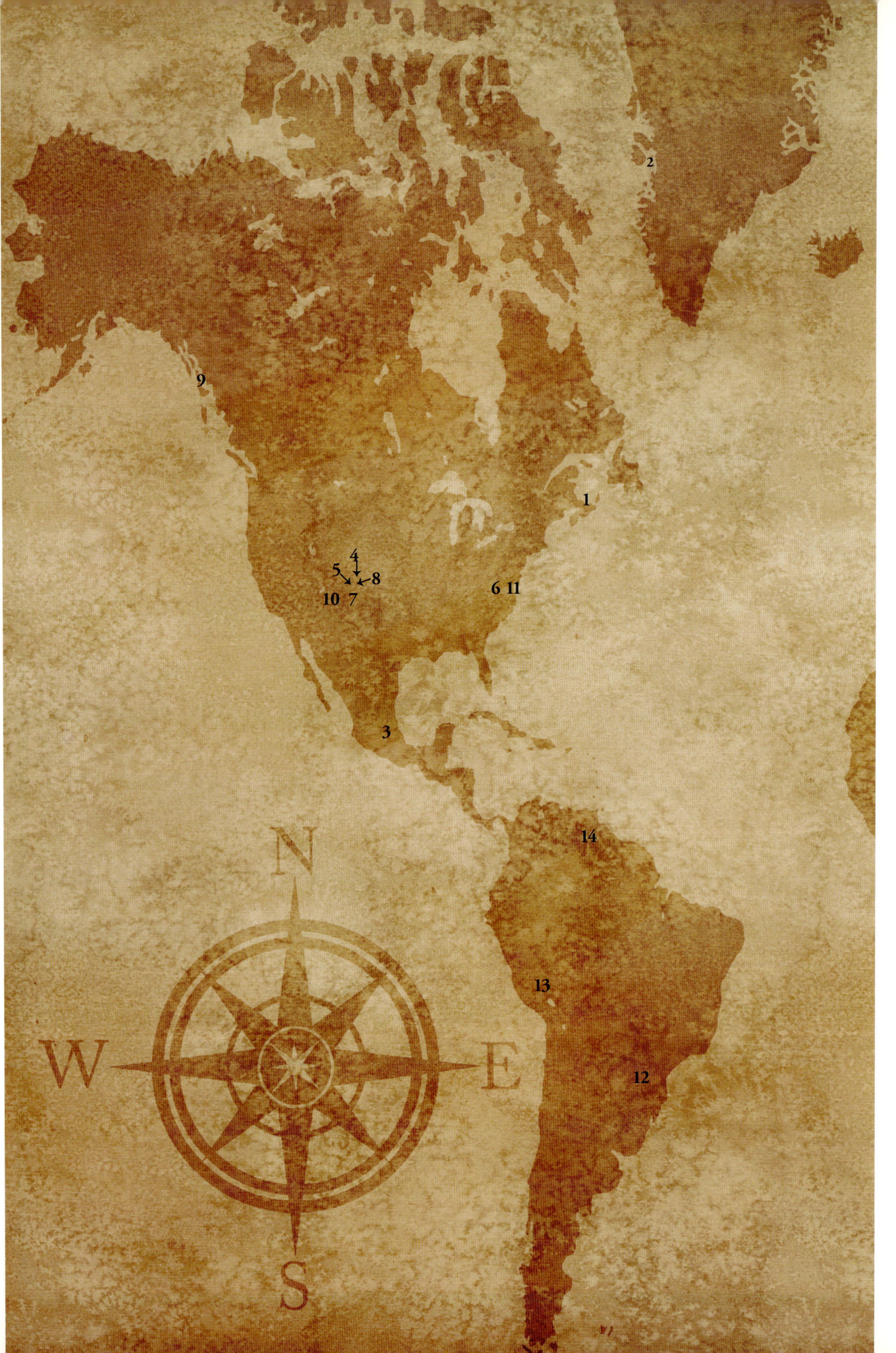

2
9
1
4
5
8
10
7
6
11
3
14
N
13
W
E
12
S

Sacred Sites of the Western Hemisphere

NORTH AMERICA

CANADA

1 Northumberland Strait

GREENLAND

2 Disko Bay

MEXICO

3 Pyramid of the Sun, Teotihuacán

UNITED STATES

4 Delicate Arch, Arches National Park, Utah

5 Dugout Ranch, Utah

6 Luray Caverns, Virginia

7 Monument Valley, Navajo Nation Reservation, Arizona/Utah

8 Mount Wilson, Colorado

9 Saanaheit Pole, Sitka National Historical Park, Alaska

10 Zion National Park, Utah

11 Washington Monument, Washington, D.C.

SOUTH AMERICA

ARGENTINA/BRAZIL

12 Iguazu Falls

PERU

13 Machu Picchu

VENEZUELA

14 Angel Falls, Canaima National Park

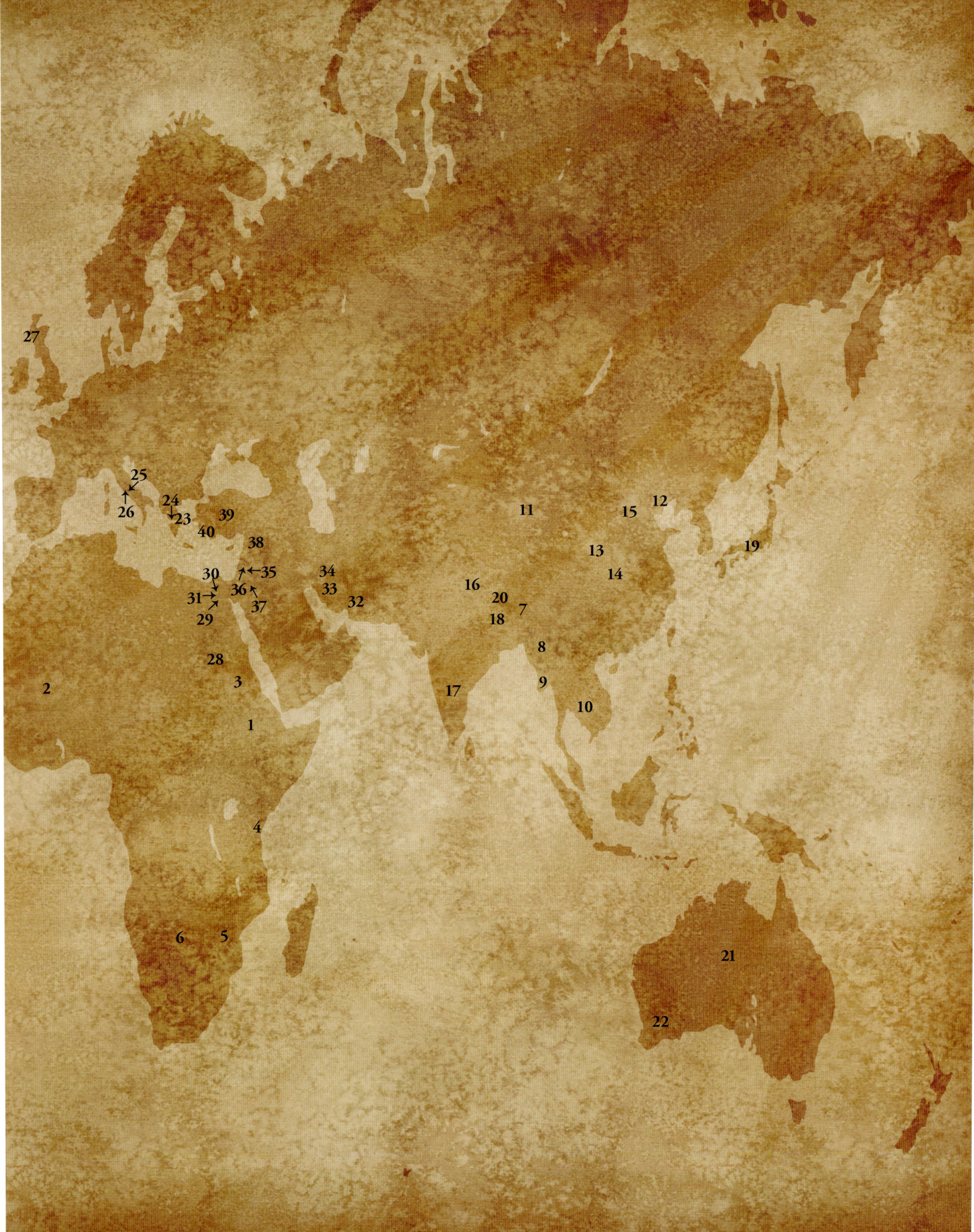

27
25
26
24
23
39
40
11
15
12
38
13
19
30
35
34
14
36
31
33
16
20
37
32
7
29
18
8
28
3
2
9
17
10
1
4
6
5
21
22

Sacred Sites of the Eastern Hemisphere

AFRICA

ETHIOPIA

1 Church of Bet Giorgis, Lalibela

MALI

2 Great Mosque of Djenné

SUDAN

3 Meroë

TANZANIA

4 Marhubi Palace Ruins, Zanzibar

ZIMBABWE

5 Great Zimbabwe National Monument

6 Victoria Falls

ASIA

BHUTAN

7 Rinpung Dzong, Paro

BURMA (MYANMAR)

8 Bagan

9 Shwedagon Temple, Yangon

CAMBODIA

10 Angkor

CHINA

11 Crescent Moon Spring, Dunhuang

12 Sacred Way of Xiaoling, Eastern Qing Tombs, Zunhua

13 Giant Wild Goose Pagoda, Xi'an

14 Three Gorges, Yangtze River

15 Yungang Grottoes, Datong

INDIA

16 Jantar Mantar, Delhi

17 Royal Center Stepped Tank and Virupaksha Temple, Hampi

18 Varanasi

JAPAN

19 Daisen-in and Saiho-ji gardens, Kyoto

NEPAL

20 Lumbini

AUSTRALIA

21 Ayers Rock, Uluru National Park

22 Wave Rock, Hyden

EUROPE

GREECE

23 Erechtheion, Parthenon, and Temple of Olympian Zeus, Athens

24 Temple of Athena, Delphi

ITALY

25 Hadrian's Villa, Tivoli

26 Via Appia Antica, Rome

SCOTLAND

27 Fingal's Cave, Staffa

MIDDLE EAST

EGYPT

28 Great Temple of Abu Simbel

29 Bent Pyramid and Red Pyramid, Dashur

30 Great Sphinx and Great Pyramid of Giza

31 Step Pyramid of Djoser, Saqqara

IRAN

32 Bam

33 Naqsh-e Rostam

34 Imam Mosque, Isfahan

ISRAEL

35 Tomb of Zechariah, Kidron Valley

36 Qumran

JORDAN

37 Petra

SYRIA

38 Tetrapylon, Palmyra

TURKEY

39 Göreme Caves and White Valley, Cappadocia

40 Temple of Apollo, Didyma

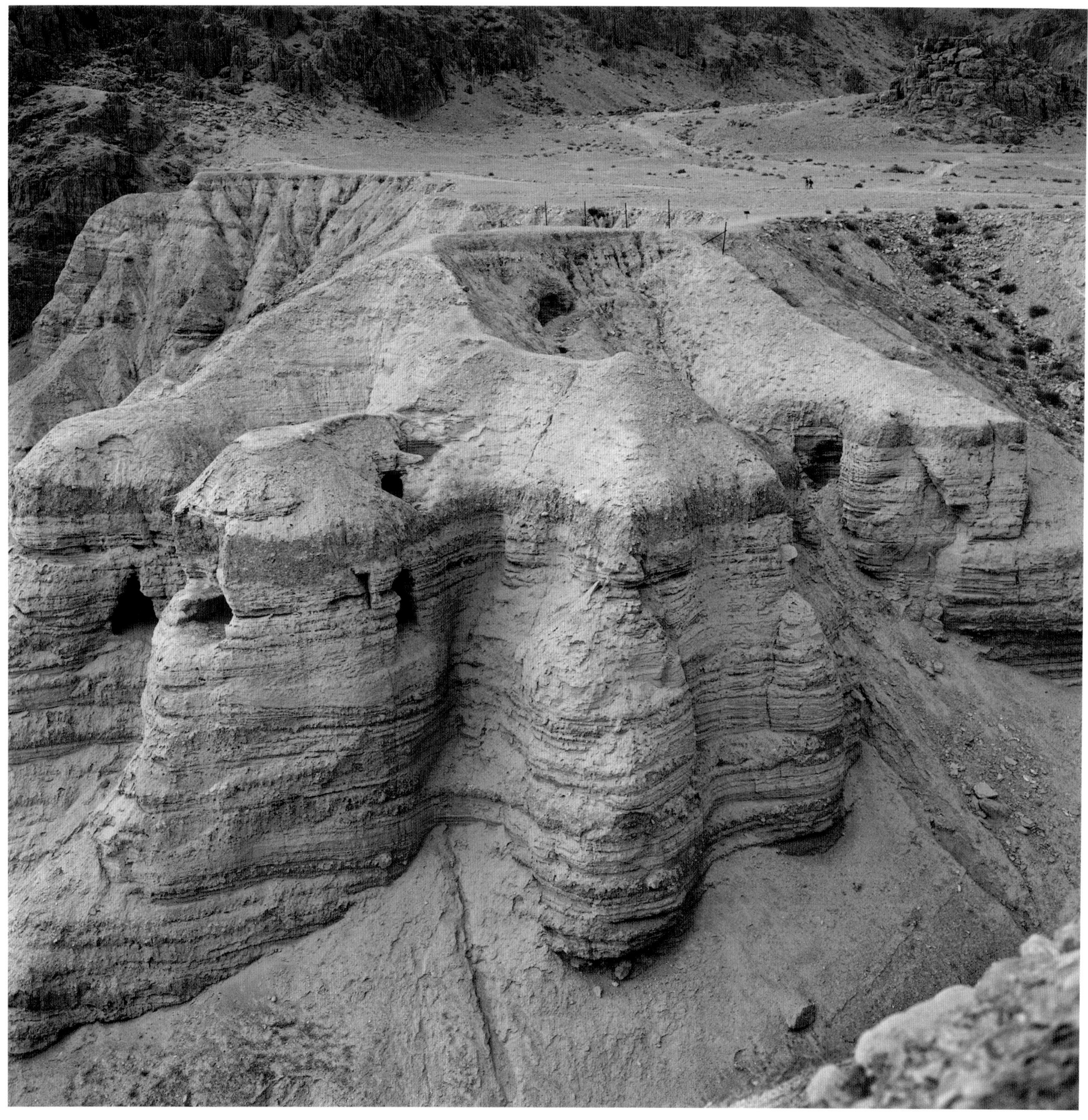

Acknowledgments

A. T. Mann

I would like to thank our editor, Barbara Berger, and also Melanie Madden and Hannah Reich, at Sterling Publishing for their editing and invaluable help in guiding this book to completion. Thanks to Judith Wheelock for reading the book and for her inspiration and support; to Ziska for her detailed comments on the text; and for the opportunity to work with Lynn Davis and her assistants Chad Kleitch and Rebeccah Johnson.

Lynn Davis

In memory of
James A. Davis and Ayrev Davis

Thank you to:

Tad Mann, Chad Kleitsch, Rebeccah Johnson, Heather Sutfin, Steve Rifkin, Andy Baugnet, Mark Sage, Joe Hartwell, Barbara Berger, the Center for Creative Photography, the Pew Charitable Trust, and the Nature Conservancy

To friends and family:

Silver, Michael Ward Stout, Eric Johnson, John Thomas, Gita Mehta, Selma Al-Radi, Lynn Nesbit, George Andreou, Phil Glass, Hennessey Knoop, Nabil Nahas, Prince Chatri Chalerm and Kamla Yukol, James Wang, Barbara Heiser, Bill Katz, Fereydoun Ave, Myles Kehoe, Karly Kehoe, and Patti Smith

To my mother, Ruth Davis, whose travels and magical suitcase inspired my dreams and opened the world to me. To my sister, Maxine Davis. And to my husband and fellow traveler, Rudy Wurlitzer.

OPPOSITE: Qumran, Israel, 1994

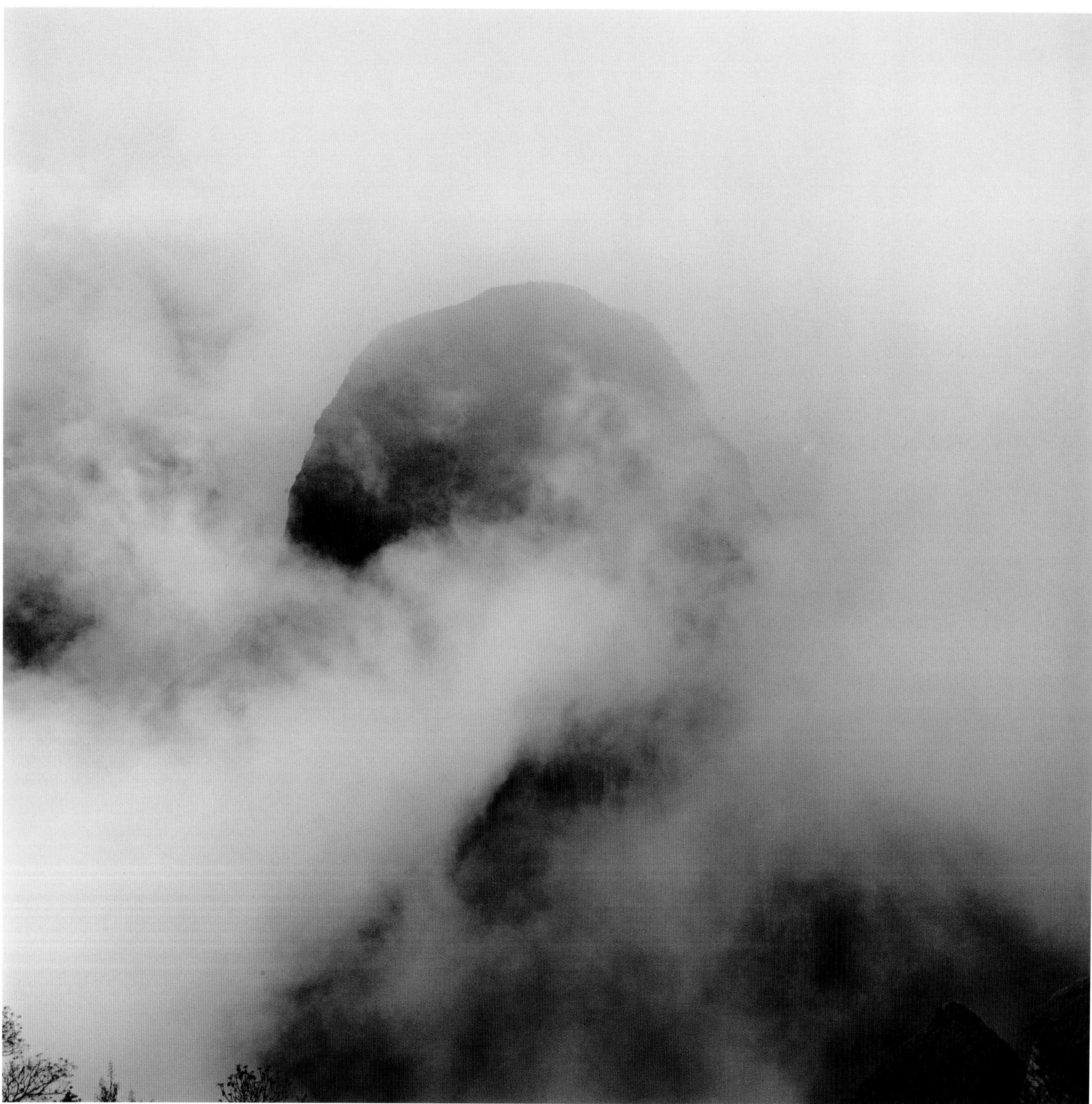

Endnotes

Front matter

[1] Roberto Calasso, *Literature and the Gods* (New York: Knopf, 2001), p. 3.

Chapter 1

[1] Stephen H. Buhner, *The Secret Teachings of Plants: The Intelligence of the Heart in the Direct Perception of Nature* (Rochester, VT: Bear & Company, 2004), p. 140.

[2] A. T. Mann, *Sacred Architecture* (London: Element Books, 1979), p. 13.

[3] Robert Lawlor, *Voices of the First Day* (Rochester, VT: Inner Traditions, 1991), p. 1.

[4] Chögyam Trungpa, *Illusion's Game: The Life and Teaching of Naropa* (Boston: Shambhala, 1994), p. 133.

[5] Ibid., p. 33.

[6] See the statement of purpose for the Forum for Architecture, Culture and Spirituality, of which the author is a member. Their website is http://faculty.arch.utah.edu/acs/.

[7] Mircea Eliade, *The Sacred and the Profane*, trans. Willard R. Trask (London: Harcourt Brace and World, 1959), p. 68.

[8] In the new physics there is even a process called "entanglement" that Einstein predicted and that essentially suggests that two subatomic particles can become entangled and inextricably linked so that even if they are separated by being in different universes, a change in one particle would instantly be reflected in the other. See Amir D. Aczel, *Entanglement* (New York: Four Walls Eight Windows, 2001).

Chapter 2

[1] Stephen H. Buhner, *The Secret Teachings of Plants: The Intelligence of the Heart in the Direct Perception of Nature* (Rochester, VT: Bear & Company, 2004), p. 150.

[2] C. G. Jung, *Archetypes of the Collective Unconscious*, trans. R. F. C. Hull (London: Routledge and Kegan Paul, 1969), p. 6.

[3] Ibid., p. 5.

[4] Thomas Moore, *The Re-Enchantment of Everyday Life* (New York, HarperPerennial, 1997), p. 41.

[5] See the recent popular books of professed atheists such as Sam Harris, Christopher Hitchens, and Richard Dawkins.

Chapter 3

[1] Quoted in John Carter Covell, *Unraveling Zen's Red Thread* (Seoul: Hollym International, 1980), p. 182.

[2] Ibid., note on p. 219.

[3] Giorgio de Santillana and Hertha von Dechend, *Hamlet's Mill* (Boston: Godine, 1977).

[4] John Carter Covell, *Unraveling Zen's Red Thread*. Jung follows, quoting Richard of St. Victor, "Do you wish to see the transfigured Christ? Ascend that mountain and learn to know yourself."

[5] May Castleberry, ed., *The New World's Old World* (Albuquerque: University of New Mexico Press), p. 154, quoting Hiram Bingham.

[6] Richard I. Burger and Lucy C. Salazar, *Machu Picchu* (New Haven: Yale University Press, 2004), p. 36.

[7] James E. McClellan and Harold Dorn, *Science and Technology in World History* (Baltimore: Johns Hopkins University Press, 2006), pp. 164–165.

[8] Meher McArthur, *Reading Buddhist Art* (London: Thames and Hudson, 2002).

[9] Marilyn M. Rhie and Robert Thurman, *Wisdom and Compassion: The Sacred Art of Tibet* (New York: Abrams, 1991).

[10] Ibid, pp. 32–33.

[11] De Santillana and von Dechend, *Hamlet's Mill*, p. 162.

[12] Michael Freeman and Roger Warner, *Angkor: The Hidden Glories* (Boston: Houghton Mifflin, 1990), p. 244; their translation of a quote from a French guidebook by Jean Commaille.

[13] Roberto Calasso, *Ka*, trans. Tim Parks (New York: Knopf, 1998), p. 119.

[14] She is often called Yin-Yang before their separation, expressed in the figure of Nu Gua, a divine being who brought civilization and order to China after the Great Flood. She rules over both Heaven and Earth, and is associated with the constellation of the Great Bear. See Sukie Colegrave, *The Spirit of the Valley* (London: Virago, 1979), pp. 31–34.

[15] Ernest J. Eitel, *Feng Shui or The Rudiments of Natural Science in China* (Cambridge: Cokaygne, 1973), pp. 57–58.

[16] Lillian Too, *Feng Shui* (Shaftesbury: Element Books, 1996), pp. 56–57.

[17] Sarah Rossbach, *Feng Shui* (London: Rider, 1984), p. 36.

[18] Stephen Skinner, *The Living Earth Manual of Feng-Shui* (London: Routledge and Kegan Paul, 1982), p. 14.

[19] Han-shan, "Cold Mountain Poems," in *Riprap and Cold Mountain Poems*, trans. Gary Snyder (San Francisco: North Point Press, 1990), p. 49.

[20] Rossbach, *Feng Shui*, pp. 36–37.

OPPOSITE: Machu Picchu, Peru, 2000

[21] Daisetz Suzuki, *Zen and Japanese Culture* (Princeton: Bollingen, 1959), p. 332.

[22] Ibid., p. 336.

[23] Werner Wolff, *Island of Death* (Whitefish, MT: Kessinger Publications, 2004), pp. 26–28.

[24] John Miksic, *Borobudur* (Hong Kong: Periplus, 1991), p. 24.

[25] The author traveled and taught on Bali in 2007 and visited Mt. Batur and its environs. He also led a tour to the ring of volcanoes on Java near the Buddhist monument Borobudur.

[26] Miksic, *Borobudur*, p. 28.

[27] Ibid., pp. 28–30.

[28] Frank Waters, *Masked Gods* (New York: Ballantine Books, 1950); and Frank Waters, *Book of the Hopi* (New York: Penguin Books, 1963).

[29] Waters, *Masked Gods*, pp. 163–165.

[30] Ibid., p. 164.

[31] Julia Meredith, "Mapping Identity: Tibetans in New Mexico and Their Incorporation into the Tri-Ethnic Myth," *Journal of the Southwest* 44 (2002).

[32] C. G. Jung, *Memories, Dreams and Reflections* (London: Collins, 1983), p. 83.

[33] Ibid., p. 237.

[34] A. T. Mann, essays in *The Roof of Europe* (Geneva: Bellerive Foundation, 1991).

[35] Rainer Maria Rilke, "The Second Elegy," in *Duino Elegies*, trans. Stephen Mitchell (Boston: Shambhala, 1992).

[36] Friedrich Nietzsche, *Thus Spoke Zarathustra*, trans. Walter Kaufmann (New York: Penguin, 1978), p. 3.

[37] Emma Jung, *The Grail Legend* (London: Hodder and Stoughton, 1970), p. 121.

[38] Ibid., p. 104.

[39] James G. Cowan, *The Aborigine Tradition* (Shaftesbury: Element, 1992), pp. 24–25.

[40] Robert Lawlor, *Voices of the First Day* (Rochester, VT: Inner Traditions, 1991), p. 1.

[41] Ibid., pp. 160–161.

[42] Elisha Kent Kane, *The United States Grinnell Expedition in Search of Sir John Franklin: A Personal Narrative* (Boston: Philips, Sampson, 1857), p. 68.

Chapter 4

[1] Joseph Campbell, *The Masks of God: Primitive Mythology* (New York: Viking Press, 1959), p. 397.

[2] Joseph Campbell, *Thou Art That: Transforming Religious Metaphor* (New York: New World Library, 2001), p. 65.

[3] Porphyry, *On the Cave of the Nymphs*, trans. Thomas Taylor (Grand Rapids, MI: Phanes, 1991), p. 25.

[4] Ibid., p. 12.

[5] Linda Schele and David Freidel, *A Forest of Kings* (New York: Quill, 1990), p. 67.

[6] Andrea Stone, *Images from the Underworld: Naj Tunich and the Tradition of Maya Cave Painting* (Austin: University of Texas Press, 1995), pp. 43–45.

[7] Graham Hancock, *Supernatural* (Scarborough, Ontario: Doubleday Canada, 2006), pp. 26–27.

[8] Ibid., p. 79.

[9] Vincent Scully, *The Earth, the Temple, and the Gods* (New Haven: Yale University Press, 1962), p. 106.

[10] Giorgio de Santillana and Hertha von Dechend, *Hamlet's Mill* (Boston: Godine, 1977), p. 57; also see Robert Temple, *The Sirius Mystery* (London: Sidgwick and Jackson, 1975), pp. 121–143.

[11] Scully, *The Earth, the Temple, and the Gods*, p. 109.

[12] Angeliki Charitonidou, *Epidaurus: The Sanctuary of Asclepios and the Museum* (Athens: Clio Editions, 1978), p. 13.

[13] Yeshe Tsogyal, *The Lotus-Born: The Life Story of Padmasambhava* (Boston: Shambhala, 1993), p. 124.

[14] "China's Hidden Cave Art," *New York Times*, June 17, 1979.

[15] Thomas Barrie, *Spiritual Path, Sacred Place* (Boston: Shambhala, 1996), p. 31.

Chapter 5

[1] Paul Negri, ed., *Metaphysical Poetry: An Anthology* (New York: Dover, 2002), p. 203.

[2] Thomas Moore, *The Re-Enchantment of Everyday Life* (New York, HarperPerennial, 1997), p. 14.

[3] A. T. Mann, *The Divine Plot: Astrology, Reincarnation, Cosmology and History* (London: Element, 1986), pp. 38–39. The book contains a list of thirty-nine cultures around the world that have flood legends.

[4] Roberto Calasso, *Ka*, trans. Tim Parks, (New York: Knopf, 1998), p. 117–118.

[5] "Flowing with the Spirit of Rumi," Coleman Barks interviewed by Joseph Roberts, on Bill Moyers's *Language of Life* series on PBS, reprinted in *Common Ground* magazine (Vancouver), June 2001.

[6] Ibid.

[7] Calasso, *Ka*, p. 116.

[8] The lotus is also a symbol of the Crown chakra at the apex of the head.

[9] Richard I. Burger and Lucy C. Salazar, *Machu Picchu* (New Haven: Yale University Press, 2004), p. 116.

[10] Carl Jung, *Alchemical Studies* (London: Routledge and Kegan Paul, 1967), p. 207.

[11] Emma Jung, *The Grail Legend* (London: Hodder and Stoughton, 1970), pp. 369–371.

[12] Ibid., p. 369, slightly abridged.

[13] Ibid., p. 139. "Stella Maris" is Latin for "star of the sea," another name for the Virgin Mary.

[14] Ralph Metzner, *The Well of Remembrance* (London: Shambhala, 1994), pp. 219–220.

[15] Louis Charpentier, *The Mysteries of Chartres Cathedral* (Steeple Bumstead, UK: RILKO Books, 1993), p. 32.

[16] M. A. R. Barker, *Klamath Directory,* University of California Publications in Linguistics 31 (Berkeley: University of California Press, 1963), p. 145.

[17] James A. Swan, *The Power of Place* (Bath: Gateway Books, 1993).

[18] From Juan Antonio Lazara, "Iguazu and the Missions," *Guia del Estudiante*, Buenos Aires, 2007.

[19] E. Bailby, "The Iguaçu Falls," *UNESCO Courier* 48 (1995): 40–43.

[20] *Bali*, Indonesian Regional Maps (Singapore: Periplus [HK] Editions, 2005).

[21] James Herron, "Really Roughing It in the Outback," *Los Angeles Times*, November 17, 2002.

[22] James G. Cowan, *The Aborigine Tradition* (Shaftesbury: Element, 1992), pp. 23–24.

[23] Ibid., p. 78.

[24] Ibid., pp. 78–81.

[25] Alec Bartholomew, *Hidden Nature: The Startling Insights of Viktor Schauberger* (London: Floris Books, 2003), p. 63.

[26] Masaru Emoto, *The Secret Life of Water* (New York: Atria Books, 2005).

[27] William Butler Yeats, "The Stolen Child" (poem).

Chapter 6

[1] From the Camelot Project of the University of Rochester.

[2] Carl Jung, *Alchemical Studies* (London: Routledge and Kegan Paul, 1967), p. 194.

[3] Heinrich Zimmer, *Myths and Symbols in Indian Art and Civilization* (Washington, DC: Pantheon, 1946), p. 67.

[4] Anna Lewington and Edward Parker, *Ancient Trees: Trees that Live for 1000 Years* (London: Collins & Brown, 1999) p. 9.

[5] Ibid.

[6] Ralph Metzner, *The Well of Remembrance* (London: Shambhala, 1994), p. 206.

[7] Linda Schele and David Freidel, *A Forest of Kings* (New York: Quill, 1990), p. 418.

[8] Schele and Freidel, *A Forest of Kings*, p. 40.

[9] John Michell, *The View over Atlantis* (London: Garnstone Press, 1972), p. 17.

[10] Ibid., p. 43.

[11] R. J. Stewart, *The Mystic Life of Merlin* (London: Arcana, 1986), p. ix; and R. J. Stewart, *The Prophetic Vision of Merlin* (London: Arcana, 1986). R. J. Stewart consulted the author during the writing of these two books in 1985 to verify their astrological and astronomical symbolism.

[12] Stewart, *The Mystic Life of Merlin*, pp. 99–100.

[13] A. T. Mann and Jane Lyle, *Sacred Sexuality* (Shaftesbury: Element, 1995), p. 135.

[14] Ibid., pp. 154–156.

[15] Metzner, *Well of Remembrance*, pp. 62–63.

[16] Ibid., p. 63.

[17] Robert Graves, *The White Goddess: A Historical Grammar of Poetic Myth* (London: Faber and Faber, 1961), p. 133.

[18] Zena Halpern, "Menorah Found in the Catskill Mountains of New York," *Ancient American* 11, no. 71 (2007): 8; and Jeff Love, *The Quantum Gods* (Tisbury: Compton Russell Element, 1976), pp. 27, 33.

[19] Graves, *The White Goddess,* pp. 144–145.

[20] Mann and Lyle, *Sacred Sexuality*, p. 176. This quotation also appears in Jung, *Alchemical Studies*, p. 307.

[21] Moyra Caldecott, *Myths of the Sacred Tree* (Rochester, VT: Destiny Books, 1993), p. 202.

[22] Ibid., p. 203.

Chapter 7

[1] Lethaby, William, *Architecture, Mysticism and Myth* (London: Architectural Press, 1974), p. 32.

[2] Richard Tarnas, *Cosmos and Psyche* (New York: Viking, 2006), pp. 94–96.

[3] Wasson et al., *Persephone's Quest* (New Haven: Yale University Press, 1986), p. 169.

[4] Walter Burkert, "Jason, Hypsipyle, and New Fire at Lemons," in *Oxford Readings in Greek Religion*, ed. Richard Buxton (Oxford: Oxford University Press, 2001).

[5] Johannes Fabricius, *Alchemy* (Copenhagen: Rosenkilde and Bagger, 1976), pp. 170–171.

[6] Heinrich Zimmer, *Myths and Symbols in Indian Art and Civilization* (Washington, DC: Pantheon, 1946), p. 152.

[7] Poem from the "Twelve Keys of Basil Valentine" (Germany, 1599) in Johannes Fabricius, *Alchemy* (Copenhagen: Rosenkilde and Bagger, 1976), p. 196.

[8] Bankei (1622–1693), Zen poet, "Song of Original Mind," in *Bankei Zen: Translations from the Record of Bankei*, trans. Peter Haskel, ed. Yoshito Hakeda (New York: Grove Press, 1994), p. 134.

[9] Roberto Calasso, *Ka*, trans. Tim Parks, (New York: Knopf, 1998), pp. 426–427.

[10] Richard Erdoes and Alfonso Ortiz, *American Indian Myths and Legends* (New York: Pantheon, 1984), p. 14.

[11] C. G. Jung, *Word and Image* (Princeton, NJ: Bollingen, 1979), p. 188.

[12] Ibid., p. 189, from his *Experimental Researches*, Collected Works 2, p. 227.

[13] Ibid., pp. 197–198.

[14] Lethaby, *Architecture, Mysticism and Myth*, pp. 227–232.

[15] John Anthony West, *Serpent in the Sky* (San Francisco: Harper and Row, 1979), p. 78.

[16] Angel Thompson, *Feng Shui* (New York: St. Martin's Griffin, 1996), p. 7.

[17] Robert Graves, *The White Goddess: A Historical Grammar of Poetic Myth* (London: Faber and Faber, 1961), p. 38.

[18] Ibid., pp. 38–39.

Chapter 8

[1] Eva Wong, trans., *Cultivating Stillness: A Taoist Manual for Transforming Body and Mind* (Boston: Shambhala, 1992), p. 18.

[2] John Michell, *City of Revelation* (London: Garnstone Press, 1972), pp. 88–89. See also John Michell, *The View over Atlantis*. (London: Garnstone Press, 1975)

[3] Carl A. Ruck, et al., *The Road to Eleusis* (Los Angeles: William Dailey Rare Books, 1998), p. 13.

[4] Ibid., p. 85.

[5] Ibid., p. 87.

[6] Ibid. The authors of the *Road to Eleusis* suggest that the wheat mold is ergot, known to have hallucinogenic qualities that trigger death and rebirth experiences in those who ingest it. One of the authors of the book is Albert Hoffman, who discovered LSD.

[7] Wong, *Cultivating Stillness*, p. xvii.

[8] Richard Hinckley Allen, *Star Names: Their Lore and Meaning* (New York: Dover, 1963), pp. 205–209.

[9] Theony Condos, trans., *Star Myths of the Greeks and Romans* (Grand Rapids, MI: Phanes Press, 1997), p. 103.

[10] Graham Hancock and Santha Faiia, *Heaven's Mirror* (New York: Crown, 1998), pp. 119–131. Hancock mentions the work of John Grigsby, a PhD candidate who made the discovery of the Angkor alignments.

[11] Michael Freeman and Roger Warner, *Angkor: The Hidden Glories* (Boston: Houghton Mifflin, 1990), p. 246; their translation of a quote from a French guidebook by Jean Commaille.

[12] Adrian Gilbert and Maurice Cotterell, *The Mayan Prophecies* (Shaftesbury: Element Books, 1995), pp. 104–106.

[13] Stephen Skinner, *Guide to the Feng Shui Compass* (London: Golden Hind Press, 2008), p. 164.

Chapter 9

[1] Giorgio de Santillana and Hertha von Dechend, *Hamlet's Mill* (Boston: Godine, 1977), p. 225.

[2] *Lost Horizon* is a 1937 film directed by Frank Capra and starring Ronald Colman and Jane Wyatt.

[3] Suzanne Cahill, *Transcendence and Divine Passion: The Queen Mother of the West in Medieval China* (Stanford, CA: Stanford University, 1993), pp. 18–20.

[4] Derek Walters, *The Complete Guide to Chinese Astrology* (London: Watkins, 2005), p. 244.

[5] Unreleased DVD of the Kalachakra Tantra teachings, Foundation for Universal Responsibility and Mystic Fire Video, Montauk, NY, 2000–2005.

[6] Alexander Berzin, "Holy Wars in Buddhism and Islam: The Myth of Shambhala (full version)," Berzin Archives, 2001 (revised 2006), http://www.berzinarchives.com/web/en/archives/advanced/kalachakra/relation_islam_hinduism/holy_wars_buddhism_islam/holy_war_buddhism_islam_shambhala_long.html.

[7] Henry David Thoreau, *Walden* (Boston: J. M. Dent & Sons, 1912), p. 263.

[8] A. T. Mann and Jane Lyle, *Sacred Sexuality* (Shaftesbury: Element, 1995).

[9] James M. Robinson, *The Nag Hammadi Library* (Leiden: E. J. Brill, 1977), p. 169.

[10] John Lamb Lash, *Not in His Image: Gnostic Vision, Sacred Ecology, and the Future of Belief* (White River Junction, VT: Chelsea Green Publishing, 2006), pp. 10–11.

[11] Ibid., pp. 6–7.

[12] These dates are approximate. E. H. Blakeney, ed. *A Smaller Classical Dictionary* (London: Dent, 1917), p. 495.

[13] Peter Dawkins, *Arcadia* (Warwick, UK: Francis Bacon Research Trust, 1988), pp. 15–17.

[14] A. T. Mann, *The Divine Plot: Astrology, Reincarnation, Cosmology and History* (London: Element, 1986), pp. 38.

[15] John K. Howat, *American Paradise: The World of the Hudson River School* (New York: Metropolitan Museum of Art, 1987).

Chapter 10

[1] Vincent Scully, *The Earth, The Temple, and The Gods* (New Haven: Yale University Press, 1962), p. 3.

[2] Rodney Rhoades and David R. Bell, *Medical Physiology* (Baltimore: Lippincott Williams and Wilkins, 1995), p. 127.

[3] W. R. Lethaby, *Architecture, Mysticism and Myth* (London, Architectural Press, 1974), p. 53.

[4] Jean Richer, *Sacred Geography of the Ancient Greeks* (Albany: State University of New York Press, 1994), pp. 82–85.

[5] Ibid., p. 73.

[6] Ibid., p. 67.

[7] Linda Schele and David Freidel, *A Forest of Kings* (New York: Quill, 1990), pp. 66–67.

[8] Ibid., p. 67.

[9] Cottie Burland, *North American Indian Mythology*

(London: Chancellor Press, 1996), pp. 63–65.

[10] Ibid., p. 129.

[11] Gerald S. Hawkins, *Stonehenge Decoded* (Garden City, NY: Doubleday, 1965), p. 138.

[12] Ibid., pp. 64–66.

[13] John Michell, *The View over Atlantis* (London: Garnstone Press, 1972), pp. 9–11.

[14] See Alfred Watkins, *The Old Straight Track* (London: Abacus, 1970), pp. 157–162, for a discussion of relevant place names.

[15] Ibid., p. 15.

[16] William Stirling, *The Canon* (London: RILKO, 1981).

[17] Douglas Heggie, *Megalithic Science* (London: Thames and Hudson, 1981), p. 37.

[18] Martin Brennan, *The Boyne Valley Vision* (Portlaoise, Ireland: Dolmen Press, 1980), back cover.

[19] Ibid., p. 24.

[20] Ibid., p. 31.

[21] Ibid., p. 32.

[22] Ibid., p. 113.

[23] Shashi Bhushan Ashri, *Delhi's Jantar Mantar Observatory* (New Delhi: Shalini, 2004), pp. 166–167.

[24] Geoffrey Cornelius and Paul Devereux, *The Secret Language of Stars and Planets* (San Francisco: Chronicle Books, 1996), p. 143.

[25] Ibid., p. xxx.

[26] Evan Hadingham, *Early Man and the Cosmos* (London: Heinemann, 1983), pp. 224–226.

[27] Ibid., pp. 171–173.

[28] Herbert Weaver, *Divining the Primary Sense* (London: Routledge and Kegan Paul, 1978), p. 112.

[29] Ibid., p. 76.

[30] Ibid., pp. 36–39.

Chapter 11

[1] Quoted in John Carter Covell, *Unraveling Zen's Red Thread* (Seoul: Hollym International, 1980), p. 41.

[2] Shin'ichi Hisamatsu, *Zen and the Fine Arts* (Kyoto: Kodansha, 1970), p. 11.

[3] Ibid., p. 11.

[4] Ibid., p. 12.

[5] Ibid., p. 53.

[6] Günther Nitschke, *From Shinto to Ando: Studies in Architectural Anthropology in Japan* (London: Academy Editions, 1993), p. 49.

[7] Ibid., p. 58.

[8] Ibid., p. 60.

[9] Patrul Rinpoche, *The Words of My Perfect Teacher*, trans. Padmakara Translation Group (San Francisco: HarperCollins, 1994), p. 56.

[10] William Wordsworth, *Intimations of Immortality from Recollections of Early Childhood* (Boston: Houghton Mifflin, 1895), p. 89.

Chapter 12

[1] William Wordsworth, "The Tables Turned," *The Poems of William Wordsworth* (London: E. Moxon, 1857), p. 361.

[2] Thomas Mann, *Joseph and His Brothers* (London: Sidgwick and Jackson, 1969), p. 247.

[3] Michael Freeman and Roger Warner, *Angkor: The Hidden Glories* (Boston: Houghton Mifflin, 1990), pp. 250–252; their translation of a quote from a French guidebook by Jean Commaille.

[4] "Flowing with the Spirit of Rumi," Coleman Barks interviewed by Joseph Roberts, on Bill Moyers's *Language of Life* series on PBS, reprinted in *Common Ground* magazine (Vancouver), June 2001.

[5] Joseph Campbell, *The Hero with a Thousand Faces* (New York: Bollingen, 1949), p. 285.

[6] Ibid., p. 285, from the *Prose Edda*, trans. Arthur Gilchrist Brodeur.

[7] A. T. Mann, *The Divine Plot: Astrology, Reincarnation, Cosmology and History* (London: Element, 1986), pp. 38.

Bibliography

Aczel, Amir D. *Entanglement.* New York: Four Walls Eight Windows, 2001.

Allen, Richard Hinckley. *Star Names: Their Lore and Meaning.* New York: Dover, 1963

Ashri, Shashi Bhushan. *Delhi's Jantar Mantar Observatory.* New Delhi: Shalini, 2004

Barker, M. A. R. *Klamath Directory.* University of California Publications in Linguistics 31. Berkeley: University of California Press, 1963.

Barrie, Thomas. *Spiritual Path, Sacred Place.* Boston: Shambhala, 1996.

Bartholomew, Alec. *Hidden Nature: The Startling Insights of Viktor Schauberger.* London: Floris Books, 2003.

Berzin, Alexander. "Holy Wars in Buddhism and Islam: The Myth of Shambhala (full version)," Berzin Archives, 2001 (revised 2006).

Blakeney, E. H., ed.. *A Smaller Classical Dictionary.* London: Dent, 1917.

Brennan, Martin. *The Boyne Valley Vision.* Portlaoise, Ireland: Dolmen Press, 1980.

Burger, Richard L., and Lucy C. Salazar. *Machu Picchu.* New Haven, CT: Yale University Press, 2004.

Burkert, Walter. "Jason, Hypsipyle, and New Fire at Lemons," in *Oxford Readings in Greek Religion,* ed. Richard Buxton. Oxford: Oxford University Press, 2001

Burland, Cottie. *North American Indian Mythology.* London: Chancellor Press, 1996.

Cahill, Suzanne. *Transcendence and Divine Passion: The Queen Mother of the West in Medieval China.* Palo Alto, CA: Stanford University, 1993.

Calasso, Roberto. *Ka.* Translated by Tim Parks. New York: Knopf, 1998.

———. *Literature and the Gods.* New York: Knopf, 2001.

Caldecott, Moyra. *Myths of the Sacred Tree.* Rochester, VT: Destiny Books, 1993.

Campbell, Joseph. *The Hero with a Thousand Faces.* New York: Bollingen, 1949.

———. *Thou Art That: Transforming Religious Metaphor.* New York: New World Library, 2001.

Castleberry, May, ed. *The New World's Old World.* Albuquerque: University of New Mexico Press, 2003.

Charitonidou, Angeliki. *Epidaurus: The Sanctuary of Asclepios and the Museum.* Athens: Clio Editions, 1978.

Charpentier, Louis. *The Mysteries of Chartres Cathedral.* London: RILKO, 1966

Conan, Michael, ed. *Sacred Gardens and Landscapes: Ritual and Agency.* Washington, DC: Dumbarton Oaks, 2007.

Condos, Theony, trans. *Star Myths of the Greeks and Romans.* Grand Rapids, MI: Phanes Press, 1997.

Cornelius, Geoffrey, and Paul Devereux. *The Secret Language of Stars and Planets.* San Francisco: Chronicle Books, 1996.

Covell, Jon Carter. *Unraveling Zen's Red Thread.* Seoul: Hollym International, 1980.

Cowan, James G. *The Aborigine Tradition.* Shaftesbury: Element, 1992.

Dawkins, Peter. *Arcadia.* Warwick, UK: Francis Bacon Research Trust, 1988.

Davis, Lynn. *Illumination.* New York: Melcher Media, 2007.

———. *Monument*. Santa Fe, NM: Arena Editions, 1999.

Eitel, Ernest J. *Feng-Shui or The Rudiments of Natural Science in China.* Cambridge: Cokaygne, 1973.

Eliade, Mircea. *Myths, Dreams and Mysteries*. Translated by Philip Mairet. London: Collins, 1974.

———. *The Sacred and the Profane*. Translated by Willard Trask. New York: Harcourt Brace and World, 1959.

Emoto, Masaru. *The Secret Life of Water*. New York: Atria Books, 2005.

Erdoes, Richard, and Alfonso Ortiz. *American Indian Myths and Legends.* New York: Pantheon, 1984.

Fabricius, Johannes. *Alchemy*. Copenhagen: Rosenkilde and Bagger, 1976.

Freeman, Michael, and Roger Warner. *Angkor: The Hidden Glories*. Boston: Houghton Mifflin, 1990.

Gates, Henry Louis, Jr. *Wonders of the African World*. With photographs by Lynn Davis. New York: Knopf, 1999.

Gilbert, Adrian, and Maurice Cotterell. *The Mayan Prophecies*. Shaftesbury: Element Books, 1995.

Godwin, Joscelyn. *Mystery Religions in the Ancient World*. London: Thames and Hudson, 1981.

Graves, Robert. *The White Goddess*. London: Faber and Faber, 1961.

Hadingham, Evan. *Early Man and the Cosmos.* London, Heinemann, 1983.

Halpern, Zena. "Menorah Found in the Catskill Mountains of New York," *Ancient American* 11, no. 71, 2007.

Hancock, Graham, and Santha Faiia. *Heaven's Mirror*. New York: Crown, 1998.

——— *Supernatural*. Scarborough, Ontario: Doubleday Canada, 2006.

Hawkins, Gerald S. *Stonehenge Decoded*. Garden City, NY: Doubleday, 1965.

Heggie, Douglas. *Megalithic Science*. London: Thames and Hudson, 1981.

Herron, James. "Really Roughing It in the Outback," *Los Angeles Times*, November 17, 2002.

Hillenbrand, Robert. *Islamic Art and Architecture*. London: Thames and Hudson, 1999.

Hisamatsu, Shin'ichi. *Zen and the Fine Arts*. Kyoto: Kodansha, 1970.

Howat, John K. *American Paradise: The World of the Hudson River School*. New York: Metropolitan Museum of Art, 1987.

Jung, C. G. *Alchemical Studies*. London: Routledge and Kegan Paul, 1967.

———. *The Archetypes and the Collective Unconscious*. Collected Works 9. London: Routledge and Kegan Paul, 1969.

———. *Memories, Dreams and Reflections*. London: Collins, 1983.

———. *Word and Image*. Princeton, NJ: Bollingen, 1979.

Jung, Emma. *The Grail Legend*. London: Hodder and Stoughton, 1970.

Kerényi, Carl. *Eleusis*. Translated by Ralph Manheim. Princeton, NJ: Princeton University Press, 1967.

Lash, John Lamb. *Not in His Image: Gnostic Vision, Sacred Ecology, and the Future of Belief.* White River Junction, VT: Chelsea Green Publishing, 2006.

Lawlor, Robert. *Voices of the First Day*. Rochester, VT: Inner Traditions, 1991.

Lazara, Juan Antonio. "Iguazu and the Missions," *Guia del Estudiante*. Buenos Aires, 2007.

Mann, A. T. *The Divine Plot*. London: Element Books, 1986.

———. *Sacred Architecture*. London: Element Books, 1993.

Mann, A. T., et al., essays in *The Roof of Europe*. Geneva: Bellerive Foundation, 1991.

Mann, A. T., and Jane Lyle. *Sacred Sexuality*. London: Element Books, 1995.

Mann, Thomas. *Joseph and His Brothers*. London: Sidgwick and Jackson, 1969.

McArthur, Meher. *Reading Buddhist Art*. London: Thames and Hudson, 2002.

McClellan, James E., and Harold Dorn. *Science and Technology in World History*. Baltimore: Johns Hopkins University Press, 2006.

Meredith. "Mapping Identity: Tibetans in New Mexico and Their Incorporation into the Tri-Ethnic Myth," *Journal of the Southwest* 44 (2002).

Metzner, Ralph. *The Well of Remembrance*. London: Shambhala, 1994.

Michell, John. *The View over Atlantis*. London: Garnstone Press, 1972.

Miksic, John. *Borobudur: Golden Tales of the Buddhas*. Hong Kong: Periplus, 1990.

Negri, Paul, ed. *Metaphysical Poetry: An Anthology*. New York: Dover, 2002.

Nietzsche, Friedrich. *Thus Spoke Zarathustra*, trans. Walter Kaufmann. New York: Penguin, 1978.

Nitschke, Günther. *From Shinto to Ando: Studies in Architectural Anthropology in Japan*. London: Academy Editions, 1993.

Porphyry. *On the Cave of the Nymphs*, trans. Thomas Taylor. Grand Rapids, MI: Phanes, 1991.

Rhie, Marilyn M., and Robert A. F. Thurman. *Wisdom and Compassion: The Sacred Art of Tibet*. New York: Abrams, 1991.

Rhoades, Rodney, and David R. Bell. *Medical Physiology*. Baltimore: Lippincott Williams and Wilkins, 1995.

Richer, Jean. *Sacred Geography of the Ancient Greeks*. Albany: State University of New York Press, 1994.

Rilke, Rainer Maria. "The Second Elegy," in *Duino Elegies*, trans. Stephen Mitchell. Boston: Shambhala, 1992.

Rinpoche Patrul. *The Words of My Perfect Teacher*, trans. Padmakara Translation Group, San Francisco: HarperCollins, 1994.

Robinson, James M. *The Nag Hammadi Library*. Leiden, E. J. Brill, 1977.

Rossbach, Sarah. *Feng Shui*. London: Rider, 1984.

Ruck, Carl A., et al. *The Road to Eleusis*. West Hollywood, CA: William Dailey Antiquarian Books, 2004.

de Santillana, Giorgio, and Hertha von Dechend. *Hamlet's Mill: An Essay Investigating the Origins of Human Knowledge and Its Transmission through Myth*. Boston: Godine, 1977.

Schele, Linda, and David Freidel. *A Forest of Kings*. New York: Quill, 1990.

Scully, Vincent. *The Earth, the Temple and the Gods*. New Haven, CT: Yale University Press, 1979.

Skinner, Stephen. *The Living Earth Manual of Feng-Shui*. London: Routledge and Kegan Paul, 1982.

———. *Guide to the Feng Shui Compass*. London: Golden Hind Press, 2008.

Stewart, R. J. *The Mystic Life of Merlin*. London: Arcana, 1986.

———. *The Prophetic Vision of Merlin*. London: Arcana, 1986.

Stirling, William. *The Canon.* London: RILKO, 1981.

Stone, Andrea J. *Images from the Underworld: Naj Tunich and the Tradition of Maya Cave Painting.* Austin: University of Texas Press, 1995.

Suzuki, Daisetz. *Zen and Japanese Culture.* Princeton, NJ: Bollingen, 1959.

Swan, James A. *The Power of Place.* Bath: Gateway Books, 1993.

Tarnas, Richard. *Cosmos and Psyche.* New York: Viking, 2006.

Temple, Robert. *The Sirius Mystery.* London: Sidgwick and Jackson, 1975.

Thompson, Angel. *Feng Shui.* New York: St. Martin's Griffin, 1996.

Thurman, Robert, and Tad Wise. *Circling the Sacred Mountain.* New York: Bantam, 1999.

Too, Lillian. *Feng Shui.* Shaftesbury: Element Books, 1996.

Trungpa, Chögyam. *Illusion's Game: The Life and Teaching of Naropa.* Boston: Shambhala, 1994.

Tsogyal, Yeshe. *The Lotus-Born.* Boudhanath: Rangjung Yeshe Publications, 2004.

Walters, Derek. *The Complete Guide to Chinese Astrology.* London: Watkins, 2005.

Wasson, Gordon, et al. *Persephone's Quest.* New Haven, CT: Yale University Press, 1986.

Waters, Frank. *Book of the Hopi.* New York: Penguin Books, 1963.

———. *Masked Gods.* New York: Ballantine Books, 1950.

Watkins, Alfred. *The Old Straight Track.* London: Abacus, 1970.

Weaver, Herbert. *Divining the Primary Sense.* London: Routledge and Kegan Paul, 1978.

West, John Anthony. *Serpent in the Sky.* San Francisco: Harper and Row, 1979.

Wolff, Werner. *Island of Death: A New Key to Easter Island's Culture.* Whitefish, MT: Kessinger Publications, 2004.

Wong, Eva, trans. *Cultivating Stillness: A Taoist Manual for Transforming Body and Mind.* Boston: Shambala, 1992.

Zimmer, Heinrich. *Myths and Symbols in Indian Art and Civilization.* New York: Bollingen, 1946.

Index

Note: Page numbers in *italics* include photographs and captions, and page numbers in **bold** indicate map-legend references.

About the Authors

Lynn Davis (b. 1944) received a BFA from the San Francisco Art Institute in 1970 and apprenticed with Berenice Abbott in the summer of 1974. She has had sixty-eight solo shows since 1980, and her work is in the collections of many museums including the Museum of Modern Art, the Whitney Museum, the J. Paul Getty Museum, the Guggenheim Museum, and the Reina Sofía in Madrid. She has photographed in forty-eight countries including Egypt, Yemen, Burma, Cambodia, Russia, Kazakhstan, China, Ethiopia, Sudan, Mali, Iran, Greenland, and, most recently, Greece and Brazil. In 2005 Davis received an Academy Award in Art from the American Academy of Arts and Letters. She lives and works in Hudson, New York and Cape Breton, Nova Scotia.

Her artist books include *Space Project, Illumination*, *American Monument*, *Monument*, *Wonders of the African World*, and *Bodywork*.

For more information, and to see additional work, visit her Web site, www.lynndavisphotography.com.

A. T. Mann (b. 1943) received a BArch from Cornell University and worked for prominent architects in New York and Rome. He is a graphic and Web site designer, painter, astrologer, and author of sixteen books on many subjects; his books have been translated into twenty languages and he lectures worldwide. He is a member of the Forum on Architecture, Culture, and Spirituality, is director of publications of the National Council of Geocosmic Research, and works regularly with Mystic Fire Video. He teaches sacred and ecological architecture and feng shui, and he works with eco-designers. He writes reports for tarot.com.

His books include *Mandala Astrological Tarot*, *The Phenomenon Book of Calendars*, *The Round Art*, *The Divine Plot*, *Sacred Architecture*, *Sacred Sexuality* (with Jane Lyle), and *A New Vision of Astrology*.

For more information, and to see additional work, visit his Web site, www.atmann.net.

A Note on the Type

Sacred Landscapes is composed largely in the classic font known as Adobe Garamond Pro. Garamond was originally designed in the sixteenth century by Parisian font designer Claude Garamond, for whom the font was named. Garamond's typefaces were likely influenced by the handwriting of monarch Francis I's librarian, Angelo Vergecio, and the Venetian old-style types in the print shops of Aldus Manutius. Today's Adobe Garamond is a revival of the original type cut by Garamond; it was created by Adobe Systems Inc. in 1987 under the direction of Robert Slimbach. The other font used is Filosofia (1996), which was designed by Zuzana Licko of the digital type foundry Emigre. Filosofia is based on the typefaces of the eighteenth-century Italian typographer Giambattista Bodoni.

Color separations by Embassy Graphics
Printing and binding by 1010 Printing International Ltd., China
Interior design by Christine Heun